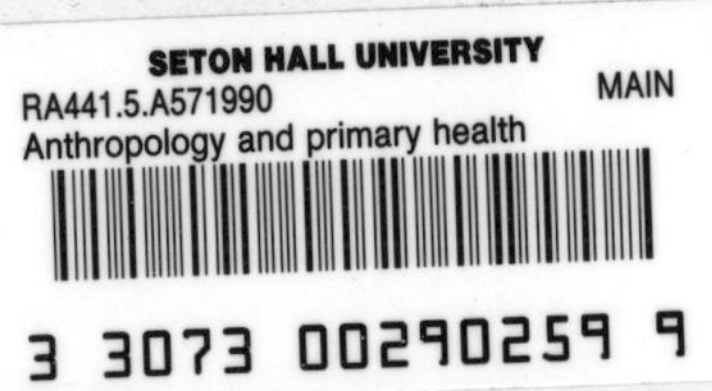

Anthropology and Primary Health Care

Anthropology and Primary Health Care

EDITED BY
Jeannine Coreil and J. Dennis Mull

Westview Press
BOULDER • SAN FRANCISCO • OXFORD

This Westview softcover edition is printed on acid-free paper and bound in library-quality, coated covers that carry the highest rating of the National Association of State Textbook Administrators, in consultation with the Association of American Publishers and the Book Manufacturers' Institute.

Published in 1990 in the United States of America by Westview Press, Inc., 5500 Central Avenue, Boulder, Colorado 80301, and in the United Kingdom by Westview Press, 36 Lonsdale Road, Summertown, Oxford OX2 7EW

Library of Congress Cataloging-in-Publication Data
Anthropology and primary health care / edited by Jeannine Coreil and J. Dennis Mull
p. cm.
Includes index.
ISBN 0-8133-8138-X
1. Medical care—Developing countries. 2. Social medicine—Developing countries. 3. Medical anthropology—Developing countries. I. Coreil, Jeannine. II. Mull, J. Dennis.
[DNLM: 1. Developing Countries. 2. Health Planning. 3. Primary Health Care. 4. Social Medicine. WA 31 A628]
RA441.5.A57 1990
362.1'09172'4—dc20
DNLM/DLC
for Library of Congress

90-12857
CIP

Printed and bound in the United States of America

∞ The paper used in this publication meets the requirements of the American National Standard for Permanence of Paper for Printed Library Materials Z39.48-1984.

10 9 8 7 6 5 4 3 2 1

Contents

Tables and Figures

Tables

Figures

Foreword

A book on anthropology and primary health care is particularly appropriate at this time. With their increasing involvement in addressing the health problems of developing countries, anthropologists and other social scientists need to learn from the experiences of others. They need to consider specific experiences or case studies in light of relevant ethnomedical models and to seek general principles of human behavior and societal organization which will aid the effort to improve health. But in addition, the improvement of health must be seen as an inter-disciplinary task. Therefore, this book should be of great value to physicians, epidemiologists, program managers, and other international health professionals. These individuals have a great need to understand the contributions that social science methodologies and perspectives and their social sciences colleagues can offer to the common struggle to improve health.

Health is an undeniable human right, yet one achieved by few in the developing world. Defined in the Constitution of the World Health Organization as "a state of physical, mental, and social well-being and not merely the absence of disease or infirmity," health stands as an important social goal, albeit one hard to measure at either an individual or a societal level. It is often taken for granted and appreciated only in its absence with the occurrence of illness; hence the tendency in most populations to ignore or undervalue actions that promote health or prevent disease and to demand medical services for even mild and self-limited illnesses. Thus, optimal preservation of health requires an active approach on the part of individuals and communities. This approach should recognize the right to health of all members of the population and must include specific actions to support health at an individual and community level. It must also include the more broad aspects of development that lead to improvements in quality of life with an emphasis on health.

The desire to achieve health for all is not new, but it has taken time for sufficient momentum to build to make it an important part of national and international policy. Even now, it is too often national or international rhetoric rather than policy. Too often other forces determine allocation of resources. The objective of "health for all" was included in the WHO Constitution in 1948 and the work of three decades led to the Declaration of Alma-Ata in which "Health for All by the Year 2000" was further established as a rallying cry. Clearly, the current stress on greater equity in health care and health status is an essential ingredient in achieving health for all.

As part of the growing commitment to equity in health, there has been increasing attention directed to concerns and health problems at the population or community level. There has been an important recognition that curative care delivered from hospitals, clinics, or physicians' offices is inadequate to meet the health needs of the population. This has led to disease control programs delivered at the community level and a new emphasis on prevention, e.g., immunizations for children, rather than cure. As experience has accumulated, both the successes and failures of these initiatives have become obvious. Interventions that are efficacious and cost-effective in controlled settings are more problematic when implemented in diverse field situations. The provision of these seemingly simple intervention technologies is in reality complex, and their potential impact is diminished by cultural, sociopolitical, and economic factors. For example, the use of oral rehydration therapy for management of diarrheal dehydration in clinical settings has led to dramatic improvements in illness outcome with reductions in cost. However, the promotion of techniques for management of diarrhea to reduce or treat dehydration at the community level has been more problematic. Furthermore, while ORT may avert a death from dehydration in a clinical setting, its potential to reduce childhood mortality in a community setting will be reduced by the continuing risk for the child of other illnesses and malnutrition. This is not to conclude that ORT is without value at the community level, but rather that the type and magnitude of effort needed to establish effective use were underestimated and the potential impact overstated. Similar examples could be raised in regard to other community-level interventions.

It is important to consider possible solutions to overcome these constraints in implementation of health interventions. In some cases, the technology must be modified to adapt to cultural, economic, or environmental conditions. In other situations, improved training or communications methods may overcome an implementation problem. Another approach is to broaden the scope of the intervention, such as promoting dietary management of diarrhea and improved infant feeding instead of focusing only on fluid therapy. Often it would seem better to take a more integrated approach to deal with specific health problems and to deliver services for multiple problems in a more comprehensive fashion. In this way, curative efforts can be linked with preventive services and community improvement.

As we learn from our experiences, health programs continue to evolve. Further progress will require thoughtful evaluation and reformulation by interdisciplinary teams. Such teams must include epidemiologic perspectives on the distribution and determinants of disease in the population and social science perspectives on the determinants of human behavior and on communications, along with clinical and management expertise. The further enhancement of intersectoral approaches will make this need for continuous examination and improvement more profound, but potentially will make such interventions even more successful.

With scarce resources, the question is not whether choices need to be made, but how and by whom will they be made. The Declaration of Alma-Ata is clear in calling for "community and individual self-reliance and participation in the planning, organization, operation and control of primary health care." The need for such involvement is compelling if health efforts are to be successful and sustained.

Health programs must be responsive to the needs that the community expresses and at the same time identify the major health problems of the population and possible means of control. Education of communities about these matters is an essential part of primary health care and of community development, since a poorly informed population cannot make the best decisions.

Anthropologists play a unique and difficult role in these rapidly evolving efforts to improve health in the developing world. They must endeavor to understand and to explain to other health colleagues the sociocultural context of illness and of health promoting behaviors. They may be called upon to use their skills to improve the implementation or impact of disease control interventions. They will wish to engage in these tasks with the broader objectives of attaining the equity, community involvement, self-determination, and sustained social change that should characterize primary health care programs. They must do this with an understanding of community health problems and available technologies, as well as perceived needs of the population. They may wish to be the advocates for the community, especially the poor and powerless, but they must also develop the ability to work with the health system, with governments, and with international agencies. As such, public health professionals can play a critical part in shaping the primary health care of the future.

Robert E. Black
Johns Hopkins School of
Hygiene and Public Health

Preface

The interdisciplinary field of anthropology in international health has shown dynamic growth and maturation since the mid-1970s. The major impetus has been the Primary Health Care (PHC) movement initiated by a WHO-sponsored conference held at Alma-Ata, U.S.S.R., in 1978, which focused global attention on the basic health needs of less developed nations. Since then, a dramatic shift in policy and priorities has occurred in Third World health programs as governments and health agencies attempt to achieve the stated Alma-Ata goal of "Health for All."

Specifically, there has been a de-emphasis on urban-based, high-technology, curative medical care, and a movement toward community-based preventive health programs that rely on low-cost appropriate technology to meet basic health needs as defined by local people through participatory processes. Planners and administrators of such programs now recognize that new approaches to health care are needed--approaches that incorporate the sociocultural and domestic contexts of health behavior. The chapters that follow demonstrate how the perspectives and methods of medical anthropology can make a unique and highly valuable contribution to this endeavor.

The emergence of anthropology in international health as a distinct field is evident in many ways. Increasing numbers of anthropologists are working and conducting research in international settings, large numbers of journal articles and project reports are being written, and more and more students are being trained in this specialty. Yet there are no books dealing with this field in a comprehensive way. Indeed, scholars continue to cite and use Benjamin Paul's 1955 *Health, Culture and Community* for lack of more recent volumes on cross-cultural health action programs. We hope that the following chapters will help remedy this lack.

In developing this book, we sought to cover the major theoretical perspectives, content areas, and methodologic approaches that presently characterize the field of anthropology and primary health care. We also wanted to provide a discussion of the field in historical perspective. Thus, the chapters are organized into five sections reflecting these content areas: overview and historical background; critical perspectives on anthropology and primary health care; extension of primary health care into the community; ethnomedical models; and issues and methods in applied research. Each section is introduced by a brief discussion of what follows.

We also sought contributions covering a wide geographical area, and thus the book draws upon studies based in Mexico (Rubel), Nicaragua (Donahue), Nigeria (Ramakrishna, Brieger, and Adeniyi), South Asia (Nichter; Mull and Mull), Indonesia (Griffiths), and New Zealand (Wood). One chapter presents findings from research carried out in the United States (Heurtin-Roberts and Reisin), demonstrating how some of the problems facing PHC in the developing world are also present in industrial nations. Four chapters (Velimirovic; Kendall; Jordan; and Pelto, Bentley, and Pelto) review relevant literature from many different geographical areas.

One sign of maturity of an emergent field is the involvement of professionals from other disciplines. Growing numbers of physicians, nurses, and other health professionals are currently engaged in anthropology and international health research. Indeed, it is significant that this book is co-edited by an anthropologist and a physician. We have benefitted from being able to draw upon each other's differing perspectives to temper the biases that might otherwise have surfaced.

We feel that presenting *multiple* perspectives on anthropology and primary health care is essential because it raises issues that can profitably be discussed to strengthen the field as a whole. Thus we have sought to include strong critical essays discussing broad macropolitical questions as well as more narrowly focused chapters dealing with important "nuts and bolts" issues. Throughout, our intent has been to present a multiplicity of voices on this exciting and promising new field, both to reflect its dynamic and emergent nature and to stimulate further consideration of its proper methods and goals.

Jeannine Coreil
J. Dennis Mull

Acknowledgements

We began working on the book four years ago, and without the support and encouragement of many friends and colleagues, we could not have survived the inevitable ups and downs of such a project to bring it through to completion. In particular we want to thank Debra Schumann, Patricia Marshall, and our families for their encouragement. The contributing authors were also very patient and supportive. Dorothy Mull volunteered to go beyond her role as a contributor to serve as an editorial consultant for the entire volume; we are grateful for her help. Finally, we wish to thank Brent A. Wynn, who did an outstanding job of developing the book format, producing the camera-ready copy, word processing, and some editing.

We dedicate the book to the poor people of the world who so generously opened their lives and hearts to the contributors, and we salute them in their struggle for health as a basic human right.

J.C.
J.D.M.

I

OVERVIEW AND HISTORICAL BACKGROUND

The two chapters in this section complement one another in providing an introduction and context for the rest of the book. Coreil traces the shifting patterns of anthropological involvement in cross-cultural public health programs over the last few decades and relates these patterns to broader trends in international development and the social sciences. Mull discusses the recent emergence of primary health care (PHC) as the focus of health action in the developing world. He shows how the PHC concept represented a truly radical departure from earlier approaches to international health, and lays out the issues that differentiate "comprehensive" from "selective" PHC. Both chapters identify challenges to the success of PHC and suggest that anthropological methods and perspectives are particularly suited to help meet these challenges.

At the same time, the two authors document the imperfect fit between the traditional holistic orientation of anthropology and the increasingly technological, quick-fix approach to problem-solving that has characterized PHC strategies in recent years. They point out that while anthropologists typically conduct broad-based qualitative studies and advocate long-term comprehensive community development, international health planning has become increasingly focused on specific, short-term interventions designed by external development agencies with little involvement of local communities. Mull argues that such interventions are unlikely to prove successful in attaining the goals of "Health for All" and suggests that they need to be combined with the best features of comprehensive PHC in future programs. Similarly, Coreil makes the case that traditional anthropological methods need to be adapted to address more focused research questions that incorporate quantitative data without compromising the strengths of anthropology in holistic problem analysis.

1

The Evolution of Anthropology in International Health

Jeannine Coreil

Introduction

One of the most important growth areas within medical anthropology over the past decade has been in the field of international community health. Recent years have witnessed a rapid increase in the number of anthropologists involved in cross-cultural public health research, and in the integration of anthropological perspectives and methods in the planning and implementation of primary health care programs. This period is reminiscent of the earlier participation of anthropologists in public health development programs during the 1950s, but changes in dominant issues, theory and method have made the current era different in important ways.

In this chapter I review the variable involvement of anthropologists in international health over the past fifty years, noting the factors within and outside the discipline which influenced the evolution of this field. The first section outlines the scope of the field and cites important literature sources. The contributions of anthropology to health programs in developing countries are then discussed from the standpoint of (1) historical changes in development work, international health and behavioral sciences; (2) research questions and conceptual bases; (3) methodological approaches; and (4) issues and challenges.

Definitions and Sources

As defined in this review, the term "international health" refers to knowledge and practice regarding health problems in less developed countries. For the most part it entails the kinds of research and programs usually categorized as public health, preventive medicine, or community health in developed countries, and has become largely synonymous with the concept of primary health care (PHC) since the Alma-Ata conference (WHO and UNICEF 1978). Pillsbury (1985: 84-86) sums up the core work of international health as problem identification and analysis, intervention, and evaluation focused on specific health problems and populations. In other words, international health is largely an applied field with practical goals. George Foster also notes that historically, "health care providers and health care recipients have represented distinct cultural, social or ethnic groups" (1982a: 189) and that therefore the field essentially addresses the cross-cultural delivery of services. International health is both a specialization among the health disciplines and a subfield of international development, giving it a somewhat broader context than other areas in which medical anthropology has been applied to real-life problems.[1]

Foster has written several important "state of the art" papers on anthropology and international health which chart the major issues as well as the variable involvement of anthropologists over the past half-century.[2] Prior to 1977 (Foster 1977) the term "international health" was not widely used in the anthropological literature, so that relevant material is somewhat difficult to find. However, one of the earliest important discussions of cross-cultural health research appeared in an article by Polgar (1962),[3] and since 1963 various reviews of the field of medical anthropology have surveyed international health research under headings such as public health, medical ecology and epidemiology, and culture change.[4] An excellent discussion of what anthropologists actually do in international health work is presented by Pillsbury (1985).[5]

In recent years the published works that have helped define the field of anthropology and international health include several special journal issues,[6] collections of case studies (van der Geest and Whyte 1988; Nichter 1989), and a monograph series summarizing anthropological and behavioral science contributions to child survival research (Pillsbury 1989a). These publications document the growing inclusion of anthropological perspectives and research methods, as well as anthropologists themselves, in programs aimed at reducing morbidity and mortality in the developing world.

Historical Perspectives

Following the reviews of anthropology in international development by Hoben (1982) and Pillsbury (1986), I will discuss anthropological involvement in international health in three broad phases: (1) the early period of active involvement (1945-1960); (2) the middle period of minimal involvement (1960-1975); and (3) the recent period of growing involvement (1975-present).

The Early Phase (1945-1960): Culture Brokers

Foster (1982a: 190) notes that the earliest role of anthropology in international health can be traced to colonial interest in the diet and health of traditional populations dating from the 1930s and 1940s, citing early works by Firth (1934), Richards (1939) and Malinowski (1945). In the same era, the U.S. National Research Council's Committee on Food Habits engaged Ruth Benedict, Margaret Mead, and others to write a *Manual for the Study of Food Habits* (1945) which addressed issues in international nutrition as an applied science. But it was not until 1950 that an anthropologist, Cora DuBois, was first hired for a formal position by an international health organization, the World Health Organization. Shortly thereafter, several anthropologists were appointed to international health posts, including Edward Wellin at the Rockefeller Foundation, Benjamin Paul at the Harvard School of Public Health, and George Foster and others at the Institute for Inter-American Affairs (the forerunner of the U.S. Agency for International Development).

The appointment of anthropologists to institutional posts paralleled the rapid expansion of public health programs worldwide as modern medicine was introduced on a large scale in many areas. The primary role of anthropologists was seen as that of identifying significant cultural barriers to the acceptance of new public health programs. The Paul casebook (1955a), although not limited to developing countries in scope, reflects this vision of the anthropologist's function. For example, Cassel's chapter (1955) highlights the difficulty in changing cultural practices (in this case food habits) which are perceived as symbols of the moral code governing interpersonal conduct, while Hsu, using the example of a cholera epidemic, emphasizes that emotional reactions in crisis situations may impede the acceptance of culture change (1955).

During this same postwar period, anthropologists were also actively participating in a wide range of community development projects as the United States expanded its foreign aid programs. The role of anthropologists in these other areas was similar to that in the health field--as Hoben put it (1982: 353), "to facilitate the diffusion of improved technology by overcoming resistance to change grounded in traditional values, institutions, and practices." The period during and after World War II was also widely recognized as the high point of anthropological and behavioral science influence in all areas of national and international policy (Weaver 1985a). Thus, the early involvement of anthropology in international health must be understood as part of a broader involvement of the behavioral sciences in development planning and evaluation in general, which in turn must be seen as a natural development in an era of growth for all fields of social science.

Middle Period (1960-75): Declining Involvement

Beginning around 1960, however, there was a steady decline in the number of anthropologists directly involved in international health and development work. This was partially due to the shift away from community development and towards technology transfer, with emphasis being placed on the urban sector instead of on rural villages. In the health field, the focus thus moved to hospital-based curative services, to secondary and tertiary care, and to the technical expertise necessary to apply advanced medical technology. One area in which anthropologists did remain involved was the dissemination of contraceptive technology, where again their job was to identify cultural barriers to acceptance of family planning (Polgar 1966, 1971, 1972; Newman 1972). This was also a time when anthropologists began to take an interest in the worldwide decline in breastfeeding (Raphael 1973), a concern than has grown steadily and has led to varied research on infant feeding.

In the 1960s and early 1970s an abundance of academic positions enticed many anthropologists into university settings, where the traditional bias against applied social science (see Mull and Mull, Chapter 14) discouraged further pursuit of applied work. Thus, their research interests shifted towards theoretical problems, as reflected in the emergence of cognitive anthropology and ethnosemantics as the dominant paradigm. Descriptive ethnomedical studies predominated in medical anthropological research. These disciplinary changes reinforced the withdrawal of anthropologists from engaging in applied work in international health.

Recent Period (1975-present): Expanded Involvement in PHC

In 1975 two important developments marked the re-entry of anthropologists into the international health scene. First, Congress passed legislation signalling new directions for foreign assistance that mandated both greater attention to the rural poor and appropriate technology to meet the needs of less developed nations. Most important, all development projects were required to include "social soundness analysis" components, which led to the employment of greater numbers of anthropologists in staff positions and on short-term assignments (Hoben 1982: 358).

Second, in the international health arena, 1975 marked the first endorsement by the World Health Organization of traditional medicine as a legitimate alternative in national health care planning, and a program in traditional medicine was established in 1978 (Velimirovic 1984; Djukanovic and Mach 1975, 1978). Since that time there has been increasing attention to the potential benefits of integrating indigenous healers in service delivery (Rubel and Sargent 1979; Pillsbury 1982; Maclean and Bannerman 1982), although some would say that this has consisted mostly of rhetoric and little action (Velimirovic, Chapter 3). Nevertheless, the establishment of the traditional medicine program within WHO created a natural place for anthropological expertise in international health.

Following closely on these developments, in 1978 WHO launched the primary health care movement at the historic Alma-Ata Conference, setting the stage for a worldwide redirection of health care to give priority to basic health services, community participation, appropriate technology and home-based care (see Mull, Chapter 2). As during the early period of the community development model, with which primary health care has much affinity (Foster 1982b), anthropological expertise became increasingly recognized as valuable to the primary health care agenda (Foster 1978). Anthropologists were engaged in research and evaluation of community and family needs, some in full-time employment with international agencies, others in short-term projects and consultation. Also around this time, a related field, water and sanitation, gained momentum, with anthropologists making important contributions regarding the role of women and the importance of community participation in program effectiveness (Elmendorf 1981, 1983).

Most recently, international efforts linked with child survival projects have incorporated substantial anthropological elements. Thus, conceptual and methodologic approaches drawn from medical anthropology have been used in operational research, program design, and evaluation (Sukkary-Stolba 1989; Pillsbury 1989b; Brownlee 1989). In particular, the emergence of social marketing as a primary child survival promotion strategy, with its emphasis on qualitative research to determine consumer perceptions, parallels the traditional anthropological concern with ethnomedical context.

In fact, the adaptation of social marketing principles to public health in general was significantly influenced by anthropological perspectives (Manoff 1985), though its main research method, the focus group interview, was drawn primarily from other social science disciplines (Coreil 1988). In other words, social marketing methodology requires understanding of existing beliefs and practices and calls for repeated analyses of the impact of the social marketing program as it may be enhanced or blunted by existing cultural elements. Thus, in a sense social marketing frequently entails activities that resemble focused and highly applied medical anthropology.

As described in the following chapter, since 1983 child survival programs have largely adopted the selective intervention approach (Walsh and Warren 1979), i.e. they have targeted specific health problems such as diarrheal diseases and immunizable diseases which account for a large proportion of mortality. Similarly, most anthropologists working in this area have focused their research narrowly, as exemplified in a recent collection of anthropological studies of diarrheal illness (Coreil and Mull 1988) and a review of anthropological research on child survival (Pillsbury 1989a). An important outgrowth of these studies focused on a single health problem has been the accumulation of a rich body of comparative data that can now be analyzed for cross-cultural patterns and variation, leading to theoretical as well as methodological contributions (see Kendall, Chapter 9; Pelto, Bentley, and Pelto, Chapter 12).

Developments within anthropology have also facilitated the involvement of anthropologists in international health over the past decade and a half. To begin with, the number of training programs in medical anthropology increased significantly, and these programs began to prepare an increasingly larger number of graduates for applied positions. At the same time, many of these medical anthropologists began to seek additional training in public health and related fields (*Medical Anthropology Quarterly* 1984) in order to learn the "culture of medicine" and the skills necessary to collaborate with health professionals. Finally, medical anthropologists began to recognize the importance of acquiring in-depth technical knowledge and experience with particular health problems to be able to fully participate in operational research and program development. In sum, medical anthropologists became more plentiful, better trained, and more prepared for multidisciplinary collaboration on health problems, putting them in a better position to respond to the need for behavioral science in international health.

Whether the present involvement of anthropologists in international health will continue to grow, or wane as in earlier years, remains to be seen. While a methodologic niche for anthropological research seems to have become somewhat institutionalized in large-scale multidisciplinary projects, the sustainability of this niche, like the health programs themselves, will depend largely on the continued availability of funding for behavioral research on the level that has characterized the child survival initiatives. It will also depend on sustained international commitment to PHC and to community-based approaches to achieving health for all. It appears that at least one important role for anthropology in the international health of the 1990s will be in addressing the sociocultural components of the "health transition," the process of behavior change that underlies improvements in health status of developing country populations.

Research Questions and Conceptual Bases

The Adversary Model

As noted above, in the 1950s, the main agenda of anthropological research in international health was to find out how to get people to adopt new health practices. The goal was to identify existing health habits and to understand how the behaviors and underlying beliefs were linked, the functions they performed, and the meaning the behaviors held for those who practiced them (Paul 1955b: 1). The desired result might be described as "an ethnography of health habits." As the main focus was on conflict between the old and new ways, and existing health practices were viewed as barriers to change, this approach came to be known as the "adversary model" (Foster 1977: 528).

> In the early analyses of the sociocultural factors that seemed to inhibit acceptance of scientific medicine by traditional peoples, anthropologists developed an 'adversary' model to explain the resistances that occurred. It was postulated that scientific and traditional medicine were locked in

battle, each trying to win (or hold on to) the allegiance of the community (Foster 1977: 528).

The adversary model was based on dualistic thinking about traditional versus modern medicine. Early writings convey the idea that adoption of new health behaviors leads to abandonment of the old, in an all or nothing fashion that might be described as "total conversion." A modified version of this view evolved into the idea of illness domains, an extension of Polgar's notion of the "separate capsule" (Polgar 1963: 412). For example, utilization of health services was assumed to depend on the type of illness: certain classes were supposedly considered appropriate for modern medicine, others for indigenous therapy, and the central research question was seen as that of identifying the circumstances under which people choose one or the other treatment system (Colson 1971).

Later studies used the hierarchy of resort framework (Romanucci-Ross 1969), which sought to explain help-seeking in terms of sequential recourse to either traditional or modern medicine after home treatment failed. The same dichotomous thinking characterized analyses of the response of traditional healers to the introduction of cosmopolitan medicine. It was assumed that healers and modern health professionals were in an adversarial position, and that the healers were by necessity forced to resist or accommodate the encroaching system (Landy 1974).

The focus on cultural barriers persisted during the 1960s and 1970s, as illustrated by the extensive research on acceptability of family planning methods (Polgar and Marshall 1976). The emphasis was on convincing the health care establishment to avoid what Polgar (1963) termed the "fallacy of the empty vessel," that is, to recognize the importance of the existing cultural system in designing and implementing new health programs.

Ecological and Decision Models

As noted above, in the 1960s and early 1970s applied anthropologists tended to be academically inclined, and some researchers with international public health interests adopted traditional epidemiological approaches and concepts from medical ecology. In other words, they examined cultural practices as "risk factors" for disease or protective against illness. This approach is documented in Hughes' review (1963) of the health effects of cultural traits such as personal hygiene, clothing, postural habits and cosmetic practices. A number of studies at this time focused specifically on the link between beliefs and domestic sanitation (Paul 1958; Khare 1962).

If we compare these models with anthropological approaches of the late 1970s and 1980s, both continuities and new developments can be noted. Recent work still emphasizes cultural context and the importance of ethnomedical data for program planning and evaluation (Kleinman 1978), but the influence of cognitive anthropology is seen in the application of systematic procedures for identifying cognitive models of disease to explain behavior. The domain of health beliefs is now recognized as complex and influenced by situational variables. Ethnomedical studies focus not only on concepts of disease, but also on illness terminology, theories of causation, folk illness categories, diagnostic criteria for evaluating symptoms, and the language of distress used to describe illness experience, all of which can be very useful for health program planning. Concepts such as "explanatory models" of illness have been linked with help-seeking behavior, patterns of distress, and social context to help us understand the "cultural construction of illness" (see, for example, Weiss 1988).

The dualistic view of health service utilization has been replaced with a multivariate decision process model (Young 1984). The focus of this approach is to identify the criteria underlying recurrent decisions across and within illness episodes, and multiple, diverse options within pluralistic health care systems are recognized (Coreil 1983). Whereas earlier studies of the help-seeking process adopted the hierarchy of resort model, one which assumed that a single pattern characterized whole societies, we now recognize that the sequence is much more complex, variable across households, subject to recurrent decisions at multiple points, and influenced by a wide range of factors including situational variables and social and economic costs.

Similarly, while earlier studies assumed substantial cultural homogeneity in the target population, later research recognizes intracultural variation (Pelto and Pelto 1975) and emphasizes variability across households even within single communities. The household has become the unit of analysis in health behavior studies as it has been increasingly recognized that the household constitutes the primary locus of decision-making which affects health status and response to illness. There has been increased interest in home management of illness and the popular sector of health care (Polgar 1963; Kleinman 1980), particularly as a result of intensive international efforts to promote home-based oral rehydration therapy for childhood diarrhea.

In short, researchers have enlarged the traditional view of households as consumers of health care to include the production of health as well (Cochrane, O'Hara, and Leslie 1980; Mosley 1987; Schumann 1988). The "household production of health" framework conceptualizes health outcomes as dependent on multiple dimensions including socioeconomic conditions, means of subsistence, household composition, dietary factors, child care patterns, and resource allocation strategies, as well as the specific health-related behaviors practiced. The central role of women and mothers as principal actors in this domain has received increasing attention.

Epidemiologic studies of risk factors and protective practices have continued to appear (Heggenhougen and Shore 1986; Janes, Stall, and Gifford 1986), and have gained greater sophistication and prominence along with the emergence of biocultural ecology as a dominant theoretical orientation in medical anthropology (Wellin 1977; McElroy and Townsend 1989; Pelto, Bentley, and Pelto, Chapter 12). By virtue of its broad scope, this latter field has become increasingly multidisciplinary, involving the behavioral, natural and biomedical sciences, and anthropologists have diversified their research skills in order to collaborate effectively with other scientists.

After decades of research focused on client populations, anthropologists have also begun to address the social organization of health care and its political-economic context as the locus of change. A critical perspective has emerged which challenges current primary health care strategies as ignoring fundamental barriers stemming from inequities in power and wealth, exclusion of local communities from effective participation in decision making, and inadequate access to services by the most needy (Heggenhougen 1984; New and Donahue 1986; Singer, Baer, and Lazarus 1990). The structure and culture of health bureaucracies at the local (Nichter 1986), national (Marchione 1984; Justice 1986) and international level (Foster 1987b) has been studied as a major impediment to the achievement of program goals (see Section II).

The Insight Model

Finally, the adversary model of directed change in international health has been increasingly replaced by what might be called the "insight model," one in which knowledge and explanation of the cultural underpinnings of health-related phenomena are applied in a positive fashion to integrate new ideas and practices with what already exists and has meaning for populations being served. Researchers look for insights into how people think about health matters, how they make choices affecting their health, and how they evaluate variable outcomes in order to maximize congruence between health innovations and what is familiar and habitual. Such insights can illuminate resistance factors, but more importantly, they can inform communication strategies to improve comprehension and retention, identify novel approaches to motivating behavior change, and enhance the credibility of new programs by demonstrating an appreciation for indigenous health culture.

For example, the Indonesian case study described by Griffiths (Chapter 8) illustrates the usefulness of insight into what motivates mothers to breastfeed their infants. While initially the breastfeeding promotion program stressed the nutritional qualities of maternal milk and had limited success, modification of the communication strategy to encourage nursing with both breasts as a way to ensure that the baby was "satisfied" proved effective in prolonging the duration of breastfeeding.

The above example demonstrates the congruence of the insight model with social marketing approaches, which seek to build communication strategies on existing motivations, using familiar concepts and vernacular language to "sell" health innovations. The insight model also has important similarities to new approaches in health education which seek to convey new ideas through "appropriate analogy" (Nichter and Nichter 1986; Nichter and Nichter 1987; Nichter 1989). This approach departs from traditional didactic instruction by incorporating cultural metaphors and analogs to maximize the congruence between popular health concepts and biomedical facts and thereby facilitate adoption of new behaviors.

Bastien (1987) provides an excellent illustration of a successful application of the metaphorical process in which Andean villagers were taught the principle of dehydration and convinced of the value of oral rehydration therapy for diarrhea through adaptation of a well-known myth about competition between rival mountains for the love of a maiden mountain. As the story goes, the rivalry led to fighting, one of the mountains was injured, and the injury led to severe water loss. Dying of dehydration, the embattled mountain appealed to the Condor for help, which was effectively delivered in the form of a special medicine (ORT).

> Basic to this approach is the assumption that this cognitive style of metaphorical knowledge has enabled Andeans to adapt and survive in the Andes for thousands of years. The premise that land and bodies reflect each other contributes to a close relationship of Andeans with their

> environment. The terrain of Andean highlands is steep and often barren, yet the people regard it as symbolic of their bodies and feed it as a mother. In similar fashion, health workers can use metaphors of animals and land to teach them about modern medicine (Bastien 1987: 85).

A similar teaching method is described by Ramakrishna, Brieger, and Adeniyi (Chapter 13), who refer to the process as "Health Belief Synthesis," that is, constructing a "bridge between scientific thought and local beliefs" to convey new ideas. In the guineaworm control program these authors discuss, community health workers and other villagers were made to understand the relationship between water quality and "weak blood" (which causes the worms to emerge) by reference to the analogy of the well-known wrath of the Yoruba divinity *Soponna*, who makes the earth hot and the streams dry during the dry season, when the quality of the water in ponds becomes visibly poor.

Anthropological studies of diarrheal diseases have also suggested the potential utility of cultural analogs for communicating the concept of rehydration (e.g. Coreil 1985; Green 1986; Bentley 1988; Nichter 1988), and WHO is currently sponsoring a field trial to test the effectiveness of an intervention based on cultural metaphors to promote oral rehydration therapy using indigenous concepts of dehydration compared to an approach based solely on biomedical notions (Herman and Bentley 1989).

Methodologic Approaches: The Ethnographic Bias

Early anthropological research in international health relied primarily on traditional ethnographic methods, usually involving a single community, extended fieldwork, participant observation, in-depth interviews and use of key informants. Findings were often presented in the "case study" format, a good example being Wellin's (1955) analysis of water boiling in a Peruvian town. Survey techniques began to be incorporated in the 1960s, but it was not until recently that quantitative methods have been systematically integrated with traditional ethnographic techniques. The community survey, varying from small to large scale, has acquired a central place in the methodologic repertoire of applied medical anthropologists. Epidemiologic methods have also been increasingly adapted to the research needs of anthropologists, along with multivariate statistical methods of data analysis (Pelto, Bentley, and Pelto, Chapter 12). The new standard of anthropological research in international health has become a distinctive mix of both quantitative and qualitative methods used to generate diverse kinds of data around a central research question.

Despite the diversification of methodologic approaches in anthropological research, international agencies continue to identify anthropologists as *qualitative* researchers skilled primarily in ethnographic techniques. As PHC program managers increasingly recognize the value of traditional anthropological approaches for program planning and evaluation (WHO/SEARO 1982; Buzzard 1984; Gray 1986; Ramalingaswami 1986), the inclusion of a qualitative component in multidisciplinary research has become commonplace. Anthropological contributions to large-scale projects are usually limited to describing ethnomedical systems related to a particular health problem. Typically, this takes place during the preliminary phase of multistage projects in which the ethnographic data is used to refine survey instruments, interpret quantitative results and guide intervention design. This is viewed as a form of cultural validity testing that can increase the practical value of survey data.

The strong identification of anthropology with qualitative methods and ethnography in particular has served to promote its use in certain areas, but in others it is viewed as a weakness. In the area of PHC operational research, behavioral science perspectives have become increasingly important, and anthropology has dominated this arena because of its cross-cultural focus. A good illustration of this involvement is the prominent role ethnographic research played in the Applied Diarrheal Diseases Research Project based at Harvard University, which has supported collaborative research projects involving social and biomedical scientists in several regions of the world (Harvard Institute for International Development 1988).

On the other hand, identification with qualitative research has generally limited the involvement of anthropologists in other aspects of international health, such as policy and planning. There are many reasons for this. For example, Hoben (1982) cites the stereotype of anthropological methods as soft and lacking rigor as a major bias against incorporating the discipline in development planning. Weaver (1985b) also notes that the tradition of long-term research in anthropological field studies has discouraged policy makers, who usually work under pressure of time, from using anthropological expertise (see also Mull and Mull, Chapter 14).

A similarly pessimistic assessment is made by Foster, who concludes that there is "little evidence that behavioral science research to date has influenced international health planning and health care delivery" (1984: 853), primarily because anthropological research findings cannot be quantified, and anthropologists have not yet learned to translate ethnomedical models into operational terms.

Furthermore, he states that "it is unrealistic to expect that behavioral information will ever play much of a role in policy and planning activities" (1987b: 1047). The possibility for changing this prospect, he argues, must come from within the organizations themselves (1987a: 716). It seems probable that as more anthropologists assume positions within health organizations, as anthropological research findings become increasingly quantified, and as qualitative research is put to greater practical use, as has occurred in recent years, we will in fact witness a greater contribution of anthropology at the policy level.

Responding to some of the methodologic biases noted above, medical anthropologists have in recent years developed more short-term research techniques variously referred to as "rapid anthropological assessment" (Scrimshaw and Hurtado 1987) and "rapid ethnographic assessment" (Bentley et al. 1988). These approaches use traditional ethnographic methods of in-depth interviews and structured observation, but in a streamlined form, and there are new additions such as the focus group interview. Through the use of these methods, a specific research question can be addressed within a time frame of several weeks. While this methodology has elicited criticism from some anthropological classicists, it has served to make anthropological background studies feasible in the early phases of international health programs. The flexibility of anthropologists in adapting their methods to the more urgent timetables of program planners and administrators has contributed much to the resurgent presence of anthropologists in international health.

While the development of more rapid field methods may revise the stereotype of anthropological research as long-term and labor intensive, international agencies continue to view anthropologists primarily as ethnographers with expertise in qualitative data collection. The ethnographer stereotype may prove to be both an asset and a liability. With the increasing recognition of the importance of cultural context to program success, opportunities for anthropological involvement in international health programs have expanded and will probably continue to do so. However, such involvement reinforces the stereotype of anthropological research as ethnographic, qualitative, and soft, and may limit participation in other phases of research. Thus the challenge, for anthropologists, is to take advantage of expanded opportunities in ethnographic research while broadening their research capabilities beyond the qualitative realm.

Issues and Challenges

While there are many important issues that need to be addressed by anthropologists as they define an appropriate role for the discipline within international health, two appear to be particularly salient at this time.

The first issue relates to the way that social science approaches are currently viewed and utilized in international health research and practice. To a large extent the recent popularity of anthropological involvement in primary health care is an extension of the "magic bullet syndrome" and "quick-fix thinking" that has characterized biomedical approaches to health problems in both developed and developing countries (Heggenhougen and Clements 1987). While purely technological solutions have clearly failed and there is now general acceptance of the importance of sociocultural context, many planners are now turning to anthropology to identify the missing piece of the puzzle. Studies are commissioned with the hope that social science can pinpoint a simple key element that can be manipulated in such a way to make the whole system work as desired. Complex analyses that outline multifactorial solutions are considered to have little utility by those in management positions.

For example, on several occasions during my work with primary health care projects in Haiti, program managers (mostly physicians) read with interest my carefully documented reports analyzing the influence of socioeconomic and ethnomedical factors on the health problem at hand, put the report aside, then asked me to pick out the "key" variable that really made a difference. My qualified answers usually failed to satisfy the person seeking a magic bullet; on one occasion a frustrated administrator then turned to one of the project data coders and asked her if she had been able to discern the supposed "missing link."

The search for simple "human factors" solutions that do not entail reorganization of the health care system or change in the sociopolitical structure of the society underlies much of the current utilization of social science in international health. Similar criticisms have been leveled at the application of social marketing strategies, which are closely allied with social science, as being yet another technological fix for health problems. By limiting the focus to a product being promoted, and by treating sociocultural and political contexts as unmodifiable environmental constraints, social marketing in practice reinforces the technologic interventionist paradigm. Thus, to be able to satisfy the demand for parsimonious explanations of health behavior without "selling out" to a reductionist development worldview represents a major challenge for anthropologists working in international health.

A second major issue facing anthropologists today has to do with the willingness of government officials to integrate popular models of illness and the folk sector of health care into national and community health initiatives. Despite paying considerable lip service to the value of local resources, health culture, and user perspectives in PHC, and acknowledging the increased involvement of social scientists in applied research over the past decade, it remains the case that program planners and implementers make only limited use of social and behavioral knowledge. The reasons for this are diverse, but resistance often derives from conflicts between professional and non-professional authority. Officials are reluctant to endorse public health actions that appear to confer legitimacy to "unorthodox" health beliefs, health behaviors, and health practitioners.

Recommendations that encourage the incorporation of popular knowledge (e.g. diarrhea is caused by worms) or traditional healers (e.g. by the training of lay birth attendants) and yet pose no challenge to the biomedical model and power structure have been accepted fairly easily. However, when the suggested element conflicts with established knowledge and political structures, opposition is the most frequent reaction. The usual recourse is to question the scientific soundness of qualitative anthropological research methods as the rationale for rejecting the recommendation.

A good example of this selective use of anthropology in PHC occurred in the Mass Media and Health Practices Project in Honduras (1980-83), which included a large ethnographic research component in the design phase. Although this project has been frequently cited as a prime example of the successful integration of anthropological knowledge in a large-scale intervention (Kendall, Foote, and Martorell 1983), on the whole the ethnographic findings were largely discarded by the medical staff directing the program.

> Initial ethnographic research was incorporated into the project, local categories for disease were part of campaign messages, and the description of the physical environment of the household developed by anthropology was accepted as valid. At the same time, especially with regard to developing the intervention strategy and the goals for the campaign, the entire portrait provided by anthropology regarding local perception and treatment of diarrhea, and local concerns about ill health in general, was not really considered. When anthropological evidence clashed with the viewpoint of medical authorities and with evidence collected from other sources, the former was not considered to be of sufficient weight to change the implementation strategy (Kendall 1989: 289-290).

Although the ethnographic findings were incorporated into the program to some extent, as in the decisions to mention "diarrhea caused by worms" in the campaign and not to promote water boiling for reducing diarrhea incidence, the project fell short of utilizing the full potential of the anthropological research. Folk categories and popular beliefs related to diarrhea were used "in a rather superficial sense when these were considered benign" (Kendall 1989: 300), while those that conflicted with medical knowledge, such as the belief in the folk illness *empacho* (which anthropological research had shown would be important to address in the ORT campaign), were rejected. Popular belief in this folk illness was viewed as a reflection of peasant ignorance which should not be legitimized. In analyzing the reasons for this failure, Kendall concludes that "some of this disregard is due to professional autonomy and the relation of the social sciences to medicine. However, some of this is also due to the perception of ethnography as subjective and unsound science" (1989: 296). The methodologic justification for discrediting anthropological research relates back to its stereotype as "soft," unrigorous, and having less weight than quantitative research, as discussed in the preceding section.

Conflicts of medical authority and power also underlie the reluctance of the medical establishment to give official recognition to traditional healers, especially those of the magico-religious type. Here I am speaking of more than simply the issue of using healers in service delivery programs, which involves a whole other set of issues. Despite a large anthropological literature documenting the importance of folk medical care from the standpoint of understanding how rural needs are currently being met (Pillsbury 1982), achieving effective control of major diseases, and assessing total family health care expenditures (Coreil 1983), official discussions of health care rarely mention the folk sector. To mention is to recognize, and recognition confers a measure of legitimacy that is not always desired.

In the course of my fieldwork in Haiti, there were two situations where I documented the unofficial involvement of traditional healers in public health practice. In the first, the healers were treating victims of an anthrax epidemic with antibiotics obtained from local pharmacies, and the healers asked to be supplied directly by the health authorities (Coreil 1980). In the second, the healers were found to be using ORT to treat diarrhea in their patients and expressed willingness to collaborate with authorities in the control of diarrheal diseases (Coreil 1988). In both instances public health officials were extremely reluctant to acknowledge what was going on; the very existence of these healers was viewed as a problem and a source of embarrassment, and the prospect of even acknowledging their independent actions appeared to confer undue positive sanction (Coreil 1989).

Apart from the issue of conflict with professional authority, programmatic incorporation of folk medical knowledge and practitioners reinforces, at least in the eyes of many Third World health professionals, the outside world's view of developing countries as lagging behind in medical modernization. National pride leads any country to want to present its best side to the rest of the world, and the professional medical communities of less technologically advanced societies often do not regard folk healing as something to be proudly displayed. Hence, the anthropological focus on popular health culture is often received with ambivalence.

Conclusion

The problems described above can be expressed as a series of challenges facing medical anthropologists working in the international health field. How can we continue to make use of anthropology's strengths in holistic and descriptive ethnomedical studies without compromising our objective of making significant contributions to health action programs? How can we take advantage of opportunities to integrate ethnographic approaches in multidisciplinary projects in a way that strengthens the role of qualitative research and avoids reinforcing negative stereotypes of anthropology? How can we meet the needs of decision-makers for sociocultural knowledge without alienating those who seek our help? How can we provide a foundation on which to base constructive programs even while policies and strategies shift to and fro in search of a magic bullet? In the long run anthropology's most important contribution may be not in the initiation phase of new health programs but in finding ways that such programs can be institutionalized and sustained over time. These dilemmas represent only a few of the many challenges facing anthropology in international health. We must find ways to bring the full value of anthropology's tradition of rich cultural insight to bear on the future of primary health care.

Acknowledgements

I would like to thank Barbara Pillsbury, Bert Pelto, Gretel Pelto, and Dorothy Mull for their helpful suggestions on this chapter.

Notes

1. Although water, sanitation, family planning, and nutrition are important aspects of international health, and of primary health care in particular, anthropological involvement in these areas is not covered in this review.

2. For example, his 1958 review of intercultural health practice identifies 11 cultural barriers and 7 motivations to change. About 20 years later, in a programmatic article entitled "Medical Anthropology and International Health Planning" (1977), he focuses on the determinants of community acceptance of modern medicine and the role of traditional healers in service delivery; and a paper on the role of medical anthropology in primary health care (Foster 1978) emphasizes erroneous stereotypes of traditional medicine (see Velimirovic, Chapter 3).

In 1982 the text of Foster's acceptance speech for the Malinowski Award was published as "Applied Anthropology and International Health: Retrospect and Prospect" (Foster 1982a), an account of the waxing and waning of anthropological involvement in international health since the 1940s. Still another article (Foster 1984) addresses the utility of anthropological research in dealing with health problems in the developing world and provides a useful review of research findings since 1950.

Most recently, Foster has written two papers dealing with international health organizations; one discusses behavioral science contributions to WHO (1987a) and the other analyzes the bureaucratic features of such organizations (1987b).

3. Both this broad overview and the book chapter published the following year (Polgar 1963) contain useful summaries of health research on the international scene. Interestingly, what is today referred to as "international" health, Polgar describes as "cross-cultural"; both terms imply the somewhat ethnocentric notion that our own culture stands aloof from the "international" or "cross-cultural" scene (Pillsbury 1985). At about the same time, Hughes wrote a comprehensive chapter on "Public Health in Non-Literate Societies" (1963) which examines specific cultural and behavioral risk factors for disease.

4. Between 1963 and 1974 four review articles appeared which bore the title "Medical Anthropology," and which included references to applied research in developing countries. In Scotch's (1963) review, international health work is discussed in a section on "Modern Public Health Programs in Different Cultural Settings." Almost a decade later Fabrega's (1972) review addresses related topics under two different headings--ethnomedical studies and medical ecology and epidemiology. A year later Colson and Selby (1974) discussed international health issues primarily under "Health Care Delivery Systems," while Lieban (1974) comments on relevant applied research in a treatment of "Medicine and Culture Change."

After 1974 the field of medical anthropology had grown and specialized to the point that subsequent reviews focused on more narrow subfields (e.g. Fabrega 1977; Worsley 1982), none specifically related to international health. For example, Worsley's (1982) review of non-Western medical systems is largely a theoretical discussion of comparative healing systems and medical pluralism.

5. Written as a chapter in a training manual in medical anthropology, it describes the work settings and kinds of employment available in international health work together with the skills needed and job-hunting strategies.

6. These developed out of American Anthropological Association meeting symposia and bore the following titles: "Anthropology and Disease Control" (Brown 1983), "Anthropology and Primary Health Care in Developing Countries" (Bloom and Reid 1984), and "Anthropological Studies of Diarrheal Illness" (Coreil and Mull 1988).

References

Bastien, Joseph 1987 *Healers of the Andes*. Salt Lake City: University of Utah Press.

Bentley, Margaret E. 1988 The Household Management of Childhood Diarrhea in Rural North India. *Social Science and Medicine* 27(1):75-85.

Bentley, Margaret E., Gretel H. Pelto, Walter L. Straus, Debra A. Schumann, Catherine Adegbola, Emanuela de la Pena, Gbolahan A. Oni, Kenneth H. Brown, and Sandra L. Huffman 1988 Rapid Ethnographic Assessment: Applications in a Diarrhea Management Program. *Social Science and Medicine* 27(1):107-116.

Bloom, Abby, and Janice Reid, eds. 1984 Anthropology and Primary Health Care in Developing Countries. Special Issue of *Social Science and Medicine*, Vol. 19, No. 3.

Brown, Peter J. 1983 Anthropology and Disease Control. Special Issue of *Medical Anthropology*, Vol. 7, No. 2.

Brownlee, A. 1989 *Breastfeeding, Weaning and Nutrition: The Behavioral Issues*. Behavioral Issues in Child Survival Programs Monograph No. 4. Prepared for the Office of Health, USAID, Washington, DC by International Health and Development Associates, December.

Buzzard, Shirley 1984 Appropriate Research for Primary Health Care: An Anthropologist's View. *Social Science and Medicine* 19(3):273-278.

Cassel, John 1955 A Comprehensive Health Program Among South African Zulu. In *Health, Culture and Community*. Benjamin D. Paul, ed. Pp. 15-42. New York: Sage.

Cochrane, S., D.J. O'Hara, and J. Leslie 1980 The Effects of Education on Health. World Bank Staff Working Paper No. 405. Washington, DC: World Bank.

Colson, Anthony C. 1971 The Differential Use of Medical Resources in Developing Countries. *Journal of Health and Social Behavior* 12:226-237.

Colson, Anthony C., and Karen E. Selby 1974 Medical Anthropology. *Annual Review of Anthropology* 3:245-262.

Coreil, Jeannine 1980 Traditional and Western Responses to an Anthrax Epidemic in Rural Haiti. *Medical Anthropology* 4:79-105.

___ 1983 Parallel Structures in Professional and Folk Health Care: A Model Applied to Rural Haiti. *Culture, Medicine and Psychiatry* 7:131-151.

___ 1985 Community Acceptance of Oral Rehydration Therapy in Haiti. Project report presented to the Pan American Health Organization, CDD Operational Research, Grant No. 107USA4.

___ 1988 Scientific Requirements of Focus Group Research in Developing Countries. Paper presented at the Society for Applied Anthropology annual meeting, Tampa, FL, April 21-23.

___ 1989 Lessons in Knowledge Utilization Learned from a Community Study of Oral Rehydration Therapy in Haiti. In *Making Ourselves Useful: Case Studies in the Utilization of Anthropological Knowledge*. John van Willigen, Barbara Rylko-Bauer, and Ann McElroy, eds. Pp. 143-158. Boulder: Westview Press.

Coreil, Jeannine, and J. Dennis Mull, eds. 1988 Anthropological Studies of Diarrheal Illness. Special Issue of *Social Science and Medicine*, Vol. 27, No. 1.

Djukanovic, V. and E. Mach, eds. 1975 *Alternative Approaches to Meeting Basic Health Needs in Developing Countries*. Geneva: WHO.

Elmendorf, Mary 1981 *Women, Water and Waste: Beyond Access*. Arlington, VA: Water and Sanitation for Health.

___ 1983 Public and Private Roles of Women in Water Supply and Sanitation Programs. *Human Organization* 42(23):195-204.

Fabrega, Horacio, Jr. 1972 Medical Anthropology. In *Biennial Review of Anthropology*. Bernard J. Siegel, ed. Pp. 167-229. Stanford, CA: Stanford University Press.

Firth, Raymond 1934 The Sociological Study of Native Diet. *Africa* 7:401-414.

Foster, George M. 1977 Medical Anthropology and International Health Planning. *Social Science and Medicine* 11:527-534.

___ 1978 The Role of Medical Anthropology in Primary Health Care. *Bulletin of the Pan American Health Organization* 12(4):335-340.

___ 1982a Applied Anthropology and International Health: Retrospect and Prospect. *Human Organization* 41(3):189-197.

___ 1982b Community Development and Primary Health Care: Their Conceptual Similarities. *Medical Anthropology* 6(3):183-195.

___ 1984 Anthropological Research Perspectives on Health Problems in Developing Countries. *Social Science and Medicine* 18(10):847-854.

___ 1987a World Health Organization Behavioral Science Research: Problems and Prospects. *Social Science and Medicine* 24(9):709-717.

___ 1987b Bureaucratic Aspects of International Health Agencies. *Social Science and Medicine* 25(9):1039-1048.

Gray, Ronald 1986 A Review of Methodological Approaches to Evaluating Health Programs. Johns Hopkins Institute for International Programs Occasional Paper, No. 1.

Green, Edward C. 1986 Diarrhea and the Social Marketing of Oral Rehydration Salts in Bangladesh. *Social Science and Medicine* 23:357-366.

Harvard Institute for International Development 1988 The Applied Diarrheal Disease Research Project: Mid-Project Report, Sept. 30, 1985-March 30, 1988.

Heggenhougen, H.K. 1984 Will Primary Health Care Efforts Be Allowed to Succeed? *Social Science and Medicine* 19(3): 217-224.

Heggenhougen, H.K., and L. Shore 1986 Cultural Components of Behavioural Epidemiology: Implications for Primary Health Care. *Social Science and Medicine* 22(11):1235-1245.

Heggenhougen, Kris, and John Clements 1987 *Acceptability of Childhood Immunization: Social Science Perspectives*. Evaluation and Planning Centre for Health Care, Pub. No. 14, London: London School of Hygiene and Tropical Medicine.

Herman, Elizabeth, and Margaret E. Bentley 1989 Adapting to the Cultural Context of Diarrhea: Ethnographic Methods for CDD Programs. Unpublished document, Johns Hopkins University, Baltimore.

Hoben, Allan 1982 Anthropologists and Development. *Annual Review of Anthropology* 11:349-375.

Hsu, Francis L.K. 1955 A Cholera Epidemic in a Chinese Town. In *Health, Culture and Community*. Benjamin D. Paul, ed. Pp. 135-154. New York: Sage.

Hughes, Charles Campbell 1963 Public Health in Non-Literate Societies. In *Man's Image in Medicine and Anthropology*. Iago Galdston, ed. Pp. 157-233. New York: International University Press.

Janes, Craig R., Ron Stall, and Sandra M. Gifford, eds. 1986 *Anthropology and Epidemiology*. Dordrecht: Reidel.

Justice, Judith 1986 *Policies, Plans and People: Culture and Health Development in Nepal*. Berkeley: University of California Press.

Kendall, Carl 1989 The Use and Non-Use of Anthropology: The Diarrheal Disease Control Program in Honduras. In *Making Ourselves Useful: Case Studies in the Utilization of Anthropological Knowledge*. John van Willigen, Barbara Rylko-Bauer, and Ann McElroy, eds. Pp. 283-303. Boulder: Westview Press.

Kendall, Carl, Dennis Foote, and Reynaldo Martorell 1984 Ethnomedicine and Oral Rehydration Therapy: A Case Study of Ethnomedical Investigation and Program Planning. *Social Science and Medicine* 19(3):253-260.

Khare, R.S. 1962 Ritual Purity and Pollution in Relation to Domestic Sanitation. *The Eastern Anthropologist* 15:125-139.

Kleinman, Arthur 1978 International Health Care Planning from an Ethnomedical Perspective: Critique and Recommendations for Change. *Medical Anthropology* 2(2):72-96.

___ 1980 *Patients and Healers in the Context of Culture*. Berkeley: University of California Press.

Landy, David 1978 Role Adaptation: Traditional Curers under the Impact of Western Medicine. *American Ethnologist* 1:103-127.

Lieban, Richard W. 1974 Medical Anthropology. In *Handbook of Social and Cultural Anthropology*. John J. Honigman, ed. Pp. 1031-1072. Chicago: Rand McNally.

Maclean, Una, and Robert H. Bannerman 1982 Introduction: Utilization of Indigenous Healers in National Health Delivery Systems. *Social Science and Medicine* 16:1815-1816.

Malinowski, Bronislaw 1945 *The Dynamics of Culture Change: An Inquiry into Race Relations in Africa*. New Haven: Yale University Press.

Manoff, Richard 1985 *Social Marketing: New Imperative for Public Health*. New York: Praeger.

Marchione, Thomas J. 1984 Evaluating Primary Health Care and Nutrition Programs in the Context of National Development. *Social Science and Medicine* 19(3:225-235.

McElroy, Ann, and Patricia Townsend 1989 *Medical Anthropology in Ecological Perspective*, 2nd ed. Boulder: Westview Press.

Medical Anthropology Quarterly 1984 Perspectives on Postdoctoral Public Health Training for Medical Anthropologists. 15(4):90-101.

Mosley, W.H. 1987 Appropriate Reproductive Health Skills and Knowledge for Physicians and Nurses in Primary Health Care Settings. Prepared for a conference on "Reproductive Health Education and Technology: Issues and Future Directions," Lausanne, Switzerland, January 25-29.

National Research Council (NRC) 1945 *Manual for the Study of Food Habits*. Washington: National Academy of Sciences, National Research Council, Bulletin 111.

New, Kong-Ming, and John M. Donahue 1986 Introduction: Strategies for Primary Health Care by the Year 2000: A Political Economic Perspective. *Human Organization* 45(2):95-96.

Newman, Lucile F. 1972 Birth Control: An Anthropological View. *Addison-Wesley Module in Anthropology* No. 27, pp. 1-21.

Nichter, Mark A. 1986 The Primary Health Center as a Social System: PHC, Social Status, and the Issue of Team-Work in South Asia. *Social Science and Medicine* 23(4):347-355.

___ 1988 From *Aralu* to ORS: Sinhalese Perceptions of Digestion, Diarrhea, and Dehydration. *Social Science and Medicine* 27(1):39-52.

___ 1989 *Anthropology and International Health: South Asian Case Studies*. Norwell, MA: Kluwer Academic Publishers.

Nichter, Mark, and Mimi Nichter 1987 Cultural Notions of Fertility in South Asia and Their Impact on Sri Lankan Family Planning Practices. *Human Organization* 46(1)18-28.

Nichter, Mimi, and Mark Nichter 1986 Health Education by Appropriate Analogy: Using the Familiar to Explain the New. *Convergence* 19(1):63-71.

Paul, Benjamin D., ed. 1955a *Health, Culture and Community*. New York: Russell Sage.

___ 1955b Introduction: Understanding the Community. In *Health, Culture and Community*. Benjamin D. Paul, ed. Pp. 1-11. New York: Russell Sage.

___ 1958 The Role of Beliefs and Customs in Sanitation Programs. *American Journal of Public Health* 48:1502-1506.

Pelto, Pertti J., and Gretel H. Pelto 1975 Intracultural Diversity: Some Theoretical Issues. *American Ethnologist* 2(1):1-18.

Pillsbury, Barbara L.K. 1982 Policy and Evaluation Perspectives on Traditional Health Practitioners in National Health Care Systems. *Social Science and Medicine* 16:1825-1834.

___ 1985 Anthropologists in International Health. In *Training Manual in Medical Anthropology*. Carole E. Hill, ed. Special Publication No. 18, pp. 84-110. Washington, DC: American Anthropological Association.

___ 1986 Making a Difference: Anthropologists in International Development. In *Anthropology and Public Policy: A Dialogue*. Special Publication No. 21, pp. 10-28. Washington, DC: American Anthropological Association.

___ 1989a (Series Coordinator) Behavioral Issues in Child Survival Programs: A Synthesis of the Literature with Recommendations for Project Design & Implementation. A monograph series prepared for the Office of Health, USAID, Washington, DC by International Health and Development Associates, December.

___ 1989b *Immunization: The Behavioral Issues*. Behavioral Issues in Child Survival Programs Monograph No. 3, Prepared for the Office of Health, USAID,

Washington, DC by International Health and Development Associates, December.

Polgar, Steven 1962 Health and Human Behavior: Areas of Interest Common to the Social and Medical Sciences. *Current Anthropology* 3(2):159-205.

___ 1963 Health Action in Cross-Cultural Perspective. In *Handbook of Medical Sociology*. Howard Freeman, Sol Levine, and Leo G. Reeder, eds. Pp. 397-419. Englewood Cliffs: Prentice-Hall.

___ 1966 Sociocultural Research in Family Planning in the United States: Review and Prospects. *Human Organization* 25(4):321-329.

___ 1971 *Culture and Population: A Collection of Current Studies*. Carolina Population Center Monograph No. 9, Cambridge: Schenkman.

___ 1972 Population History and Population Policies from an Anthropological Perspective. *Current Anthropology* 13(2):203-211.

Polgar, Steven, and John F. Marshall 1976 The Search for Culturally Acceptable Fertility Regulating Methods. In *Culture, Natality and Family Planning*. J.F. Marshall and S. Polgar, eds. Pp. 204-218. Carolina Population Center, University of North Carolina, Chapel Hill.

Ramalingaswami, V. 1986 The Art of the Possible. *Social Science and Medicine* 22:1097-1103.

Raphael, Dana 1973 The Role of Breastfeeding in a Bottle-Oriented World. *Ecology of Food and Nutrition* 2:121-126.

Richards, Audrey I. 1939 *Land, Labour and Diet in Northern Rhodesia: An Economic Study of the Bemba Tribe*. London: Oxford University Press for the International African Institute.

Romanucci-Ross, Lola 1969 The Hierarchy of Resort in Curative Practices: The Admiralty Islands, Melanesia. *Journal of Health and Social Behavior* 10:201-209.

Rubel Arthur J., and Carolyn Sargent 1979 Introduction to Parallel Medical Systems: Papers From a Workshop on "The Healing Process." *Social Science and Medicine* 13B:3-6.

Schumann, Debra, Organizer 1988 The Household Production of Health. Symposium at the American Anthropological Association annual meeting, Chicago, November 18-22.

Scotch, Norman A. 1963 Medical Anthropology. In *Biennial Review of Anthropology*. Bernard J. Siegel, ed. Pp. 30-68. Stanford, CA: Stanford University Press.

Scrimshaw, Susan C.M., and Elena Hurtado 1987 *Rapid Assessment Procedures for Nutrition and Primary Health Care*. Los Angeles: U.C.L.A. Latin American Center Publications.

Singer, M., H.A. Baer, and E. Lazarus, eds. 1990. Critical Medical Anthropology: Theory and Research. Special Issue of *Social Science and Medicine* Vol. 30, No. 2.

Sukkary-Stolba, S. 1989 *Oral Rehydration Therapy: The Behavioral Issues*. Behavioral Issues in Child Survival Monograph No. 1. Prepared for the Office of Health, USAID, Washington, DC by International Health and Development and Associates, December.

van der Geest, S., and S.R. Whyte, eds. 1988 *The Context of Medicines in Developing Countries: Studies in Pharmaceutical Anthropology*. Dordrecht: Reidel.

Velimirovic, Boris 1984 Traditional Medicine Is Not Primary Health Care, A Polemic. Part I: *Curare* 7:61-79. Part II: *Curare* 7:85-93.

Walsh, Julia A., and Kenneth S. Warren 1979 Selective Primary Health Care: An Interim Strategy for Disease Control in Developing Countries. *New England Journal of Medicine* 301:976-974.

Weaver, Thomas 1985a Anthropology as a Policy Science: Part I, A Critique. *Human Organization* 44(2):97-105

___ 1985b Anthropology as a Policy Science: Part II, Development and Training. *Human Organization* 44(3): 197-205.

Weiss, Mitchell G. 1988 Cultural Models of Diarrheal Illness: Conceptual Framework and Review. *Social Science and Medicine* 27(1):5-16.

Wellin, Edward 1955 Water Boiling in a Peruvian Town. In *Health, Culture and Community*. Benjamin D. Paul, ed. Pp. 71-103. New York: Russell Sage.

___ 1977 Theoretical Orientations in Medical Anthropology: Continuity and Change Over the Past Half-Century. In *Culture, Disease and Healing: Studies in Medical Anthropology*. David Landy, ed. Pp. 47-58. New York: MacMillan.

WHO/SEARO 1982 Appropriate Technologies for Behavioural Science Research on Health Problems. Report of an Inter-Country Consultation, 1-11 December 1981, SEA/HE/119, SEA/RES/47. New Delhi: World Health Organization.

WHO and UNICEF 1978 Primary Health Care: Report of the International Conference on Primary Health Care, Alma-Ata, USSR, 6-12 September 1978.

Worsley, Peter 1982 Non-Western Medical Systems. *Annual Review of Anthropology* 11:315-348.

Young, James C. 1981 *Medical Choice in a Mexican Village*. New Brunswick: Rutgers University Press.

2

The Primary Health Care Dialectic: History, Rhetoric, and Reality

J. Dennis Mull

Introduction

Until the middle of the 20th century, biomedically-oriented health care in the developing world consisted largely of attempts to import or cultivate hospital-centered medicine as it had evolved in the wealthier industrialized nations. These efforts were initiated by different organizations in different parts of the world. In Africa, the prime instigators were missionary groups; in Asia, government institutions; and in Latin America, a mixture of the two. Although these initiatives seemed promising at the outset, they ultimately proved to be of negligible benefit to the poor people who constitute the majority of the population in developing countries.

Relics of the commitments made in that early era linger on, partly for political reasons. Thus, ivory towers better described as "disease palaces" (Mahler 1974) still dot the developing world--high-technology facilities usually located in cities far from the rural areas where most people live (cf. Morley 1973). By the 1950s, however, planners and administrators worldwide realized that the hospital-based approach to health care had failed. In the two decades that followed, the World Health Organization and other international agencies tried to remedy the deficiencies and inequities of that earlier model via highly targeted programs aimed at eliminating certain dread diseases such as malaria and schistosomiasis. However, these efforts too met with little success. It was in the wake of these frustrating disappointments that the primary health care (PHC) movement was born.

At an international conference held in Alma-Ata in the U.S.S.R. in 1978, WHO and UNICEF introduced the term "primary health care"

(PHC) and issued a declaration that this was *the* approach that countries of the world should adopt in order to reach a stated goal of achieving "Health for All by the Year 2000" (WHO/UNICEF 1978). As defined in the Alma-Ata declaration, PHC was to be truly comprehensive. It was to consist of essential health care made universally accessible to individuals and families by means acceptable to them, with their full participation, and at a cost that they, their community, and the country as a whole could afford. In an effort to address the world's major health needs, PHC was to provide preventive, curative, and rehabilitative services consisting of at least the following eight components:

* Health education enabling people to prevent and deal with problems;
* Basic sanitation and an adequate source of safe water;
* Healthful nutrition and a secure food supply;
* Maternal and child health care, including family planning;
* Immunization against the major infectious diseases;
* Prevention of endemic diseases;
* Appropriate treatment of common ailments;
* A supply of essential medications.

Like many such events, this now famous programmatic launching of "Health for All by the Year 2000" really represented less a birth than an endorsement of an idea whose time, by popular consensus, had come. A brief review of the events preceding Alma-Ata will be presented here to help illuminate how unanimity could be so readily achieved around so ambitious an international objective. This will be followed by a summary of the evolution of the PHC movement after 1978 and the controversial issues that have arisen in its wake. Special attention will be given to the continuing debate over the relative merits of the two major approaches to PHC, i.e. comprehensive, or horizontal, PHC (CPHC) and selective, or vertical, PHC (SPHC). This debate has been the focus of many articles (notably Walsh and Warren 1979; Gish 1982; Rifkin and Walt 1986 and 1988; Walsh 1988; and Warren 1988).

Rather than recapitulating all of the arguments in favor of one or the other approach, this chapter will summarize major factors that have influenced international perspectives on PHC over the years. It is hoped that this summary will provide a useful background for the chapters that follow as each addresses a particular aspect of PHC. Many of the problems raised in those chapters reflect basic challenges facing PHC generally as it attempts to fulfill its ambitious goal of providing "health for all," and such challenges cannot be fully understood in isolation from the larger social, economic, and political issues that surround them. Implicitly, then, one aim of the present review is to suggest that insights drawn from holistically-oriented disciplines such as medical anthropology can make an important contribution to the evolution of truly effective, culturally appropriate primary health care.

Bracketed here, however, will be any extensive consideration of the wider world context in which international health programs have expanded to their present order of magnitude. This context would include such well-known entities as the decolonization struggles that took place around the time of World War II and what many would call the "neo-colonialist" development initiatives that followed. The not-so-hidden linkages between medical "assistance" to the developing world by industrialized nations via aid organizations and those nations' political agendas have been discussed at length by others, for example by Hancock (1989). Donahue (Chapter 4) provides a related critique of *biomedical* hegemony via a closeup look at power relations within one developing country and suggests productive ways in which anthropologists might respond. In the final chapter of the present volume, Mull and Mull discuss the conflicted nature of anthropologists' involvement in research financed by aid organizations whose political stance and aims they may not share.

Mid-Century Vertical Programs Before PHC

Turning now from these larger issues to consider the history of PHC, one can see that the narrowly-focused international health programs of the 1950s and 1960s targeting specific diseases were organized in similar ways although their objectives differed. The U.S. Peace Corps waged war on tuberculosis in Latin America; WHO sponsored worldwide campaigns against malaria and schistosomiasis; and a consortium of international agencies, including the Center for Disease Control in Atlanta, conducted a drive to eliminate smallpox from the face of the earth. These initiatives came to be known as "vertical programs" for two main reasons. First of all, most of them were paid for and directed by people from outside the target population; second, they were organized so that they operated from the top down to the field worker level rather than being integrated with other programs along the way.

This "vertical" approach had the advantage of fostering efficiency and accountability, so that those trying to run the programs had a minimum of distractions and annoyances. The outcome of these activities varied considerably, however. Thus, although the anti-smallpox campaign was one of the greatest success stories in the history of medicine (see Henderson 1976), most initiatives of this type were failures.

The family planning program in India, for example, ran for a decade during the 1960s, yet at the end of that period, birthrates were higher than they were when it began. The international effort to eradicate schistosomiasis met a similar fate as expanded crop irrigation aided food production but at the same time spread the disease. Campaigns against trachoma and leprosy fared no better. The global malaria eradication drive, which was the largest and most ambitious of all the vertical programs and was the focus of WHO's efforts for ten years, likewise ended in failure: at the end of the decade, malaria rates were either unchanged or even higher than before in most countries where the program had been implemented. This latter debacle in particular did much to fuel the fires of support for PHC at Alma-Ata.

There were other problems with the vertical model of health care. Most notably, it did nothing to remedy the basic health problems that had persisted despite the "disease palace" approach. As suggested above, the majority of people in developing countries, living mainly in rural areas, continued to lack access to curative medicine and saw no hope that the extremely high morbidity and mortality rates among their children might ever be lowered. The resultant widespread popular discontent with the state of curative health care led several such countries (notably Indonesia, Kenya, and the Philippines) to experiment with providing comprehensive and integrated basic health services in the 1960s.

These services varied from country to country, ranging from simple community-based preventive and curative measures carried out by local people with minimal training to fully integrated systems linking community health workers with referral-driven health centers staffed by professionals and backed by regional hospitals. They were all comprehensive in intent, however, and by the late 1970s, many other countries were considering implementing programs shaped by the same underlying philosophy. As the Alma-Ata meeting drew near, it was clear that such strategies had attracted global support as a possible way to rectify inequities in the delivery of health services in the developing world.

The Birth of Comprehensive PHC

Individuals who were part of the international health leadership in the mid-1970s have indicated that the mood of WHO officials at that time was one of disappointment and even despair (Newell 1988). Several of their vertical initiatives had been unsuccessful, and the malaria program's spectacular failure had all but ruined the organization's international credibility. Health leaders were ready for an entirely new approach, and they were galvanized by the social justice ethic implicit in a resolution to strive for "Health for All by the Year 2000." As a result, the resolution was unanimously approved by 60 international organizations and by 138 member nations of WHO represented at the Alma-Ata conference. Thus began the movement that gave new life and hope not only to WHO but to the international health leadership in general, and with it came a highly contagious, almost religious fervor. Indeed, very few concepts in the annals of health care have ever enjoyed such universal endorsement.

The agenda for achieving Health for All--or HFA, as it came to be known--was an ambitious one. Strikingly idealistic and remarkably unfettered by talk of fiscal constraints, much less tempered by political considerations, the Alma-Ata declaration aimed to achieve not just health in the sense of freedom from disease, but a state of positive well-being for everyone in the world by the end of the 20th century. The proposed means for achieving this were extremely comprehensive and included not only providing conventional preventive health services, but making safe water available to everyone, improving roads so that commerce, education, and agriculture could flourish, and bringing modern curative medicine to remote locales. A suggestion was even made that resources be taken away from the military and that warfare be ended so that funding of these programs would be more feasible (WHO/UNICEF 1978:5).

The centerpiece of the Health-for-All proposal was its plan for comprehensive primary health care delivery--a plan that was proposed in 1978 and further defined in WHO publications over the next two years (WHO 1979). Comprehensive primary health care, or CPHC, had multiple programmatic components that represented a drastic change from the doctor-centered urban hospital approach to health that had previously dominated most of the developing world. First of all, it was to be all-pervasive, beginning with a village or community health worker (CHW) at the local level who was to be chosen by his or her neighbors and whose activities were to be responsive to the wishes of the community itself (see Wood, Chapter 6, for a detailed discussion).

After being trained for a limited time period, sometimes for only a few weeks, the CHW was to provide basic preventive health services such as growth monitoring as well as simple curative treatment. He or she would refer difficult or complex cases to a somewhat more skilled paraprofessional who might be known as a lady health visitor (LHV) or a community health nurse (CHN), and this individual would be available to the CHW for clinical consultation and administrative direction. Above these health workers would be another tier of expertise in the form of regional nurses or general practice physicians working in conjunction with health teams who would provide a still higher level of clinical referral and administrative supervision. Finally, at the very top would be district hospitals and management centers to which the most difficult clinical cases could be referred, and where field program activities could be coordinated with the central government.

Thus, CPHC was intended to provide an integrated system of clinical medical care to *everyone* through a network of consultation, service, and referral--a network extending from the village health worker to the hospital, with supervision and direction coming from centralized health professionals and administrators. Beyond this curative aspect of CPHC, six specific preventive programs were mandated as being of prime importance in reducing the need for clinical care. These programs were perhaps best codified by UNICEF, which coined the acronym GOBI-FF from the initial letters of their names to refer to them as a unit--G for "Growth monitoring," O for "Oral rehydration therapy," and so on. Since these programs have been adopted by virtually all organizations involved in international health and form the foundation of current PHC programs, they are briefly described below.

1. Growth monitoring. Growth monitoring is based on the principle that documenting growth is the simplest way to assess a child's nutritional status--especially during the first five years of life, the period of greatest vulnerability. Briefly stated, a child who is in good health shows a steady increase in height and weight. For efficiency, most growth monitoring programs follow the most sensitive indicator of health status--the child's weight as a function of age--and plot this weight on a small card chart that is used only for that individual child. Printed on the chart are standard curves representing international norms and varying degrees of malnutrition. When a child fails to exhibit growth on two or more successive (usually monthly) weighings, or when the "weight line" starts downward, there is cause for concern and possible intervention.

Varying degrees of malnutrition are associated with defined levels of risk. For example, the risk of death among children suffering from second-degree malnutrition, the intermediate level, was shown to be more than 20% in one study, while mortality among those with third-degree malnutrition, the most severe form, can be as high as 60% (Gómez et al. 1956:77, 81). The usefulness of the growth chart lies in its simplicity; it enables a mother to be an informed partner in evaluating her child's health status. There are other means of assessing nutrition and growth, such as measuring the child's arm circumference or skin-fold thickness, but these methods are more complex and have been less popular than monitoring weight for age.

2. Oral rehydration therapy. This simple technology involves the oral administration of solutions made with packaged rehydration salts and glucose (ORS) or with household salt and sugar (SSS). Oral rehydration therapy, known as ORT, is intended to prevent death from dehydration in children with diarrhea. (An estimated 4 to 5 million children a year die from diarrhea, and in most cases it is the dehydration rather than the diarrhea-causing infection that kills them.) ORT works because of a physiological linkage between the intestinal absorption of salt and sugar and the absorption of water. Its appeal is that mothers can administer it themselves and death can thus be prevented without the involvement of doctors or hospitals. The social science literature indicates, however, that widespread and correct use of ORT is not easily achieved (Coreil and Mull 1988).

3. Breastfeeding. Breast is best, compared to bottlefeeding of infants. First of all, human breastmilk is cheaper than other milks. It is also better for the child, both because it is more nutritious and because it imparts immunity to infection. An additional benefit is that roughly two-thirds of breastfeeding mothers do not ovulate, and therefore breastfeeding is a statistically helpful if individually risky form of birth control in settings where other methods may not be available or acceptable (Jelliffe and Jelliffe 1978; Huffman and Lamphere 1984). Bottlefeeding not only lacks these virtues but actually perpetrates disease because of the contaminated water frequently used in preparation, the often-dirty environment in which feeding takes place, and the widespread lack of refrigeration in the developing world. Yet mothers in many areas do not breastfeed, for a variety of reasons (Brownlee 1989).

4. Immunization. In developing countries, approximately 5 million children per year die from vaccine-preventable causes. Hence, mass immunization through such programs as WHO's very successful Expanded Program on Immunization (EPI) has been a cornerstone of virtually all PHC programs. The cost of immunizing a child against six major diseases--measles, polio, diphtheria, tetanus, pertussis, and tuberculosis--is on the average only about five dollars, and this cost is often covered by outside funding agencies. Immunization has been difficult to implement in many developing countries, however. One problem has been nonacceptance of immunization for a variety of reasons, i.e. social and cultural barriers (Heggenhougen and Clements 1987; Pillsbury 1989; Nichter, this volume). Other impediments include the difficulty of keeping live virus vaccines frozen or cold all the way from the manufacturer to the village, as well as the need for large quantities of sterile needles and syringes, to say nothing of vehicles to carry health workers to remote sites.

5. Family planning. Family planning--sometimes referred to as family spacing--remains a focus of public health concern for obvious reasons. The time interval for population doubling in the poorest countries ranges from 16

to 50 years, as compared with 100 years for most Western nations and 1,000 years for Sweden. Thus the poorest countries literally outgrow their own successes in agriculture and economics; and many--especially in Africa--are getting poorer year after year (Bell and Reich 1988). For example, Africa's per capita income shrank by almost 4% between 1980 and 1988 (*The Economist* 1989:40).

Beyond economic considerations, the health of both mothers and children are influenced by family size, or, more accurately, by birth spacing. If there are at least two years between pregnancies, not only is the mother better able to recoup her own physiological losses, but children have a greater chance of being well cared for, of being breastfed longer, and of being taller and heavier when they grow up. In countries where the average birth interval is less than two years, infant mortality is usually high (Hobcraft et al. 1983; Morley and Lovel 1986:112).

6. Food supplements. The second "F" of GOBI-FF refers to food supplement programs, but the meaning of the term has changed somewhat over the years. In the late 1970s and early 1980s, it referred mainly to the introduction of "outside" foods, frequently donated, to remedy nutritional deficiencies in a particular population. Most such programs were unsuccessful because of their cost, however, and so they have been largely discontinued except when famines have managed to generate international support, as in Ethiopia and sub-Saharan Africa in recent years. (Particularly in such settings, Vitamin A supplementation has also received considerable attention, not only as a means of preventing blindness but also as a possible way to reduce general morbidity and mortality at low cost.)

Today, the term "food supplementation" primarily refers to weaning foods, which are usually simply local indigenous foods that mothers are advised to give to their infants after about four months of age when breastmilk alone is no longer nutritionally adequate for infant growth. See Griffiths, this volume, for a description of a successful intervention of this type.

7. Female literacy--the forgotten F. Occasionally one sees the GOBI-FF acronym written with a third F standing for female literacy. Studies have shown that in developing countries where many mothers are illiterate, infant mortality rates are often very high (Ware 1984). It is not certain that there is any causal connection involved, since factors such as poverty may underlie both phenomena (Cleland and van Ginneken 1988; MacCormack 1988), but if there is such a connection, a mother's literacy may enhance child survival because of the empowerment that takes place when girls go to school and learn to make decisions for themselves (Caldwell 1981). In a comprehensive analysis of the relative benefit to *women* of the various components of GOBI-FF--a perspective that has received relatively little attention from health planners, who have focused on ***children's*** needs despite the fact that mothers usually are the caregivers--Leslie et al. (1988) conclude that female education is probably the single most valuable element in the long term, surpassing even family planning.

Implementation of female literacy, however, requires not only a massive investment in schools and teachers but also, in many countries, a radical change in social conventions and fundamental power relationships. Predictably, the (largely male) international health leadership often advocates this final F in a somewhat muted fashion as compared to the rest of the GOBI-FF interventions.

Problems in the Delivery of Comprehensive PHC

After several years of enthusiastic response to the appeal of the Health-for-All movement, problems began to emerge. In much of the developing world, for example, entities such as road-building, water treatment plants, and sanitation are not under the control of health planners, and at least equally important, such projects are very expensive. As a result, some of the more ambitious goals of the 1978 version of CPHC have been abandoned, even at the rhetorical level, and a more purely health-oriented form of primary health care, sometimes called "Basic PHC," has come into being. However, the viability of even this relatively modest type of program has recently been questioned as the high cost of *any* form of comprehensive health care has become increasingly manifest.

One of the earliest doubters was Chabot (1984), who argued that at a cost of ten dollars per person to set up, and two dollars per person per year to maintain, comprehensive PHC was simply not economically feasible in developing countries able to spend only one dollar per person per year on health. At about the same time, a paper by Islam and Bachman (1983) similarly noted the minuscule resources allocated to health in Bangladesh compared to the staggering amounts (30% of the national budget) committed to maintaining a massive military and police organization. The authors questioned whether CPHC could succeed in such a context, particularly since 70% of the health expenditure was going to the cities while 90% of the population lived in rural areas.

It seems clear that in much of the developing world, comprehensive programs will not be truly successful unless there is a substantial reorientation of political thinking and resource allocation (Mahler 1988). In the introduction to their book entitled *Practising Health for All*, Morley, Rohde, and Williams (1983) point out the need for an unswerving commitment to community control and social justice. These authors cite the example of China, which achieved a model primary health care program only after its revolution had taken place. At that time, food production was radically reorganized, family planning was made mandatory, drug abuse was virtually eradicated, and cadres of rural health workers were created who were not only selected by their neighbors but continued in their jobs only if those neighbor-clients were satisfied.

Other countries and regions with a good claim to having achieved truly comprehensive PHC are Cuba, Nicaragua, Kerala State in India, and Sri Lanka. Significantly, all have governments that have gone through a socialist or communist transformation with subsequent reallocation of resources toward the poor, and all espouse political empowerment at the community level. In most developing countries, however, Chinese-style revolution has not taken place, and it has been very difficult to integrate primary health care programs with existing government agencies, to ensure meaningful community participation, and to achieve true coordination of health care activities from bottom to top.

Recognizing these problems, WHO held a conference in New Delhi in 1984 to discuss how a transition could be made from vertical programs to integrated, comprehensive PHC. Most people at the conference considered that the most important prerequisite for successful CPHC, and yet the most difficult to achieve, was the establishment of an infrastructure consisting not only of material resources but also of trained personnel (Dr. John H. Bryant, personal communication). Unfortunately, there have been only a few major success stories in CPHC since the 1984 conference; in fact, supporters of the concept have dwindled since that time.

The reasons for this are varied. Some critics complain that from the start, CPHC was too ambitious. They contend that the money never was there in the first place to deliver the promise of comprehensive primary health care in the developing world, and that failed promises have led to a rising tide of disillusionment (*The Economist* 1986; Bourne 1987). It is certainly true that CPHC always seemed to evoke more enthusiasm from international agencies than from governments of developing countries. Many such governments seemed to have mixed feelings about it, endorsing the *idea* of CPHC but never putting it into practice.

Very early on, the political right wing among the international health leadership sensed these difficulties and proposed an alternate model which has come to be known as selective primary health care (SPHC). This model has gained support in recent years but has also been severely criticized. A brief history of the SPHC movement follows.

Advocates of Selective PHC Join the HFA Movement

Only a year after the enthusiastic launching of "Health for All" in 1978, the opposition threw down the gauntlet in the form of a paper entitled "Selective Primary Health Care: An Interim Strategy for Disease Control in Developing Countries" (Walsh and Warren 1979). This paper was subsequently reprinted in *Social Science and Medicine*, indicating its relevance for the social science world, and since then it has become an ideological focal point for the ongoing debate over which concept of primary health care--comprehensive or selective--is most useful and appropriate in the developing world.

Walsh and Warren argued that the broad goals of the CPHC programs were too expensive, too ambitious, and basically unattainable. Not surprisingly, in view of Warren's position as a director of the Rockefeller Foundation, the paper seemed to reflect a "funding agency" point of view. In other words, it advocated dealing with measurable disease entities so that quantifiable results could be produced at the lowest possible cost. "Selective" PHC, then, would concentrate on such matters as encouraging breastfeeding, implementing oral rehydration therapy for diarrhea, and immunizing people against the vaccine-preventable diseases. Diseases that were very common but also costly or difficult to treat, such as tuberculosis, would not be targeted. In short, SPHC was to emphasize cost-effectiveness (Evans, Hall, and Waxford 1981).

SPHC held much appeal for funding agencies. The fact that it was based on numbers, starting with prevalence and incidence of disease as defined by field surveys and lending itself to repeat surveys to show the measurable impact of health interventions, made it attractive to those with a management frame of mind and/or a pocketbook to protect. Articles appeared assessing the cost-effectiveness of different types of health programs based on the cost per death averted. For example, it was judged that an immunization drive or an oral rehydration therapy program might cost between $100 and $200 per death prevented, while in some comprehensive PHC programs, it might cost as much as $320 to prevent a death (Shepard 1983).

The controllable, relatively easy to implement SPHC programs appealed to the international health organizations despite their verbal commitment to the concept of comprehensive PHC. In time, GOBI-FF became not just a component of the drive toward "Health for All," it all but *became* primary health care in the minds of the international health leadership. Thus, both the UNICEF GOBI-FF campaigns and the "child survival programs" of the U.S. Agency for International Development embody tacit acceptance of verticalized

PHC. Even WHO, which seemed critical and defensive for years following the emergence of the SPHC concept, has now put most of its resources and energies into vertical programs such as the Expanded Program on Immunization (EPI) and the Program for Control of Diarrheal Diseases (CDD), which emphasizes oral rehydration therapy.

International agencies find these vertical programs attractive not only because of their quantifiability and lower cost, but also because they do not require of governments a revolution in political thinking and resource commitment. WHO itself, while sounding idealistic in meetings such as the one held in Alma-Ata, is in fact quite pragmatic in attempting to get along with governments that neither allocate resources to the neediest nor support social change such as advances in female literacy. As noted above, the bulk of WHO's own funding has been committed to selective rather than comprehensive PHC programs, although public acknowledgement of this is not likely to be forthcoming.

Problems with Selective PHC

Problems, like causes, are to some extent in the eye of the beholder. Most people who are dissatisfied with selective PHC fall into one or the other of two groups. First are the consumers, though they rarely know the name of what they are criticizing. These are the poor and disenfranchised in the developing world who continue to suffer from the same ill health and lack of access to medical care that they experienced in the vertical program era of the 1950s and 1960s. (Indeed, SPHC has been called "old wine in new bottles" [Gish 1982; see also Gish 1979].) Second are those who might be characterized as the "ideological left" in the Health-for-All movement. Unlike the poor, these people are able to articulate their concerns in the literature, and a recent special issue of *Social Science and Medicine* (26[9], 1988) contains some of the most interesting and powerful critiques of SPHC that have ever appeared in print.

For example, in that issue a charter member of the PHC movement (Newell) questions whether SPHC can do anything other than destroy the essence of PHC, which he defines as the empowerment of the community to become actively involved in health care programs. Like Rifkin and Walt (1986), he argues that SPHC does not leave anything of lasting value behind once the specific intervention has ended. In another article in the same issue, Nabarro and Chinnock (1988) even question the scientific merit of growth monitoring, which is the very cornerstone of GOBI-FF. While the powerful advocates of SPHC are not likely to be swayed by such a critique, the vitality of the authors' argument raises new questions about the effectiveness and appropriateness of other such vertical programs, programs that have been considered virtually sacrosanct until now.

Most of the social scientists who have examined selective PHC and contrasted it with comprehensive PHC have found it lacking in appeal both from a development standpoint, i.e. as a long-range solution to health problems and lack of community resources in the developing world, and from the strictly humanitarian perspective that people should be provided with the curative medicine they need and want (Berman 1982; Unger and Killingsworth 1983; Heggenhougen 1984). In addition, SPHC in the form of GOBI-FF is almost exclusively limited to children, and (very secondarily; cf. Rosenfield and Maine 1985) to women of childbearing age; the needs of other segments of the population are virtually ignored.

Nevertheless, most of the projects funded by international health agencies in recent years have been SPHC-oriented, and there is little likelihood of any immediate change in this trend. For instance, as of 1990 the organizations' focus was on acute respiratory infection and it appeared that the next health problem to be addressed would be that of maternal mortality during pregnancy and childbirth. (Historically, SPHC has given little attention to women's health problems except as they are related to reproductive function--a narrowness of vision that has generated considerable criticism [Baumslag 1985]).

PHC Today: A Pragmatic Fusion of CPHC and SPHC

Table 2.1 summarizes the advantages and disadvantages of the two major approaches to primary health care, CPHC and SPHC, from the standpoint of program management and impact. As noted above, selective programs appeal to international health organizations, funding agencies, and governments of developing countries not only because they are relatively easy to administer, simple, and low-cost, but also because they do not threaten the political status quo. Comprehensive PHC, on the other hand, retains the allegiance of idealists (or, as some would put it, the clear-sighted) because it empowers the community, promises to bring about lasting improvement in general health status, and gives people hope for respite from illness when curative care is required.

As of this writing, it appears that there will be a continued effort to combine SPHC and CPHC pragmatically in many developing countries and that the two factions may eventually be reconciled. Rifkin and Walt report (1988) that a shifting and softening of position has already taken place; indeed, staunch advocates of SPHC such as Walsh (1988) and Warren (1988) have urged that infrastructure and curative medicine be developed along with selective PHC programs, that cultural factors be considered, and that communities be involved.

Predictably, some of those who contributed substantially to the growth of the "Basic PHC" movement and who have remained active in international health initiatives have denied that there are any real differences between the two camps (Taylor and Jolly 1988; Kendall 1988). Kendall, for example, reports that in nine Latin American countries surveyed, local health workers handling diarrhea control activities were involved in other primary care interventions as well, and thus the diarrhea programs were not really "vertical" (1988:21). In corridor conversations, some even express the view that the entire "selective vs. comprehensive" debate has been overblown by people who simply want to publish articles (Jeannine Coreil, personal communication). However, the present author feels that most social scientists would agree with Newell (and Wisner 1988) that SPHC and CPHC are not only different but incompatible--that SPHC could in fact stifle and even destroy the more revolutionary and hence more difficult evolution of CPHC.

In a recent article, Mosley (1988) has called for a compromise based on the nature of the health problem to be addressed rather than on any particular *a priori* theoretical orientation. He argues, for example, that one could target tetanus for eradication through immunization (a vertical approach) and at the same time attack child malnutrition via provision of safe water, adequate food, health education of mothers, and the like (a comprehensive approach). In other words, he asserts that the approach should follow from the problem. This argument has some appeal, but unfortunately the reader senses in his article a somewhat lukewarm commitment to community empowerment, and even an "end justifies the means" mentality that many will find unacceptable.

The Future

If past is prologue, SPHC is likely to continue to dominate the primary health care movement. The literal and figurative revolutions that many feel are necessary for comprehensive PHC to be implemented have not occurred and do not seem imminent. Recent changes in the WHO leadership also suggest that vertical PHC programs will retain their current position of prominence. Thus, SPHC would appear to be in a mode of continued ascendancy, but with almost nobody completely happy about the fact, least of all idealists, experienced field workers, most social scientists, and the poor people of the developing world.

For those trying to decide which side to take, Rifkin and Walt (1986) have offered a useful perspective. They argue that the critical element in comprehensive PHC is *process*, and that it is the process itself which leads to the empowerment of the people. The logical corollary is that programs which do not confer empowerment, such as the SPHC vertical programs, fail in the same way that programs based on the importation of foreign food supplements fail. They may help temporarily, but there is nothing of lasting value left behind--no way for people to take care of the problems by themselves in the future, when external funding has been withdrawn and they are left with only their own resources to draw on. Growth monitoring is an excellent example of this. In both Mexico and Pakistan, the present author has observed that unless mothers understand what it is all about--and "buy into it"--they revert to bottlefeeding and other undesirable practices as soon as the growth monitoring team has departed.

Despite the misgivings of many, the current pattern of mixing a large number of vertical elements with a small number of comprehensive elements in the same PHC program is likely to continue in many developing countries that do not want to abandon CPHC but are unable or unwilling to support it fully. In such cases, community participation in program planning is often claimed where it does not in fact exist. Here, as frequently in the history of PHC, rhetoric is likely to be in conflict with observable reality, and one is well advised to look beyond mere allegations in order to discover the truth.

Anthropologists can be particularly helpful in this regard, not only in fact-finding but in furthering community involvement in PHC efforts. Even advocates of selective PHC admit that ideally, the community should be involved in identifying health problems, designing solutions, evaluating successes and failures, and directing any needed changes. Yet most health workers lack any knowledge of how to implement meaningful community participation in PHC initiatives, the entire process is fraught with hazards (cf. Paul and Demarest 1984), and the fact is that it has never even been tried in most of the developing world. There are a variety of reasons for this, and anthropologists can help to illuminate them.

Further, while social scientists have historically been called in to explain people's beliefs and practices with the aim of inducing them to do what health workers and governments want, there is no reason why they cannot also serve as community advocates (see Donahue, Chapter 4). In the present author's view, they can and should focus the attention of the international health leadership on the highly divergent implications of the two divergent approaches to PHC, and particularly on the undesirable dependency that results when, as the old maxim has it, a man is given a fish to eat rather than being taught how to fish for himself.

It is certain that vertical PHC programs save lives. In some cases they may even, as one writer has argued, provide a focus for local people's efforts, enhance morale, and thus contribute to the eventual development of a self-sustaining health infrastructure (Foster 1985: 105). But vertical programs are wholly inadequate as the sole or even the main response to the massive array of diseases and mishaps threatening the well-being of millions in the developing world on a daily basis. Recently it has been suggested that some of the cultural values embedded in the Alma-Ata declaration, such as the emphasis placed on self-reliance, are Eurocentric (see van der Geest et al. 1990). However this may be, the fact is that in the absence of dependable, locally accessible preventive *and curative* health services--i.e. in the absence of comprehensive PHC as envisioned by the founders of the "Health for All" movement--human lives will remain vulnerable to needless impairment, dissatisfaction will continue, and true community empowerment will not be realized.

Acknowledgements

The author is grateful to an anonymous reviewer and to Dorothy Mull for providing insights that helped to broaden the scope of the discussion.

Table 2.1

Comprehensive vs. Selective PHC: Contrasting Positions on the Major Issues

Issue	Comprehensive PHC	Selective PHC
Water purity	A must--80% of disease in developing world is caused by impure water.	Too expensive.
Broadly integrated health infrastructure	The cornerstone of HFA/ PHC. Total government support and complete integration of horizontal and vertical infrastructure structure is mandatory.	Impractical--requires decentralization, new personnel and training, changed allocation of funds. Governments won't do this.
Narrowly targeted, highly-focused vertical programs, e.g. immunization campaigns	Do not make a lasting difference. May eliminate death from one cause, e.g. measles, but the child will die of something else, e.g. pneumonia (so-called "replacement mortality").	The cornerstone of selective PHC. More scientific, more cost effective, more con- trollable, and more doable because not dependent on local infrastructure.
Community involve- ment in program control	The essence of successful PHC. The *process* is vital because it empowers the community. Should not be seen as merely an alternative way to provide service.	Impractical--would require a revolution in many countries. Threatens status quo. Requires expertise not available in most of the developing world.

References

Baumslag, N. 1985 Women's Status and Health: World Considerations. In *Advances in International Maternal and Child Health*, Vol. 5. D.B. Jelliffe and E.F.P. Jelliffe, eds. Pp. 1-26. Oxford: Clarendon Press.

Bell, D.E., and M.R. Reich, eds. 1988 *Health, Nutrition, and Economic Crises: Approaches to Policy in the Third World*. Dover, MA: Auburn House Publishing Company.

Berman, P.A. 1982 Selective Primary Health Care: Is Efficient Sufficient? *Social Science and Medicine* 116:1054-1094.

Bourne, P. 1987 Beyond the Barefoot Doctor: The Unfilled Promise of Primary Health Care. *Development International* 1(3):32-35.

Brownlee, A. 1989 *Breastfeeding, Weaning and Nutrition: The Behavioral Issues*. Behavioral Issues in Child Survival Programs, Monograph No. 4. Washington, DC: USAID.

Caldwell, J.C. 1981 Maternal Education as a Factor in Child Mortality. *World Health Forum* 2(1):75-78.

Chabot, H.T.J. 1984 Primary Health Care Will Fail If We Do Not Change Our Approach. *The Lancet* 1:340-341.

Cleland, J.C., and J.K. van Ginneken 1988 Maternal Education and Child Survival in Developing Countries: The Search for Pathways of Influence. *Social Science and Medicine* 27(12):1357-1368.

Coreil, J., and J.D. Mull, eds. 1988 Anthropological Studies of Diarrheal Illness. *Social Science and Medicine*, Special Issue 27(1).

Economist, The 1986 Primary Health Care Is Not Curing African Ills. Pp. 97-100. May 31.

___ 1989 The Third World. Pp. 3-58. September 23.

Evans, J.R., K.L. Hall, and J. Waxford 1981 Health Care in the Developing World: Problems of Scarcity and Choice. (Shattuck Lecture.) *The New England Journal of Medicine* 305:1117-1127.

Foster, S.O. 1985 Ten Priorities for Child Health. In *Advances in International Maternal and Child Health*, Vol. 5. D.B. Jelliffe and E.F.P. Jelliffe, eds. Pp. 97-110. Oxford: Clarendon Press.

Gish, O. 1979 The Political Economy of PHC and "Health by the People": An Historical Explanation. *Social Science and Medicine* 19:217-224.

___ 1982 Selective PHC: Old Wine in New Bottles. *Social Science and Medicine* 16:1049-1063.

Gómez, F., R.R. Galván, S. Frenk, J.C. Muñoz, R. Chávez, and J. Vázquez 1956 Mortality in Second and Third Degree Malnutrition. *The Journal of Tropical Pediatrics*, September:77-83.

Hancock, G. 1989 *Lords of Poverty: The Power, Prestige, and Corruption of the International Aid Business*. New York: The Atlantic Monthly Press.

Heggenhougen, H.K. 1984 Will Primary Health Care Efforts Be Allowed to Succeed? *Social Science and Medicine* 19:217-224.

Heggenhougen, K., and J. Clements 1987 *Acceptability of Childhood Immunization: Social Science Perspectives*. EPC Publication No. 14. London: Evaluation and Planning Centre for Health Care, London School of Hygiene and Tropical Medicine.

Henderson, D.A. 1976 The Eradication of Smallpox. *Scientific American* 245(4)(October):25-33.

Hobcraft, J., J.W. McDonald, and S.O. Rutstein 1983 Child-Spacing Effects on Infant and Early Child Mortality. *Population Index* 49(4):585-618.

Huffman, S.L., and B.B. Lamphere 1984 Breastfeeding Performance and Child Survival. In *Child Survival: Strategies for Research*. W.H. Mosley and L.C. Chen, eds. Pp. 93-116. Cambridge: Cambridge University Press.

Islam, K., and S. Bachman 1983 PHC in Bangladesh--Too Much to Ask? *Social Science and Medicine* 117:1463-1466.

Jelliffe, D.B., and E.F.P. Jelliffe 1978 *Human Milk in the Modern World*. Oxford: Oxford University Press.

Kendall, C. 1988 The Implementation of a Diarrheal Disease Control Program in Honduras: Is It "Selective Primary Health Care" or "Integrated Primary Health Care"? *Social Science and Medicine* 27(1):17-23.

Leslie, J., M. Lycette, and M. Buvinic 1988 Weathering Economic Crises: The Crucial Role of Women in Health. In *Health, Nutrition, and Economic Crises: Approaches to Policy in the Third World*. D.E. Bell and M.R. Reich, eds. Pp. 307-348. Dover, MA: Auburn House Publishing Company.

MacCormack, C.P. 1988 Health and the Social Power of Women. *Social Science and Medicine* 26(7):677-683.

Mahler, H. 1974 Keynote Address. National Council for International Health International Health Conference. Reston, VA.

___ 1988 Present Status of WHO's Initiative: "Health for All by the Year 2000." *Annual Review of Public Health* 9:71-97.

Morley, D. 1973 *Paediatric Priorities in the Developing World*. London: Butterworths.

Morley, D., J.E. Rohde, and G. Williams 1983 *Practising Health for All*. New York: Oxford University Press.

Morley, D., and H. Lovel 1986 *My Name is Today*. London: MacMillan.

Mosley, W.H. 1988 Is There a Middle Way? Categorical Programs for PHC. *Social Science and Medicine* 26(9):907-908.

Nabarro, D., and P. Chinnock 1988 Growth Monitoring--Inappropriate Promotion of an Appropriate Technology. *Social Science and Medicine* 26(9):941-948.

Newell, K.W. 1988 Selective Primary Health Care: The Counter Revolution. *Social Science and Medicine* 26(9):903-906.

Paul, B.D., and W.J. Demarest 1984 Citizen Participation Overplanned: The Case of a Health Project in the Guatemalan Community of San Pedro la Laguna. *Social Science and Medicine* 19(3):185-192.

Pillsbury, B. 1989 *Immunization: The Behavioral Issues*. Behavioral Issues in Child Survival Programs, Monograph No. 3. Washington, DC: USAID.

Rifkin, S.B., and G. Walt 1986 Why Health Improves: Defining the Issues Concerning "Comprehensive Primary Health Care" and "Selective Primary Health Care." *Social Science and Medicine* 23:559-566.

___ 1988 The Debate on Selective or Comprehensive Primary Health Care. (Editorial.) *Social Science and Medicine* 26(9):877-878.

Rosenfield, A., and D. Maine 1985 Maternal Mortality--A Neglected Tragedy: Where is the M in MCH? *The Lancet*, 83-85, July 13.

Shepard D.S. 1983 Procedures for Assessing the Cost Effectiveness of a Diarrheal Disease Control Program Based on Oral Rehydration Therapy. *Abstracts of the Annual Meeting of the American Public Health Association*. Pp. 128-130.

Taylor, C., and R. Jolly 1988 The Straw Men of Primary Health Care. *Social Science and Medicine* 26(9):971-977.

Unger, J.P., and S.R. Killingsworth 1983 Selective Primary Health Care: A Critical Review of Methods and Results. *Social Science and Medicine* 22:1001-1013.

van der Geest, S., J.D. Speckmann, and P.H. Streefland 1990 Primary Health Care in a Multi-Level Perspective: Towards a Research Agenda. *Social Science and Medicine* 30(9):1025-1034.

Walsh, J.A. 1988 Selectivity Within Primary Health Care. *Social Science and Medicine* 26(9):899-902.

Walsh, J.A., and K.S. Warren 1979 Selective Primary Health Care: An Interim Strategy for Disease Control in Developing Countries. *The New England Journal of Medicine* 301:967-974. Reprinted in *Social Science and Medicine* 14C:145-155, 1980.

Ware, H. 1984 Effects of Maternal Education, Women's Roles, and Child Care on Child Mortality. In *Child Survival: Strategies for Research*. W.H. Mosley and L.C. Chen, eds. Pp. 191-214. Cambridge: Cambridge University Press.

Warren, K.S. 1988 The Evolution of Selective Primary Health Care. *Social Science and Medicine* 26(9):891-898.

WHO 1979 *Formulating Strategies for Health for All by the Year 2000: Guiding Principles and Essential Issues*. Geneva.

WHO/UNICEF 1978 *Primary Health Care*. Report of the International Conference on Primary Health Care, Alma-Ata, U.S.S.R., 6-12 September. Geneva.

Wisner, B. 1988 GOBI versus PHC? Some Dangers of Selective Primary Health Care. *Social Science and Medicine* 26(9):963-969.

II

CRITICAL PERSPECTIVES

The very urgency and severity of health problems in developing nations has led some anthropologists to focus their research rather narrowly on solving these problems instead of questioning the goals of donor agencies that underwrite such research. In a reaction against this narrowness, a new set of perspectives associated with the "critical medical anthropology" movement (CMA) has called attention on the political-economic context of health conditions, challenging anthropologists to recognize the macro-level systemic forces underlying health problems. Specifically, CMA points to the often-overlooked power relationships that bind communities with larger bureaucratic organizations and commercial interests. It requires that anthropologist "study up" and seek answers that call for change in the ways that health care is currently organized. Instead of finding ways to change people's behavior to fulfill goals set by external organizations, critical research seeks to empower communities and "beneficiaries" toward goals of self-determination and greater equity in the distribution of resources and power. As such, it is closely related to the larger sphere of activities which loosely fall within the rubric of "community participation" in PHC.

Two of the chapters included in this section are basically written from the critical perspective that has just been outlined. The remaining chapter, however, is "critical" in a different sense. Velimirovic, a physician who worked for WHO for many years, argues strongly against the WHO Programme on Traditional Medicine, which, as Coreil notes in the first chapter of this volume, was a significant factor in the re-entry of anthropologists into international health research. Velimirovic finds that traditional medicine initiatives have had very little success and questions whether the integration of traditional and Western medicine is really possible. Further, citing Batalla's 1966 argument along similar lines (see references for Velimirovic's chapter), he faults anthropologists for naive "wishful thinking" and a romantic bias toward preserving traditional culture regardless of its objective value.

Several ways in which anthropologists can go beyond mere uncritical celebration of tradition are outlined by Donahue, who calls on them to use their knowledge and professional stature to empower the communities they study. Donahue criticizes what some have seen as "academic colonialism," that is, conducting research that advances one's academic career but is of little or no practical use to the people among whom the research is carried out. He argues that anthropologists should challenge the dominance of PHC programs by health professionals and should be strong community advocates. They should share their understandings of how power is manipulated within the system and how it can be mobilized for change toward community-identified goals. These arguments are illustrated through an analysis of Nicaragua's post-revolution efforts to develop participatory community-based primary health care.

In the final chapter of the section, Jordan provides a counterbalance to Velimirovic's polemic against the value of traditional healers in primary health care. She points out that one of the tenets of PHC is reliance on appropriate technology that is compatible with local culture and resources, yet the criteria for determining what is appropriate technology have remained ill-defined. In making this point, she examines the introduction of modern obstetrical practices in developing countries from the standpoint of its impact on power relations and the social distribution of knowledge in the childbirth process. She argues that the replacement of traditional birthing practices and artifacts with high technology procedures has transformed a formerly female-centered activity characterized by shared knowledge into a male dominated specialty requiring privileged authoritative knowledge. In this case "biomedical colonization of communities" is seen as the unfortunate byproduct of well-minded efforts to extend medical coverage to rural areas. Jordan makes a plea for a more humane childbirth experience that avoids unnecessary advanced technology and its attendant hierarchical distribution of knowledge and power.

3

Is Integration of Traditional and Western Medicine Really Possible?

Boris Velimirovic

Introduction

The Programme on Traditional Medicine (TM) of the World Health Organization (WHO), endorsing the use of traditional practitioners in national health systems, formally came into being in 1978. It is one of the few WHO initiatives that has not met with universal approval. The director of the programme has explained that it came into being because of two main factors: the changed political power that in much of the world accompanied national independence; and the minimal resources that were and are available to address development issues such as the extension of health care to people who lack it. As he put it, "The first factor is related to national group pride and is associated with past heritage and newly gained national independence. The second factor is linked to utilization of all available resources" (Akerele 1983).

The history of the TM programme from its genesis in 1969 to its formal adoption by the 30th World Health Assembly has previously been analyzed in detail by the author (Velimirovic 1984). Although WHO's aims were always laudable, there have also been consistent weaknesses in the conceptualization of the programme. Most notably, a universally acceptable definition of TM has never been agreed on. Thus a definition of TM as is

> the sum of all the knowledge and practices, whether explicable or not, used in diagnosis, prevention and elimination of physical, mental or social imbalance and relying exclusively on practical experience and observation handed down from generation to generation, whether verbally or in writing (AFRO Technical Report Series 1976: 3-4)

was implicitly adopted by the WHO Working Group on Traditional Medicine (WHO 1978). However, this definition was originally drawn up for the African context, and Africa, with its vast array of beliefs and practices, is very different from countries such as China, India, Sri Lanka, and Pakistan, where organized systems of TM have existed for centuries if not millennia.

Significantly, anthropologists, whose presence might have tempered such overgeneralizations, were absent both from the WHO Working Group itself and from the group of 12 WHO Secretariat members who attended the meeting. In fact, no medical anthropologists participated at any stage during the development of the WHO TM Programme. Even more surprising, there were no medical anthropologists among the editors of the WHO-published book entitled *Traditional Medicine and Health Care Coverage* (Bannerman et al. 1983), a book that uncritically advocated TM.

The Story of a Report

The report of the WHO Working Group on Traditional Medicine (WHO 1978) is highly unusual among such technical reports in its lack of balance. On one hand, the authors seem to be aware of the deficiencies of TM. For example, they comment that

> traditional medicine in some developing countries has tended to stagnate through not exploiting the rapid discoveries of science and technology for its own development. [Thus] it has kept a slow pace of change in comparison with medicine as practiced in the industrialized countries, which keeps abreast of scientific and technological innovations to the extent that it is often exclusively referred to as modern medicine.

In fact, TM has not helped indigenous people against cholera and other enteric infections, sleeping sickness, yellow fever, leprosy, schistosomiasis, trachoma, onchocercosis, malaria, tuberculosis, and other diseases which have decimated the people. It has not prevented death rates still averaging 93 per 1,000 births and rates of infant mortality as high as 200 per 1,000 in some developing countries.

Nevertheless, the authors conclude by stating, without a trace of skepticism, that

> traditional medicine has been shown to have intrinsic utility, it should be promoted, and its potential developed for the wider use and benefit of mankind. It is already the people's own health care system and is well accepted by them. It has certain advantages over imported systems of

> medicine in any setting because, as an integral part of the people's culture, it is particularly effective in solving certain cultural health problems. It has and does freely contribute to scientific and universal medicine (WHO 1978).

There are, of course, many examples of illness perception, medical beliefs, and behavioral risk factors being influenced by culture *sensu lato* and culture certainly figures in therapeutic choice. However, what is not admitted in the report is that the cultural beliefs and practices are often detrimental to good health and that TM is so intertwined with culture that in is in fact part of the problem. As Halfdan Mahler, former Director-General of WHO, has himself put it, "Culture (together with illiteracy and apathy) has been used all too often as an excuse for a lack of action" (Mahler 1978, 1983).

Change brought about by an active process of education is clearly needed. Efforts by teachers, community workers, civic and religious leaders, trade unions, women's organizations, and the mass media should all be used to enlighten people about major health problems and the most appropriate way to deal with them. In particular, there is a need for modification of beliefs about disease causation and proper treatment. People must learn that tuberculosis does not result when a man or woman with fever indulges in sexual intercourse, that leprosy and blindness are not punishments for the sins of a previous life, and that disease is not caused by eating food touched by a person of low caste, or by eating in the morning before taking a ritual ablution, or as the result of the wrath of evil spirits, or by the evil eye, or by sorcery. Only after a child has been properly vaccinated or treated for tuberculosis, malaria, or leprosy should one consider the question of whether to encourage the wearing of "protective" glass beads or the worship of a local disease deity.

To regard TM as the solution to bringing "health to all by the year 2000" is no more than wishful thinking. Certainly most herbalists do no harm; bone-setters can sometimes be as effective as orthopedists; thorn-pullers, boil-lancers and barber-surgeons can sometimes help. But despite the fact that such practitioners may have some limited effectiveness in easing discomfort, most objective observers remain skeptical. For example, Roemer (1976) writes that "their overall impact today on the health of the people must be considered negative."

Integration of What?

The 1978 WHO report advocated the integration of TM into official medicine, praising its

> unique and holistic approach--i.e., that of viewing man in his totality within a wide ecological spectrum and of emphasizing the viewpoint that ill health or disease is brought about by an imbalance, or disequilibrium, of man in his total ecological system and not only by the causative agent and pathogenic evolution (WHO 1978).

This "holistic approach" is the rallying-cry of the integrationist wave and has been discussed in detail elsewhere (Velimirovic 1984). The term suggests that TM is concerned with the patient's mind and soul, whereas biomedicine is not. But measles can be prevented only by vaccination and not by drinking urine, and polio is not caused by disturbance in a person's spiritual environment. Indigenous healers can of course be valuable in addressing people's concerns about community customs and religious beliefs. But to call these customs and beliefs a "total ecological system" is clearly inaccurate and amounts to semantic sloppiness.

Jumping on the Bandwagon

The 1978 report identified a need for more research on TM both to collect information and to "improve methods, techniques, and the composition of traditional medicaments." The ultimate goal was to

> communicate such knowledge to the political decision-makers and professional personnel employing other systems of medicine, and eventually to motivate them to accept and actively participate in the application of traditional medicine in public health care systems.

Even while the research was being carried out, however, an "educational revolution" was to take place involving curricular reforms and revised training programmes for health personnel (WHO 1978).

Further, WHO encouraged the immediate incorporation of traditional practitioners into community development programmes. People were to be taught that traditional remedies were not second-rate medicine and traditional practitioners were to be trained in primary health care techniques. In short, even before research had been completed, TM had become respectable and many were already identifying it with "community participation" in primary health care.[1]

But instead of an "educational revolution," an educational counter-revolution was going on. Integration of TM into official medicine was questionable for a variety of reasons: (1) it does not offer reciprocal benefits to each system, but unilaterally benefits TM; (2) it does not improve health knowledge; and (3) it does not enhance the quality of medical practitioners--or does so only moderately, and, again, unilaterally.

Even WHO admitted that there were likely to be profound problems as the result of its recommendation, including

> payment of lip-service to the integration process, fear of the possibly harmful iatrogenic effects of traditional medicine, doubtful status of the products of integrated training in . . . social and professional hierarchies, resistance by intransigent advocates of one or another system, [and] fear of litigation, since the legal apparatus tends to protect only the entrenched system, to encourage monopoly, and even to proscribe other systems (WHO 1978).

Thus the 1978 report states that it would be necessary to obtain "*prior* guarantees of material and financial support" from health authorities (emphasis added).

Clearly, the authors were aware that such authorities would be reluctant to comply with the WHO integration recommendations in the absence of objective evidence in their favor. Elsewhere (Velimirovic 1982) it has been argued that to be convincing, such evidence must be based on "systematic and unbiased observation." Surely this is the minimum requirement before one can present one's findings to the government officials who make decisions about health care. "What is needed, therefore, is a body of tested hard facts to clarify the role of TM today" (Velimirovic 1982).

Unfortunately, the language of the WHO report itself is not unbiased and objective. For example, we read that

> the tremendous success of the Chinese experience in the integration of Western medicine and Chinese traditional medicine continues to provide the shining example of the potential which lies in integration (WHO 1978).

In fact, this claim was contested even in China (Sidel and Sidel 1982). The report also contains recommendations that can only be described as involving interference in the internal affairs of sovereign nations. Pointing out that the greatest resistance to integration of TM often comes from intransigent decision-makers, the authors recommend, among other measures, "*replacement* of existing council or board members with *more receptive* people who would appreciate the need for change to meet present-day exigencies" (WHO 1978) (emphasis added).

Thus, even while recognizing that there are "fundamental differences" between the concepts of life, health and disease propounded by TM and those held in modern scientific medicine, and that "commercial motives control the modes of practice in certain settings" (WHO 1978), the report uncritically advocates the outright integration of the two medical systems. It does so without stating how this should be accomplished or questioning whether integration is feasible in all but exceptional situations. It seems clear that certain receptive TBAs could be trained to use clean dressings on the umbilical stump rather that cow dung (Velimirovic and Velimirovic 1978) and to promote oral rehydration therapy. But should modern physicians be trained in Ayurveda, Siddha, Unani, and other such traditions all over the world? The report is silent about matters of this kind. After all, although modern medicine should respect cultural practices, even in the face of hakims using stethoscopes in ritual fashion without understanding what they hear, it cannot compromise on the basic principles of science.

Stereotypes

Foster (1978) warns against uncritical acceptance of several stereotypes about TM that have been popularized over the past generation. His comments are worth quoting at length for they highlight the drawbacks of using traditional healers in contemporary health programmes:

> *One of the principal arguments advanced in favor of co-opting traditional curers is that they know the family background of their patients* and can hence weigh psychological as well as clinical factors in deciding what to do. In relatively isolated peasant villages, this is certainly true. But many areas are increasingly subject to population movements. Traditional healers [in those areas] inevitably will know much less about most of their patients than in stable villages.

Foster goes on to say that even in such stable villages, patients with specific folk disease tend to be treated in standardized ways, and "knowledge of the family plays a minimal role in the therapy. Hence, this argument would appear to be far weaker than it is often thought to be."

Two other stereotypes disputed by Foster are:

> ***Traditional curers are relatively old, highly respected people in every community and because of their status they should be valuable allies in primary health care.*** It is certainly true that elderly herbalists with a profound knowledge of traditional remedies, or famous shamans, inspire confidence in their patients. But to assume that because they fulfill this role well in a traditional setting they will do so in another setting is careless generalizing. Aguirre Beltrán (1978), whose practical experience in introducing health services to traditional people is unrivaled . . . [was] astonished to find enormous resistance to this approach. Old people were found not to be the best intermediaries for socio-cultural change. Specialized health training for young literate people proved to be a more practical approach.
>
> *Traditional peoples dichotomize illness into two categories: the first, illnesses that physicians quickly cure; the second, "folk" illnesses, the very existence of which physicians deny.* This . . . does appear to have had some validity in the early years following the introduction of modern medicine but, after a fairly short time, it no longer has much predictive value.

The striking thing, in many parts of the world today, is that where the services of a physician have been available for a sufficient length of time and are accessible, the physician is the first choice of most people for most complaints (López 1978; Velimirovic 1972).

Finally, foster disputes the stereotype that:

> ***physicians practicing in traditional settings have difficulties in communicating with their patients.*** Probably many researchers are guilty of underestimating the insight and sensitivity that physicians . . . display when many of their patients are traditional people (Foster 1978).

As for official medical roles for traditional curers, Foster writes,

> In asking this question, it is natural to consider experience gained to date. Most of it is limited to two areas: the upgrading of indigenous midwives, and the use of traditional curers for mental illness. But success with midwives and mental illness treatment does not necessarily mean that other curers can easily be incorporated into official health services.
>
> In the case of pregnancy, both midwife and physician agree about the onset of the condition, its course and duration, and its probable outcome. In the absence of complications, both do about the same thing. With respect to the treatment of mental illness, the symbolic and supportive roles of traditional curers do often seem to lead to successful outcomes, at least to the alleviation of symptoms in sufficient degree so that a patient can continue to live at home.
>
> But beyond these two fields, the problems become more difficult. When the physician diagnoses a malignant tumor requiring surgery, and the medicine man an intruded disease object that can be removed by sucking, are there real grounds for cooperation?

Yet another false assumption is that traditional curers continue to be produced at the same rate as in the past. Abundant evidence indicates that this is not the case (Foster 1978; Barbee 1986). Thus the most viable alternative to incorporating traditional curers into official medicine may well be to train people who are full participants in their own cultures instead (Justice 1978).

Apprehension about the Measuring Rods

The growing interest in TM after its endorsement by WHO is evidenced by the flood of books and lay publications that have appeared on this topic. While welcoming this interest, at the same time WHO seems apprehensive about possible negative side effects of the process that have been set in motion. Thus the director of the WHO TM Programme has said that it is "imperative" that WHO evaluate the programme. Though he goes on to say that "such a critical analysis will serve to identify, classify, and develop the different disciplines involved, and map out clear ground for further programme growth," his comments make it very clear that the TM initiative was launched without major questions having been asked and answered. For example, he states that what is needed is:

- Evaluation of TM and practices to separate myths from reality.
- Research into traditional medicine as part of a national health system, as not much is known (Akerele 1983).

This is what medical anthropologists have maintained all along.

Primary Health Care versus Unrealistic Expectations

Clearly, the WHO TM initiative was grounded in a desire to extend health care to all. Large numbers of people in the developing world still have no recourse to modern medical attention, and with the doubling of the world population every 32 years, the situation is very serious indeed. Thus WHO's sincerity is unquestionable. Nevertheless, the TM initiative was a mistake in the otherwise laudable drive to reach a worthy goal. Humanitarian sentiments, coupled with political pressure from countries where systems of TM have operated for centuries, successfully pushed the resolution through at the WHO Assembly.[2] The political influences underlying TM maintenance in some countries are well-documented.[3]

Contrary to the intention of its proponents, the WHO initiative actually detracted from the goal of assuring adequate primary health care for all. Far from being a step forward, it was a step back. It created unrealistic expectations that since "something was being done," all would be well. It tended to institutionalize the status quo and thus to create a double standard--one for rural areas (largely TM) and another for urban centers (largely biomedicine). It seemed to assume that nothing could change in the years ahead--that even in countries where half the population was under 15 years old, new providers could not be educated and staff could not be rapidly trained. Thus the TM initiative was inconsistent with WHO's own drive to develop adequate primary health services.

As has been documented in many publications (WHO 1979; PAHO 1978), there is no need either to copy a Western model or to settle for low-quality care in coping with the health problems of the developing world. Indigenous healers might perhaps be incorporated into a modern health care system in some places, but they are not the only answer to lack of coverage. What is needed is the imagination and the will to institute basic, low-cost health measures appropriate for a particular country's culture and level of socioeconomic development. For these measures to succeed, transformation of the social structure may be a precondition; and in that process TM is marginal at best or a hindrance at worst (Velimirovic 1982).

The possible use of traditional practitioners to dispense oral rehydration salts (ORS) for treatment of diarrhoea may be mentioned as an example. It is understandable that proponents of TM want to enhance the respect of traditional practitioners by giving them a truly effective treatment tool. However, it is very difficult to train such practitioners to dispense ORS safely and effectively, and in any case they obviously cannot solve supply and distribution problems. Further, with rare exceptions, the people themselves increasingly prefer not to patronize such practitioners where reasonable alternatives exist. The trend, as Roemer writes, is towards "reduction of the dependence of rural people on primitive medicine and a heightened utilization of scientific services" (Roemer 1976: 67).

In an increasingly politicized WHO, the 1978 resolution on TM cannot now be reversed. However, recent organizational documents have had a somewhat sober, more realistic tone vis-à-vis TM. Thus in the 90 page *Global Strategy for Health for All by the Year 2000* (WHO 1981), TM is mentioned only very discreetly and in rather vague terms. WHO's emphasis in that publication is on the training and retraining of health workers, and on community involvement. In fact, the document does not even mention integration.[4] Rather,

WHO's TM effort today appears to be concentrated on research in herbal therapy and use of traditional birth attendants (TBAs) where feasible.

What Health Care for the People?

However, some WHO officials adopt a laissez-faire attitude, asking what damage is done if people continue to use TM in the absence of something better. After all, they argue, people are well able to distinguish situations where TM can be useful (i.e. for minor or chronic ailments) from ones where scientific medicine is needed. Therefore, why not let TM diminish the burden on health services? It is true that some people might use both folk and professional care, but what is wrong with that?

A good answer to these questions is found in the preamble of the WHO Constitution itself, where it is stated that:

> Governments have a responsibility for the health of their people which can be fulfilled only by the provision of adequate health and social measures. . . . This can be achieved, *inter alia*, through the establishment of a *nation-wide* provision . . . of *skilled*, universally available preventive and curative medical care, [and through] the extensive application in every country of the results of *progress in world medical research* (emphasis added).

Given these words, can governments be neutral about what kind of health care their people receive? And can WHO itself afford to be neutral? It is true that WHO's role in legislative and administrative decisions about health care is and should be very limited indeed, since these matters lie within the jurisdiction of the different nations. However, WHO has a responsibility to do scientific studies that would help governments to make such decisions. With respect to TM, WHO should be conducting just such research instead of functioning solely as an advocate.

The question to be clearly and dispassionately answered in each case is, "How useful are particular practices, skills and personnel against the identifiable [health] problems?" (Young 1983). The present author is confident that research results will rule out TM as a viable alternative in developing countries. Instead, solutions will be found within the realm of modern medicine in the form of cheaper, less bureaucratic ways to organize care and the teaching of better skills.

Follow-Up

The foregoing thoughts were first presented in 1984 (Velimirovic 1984). A review six years later for the present publication shows that there is nothing to retract, but obviously there are new facts and considerations to be added.

Ten years after the use of traditional medical practitioners in national health systems was endorsed by WHO, the head of the TM Programme commented that

> there are still many countries where only lip service is being paid to this principle. Other countries have initiated programmes that have had to be abandoned because they were introduced without the necessary preparatory policy formulation and appropriate strategies for implementation (Akerele 1987).

In short, the overall results of the TM Programme were seen as being meager, and that is still the case. More and more, objective evaluation of TM is being called for so that it can either be recommended with confidence or, on the other hand, dismissed. As noted above, plant medicines and TBAs have been of special interest to WHO.

Traditional Materia Medica

Unfortunately, evaluation of traditional herbal remedies is very costly and time-consuming, and it may also be superfluous. Many of the proponents of such research have apparently overlooked the fact that most of the major pharmaceutical companies have done extensive studies over the past 20 years on innumerable plants claimed to have curative properties. Computerized programmes were developed to generate lists of plants thought to be effective for the same disease by more than one ethnic group (Velimirovic and Velimirovic 1980). Collecting expeditions were organized; herbalists and other experts were interviewed; and animal experiments were conducted. In short, significant resources were invested. Research of this nature calls for very complicated equipment, a lengthy time commitment (it takes 5 to 8 years to develop a new drug), and considerable financial means. Today it could cost 9 to 18 million U.S. dollars to bring a new drug to market (Douglas 1979). Are governments in the developing world willing and able to underwrite investments of this magnitude?

WHO's efforts to strengthen local research capabilities are commendable, but unfortunately such efforts are often subverted as various foreign institutes scramble for available funds. Whereas the extraction and conversion of raw material or the production of simple drugs could be efficiently achieved in a relatively small factory employing a limited number of expert personnel, budgets become bloated as the institutes pursue their own agendas. Further, although traditional medicines may be useful in treating common, self-limiting ailments and psychosomatic disorders (Gunaratne 1980), with the exception of quinine they are virtually useless against the infectious and parasitic diseases which affect millions of people in the developing world. For these diseases, modern chemical drugs, ORS, and vaccines are the only realistic solution. Thus one of the investigators in a project that trained herbalists in the Philippines later admitted that the project might well have been an anachronism (Caragay 1982).

Traditional Birth Attendants

Other than research on herbal medicine, the best-known part of the WHO TM programme is the training of TBAs in aseptic delivery techniques and simple antenatal and postnatal care. Although these activities seem promising, their success has not been systematically evaluated (Velimirovic and Velimirovic 1978).

Further, there is evidence that use of TBAs is declining. For example, in Mexico City in 1959, some 33.3% of expectant mothers were attended by a TBA while 66.5% were cared for by institutions or trained professionals. The majority of women who chose a TBA (86.3%) reported they did so for cultural reasons such as confidence in the TBA. Seventeen years later, in 1976, a similar survey conducted in the same district showed that only 5% of mothers were attended by TBAs, while institutional births had increased to 88.7%. The reported reasons for using TBAs in the second survey were less related to positive preferences and more to fear of medical institutions because of such things as the inability of the family to attend the birth, unfriendly attitudes on the part of physicians and nurses, and lack of anyone to care for children left at home (Hernández de Sándoval n.d.).

Another issue is the proper content of TBA training courses. Some feel that TBAs should be taught new methods and concepts while others argue that the main focus should be on eliminating harmful practices. In addition one must bear in mind that some governments totally rejected the idea of training TBAs at all (Diesch

1976; Johns Hopkins University 1980; Verderese 1973). Others want to replace them as soon as possible by a type of caregiver intermediate between a TBA and a professional midwife (WHO 1975). In fact, only eight out of 18 African governments for which data are available officially recognize TBAs.

Critics of TBA training programmes point out that countries favoring TBAs tend to be those that lack the political will to take bolder steps in reorganizing health care delivery. In such a context, TBA training is at best a diversionary step, creating the impression that something is being done but actually postponing more fundamental changes in societal structures.

As noted above, despite the operation of many TBA training programmes over the years and the publication of numerous reports on those programmes, there is virtually nothing approaching systematic evaluation. Even when WHO reviewed programmes in 45 countries, no evaluation results were reported. It is therefore not known whether or not TBA training programmes have been successful. More than anecdotal reports are needed to assess the impact of training on such matters as the rate of childbirth-related infections and complications, prematurity, maternal mortality and morbidity, and referral to professional services such as family planning--in short, on TBA efficiency and effectiveness.

However, the scant data thus far available suggest the persistence of multiple difficulties and relatively low TBA utilization of their training experiences. For example, TBAs have had little impact on the acceptance of family planning in Pakistan and Bangladesh (Johns Hopkins University 1980), and the same is true in Indonesia, Malaysia, and the Philippines.

The basic problem is that comprehensive maternal and child health care requires much more than just delivering a baby. It includes pre- and postnatal care of the mothers, newborn care, family planning, immunization, nutritional guidance, and careful follow-up of infants and children under five years old. This is more than a TBA can provide--even one with optimal training. Given this fact, it appears to some critics that TBA training is an unnecessary duplication of effort, since other health personnel will have to be trained to perform these functions in any case.

White Coats and Stethoscopes for All?

A decade after the endorsement of TM, we find a tacit admission that integration of TM into national health care systems has not been very successful. Instead of an evaluation of integration efforts, there is only a list of what *should* be done in the future.

> Traditional practitioners *should* become involved in the process which strengthens links between traditional medicine and the health delivery system. They *should* be involved in the planning, implementation and evaluation of community health activities so as to enhance working relationships between themselves and other members of the health team. First and foremost, of course, the traditional practitioners *should* be involved in the evaluation of their own practices so as to facilitate the ready acceptance by their peers of suggestions for changes, including the assumption of new responsibilities--for example, in health education (Akerele 1987) (emphasis added).

What this implies is that little or no integration has actually taken place.

Despite all the official endorsements, most countries have not shown enthusiasm for integration of traditional healers into their national health care systems. In Africa, for example, the concept of integration has been fully accepted only in Ethiopia, and even there, changes have been very slow. The Ethiopian government is differentiating among various classes of healers and remedies and requests evidence of their efficacy before endorsing them. Ironically, perhaps, the major outcome of these integration efforts is that some prominent traditional healers[5] in Ethiopia now own private clinics with beds (Werner 1987).

Another detriment to integration is that TM is often not as popular with the people themselves as health planners believe. For example, a writer on Nepal comments that such planners have

> mistakenly assumed that rural clients passively believe in and obey traditional practitioners. Many times, people [mention] that their traditional 'medicines' are not very good, and that their traditional practitioners are not always dependable healers (Stone 1986).

One recalls Foster's comments along the same lines (1978).

Further, the payoff from integration efforts may not justify the effort involved. For example, in Swaziland, a pilot project brought together nurses and traditional healers in a training workshop. The president of the Traditional Healers' Society and a practicing traditional doctor later wrote a most optimistic report recommending that such healers be taught to prevent and control eight childhood afflictions: diarrhoea, measles, whooping cough, tetanus, diphtheria, polio, malnutrition, and malaria. While the nurses' efforts to persuade traditional healers to use oral rehydration salts for diarrhoea are noted, the report does not mention the seven other diseases. However, the need for diarrhoea education in particular is evident from researchers' comments that

> Traditional treatment methods for diarrhoea vary widely in Swaziland. Divining may be used to determine the cause, herbal medicines are usually prescribed to harden stools, therapeutic vapor inhalation or traditional 'vaccinations' and cleansing the stomach and/or intestines by purges and enemas is often practiced. Purges and enemas given to young children usually cause further dehydration and sometimes result in death (Hoff and Maseko 1986: 414).

Two months after the Swaziland workshop was held, 60% of the traditional healers who had been present reported that they had referred patients with diarrhoea and vomiting to a clinic, whereas only 38% in the control group did so. Although the results were of questionable validity since they were largely self-reported, there is no doubt that if such practitioners were in fact converted to modern treatment of diarrhoea, the effort was worthwhile. However, a great deal of time was required to design and prepare the workshop sessions. Considering that there are between 5,000 and 8,000 traditional healers in Swaziland (Green and Makhubu 1984), some two or three hundred such workshops would be needed to cover the entire country. Would not the training of schoolteachers, mothers, and others in the community be a more efficient strategy? Already, radio health programmes concerned with diarrhoea attract many female listeners (Green 1985).

Elsewhere in Africa, opposition to TM has been expressed. For example, in Botswana there was resistance to collaboration with traditional healers among nurses, who are the backbone of the health care system in that country (Barbee 1986). In Nigeria, a survey of attitudes toward integration showed that 29% of doctors and 42% of medical students did not favor it. Moreover, most of those who favored it did so only conditionally. They felt that it should take place only under one or more of the following circumstances: in separate or special institutions; in certain fields such as psychiatry and orthopaedics; at the primary health care level; for purposes of research on herbs; after thorough study and standardization; and if adequately monitored. Further, both doctors and students condemned traditional healers who were guilty of charlatanism, witchcraft, reluctance to refer patients, and, most importantly, failure to acknowledge the limits of their skills and competence (Chiwuzie, Okoje, et al. 1987).

Oyeneye (1985) notes that TM in Nigeria has undergone tremendous changes over the past decade. Some traditional practitioners now have clean, modern clinics with waiting rooms, clerk-cashiers, secretaries, and attendants.[6] They may wear white coats and use stethoscopes, and many erect signposts to advertise themselves. Further, "in the past, traditional medical practitioners produced herbal concoctions on order. Today, a large proportion of medicines are prepared with the use of machines . . . and bottled ahead of time" (Oyeneye 1985). The author (a sociologist) acknowledges that such practitioners should be monitored and their remedies objectively evaluated, but he obviously does not recognize the cost and effort that would be involved. One need not, in fact, either endorse such practitioners or else "wait until there are adequate numbers of Western trained doctors before a significant segment can have access to health care" as some believe (Mabogunje 1981). Rather, the wise solution would be to train intermediary low cost personnel such as schoolteachers as stated above.

Chinese Medicine and TM

Since the integrationists usually cite the Chinese model as their *pièce de résistance*, it will be examined in some detail here. In 1983, WHO held seminars to give people a chance to study the use of traditional Chinese medicine in primary health care (see the extensive writings of Croizier (1973), which will be drawn on in the following account).

At the time of the Revolution there were probably fewer than 20,000 modern-trained physicians in China (Shon-tse 1957), and they were heavily concentrated in a few urban centers. "The vast countryside [was] almost entirely devoid of any kind of modern medical care." On the other hand, by 1955, the Peking government had registered 486,700 traditional doctors. At first the revolutionaries rejected traditional medicine as a particularly noxious part of the old culture and society. In 1944, for example, Mao Tse-tung said that modern-trained doctors were "of course superior to the doctors of old type," and he urged them to unite with and raise the scientific level of traditional practitioners in order to better serve the people (Mao 1969). The official goal was that of upgrading the skills of the traditional practitioners while "trying to train a sufficient number of modern physicians to replace them as soon as possible" (Anonymous, Chinese Medical Journal 1949).

> In 1954 the Chinese medical world was shaken by a rigorous Party-led campaign to raise the status of traditional medicine. This included denunciation of modern-trained doctors and Ministry of Health leaders for despising and belittling the medical legacy of the Motherland (Croizier 1973).

Traditional practitioners were brought to modern hospitals and clinics for retraining, special wards were set aside for acupuncture and herbal medicine, and Western doctors were invited to take courses in TM.

Support for TM was at its height during the revolutionary zeal of the Great Leap Forward between 1957 and 1959. Research papers disappeared from the *Chinese Medical Journal* and were supplanted by praise for TM and the thoughts of Mao Tse-tung. Acupuncture anesthesia seems to have been used for the first time in 1958, and in the same year, thirteen medical colleges for TM opened. The aim was to create a new type of "integrated" medicine.

The emphasis on TM declined somewhat when the extremist policies of the Great Leap Forward waned, but the campaign for TM restarted with new vigor during the Cultural Revolution of 1965-1966. Few medical journals appeared during that era. The news media, however, published stories of the miraculous effects of acupuncture when applied by a politically-conscious healer "who had learned the art by practicing on himself." This renewed stress on supposedly "traditional" therapies culminated in 1971-1972; and at about the same time, China rejoined WHO (Croizier 1973).

However, the medicine that emerged from the Cultural Revolution was not traditional medicine at all (Unschuld 1973). Instead, the Chinese had found a way to keep its name and appearance while really training a new force of paramedical workers, the so-called "barefoot doctors." The plan was that, as their standard of performance improved, these workers would become increasingly like modern medical practitioners (Croizier 1973). Few people know that the barefoot doctors formed not a traditional but a new category of health personnel.

During the regime of the Gang of Four (1973-1976) the status of TM was variable. It lost prestige in China after Mao's death in 1976, but it was strongly propagated by the Chinese Vice-Director of WHO. In the early 1980s, a series of exposés having to do with TM appeared in the Chinese press. For example, Wen-Hui Bao wrote that patients were regarded as serving the aims of the treatment methods rather than the treatment serving the patients, that physicians and nurses refused acupuncture for themselves, and that analgesics were given and hypnosis was performed in addition to the so-called acupuncture "anesthesia." The latter was called a much-exaggerated creation of the Gang of Four (Spiegel 1980).

The final political verdict on acupuncture has not yet been given. Not surprisingly, the Chinese Hospital for TM defends it. However, since 1975, scientific and not acupuncture anesthesia has been used in almost all surgical operations. The same has been true in the border conflict with Viet Nam, where only 1% of people injured are treated with accupuncture. Today, only 10% of the physicians in China use TM (Simen 1981), and in 1988 it was reported that no modern-trained physician was a member of the Chinese acupuncture society.

In general, older people prefer Chinese medicine, younger people prefer Western medicine, and both age groups tend to prefer the latter for acute conditions. When the contents of medical bags carried by barefoot doctors were inspected, it was found that nearly 80% of the more than 40 medicinal items present were Western medical products (Lee 1982). It is true that unlike the commune health clinics, the brigade medical stations stress the use of Chinese drugs, but this is primarily for economic reasons: the more expensive Western medicines are reserved for emergencies.

One problem with TM is that it is usually unsupervised and uncontrolled, and under these conditions its quality is unpredictable. This is been the case in Hong Kong, where many Chinese-style practitioners are, in fact, "quacks" (Lee 1975). It is true that among the five million people in Hong Kong, 90% of whom are Chinese, there are still some who use TM. However, the overwhelming majority patronize the government's scientific medical services. Use of such services has doubled in the past decade despite all of the WHO proclamation about the virtues of traditional medicine.

In recent years, the Chinese Government has emphasized the importance of systematic evaluation of traditional methods of treatment (Xiao 1986), indicating a degree of skepticism about the merits of TM. Patterns of resort in China also suggest that TM's popularity is waning. For example, at a WHO seminar held in Yexian County in June 1982, it was reported that of 186 beds in one hospital, only six were reserved for TM. There were 44 Western-trained physicians, but only one traditional doctor on staff. Only 7% of the outpatient consultations and 1.6% of the inpatient consultations involved TM (WHO 1983).

What is now clear, but was not obvious in the past, is that the Chinese policy was always rather pragmatic. Traditional practitioners were used when they were needed, but only as a stop-gap resource until sufficient numbers of health workers could be trained according to the Western system. Thus the official policy favoring the integration of Western and Chinese medicine has not been fully implemented and probably never will be. Two theorists have suggested that the reason lies in the structural impossibility of synthesizing the two medical systems (Unschuld 1980; Bibeau 1985). Developments in China were not only based on conditions unique to that country, but were also misinterpreted in other parts of the world. The Chinese model, then, cannot reasonably be regarded as exportable to other countries.

Some Initial Objectives Recalled

According to a WHO Executive Board Document (Djukanovic and Mach 1975), WHO's original objective with regard to TM was simply

> to collect data on traditional healers and indigenous systems of medicine, to analyze this information, to determine the relevance of traditional healing to primary health care needs of the various populations, and to suggest the main directions for action with special regard to the training and utilization of traditional healers in the health system.

Nowhere does this document state that the aim was to be integration and only once is such a word as "coordination" mentioned. However, a somewhat later WHO document (1976) mentions integration twice among the objectives to be sought.

There were certain irregularities connected with this latter document. First of all, representatives from the various WHO regions did *not* unanimously endorse it. They were unable to agree about the *a priori* emphasis put on integration and they requested clarification of WHO's primary objectives. They were either the immediate integration of the traditional and modern health systems even before research studies were carried out, or the development of health manpower resources to provide rural, underserved populations with medical care.

In response to the first request, it was stated that there was insufficient knowledge to carry out such an integration attempt. This is still true in 1990! As for the second request, it was pointed out that in terms of both attitudes and numbers, fully-trained medical practitioners could not solve the problems of rural areas. Other solutions, however, were suggested, including the shortening of medical school curricula and the use of paramedics, health assistants, midwives, schoolteachers, community nurses, barefoot doctors, and health visitors. These suggestions still have much to recommend them.

Some Research Deficits

Strangely enough, literature on TM rarely focuses on the serious health risks posed by many traditional practices Such practices include giving birth in unhygienic places because the delivery process is considered ritually impure and trying to hasten a prolonged labor by having the woman confess to marital infidelity that supposedly caused the difficulty. Similarly, there is little documentation available regarding female circumcision despite the fact that between 30 and 85 million women, principally in Africa, are estimated to be circumcised, and several thousand new operations are performed each day (WHO 1986).[7] Very little research has been done on the sexual experience of such women, a subject surrounded by taboos and inhibitions, or on how circumcision underlines women's generally low social status or impairs their health. One may note that the operation is not only culturally sanctioned, but also is a principal source of income for TBAs and even for professional midwives (WHO 1986). Thus, no mere retraining of TBAs will easily put a stop to this practice.

Traditional Medicine and Viral Disease

The global appearance of AIDS provides a natural test case for the role of TM in enhancing or detracting from public health. In Africa, the very heartland of TM, local curers initially claimed that they could cure "slim" since it was caused by "very powerful witches." Some of these healers, unfortunately, have themselves since succumbed to the disease. However, it was a scientifically-trained Ugandan district medical officer who first made the connection between "slim disease" and AIDS and thus clarified its true mode of transmission (Hooper 1987). TM contributed nothing to this discovery.

In fact, one cannot help wondering about the possible role of traditional rituals involving perforation, incision, scarification, male and female circumcision, tatooage, and the like in spreading the AIDS virus. Of course, this mode of transmission would be of only secondary importance and would be difficult to prove. However, what does seem clear is that endorsements of TM have strengthened the untrained practitioners of "hybrid" medicine who give unnecessary injections for a variety of ills, armed with one needle, discarded syringes, and discarded vials that once held antibiotics but have been refilled with water. Such injections, unassociated with drug abuse, were judged to have been of importance in AIDS transmission in Haiti and Zaire (WHO 1984). Studies in Zaire have already linked seropositivity with the number of injections received by patients (Mann 1986; Feldmann 1986), and it has been stated that in Kenya,

> Infection via this route is a major problem both in legitimate medical facilities . . . and on the street. The cultural preference given to the injection as a mode of treatment has spawned a host of profiteers at the grass-roots level. If one considers that an estimated 75 percent of the population use folk healers, the possible magnitude of the problem becomes apparent (Fortin 1987).

As Biggar (1986) has pointed out, this possible mode of transmission of AIDS urgently needs further study.

Injections by folk healers and practitioners of hybrid medicine may also figure in the spread of hepatitis B and primary liver cancer, both so disproportionately prevalent in the developing world. By the time WHO endorsed TM in 1978, the mode of transmission of hepatitis B was well known. Yet no warning voice was raised about this practice! Today, indiscriminate use of syringes and needles by laymen continues to be widely reported by medical professionals, ethnologists, and travellers. So, for example, Naipaul (1980; 1981) has described a *marchande*, or small retailer, in Zaire buying simple things for resale to fisherfolk. Among them, along with pencils, razor blades, soap, clothes, cooking pots, and enamel basins, were *syringes*.[8]

Again, it must be stressed that the health risks associated with TM have been largely ignored in policy discussions. Studies of these matters by medical anthropologists could supply crucially-needed information. It is disturbing that when the AIDS epidemic took hold in Africa, so much was known about kinship patterns and basket weaving and so little about sex customs or other risk-related practices.

Wishful Thinking

Anthropologists have been slow to criticize traditional practices of whatever kind, however. Of the hundreds of articles they have written on TM, most have been guided by optimism and, as Sutherland (1982) says, "such creeds as ethnomethodology, where nothing is true but thinking makes it so." The latter characterization is an oversimplification, of course, but it is true that even today, much anthropological writing on TM lacks objectivity and resembles an act of faith more than an attempt at scientific analysis. Further, one notices that enthusiasm for TM seems to be greater as the writer's distance from daily lived experience in these developing countries increases.

For example, in 1985 a five-month course for traditional healers and primary health care workers was started in Ghana with German financing. Giving no supporting evidence, the author of a report on this project (Fink 1987) asserts that traditional healers could represent a new way to provide national health care. Similarly, a study of traditional remedies for skin infection used in Chiapas, Mexico, concludes with the enthusiastic but unsupported claim that TM "can become a practical means for the detection and treatment of essential health problems" (Esquirel and Zolla 1986). In fact, uncritical belief in the efficacy of traditional remedies has been the general rule (see for example Scarpa 1987). Some respected scholars even protest against limiting TM to peripheral rural areas because this implies that it is expected to disappear with the advance of modern medicine (Bibeau 1985), and others disagree with the WHO proposal that African traditional healers be retrained as front line health workers (Djukanovic and Mach 1975). These theorists go even further than the Chinese did, advocating the maintenance of the TM system in its entirety and claiming that a radical new approach to traditional medicine is emerging (Bibeau 1985).

Epilogue

In summary, twelve years after the WHO Resolution on TM, key questions remain unanswered. How could traditional health practitioners be included in national health services? How could an appropriate organizational structure be created? How could health professionals be persuaded to support TM programmes? How would health legislation operate in such a context? How could a national drug policy be revised to include traditional remedies? How could research and development on TM be carried out? Finally, how would TM activities be financed? It is clear that the WHO endorsement of TM was intended as a pragmatic measure to help solve the problem of insufficient health care coverage. However, enthusiastic anthropologists have reinterpreted the initiative in accordance with their own biases toward cultural maintenance of diversity for its own sake (Werner 1985; Bibeau 1978; Kinkela, Bibeau, and Corin 1982; Rappaport 1980; Aluwihare 1982). This conservative bias was noted years ago by Batalla (1966) in his critique of applied anthropology generally.

One hopes that governments will support the WHO primary health goals (WHO 1981) but not assume that TM must necessarily be embraced as well. WHO itself has come to recognize that TM takes many forms and should not receive blanket endorsement. As the director of the WHO TM Programme himself put it in 1987,

> It is . . . important to distinguish between the formalized traditional systems of medicine, such as Ayurveda, Unani, and traditional Chinese medicines, each of which have a well-defined and fully documented philosophy and educational content, and the types of traditional medicine that are handed down from generation to generation by word of mouth. . . . [Some] methods and beliefs are so diverse as to preclude their incorporation into any formal system. Individual governments will have to decide on what place, if any, to accord them (Akerele 1987).

We submit that the place should be minimal and that the TM initiative itself was well-intended but misguided. It is time to realize that it has contributed virtually nothing to solving the monumental health problems of the developing world.[9]

Notes

1. One of the proponents of integration has been the U.S. Agency for International Development Office of Health, known for its generous funding.

2. For a resolution to be presented, it is usually enough to have the backing of a handful of countries. Approval of such a resolution is then normally achieved by acclamation, as was the case with TM; an actual vote is rarely taken. Even if there is a vote, countries that in reality consider the resolution irrelevant may either abstain or vote in favor out of mere courtesy. Resolutions do not require any action, but once approved, they gain respectability.

3. Immediately after India emerged as an independent nation, a demand arose for Ayurveda to be the national system of health care. This occurred despite the fact that the vast majority of students of Ayurveda have failed to complete secondary school, and, being unable to gain admission to other professional schools, attend Ayurvedic colleges as a last resort. Moreover, pure Ayurveda cannot possibly cope with the major public health needs of rural India. In fact, for the last forty years, Ayurvedic medical education has in reality been an integrated or mixed system in which both Ayurvedic and modern medical subjects are taught. Both pure Ayurvedists and proponents of scientific medicine agree that this system has produced thousands of poorly-trained health practitioners unqualified in either system but using dangerous drugs about which they have inadequate knowledge. (Based on unpublished research by P.R. Brass 1976).

4. The best PHC village handbooks ever to be published did not originate from WHO but from the U.S.-based Hesperian Foundation. Examples are David Werner's *Where There Is No Doctor*, the most widely-used health care manual in the world, printed in 20 languages, and his *Helping Health Workers Learn*. WHO

has produced a much less successful hybrid book, *The Primary Health Worker: Working Guide for Training, Guidelines for Adaption* (Geneva, 1980).

5. The term "traditional healer" is often applied so generally as to blur the distinctions among the many existing varieties of such healers. There is also confusion in the literature regarding the term "shaman," as Morris (1986) has cogently shown for Malawi.

6. Despite the apparent "progress" represented by these developments, one must recall that even a simple herbalist is likely to charge a worker a day's pay for medicines to cure problems with sexual potency, protect body or house, or counteract sorcery and witchcraft (cf. Morris 1986).

7. See also *Traditional Practices Affecting the Health of Women and Children. Female Circumcision, Childhood Marriage, Nutritional Taboos, etc.* (WHO/EMRO Technical Publication No. 2, Vol. 1: Report of a Seminar (Khartoum, 1979). Alexandria: WHO Regional Office for the Eastern Mediterranean, 1979 and Vol. 2: Background Papers to the WHO Seminar. Alexandria, WHO Regional Office for the Eastern Mediterranean, 1982.

8. Whether vaccination campaigns in the developing world have also contributed to the spread of AIDS remains a matter of conjecture. No instances of immunization-related spread of HIV have yet been reported, and certainly if needles and syringes are properly sterilized, the risk of transmission is zero (La Force 1986). Where important immunization programmes in Africa are at risk, it is in everybody's interest not to create unwarranted anxiety. However, in Zaire the present author has seen vaccination campaigns where hundreds of people have been injected in turn by a single unsterilized needle in spite of warnings against this practice.

9. Despite the critique of TM presented here, the author applauds WHO's primary health care goals and its quest to improve human health. After all, he has spent almost 20 years working for WHO in five of the six WHO regions of the world.

References

African Regional Office of the WHO (AFRO) Technical Report Series 1976 No. 1, African Traditional Medicine, Report of the Regional Expert Committee. Brazzaville (Congo): WHO.

Aguirre Beltrán, G. 1978 Training Programs in Intercultural Medicine. In *Modern Medicine and Medical Anthropology in the United States-Mexico Border Population*. B. Velimirovic, ed. Pp. 10-13. PAHO/WHO: Washington.

Akerele, O. 1983 Which Way for Traditional Medicine? *World Health*, 3-4.

___ 1987 The Best of Both Worlds; Bringing Traditional Medicine Up to Date. *Social Science and Medicine* 24(2):177-181.

Aluwihare, A.P.R. 1982 Traditional and Western Medicine Working in Tandem. *World Health Forum* 3(4):450-451.

Anonymous 1949 Outline of Plans of Future Medical Work in China. *Chinese Medical Journal*, 35, September.

Bannerman, R.H., J. Burton, and Ch'en Wen-Chiech, eds. 1983 *Traditional Medicine and Health Care Coverage: A Reader for Health Administrations and Practitioners*. Geneva: WHO.

Barbee, E. 1986 Biomedical Resistance to Ethnomedicine in Botswana. *Social Science and Medicine* 22(1):75-80.

Batalla, G.B. 1966 Conservative Thought in Applied Anthropology. *Human Organization* 25:89-92.

Bibeau, G. 1978 The World Health Organization in Encounter with African Traditional Medicine: Theoretical Conceptions and Practical Strategies. In *African Therapeutic Systems*. J.A.A. Ayoade, I.F. Harrison, D.M. Warren, and Z. Ademuwagun, eds. Waltham, MA: Crossroads Press.

___ 1985 From China to Africa: The Same Impossible Synthesis Between Traditional and Western Medicines. *Social Science and Medicine* 21(8):937-943.

Biggar, R.J. 1986 The AIDS-Problem in Africa. *Lancet* 1(8472): 79-82.

Caragay, R.N. 1982 Training Indigenous Health Workers: A Philippine Experience. *World Health Forum* 3(2):159-163.

Chiwuzie, U.F., O. Okoje, et al. 1987 Traditional Practitioners are Here to Stay. *World Health Forum* 8:240-444.

Croizier, R.C. 1973 Traditional Medicine as a Basis for Chinese Medical Practice. In *Medicine and Public Health in the People's Republic of China*. J.R. Quinn, ed. Pp. 3-21. Washington: U.S. Department of Health, Education and Welfare.

Diesch, P. 1976 In Traditional Medicine and Its Role in the Development of Health Services in South East Asia Region. WHO Doc. SEA/OMC/Traditional Medicine Meeting / 3:1-3. Interregional Congress on the Traditional Medicine Program, October 4-8. New Delhi: WHO.

Djukanovic V., and E.P. Mach, eds. 1975 *Alternative Approaches to Meeting Basic Health Needs in Developing Countries. A Joint UNICEF/WHO Study*. Geneva: WHO.

Douglas, R.D. 1979 National Drug Policies, More State Intervention or Less? *World Medicine* 14(21):29-36.

Esquirel, M., and C. Zolla 1986 Dermatological Diseases in Mexican Traditional Medicine. *Bulletin of the PAHO* 101(4):339-347.

Feldmann, D.A. 1986 Anthropology, AIDS and Africa. *Medical Anthropological Quarterly* 17:38-40.

Fink, H. 1987 Traditionelle Medizin und Primary Health Care. *Entwicklung und Zusammenarbeit* 3:19-21. Bonn.

Fortin, A.J. 1987 The Politics of AIDS in Kenya. *Third World Quarterly*, :900-919.

Foster, G. 1978 Preface to *Modern Medicine and Medical Anthropology in the United States-Mexico Border Population*. B. Velimirovic, ed. Pp. 4-11. Washington: PAHO/WHO.

Green, E. 1985 Traditional Healers, Mothers and Childhood Diarrheal Disease in Swaziland: The Interface of Anthropology and Health Education. *Social Science and Medicine* 20(3):277-385.

Green, E., and L. Makhubu 1984 Traditional Healers in Swaziland: Toward Improved Cooperation Between the Traditional and Modern Health Service. *Social Science and Medicine* 18:1071-1079.

Gunaratne, H.V.T. 1980 Bringing Down Drug Costs: The Sri Lankan Example. *World Health Forum* 1(1,2):117-122.

Hernández de Sándoval, G. n.d. Evaluación de la Atención Obstétrica en el IX. Distrito Sanitario en el Distrito Federal en los Años 1959-1976. VIII Congreso

Internacional de Medicina Preventiva y Social. México: Escuela de Salud Pública.

Hoff, W., and D. Nhlavana Maseko 1986 Nurses and Traditional Healers Join Hands. *World Health Forum* 7:412-416.

Hooper, E. 1987 AIDS in Uganda. *Swiss Review of World Affairs*, 24-27, July.

Johns Hopkins University 1980 Traditional Midwives and Family Planning. *Population Reports I*, Series VIII, 3(22):437-438, 439-448.

Justice, W.L. 1978 Training Across Cultural Barriers: The Experience of the Indian Health Services with the Community Health Medical Training Programme. In *Modern Medicine and Medical Anthropology in the United States-Mexico Border Population*. B. Velimirovic, ed. Pp. 96-108. Washington: PAHO/WHO.

Kinkela, N., G. Bibeau, and F. Corin 1982 Steps Towards a New System of Public Health in Zaire. In *African Therapeutic Systems*. J.A.A. Ayoade, I.F. Harrison, D.M. Warren, and Z. Ademuwagun eds. Waltham, MA: Crossroads Press.

La Force, M. 1986 Immunization of Children Infected with Human Immunodeficiency Virus. WHO Document WHO/EDI/GEX/86/6, Rev. 1. Geneva: WHO.

Lee, R.P.L. 1975 Towards a Convergence of Modern Western and Traditional Chinese Medical Services in Hong Kong. In *Topias and Utopias in Health: Policy Studies*. S.R. Ingma and E.A. Thomas, eds. P. 394. Mouton: The Hague.

___ 1982 Chinese and Western Medical Care in China's Rural Communes. *World Health Forum*, 3(3):301-306.

López, A.A. 1978 Medical Anthropology in a Border Context. In *Modern Medicine and Medical Anthropology in the United States-Mexico Border Population*. B. Velimirovic, ed. Pp. 43-48. Washington: PAHO/WHO.

Mabogunje, A.L. 1981 *The Development Process*. Pp. 334-337. London: Hutchinson.

Mahler, H. 1978 Promotion of Primary Health Care in Member Countries of WHO. *Public Health Reports* 93(2):107.

___ 1983 Health for All--Everyone's Concern. *World Health* 2-4, April-May.

Mann, J.M. 1986 Epidemiology of LAV/HTLV-III in Africa. Paper presented at the Second International Conference on AIDS, Paris.

Mao Tse-Tung 1969 *Selected Works*. Pp. 3, 215-218, and 236. Peking: Foreign Language Press.

Morris, B. 1986 Herbalism and Divination in Southern Malawi. *Social Science and Medicine* 23(4):367-377.

Naipaul, V.S. 1980 *A Bend in the River*. P. 11. Harmondsworth, England: Penguin Books.

___ 1981 *A New King for the Congo: Mobutu and the Nihilism of Africa*. P. 117. Harmondsworth, England: Penguin Books.

Oyeneye, O. 1985 Mobilizing Indigenous Resources for Primary Health Care in Nigeria: A Note on the Place of Traditional Medicine. *Social Science and Medicine* 20(1):67-69.

Pan American Health Organization 1978 Utilization of Auxiliaries and Community Leaders in Health Programmes in Rural Areas. Report of a Meeting. Houston, TX. PAHO Scientific Publication No. 296. Washington: PAHO.

Rappaport, H. 1980 The Integration of Scientific and Traditional Healing; the Problem of De-mystification. In *Traditional Health Care Delivery in Contemporary Africa*. P. Ulin and M. Segall, eds. Pp. 81-98. Syracuse, NY: Syracuse University Press.

Roemer, M.I. 1976 *Health Care System in World Perspective*. P. 67. Ann Arbor: Health Administration Press, University of Michigan.

Scarpa, A. 1987 The "Serpent-Stone" or the "Black Stone." *Social Science and Medicine* 25(3):229-230.

Shon-tse, Jen-min 1957 *People Handbook*. P. 608. Peking.

Sidel R., and V. Sidel 1982 *The Health of China: Current Conflicts in Medical and Human Services for One Billion People*. Boston: Beacon Press.

Simen, R.H. 1981 Impulse aus Chinas alter Medizin. *Medizinische Welt* 32(12):3.

Spiegel, B.W. 1980 *Schreckliche Schmerzen*. 34(50):160-163.

Stone, L. 1986 Primary Health Care for Whom? Village Perspective from Nepal. *Social Science and Medicine* 22(3):293-302.

Sutherland, S. 1982 Curing Nonsense. *Nature* 300(5888):118-199.

Unschuld, P. 1980 *Medizin in China*. Eine Ideengeschichte. München: Beck.

___ 1973 The Social Organization and Ecology of Medical Practice in Taiwan. In *Medicine and Public Health in the People's Republic of China*. J.R. Quinn, ed. Washington: U.S. Department of Health, Education and Welfare.

Velimirovic, B. 1984 Traditional Medicine is Not Primary Health Care, A Polemic. Part I: *Curare* 7:61-79; Part II: *Curare* 7:85-93.

Velimirovic, H. 1972 Krankenheilung bei zwei Philippinischen Gruppen, bei den Tagalog am Taalsee in Batangas und den Kankanai-Igorot in der Provinz Benguet auf Luzon. Dissertation, Freie Universität, Berlin-West.

___ 1982 Round Table. Traditional Medicine in Modern Health Care. *World Health Forum* 3(1):24-26.

Velimirovic, H., and B. Velimirovic 1978 Use of Traditional Birth Attendants. *Curare* 1:85-96.

___ 1978 The Role of Traditional Birth Attendants in Health Services. *Curare* 2:85-96.

___ 1980 Do Traditional Plant Medicines Have a Future in Third World Countries? *Curare* 3:173-191.

Verderese, M.L. 1973 Report of Review and Analysis of Information and Data on Traditional Birth Attendants. Geneva: WHO, March 13-20.

Verderese, M.L., and L.M. Turnbull 1975 The Traditional Birth Attendant in Maternal and Child Health and Family Planning. Geneva: WHO.

Werner, R. 1985 Entwicklungshilfe im Gesundheitswesen--Grundlagen einer ethnospezifischen Gesundheitssystem-Analyze. *Das Öffentliche Gesundheits-Wesen* 47:125-129, Stuttgart: G. Thieme.

___ 1987 Öffentliches Gesundheitswesen und Traditionelle Medizin in Äthiopien. *Das Öffentliche Gesundheits-Wesen* 48:36-40.

World Health Organization 1975 Training and Supervision of Traditional Birth Attendants. Report of a Study Group. Brazzaville, December 9-12. Regional Office for Africa. Geneva.

___ 1976 Traditional Medicine and Its Role in the Development of Health Services in South East Asia Region. WHO Doc. SEA/OMC/Traditional Medicine Meeting / 3:1-3. Interregional Congress Traditional Medicine Program, October 4-8. New Delhi.

___ 1978 Promotion and Development of Traditional Medicine. Technical Report Series No. 622. Geneva.

___ 1979 *Training and Utilization of Auxiliary Personnel for Rural Health Teams in Developing Countries*. Report of a WHO Expert Committee TRS 633. Geneva.

___ 1981 Global Strategy for Health for All by the Year 2000. Geneva.

___ 1983 *Primary Health Care: The Chinese Experience*. Report of an Interregional Seminar. Yexian County, June 13-26, 1982, Geneva.

___ 1984 AIDS Emergencies. Report of a WHO Meeting. Geneva: November 22-25, 1983. WHO Document STD. Geneva.

___ 1986 A Traditional Practice that Threatens Health--Female Circumcision. *WHO Chronicle* 40(1):31-36.

Xiao, Pei-Gen 1986 Medicinal Plants: The Chinese Approach. *World Health Forum* 7:84-85.

Young, A. 1983 The Relevance of Traditional Medical Cultures to Modern Primary Health Care. *Social Science and Medicine* 17:(16):1205-1211.

4

The Role of Anthropologists in Primary Health Care: Reconciling Professional and Community Interests

John M. Donahue

Introduction

Anthropologists working in primary health care (PHC) find themselves in a variety of social settings and exercising quite diverse roles. Some find themselves working in community-based applied research projects, as is described by Paul (1955), Tax (1958), and Holmberg and Lasswell (1962). Others are within international health organizations such as WHO, PAHO, and UNICEF, or in governmental agencies such as USAID (Foster 1977, 1982). Anthropologists can also be found in increasing numbers as consultants or employees within private voluntary organizations (PVOs) (Pillsbury 1985).

Efforts to implement the now famous Declaration of Alma-Ata (1978) have increased the visibility and utility of anthropology among health professionals worldwide. Primary health care (PHC) strategies now include the use of local healers, different kinds of health workers, traditional medicines, and community participation (Neumann and Lauro 1982). For the most part, these strategies overlap many topics of interest and research within medical anthropology. We should not be surprised, then, that primary health care professionals have increasingly turned to anthropological research for insights into questions dealing with community organization, traditional medical beliefs and folk healing (Martin 1983).

As anthropologists are invited into national and international health organizations, they become aware of the bureaucratic and organizational constraints on the implementation of a community-based health care program (Pillsbury 1982). Reasons for the difficulty in bridging policy and practice include the nature of bureaucratic culture (Justice 1986), the resistance of local political elites to grass-roots community organization (Werner 1980; Heggenhougen 1984), lack of political organization among traditional practitioners (Janzen 1978), fundamental differences between traditional and modern medical world views and treatments (Young 1983), and even their incompatibility (Kleinman and Sung 1979: 24-25).

Other obstacles to bridging policy and practice in primary health care exist within the national and international health organizations themselves. Among these is a clinical model of PHC advocated by medical professionals who tend to exercise professional control within these health organizations. Professional dominance is an issue often discussed among medical sociologists (Freidson 1970, 1984; Starr 1982; Ugalde 1979, 1980). As anthropologists move more into clinical and institutional settings, they are documenting how bureaucratic culture (Justice 1986) or professional dominance in the clinical model of primary health care (Donahue 1986a) impinges on many areas of anthropological concern, be they community participation, midwifery, traditional healing, or the training of community health workers (CHWs).

This essay explores two broad strategies which anthropologists might employ to ensure a balance between clinical and community approaches to primary health care. One is to work with the medical profession in institutional settings in an effort to broaden primary health care efforts beyond narrow clinical definitions. The other is to work with communities in their efforts to organize more appropriate health initiatives. Both strategies demand an understanding of the nature of professional dominance.

Professional Dominance

The issue of professional dominance is a major subject of sociological investigation both in general (Freidson 1970, 1984) and as manifested in health programs (Ugalde 1979, 1980). Among anthropologists who have worked as consultants to national and international health organizations, George Foster is among the most widely published on the subject. In the late 1960s Foster (1969: 104) noted that professionals in development programs were subject to the policy directives of national governments, the constraints of administrative bureaucracies, and the demands of their own professions. Reflecting on medical anthropology and international health planning, Foster (1977: 528) notes that health professionals easily accept the premise that the principal barriers to health care lie within the target group. On the other hand, the assumption that the barriers to improved health programs also are found "in the cultures of bureaucracies, the assumptions of the medical profession, and in the psychological makeup of the specialists who participate in these programs . . . is stoutly resisted by many."

Foster (1982) returned to this general theme in a lecture given at the time of his acceptance of the Malinowski Award. "Rarely, if ever," he said, "is the question asked, 'How can anthropologists help to change bureaucratic behavior that inhibits the design and operation of the best possible health care systems?'." He said that he had found that most health care personnel with whom he had worked in recent years appeared genuinely surprised at this question, but not all. "And those who do recognize the importance of bureaucratic factors in health care delivery feel--realistically, I suspect--that this is a constant about which little can be done." He concluded, "If changing behavior will result in effective primary health care, it must be the community, not bureaucratic behavior, that changes" (1982: 194). Some years later Foster (1987) noted how the dominance of the medical profession was (and is) exercised in the grant-review process within the World Health Organization, a process which effectively excludes important anthropological methodologies and contributions.[1]

Drawing on extensive experience with anthropologists in international health, Pillsbury (1985: 95) concludes that some who have successfully integrated themselves into interdisciplinary health teams "may still feel unduly disregarded by those physicians who consider themselves to be the guardians of health." Recently, more detailed anthropological critiques of medical hegemony in PHC efforts in Latin America have appeared for Bolivia (Crandon 1983) and for Nicaragua (Donahue 1986b). In the following analysis, I will focus on several areas of traditional anthropological concern in primary health care. Each case will suggest how anthropologists within health organizations or in local communities might work with health administrators, planners and community groups interested in a more community-based PHC program.

First, these case studies must be placed in a broader historical and comparative context. The evolution of the professionally dominated clinical model of health care in the United States provides such a framework.

Folk Healers and the Emergence of Professional Dominance

The history of folk healers in the medical division of labor in the United States can shed light on current relations between health professionals and non-professionals in the developing world.

In 19th-century America, the relationship between medical professionals and folk healers was viewed as a competition between medical occupations. The eclectics and the homeopaths, as well as lay practitioners such as herbalists, bone-setters, midwives and faith healers, were included among the folk healers (Starr 1982: 47-48, 96-99). Orthodox physicians had little competitive edge over the other medical occupations until the end of the 19th century. The growing legitimacy of scientific, clinical medicine increased the cultural authority of orthodox practitioners in the minds of the public (Starr 1982: 59). Eventually orthodox physicians were able to turn this technical advantage into professional dominance over other medical occupations. The rise of medical professionalism in 19th-century America is closely tied to the ability of physicians, as an occupational group, to control access into medical institutions such as hospitals and medical schools. The medical profession found that through licensing and accreditation they were able to attain more solidarity within their ranks as well as better control the relations of their colleagues with other medical occupations, including folk healers.

Professions are normally considered occupational groups characterized by "some configuration of concrete, usually legally sustained, privileges" (Saks 1983: 17). The domination of one occupation over another arises from the structure of the occupation itself. Medical professionals pursue their careers in "concrete, historically located institutions" (Freidson 1970: 155). In the case of the United States and in many developing countries today, those institutions include medical schools, hospitals, and clinics. In effect, these institutional ties have allowed medical practitioners to gain and maintain a monopoly over the practice of medicine--an ascendancy over lay health practitioners and other medical professionals as well.[2] Freidson notes that professionals' pride in their work often translates into an attitude of superiority over other health occupations and lay clients (1970: 156). He concludes that since those weaknesses stem from professionalism itself, "professions cannot be expected to be able to rectify them" (1970: 156).

In terms of the present discussion, we might expect resistance on the part of the medical profession, as a corporate group, to the organization of primary health care efforts outside of clinical settings and not under their direct supervision.[3] In such circumstances the anthropologist might assume the role of cultural broker between advocates of the clinical and the popular primary care models.[4] Indeed, anthropologists, health educators, and physicians who transcend narrowly defined professional roles may provide the nucleus for a revitalized PHC.[5] Such a team approach could alter the balance of power in favor of a community-based rather than an institutionally based and professionally dominated primary health care program.

Towards a Community-Based Primary Health Care Program

One of the first steps to organizing a community-based primary health care program would be to involve traditional healers, midwives, and community health workers. Anthropologists are not unanimous on the utility of this strategy, however. Armed with the distinction between "disease" which can be cured and "illness" which demands healing, Kleinman and Sung (1979: 24-25) conclude that "most indigenous practitioners (especially sacred practitioners) cannot be trained to systematically recognize, refer or treat disease. They cannot be incorporated into modern health care organizations."

For his part, Foster (1977) envisions the eventual co-opting of traditional healers into the medical system. He views traditional healers as transitional figures who may eventually become community health workers or whose roles may at least merge with that of the CHW. A third (and the most common) opinion in the anthropological literature is that physicians, traditional healers, midwives and CHWs should enter into a "therapeutic alliance" in which non-physicians would be employed in culturally appropriate therapies where the biomedical paradigm fails to address culture-specific illnesses (Engel 1977). Here research tends to focus upon levels of care, the special cognitions and roles of traditional healers and of medical professionals, and the points of possible articulation between the two (Coreil 1983; Kleinman 1980; Young 1983).

Case Studies

Bastien (1987) describes the use of an alliance strategy between CHWs and physicians in the Bolivian altiplano. In that case, the anthropologist and a Bolivian physician carried out a series of workshops in which health professionals, midwives, traditional healers, and community residents engaged in a dialogue on local health needs in the areas of traditional birthing techniques, herbal medicine, and appropriate medical technologies such as sterilization and oral rehydration therapy. Out of that experience there emerged a health education methodology based on the integration of folk categories of disease, symptoms, causes, and treatments with their counterparts in modern medicine. For example, in a discussion of diarrhea, participants were asked to choose a point of articulation between the two medical systems on which to focus their educational efforts. They decided to focus on changing the traditional treatment, but concluded that diarrhea could only be treated with a combination of native cures and a rehydration formula.

The final step was the design of a culturally relevant instructional guide. The concept of rehydration was explained by adapting a local legend in which two mountains vie for the love of a maiden mountain. During their struggle, one mountain is visited by a plague of gophers, leaving it dry and dying for lack of springs, but the mountain is saved when a condor brings it a solution of sugar and salt made from ingredients that are brought from various local sources. The participants in the workshop were taught to lead community members in a dialogue on the application of the myth to the rehydration of people suffering from the effects of diarrhea.

The case just described suggests several lessons for anthropologists and others interested in a community-based primary health care program. In the first place, anthropologists can provide direct feedback to the community which they have studied. Their knowledge of the structural-cognitive systems of both the traditional and the modern medical systems allows them to find points of articulation between the two. In the above case, the local CHWs reflected on their native categories of disease etiology and treatment and then on their medical knowledge of diarrhea and oral rehydration therapy.

The role of anthropologists in such cases is that of cultural broker. This role distinguishes them from the "academic colonialist" who studies a community, expropriates the knowledge gained, and uses it to further his or her career, but without any appreciable benefit or feedback to the community (Fals-Borda 1970; Stavenhagen 1971). In other words, the cultural information that anthropologists gather can provide the people studied with a comprehensive and systematic understanding of themselves and their world. Such an understanding, be it in the hands of the career anthropologist, politicians, health bureaucrats, or the community, is power. By providing feedback to the community, the anthropologist can serve community interests as well as other professional or policy goals.

In addition to adopting the role of "culture broker," anthropologists may also participate in the organization of direct health services for community members (New and Hessler 1972; Donahue 1979). This role, of course, depends on the availability of public or private funds for community health care, the level of consumer organization, and the response of the medical establishment to community health initiatives (Gordon 1969; Zwick 1974).

The role of the anthropologist vis-à-vis the health care establishment needs continual redefinition. While it is not at all clear that "a great deal of the commonly-cited anthropological literature dealing with the introduction of Western medicine into traditional societies is either out of date, or no longer relevant" (Foster 1977: 529), the question "How can anthropologists help to change bureaucratic behavior that inhibits the design and operation of the best possible health care systems?" (Foster 1982: 193) seems quite apropos (Justice 1986: 151-152). In fact, the question of how to integrate folk and modern medicine and the question of how to change bureaucratic obstacles to that integration are linked. The following case described by Bastien (1987) suggests that the two issues can be addressed together.

When, at the invitation of the anthropologist, Bolivian doctors witnessed a birth attended by an Aymara midwife, several suggestions for changing standard operating procedures in the clinic delivery room were made and accepted. Dialogue with the midwives also generated ideas for changes that the midwives could introduce to improve their home delivery techniques and still conform to cultural norms. Anthropologists may best initiate change among health administrators and providers by structuring dialogues between patients and physicians in which the cultural knowledge of both medical systems, the folk and the bureaucratic, are mediated, shared and, when necessary, critiqued.[6]

Another lesson for anthropologists who promote the "therapeutic alliance" is suggested by Crandon's (1987: 1012) criticism of Bastien's work. "Bastien describes a project in which Qollahuaya medical concepts were appropriated to gain compliance with a much needed oral rehydration program. This effort saves lives, yet the use of indigenous concepts to extract compliance with a hegemonic medical system implies the eventual eradication of the indigenous tradition, or its transformation and subordinate incorporation into the cosmopolitan system." Crandon's position is reminiscent of that of Singer (1977: 20), who argued that traditional medicine makes the individual "through the mediation of the healer, once again a member of the culture, that is the colonial culture." For Crandon the problem is that such a therapeutic alliance might well result in the subordination of the traditional medical system to a "hegemonic medical system." Her assumption that change will occur only in the traditional system is more appropriately an empirical question, however. In the Bastien case, change operated in both directions and within both systems. Nevertheless, Crandon's concern reflects what are, in fact, differential power relations between practitioners of Western and of folk medicine.

While there seems to be good evidence to suggest that people will use modern medicine as it becomes more accessible in economic and geographical terms (Donahue 1986b), cultural and ideological obstacles must still be addressed. Ironically, anthropologists have identified more of those obstacles within the client communities and among lay practitioners than among medical professionals. It is time to redress the imbalance.

Beyond Professional Dominance

In one sense, anthropologists doing research in primary health care find themselves in the midst of an ongoing dialectic. Following Navarro (1977: 115) we might argue that the configuration of power relations in a health system might result from the relative interplay of two forces. The one, a centripetal force, moves the health system toward the political centralization of power by dominant groups and classes. The other, a centrifugal force, is determined by the democratization and decentralization of the system. In turn, this democratizing force engenders other centrifugal forces such as deprofessionalization, despecialization, and an emphasis on rural areas and community health care. Anthropologists and those who seek a community-based PHC system usually identify more with the centrifugal forces at work in the health system. Their feedback to the community might strengthen the hand of advocates for the decentralization of the health care system and encourage "community-supportive" rather than "community-oppressive" programs in primary health care (Werner 1980).

Research strategies within the "political economy of health" model might attempt to describe how cultural models of health and illness serve to maintain or change existing power relations within a community.[7] Such knowledge, in the hands of subordinate groups, could suggest to them ways and means of creating more equitable relationships with health planners, health administrators, and medical professionals. For this to happen, the anthropologist would need to analyze how "corporate categories" such as traditional healers, midwives, or even CHWs could be organized into "corporate groups" (Janzen 1978) powerful enough to initiate dialogue with and not be co-opted by other corporate groups such as medical societies or health bureaucracies.

In those cases where health bureaucracies provide social and cultural legitimacy to organized groups of traditional healers, midwives, and CHWs, the role of the anthropologist might shift to that of serving as a consultant to the newly emergent groups. Such a situation emerged in Nicaragua after the revolution of 1979. Some historical background will provide the context for the case and discussion that follows.

Background to the Nicaraguan Case

In 1980 a decision was made within the newly created Nicaraguan National Unified Health System (SNUS) to institutionalize popular participation in the planning and implementation of health care delivery (Donahue 1983, 1986b; Garfield and Williams 1989). The organization within the Ministry of Health that was charged with this task was the Division of Communication and Popular Education in Health (DECOPS). The organizational structure of participation included the creation of Popular Health Councils (*Consejos Populares de Salud*, CPSs) at local, regional and national levels. Several voluntary associations, called mass organizations (*organizaciones de masas*), participated in health planning and delivery. The most active organizations in the health sector have been the Sandinista Defense Committees (CDSs) and the Luisa Amanda Espinoza National Association of Nicaraguan Women (*Asociación de Mujeres Nicaraguenses 'Luisa Amanda Espinoza*,' AMNLAE). The Defense Committees have a geographic constituency at the neighborhood or rural sector level, and the Women's Association focuses its concerns directly on how women might contribute to the revolutionary process.

Other organizations have occupational memberships, such as the Federation of Health Workers (FETSALUD), the Confederation of Sandinista Workers (CST), the National Association of Nicaraguan Educators (ANDEN) and the Association of Agricultural Workers (ATC). The Sandinista Youth "19th of July" (JS19J) and the Sandinista Children's Association (ANS) incorporate children and young people into the reform programs. The Parent's Association (APF) addresses educational and other familial matters. Figure 4.1 illustrates the organization of participation in health within the Popular Health Councils.

The Division of Communication and Popular Education in Health originally had intended the Health Councils to be made up exclusively of the popular organizations. They could thereby better negotiate community health concerns and strategies with the Ministry of Health as a partner in planning. However, with the emergence of the mass drug administration programs (popular health days) in 1981, the Health Councils became a joint body of representatives from the popular organizations and the Ministry. The effect was to dilute the independent planning and evaluation function of the popular organizations within the Health Councils. The Councils were subordinated to the centralized planning of the Ministry while the popular organizations were more involved in the staging of the health work days (Keyzer and Ulate 1981: 133). The mass drug administration programs became arenas in which the Popular Health Councils and health promoters first experienced attempts at professional control (Donahue 1983). This did not sit well with many volunteers and health educators. The stage was set for other tests of professional control.

Case Study

After the first national mass drug administration programs of 1981 and 1982, the Popular Health Councils turned their attention to the exercise of some control over health institutions and health personnel. That change in focus can be observed in an analysis of the meetings of several Health Councils in northern Nicaragua. These meetings reveal the range of challenges to professional control which the Popular Health Councils, as a participatory strategy, allowed to surface, to stimulate discussion, and to be acted upon.[8] The major themes included the training of CHWs (called *Brigadistas de Salud*, Health *Brigadistas*), the supervision and evaluation of medical personnel, and the coordination of the regional popular health days. I will take up these themes in order.

One major issue was the relationship between professional personnel and the training of non-professional Health *Brigadistas*. There was agreement that *Brigadista* training should include aspects of preventive medicine, recording of vital statistics, reproduction, mother-child care, and occupational health care. The program, designed for the rural areas, was first piloted in an urban neighborhood. Medical personnel from the local clinic provided the training. *Brigadista* selection was made on the basis of a profile of traits jointly developed by the National Popular Health Council, the Nicaraguan Women's Association, and the Ministry of Health. All agreed that *Brigadistas* should be designated as such, so that their health responsibilities would not conflict with other tasks. (The latter seems to have been precipitated by the fact that some volunteers entered the training program as a way to fulfill service prerequisites for Party membership. Party obligations might otherwise compete with the health tasks of the volunteers.)

A second, and potentially the most sensitive of the issues raised in the health council meetings, was the evaluation and supervision of medical personnel in the area clinics and hospitals. The Popular Health Council requested that the Ministry advise it when evaluations were to be held. They stipulated that health personnel should be evaluated on their performance in the areas of preventive medicine and popular education.

One clinic was singled out for specific criticisms. Council members pointed out that physicians were not keeping their hours in the clinic of El Carmen and patients were often treated in a condescending manner. To provide for more accountability in provider-patient relationships, the Health Council agreed to recommend that all health personnel wear name tags for easier identification. Another complaint was that some people had to wait in line while others were allowed to go forward because of favoritism (*el amigüismo*). Members of the Health Council asked that the clinic look for more efficient ways to handle the patient load. They recommended increased use of volunteers in clerical tasks. Another criticism of the care provided at the clinic related to acute care and quality of service. Eye and hand lacerations (mostly acquired in cutting and loading sugar cane) were not treated as emergencies and referrals to specialists took up to three months.

Furthermore, it was claimed that local hospital personnel in El Arroyo refused to accept women in labor who had not yet dilated to 5 cm. Health Council members argued that the inflexible application of that norm was not congruent with the felt needs of the patients. The Council recommended that the directors of the area clinics meet with the hospital director to seek ways to improve the quality of obstetric care and the utilization of the obstetrics ward.

A third issue centered on the use of local folk healers. The Popular Health Council of the rural district of Rio Viejo in Northern Nicaragua had asked the Regional Office of the Ministry to assign the local folk healer to their newly constructed health post. At about the same time, the Ministry of Health had ordered a folk healer in another village to stop practicing medicine there. The people from that village had written a letter of complaint to *La Barricada*, the national newspaper of the Sandinista Party. The Departmental Health Council responded by commissioning the Women's Association to take a census of all practitioners of folk medicine (*los recursos empíricos*) in the Department.

These events seem to have precipitated a special meeting of the Popular Organizations and the Ministry in the county seat of El Arroyo on April 12, 1982. The objective of the meeting was to formulate a general policy towards folk healers. The discussion revealed that lay members of the community held quite different opinions of the social and cultural authority of folk healers compared with the physician in the local clinic.

The participants offered what amounted to common complaints against the professional practitioners of medicine in rural areas.

> The folk healer is available day and night; the physician only during the day. . . . The healer makes home visits while the physician never moves from the clinic. . . . The healer is a confidant and gives emotional support to the patient. . . . The folk healer's practice of medicine is more in accord with the beliefs and expectations of the people. . . . The healer shares his/her knowledge, but the doctor does not explain or educate anyone about the nature of the illness or the reason for the treatment. . . . The people can tell the difference between the illnesses which folk healers can treat and those they cannot, but people often consult only healers because professional health services are not available. . . .

The meeting had the effect of forestalling further action against the folk healers by the Ministry.

Discussion of the Case

Anthropologists who, as consultants, have worked with various ministries of health in the Third World can attest to the nearly universal presence of two organizational schema, that of the administrative hierarchy of the ministry, and that of the referral system. These two structures, often found in diagram form on wall charts or in National Health Plans, have been referred to as the "pyramid" and the "octopus."[9] Both of these administrative and health delivery bureaucracies can be found in Nicaragua. They are the "concrete, historically located institutions" (Freidson 1970: 155) within which the medical profession typically exercises its professional control over community-based PHC programs.

What is different in the Nicaraguan case is that the Ministry of Health has constituted yet a third structure influencing the decision-making process. The Popular Health Councils at local, regional and national levels act as a "lever" which can be used to move the administrative "pyramid" and the referral "octopus" to function in an arena larger than what their particular bureaucratic or professional interests might dictate. The CHWs likewise have institutional advocates within the Ministry of Health at both national and regional levels in the Division of Communication and Popular Education in Health. That Division is made up of health educators whose activities, while coordinated with the other Divisions within the Ministry, are less under the control of the medical profession.

The result is a healthy tension between professional and popular health agendas, or, to use Navarro's terms, between "centripetal" and "centrifugal" forces within the health care system (1977: 115). The Division of Communication and Popular Education in Health, along with the Popular Health Councils and local Health Educators, maintain that dialectic in Nicaragua. Lack of such tension would probably mean that the medical profession had reestablished its hegemony in the system.

If the dialectic between community-based and institutionally based primary health care is to exist, an effective division of labor between medical professionals and lay practitioners may have to be organized by a third party. In the case of Nicaragua the broker role was played by the Division of Communication and Popular Education in Health and the Popular Health Councils. One effect of the Sandinista reorganization of the health sector was the bureaucratic legitimation of health education and community participation, both important components of primary health care.

Conclusion

Anthropologists can serve community-based programs in primary health care by giving more attention to the social fact of professional dominance where it exists and by seeking ways to achieve a balance between professional and community interests. Physicians are able to pursue their professional agendas precisely because their own organizations allow them to wield much influence within the health bureaucracy, both in terms of administration and in terms of referral. Anthropologists who understand the workings of health bureaucracies and professions may find themselves in a position to make their research useful to emergent groups of lay practitioners and community health committees. Anthropologists may also find themselves in a position to encourage communities and lay practitioners to organize themselves. In this way non-professionals could be helped to create an organizational base from which to influence the health system. One might expect that such a vantage point would give them a better chance of changing bureaucratic behavior to conform more to the goals of primary health care.

On the other hand, anthropologists and health professionals *within* the administrative bureaucracies may be in a position to shape the interior of the PHC program to better conform to community needs and agendas. They are in a strategic position to argue that the sharing of administrative power with local communities will enhance the health goals of the institution and the needs of the community. The case of Nicaragua suggests that the sharing of power is more apt to take place when there is pressure for change both from inside and from outside the health bureaucracy. Once the issue of power and its organization is addressed, the varying interests in and contributions to primary health care of anthropologists, community groups, lay practitioners, and medical professionals may be more easily reconciled.

Notes

1. Foster (1987) in part ascribes the meager contribution of behavioral and anthropological methodologies to health-related research within the WHO to the fact that review committees are composed almost entirely of physicians who favor research designs that use survey methods to test hypotheses. Justice (1986: 135) reports that planners tend to dismiss the reports of some anthropologists as being "too negative," and the cultural data as "too soft" for use in technical reports.

2. I use the term "lay practitioner" as a general label for all non-professionals working in PHC, including folk healers such as herbalists, midwives, and CHWs. While it is necessary to recognize the important distinctions among them (Young 1983: 1206; Coreil 1983; Kleinman and Sung 1979: 25), from the point of view of professional dominance, the subordinate status of each is to some degree an obstacle to their effective use in PHC programs. Similarly, other health professionals such as nurses face the same issue of professional dominance by physicians.

3. Young (1983) predicts strong professional resistance to the integration of traditional healers into clinical settings. Scholl (1985: 213) cites the views of administrators such as the Director of PHC in Nicaragua that CHWs should be used in a curative role only until enough professionals can be trained to replace them. [See Wood, Chapter 6, for a discussion of similar attitudes among physicians in New Zealand.--Eds.]

4. The "popular" model of primary health care differs from the clinical model in several respects. (1) Cultural authority is shifted from the medical professional to the community. (2) Organizational realignments move the health delivery system beyond the area clinic. (3) An expanded role and coverage is given to the CHW. (4) The relationship of physician-nurse-CHW in the areas of supervision and evaluation is redefined. For an extended discussion of how the criteria of the popular health model are implemented in Nicaragua, see Donahue (1986b).

5. This is not to say that individual health professionals will not support the integration of traditional healers into clinical settings. Bastien (1987) encountered both Bolivian physicians who were supportive of the workshop-dialogues and

others who refused to participate. Ellsberg (1983) notes that the PHC program on the Atlantic coast of Nicaragua had the full cooperation of medical personnel in that region. Finally, Singer, Baer and Lazarus (1990: vi) also point out that, as a group, physicians "serve to articulate the relationship between the ruling and the subordinate class. As such, biomedicine is contradictory and an arena of conflict. And some of the conflict is between the ruling class and the biomedical professionals, who can have opposed as well as shared interests."

6. In her analysis of the training of midwives in the Yucatan, Jordan (Chapter 5) describes how participants learned the language of the professionals, but the reverse did not occur. In fact, the medical jargon and procedures functioned to maintain asymmetrical power relations between the instructors and the midwives. The women in the course learned less about midwifery than about how to relate to the professional power structure, including its need for statistical data for reports to funding agencies. Justice (1986) suggests that anthropologists provide health planners with analyses of how their bureaucratic culture might obstruct the view of others' cultures.

7. The emergence of "the political economy of health" or "critical medical anthropology" movement in medical anthropology provides a fresh perspective in which to study how international power relations and national class relations affect medical systems at all levels--international, national, administrative, local, and even the provider-patient relationship itself (Baer, Singer, and Johnson 1986; Crandon 1983; Donahue 1989; Morgan 1987, 1989, 1990; New and Donahue 1986; Singer, Baer, and Lazarus 1990; Stebbins 1986; Whiteford 1990).

8. For an extended discussion of the conflict between professional and popular models of PHC in Nicaragua, see Donahue (1986b).

9. I am indebted to Dr. James Morrissey for these analogies.

Figure 4.1

Structure of Popular Participation in Health in Nicaragua

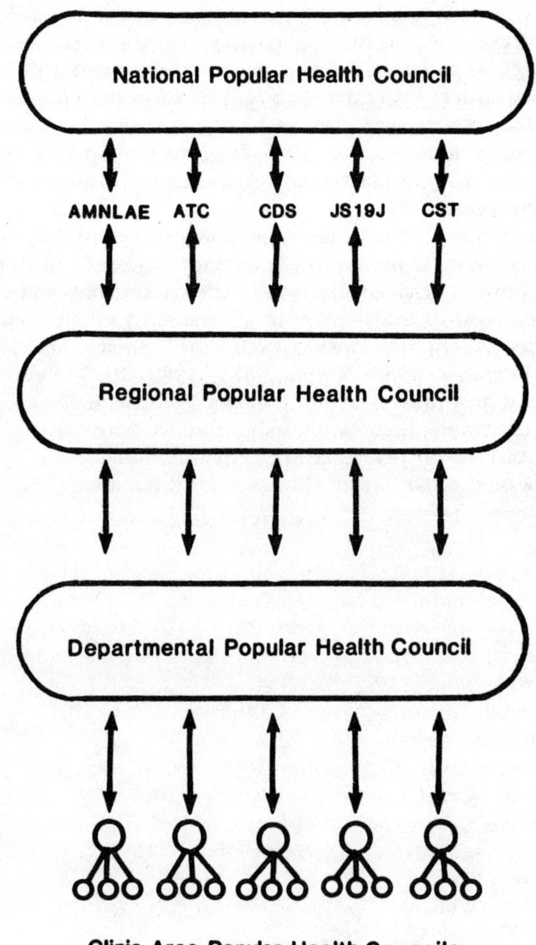

References

Baer, H., M. Singer, and J.H. Johnson 1986 Introduction: Toward a Critical Medical Anthropology. *Social Science and Medicine* 23(2):95-98.

Bastien, J. 1987 Cross-Cultural Communication Between Doctors and Peasants in Bolivia. *Social Science and Medicine* 24(12):1109-1118.

Coreil, J. 1983 Parallel Structures in Professional and Folk Health Care: A Model Applied to Rural Haiti. *Culture, Medicine and Psychiatry* 7:131-151.

Crandon, L. 1983 Grass Roots, Herbs, Promotors and Preventions: A Re-Evaluation of Contemporary International Health Care Planning. The Bolivian Case. *Social Science and Medicine* 17(17):1281-1289.

___ 1987 Beyond the Cure: Anthropological Inquiries in Medical Theories and Epistemologies. Introduction. *Social Science and Medicine* 24(12):1012.

Donahue, J.M. 1979 Not Any Doctor, But My Doctor: Community Control of Health Care in a San Antonio Barrio. Paper read at the Annual Meeting of the American Anthropological Association, Cincinnati, Ohio. Nov. 27-Dec. 2

___ 1983 The Politics of Health Care in Nicaragua Before and After the Revolution of 1979. *Human Organization* 42(3):264-272.

___ 1986a The Profession and the People: Primary Health Care in Nicaragua. *Human Organization* 45(2):96-103.

___ 1986b *The Nicaraguan Revolution in Health: From Somoza to the Sandinistas*. South Hadley, MA: Bergin and Garvey.

___ 1989 International Organizations, Health Services, and Nation Building in Nicaragua. *Medical Anthropology Quarterly*, New Series 3(3):258-269.

Ellsberg, M.C. 1983 Trail Blazing on the Atlantic Coast. *Science for the People* 15(6):14-19.

Engel, G. L. 1977 The Need For a New Medical Model: A Challenge for Biomedicine. *Science* 196(4286):129-136.

Fals-Borda, O. 1970 *Ciencia Propria y Colonialismo Intelectual. Primera Edición*. México: Editorial Nuestro Tiempo.

Foster, G. 1969 *Applied Anthropology*. Boston: Little, Brown.

___ 1977 Medical Anthropology and International Health Planning. *Social Science and Medicine* 11(10):527-534.

___ 1982 Applied Anthropology and International Health: Retrospect and Prospect. *Human Organization* 41(3):189-197.

___ 1987 World Health Organization Behavioral Science Research: Problems and Prospects. *Social Science and Medicine* 24(9):709-717.

Freidson, E. 1970 *Professional Dominance*. New York: Atherton Press.

___ 1984 The Changing Nature of Professional Control. *The Annual Review of Sociology* 10:1-20.

Garfield, R., and G. Williams 1989 *Health and Revolution: The Nicaraguan Experience*. Oxford: Oxfam.

Gordon, J.B. 1969 The Politics of Community Medicine Projects: Conflict Analysis. *Medical Care* 7:419-428.

Heggenhougen, H.K. 1984 Will Primary Health Care Efforts be Allowed to Succeed? *Social Science and Medicine* 19(3):217-224.

Holmberg, A.R., and H.D. Lasswell 1962 Community and Regional Development: The Joint Cornell- Peru Experiment. *Human Organization* 21:107-124.

Janzen, J. 1978 The Comparative Study of Medical Systems as Changing Social Systems. *Social Science and Medicine* 12(2b):121-129.

Justice, J. 1986 *Policies, Plans, and People: Culture and Health Development in Nepal*. Berkeley: University of California Press.

Keyzer, B. de, and J. Ulate 1981 Educación, Participación en Salud e Ideologia: Nicaragua Pasado y Presente. *Revista Centroamericana de Ciencias de la Salud Número* 19.

Kleinman, A. 1980 *Patients and Healers in the Context of Culture*. Berkeley: University of California Press.

Kleinman, A., and L.H. Sung 1979 Why Do Indigenous Practitioners Successfully Heal? *Social Science and Medicine* 13B(1):7-26.

Martin, P. 1983 *Primary Health Care Issues: Community Participation in Primary Health Care*. Series 1, Number 5. Washington: American Public Health Association.

Morgan, L. 1987 Dependency Theory in the Political Economy of Health: An Anthropological Critique. *Medical Anthropology Quarterly*, New Series 1(2):131-154.

___ 1989 "Political Will" and Community Participation in Costa Rican Primary Health Care. *Medical Anthropology Quarterly*, New Series 3(3):232-245.

___ 1990 International Politics and Primary Health Care in Costa Rica. *Social Science and Medicine* 30(2):211-219.

Navarro, V. 1977 *Social Security and Medicine in the USSR: A Marxist Critique*. Lexington, MA: Lexington Books.

Neumann, A.K., and P. Lauro 1982 Ethnomedicine and Biomedicine Linking. *Social Science and Medicine* 16(21):1817-1824.

New, P.K.-M., and J. Donahue 1986 Introduction: Strategies for Primary Health Care by the Year 2000: A Political Economic Perspective. *Human Organization* 45(2):95-96.

New, P.K.-M., and R.M. Hessler 1972 Neighborhood Health Center: Traditional Health Care at an Outpost. *Inquiry* 9(4):45-58.

Paul, B. 1955 *Health, Culture, and Community: Case Studies of Public Reactions to Health Programs*. New York: Russell Sage Foundation.

Pillsbury, B. 1982 Policy and Evaluation Perspectives on Traditional Health Practitioners in National Health Care Systems. *Social Science and Medicine* 16(21):1825-1834.

___ 1985 Anthropologists in International Health. In *Training Manual in Medical Anthropology*. C. Hill, ed. Pp. 84-110. Special Publication No. 18 of the Society for Applied Anthropology. Washington: American Anthropological Association.

Saks, M. 1983 Removing the Blinkers? A Critique of Recent Contributions to the Sociology of Professions. *Sociological Review* 31(1)1-21.

Scholl, E.A. 1985 An Assessment of Community Health Workers in Nicaragua. *Social Science and Medicine* 20(3):207-214.

Singer, M., H. Baer, and E. Lazarus 1990 Introduction. Critical Medical Anthropology in Question. *Social Science and Medicine* 30(2):v-viii.

Singer, P., ed. 1977 *Traditional Healing: New Science or New Colonialism?: Essays in Critique of Medical Anthropology*. Buffalo, NY: The Conch Magazine Limited.

Starr, P. 1982 *The Social Transformation of American Medicine*. New York: Basic Books.

Stavenhagen, R. 1971 Decolonizing Applied Social Sciences. *Human Organization* 30:333-357.

Stebbins, K. 1986 Politics, Economics and Health Services in Rural Oaxaca, Mexico. *Human Organization* 45(2):112-119.

Tax, S. 1958 Values in Action: The Fox Project. *Human Organization* 17:17-20.

Ugalde, A. 1979 The Role of the Medical Profession in Public Health Policy Making: The Case of Colombia. *Social Science and Medicine* 13C:109-119.

___ 1980 Physician's Control of the Health Sector: Professional Values and Economic Interests. *Social Science and Medicine* 14A:435-444.

Werner, D. 1980 The Village Health Care Programme: Community-Supportive or Community-Oppressive? An Examination of Rural Health Programs in Latin America. *Contact* 57(August):2-16.

Whiteford, L. 1990 A Question of Adequacy: Primary Health Care in the Dominican Republic. *Social Science and Medicine* 30(2):221-226.

Young, A. 1983 The Relevance of Traditional Medical Cultures to Modern Primary Health Care. *Social Science and Medicine* 17(16):1205-1211.

Zwick, D.I. 1974 Some Accomplishments and Findings of Neighborhood Health Centers. In *Neighborhood Health Centers*. Pp. 69-90. R.M. Hollister, B.M. Kramer, and S.S. Bellin, eds. Lexington, MA: Lexington Books.

5

Technology and the Social Distribution of Knowledge: Issues for Primary Health Care in Developing Countries

Brigitte Jordan

Introduction

In many countries of the Third World, strategies for development include massive efforts to improve maternal and child health (MCH). While family planning is often considered the major vehicle for such improvements, a second important component of development in the health care sector is the "upgrading" of perinatal services to conform more closely to those of developed countries. This includes the importation of obstetric technology[1] and of technology-dependent obstetric procedures such as hospital deliveries, pharmacologically managed labors, the use of ultrasound and electronic fetal monitoring, induction of labor, instrumental and surgical delivery, and the care of premature and sick infants in intensive care units. While it is clear that such facilities and technologies will lower some kinds of mortality and morbidity, their importation often also has unforeseen and unassessed negative effects. Beyond that, the replacement of traditional "low technology" raises fundamental questions about concomitant transformations in the nature of knowledge about the birth process, which in turn affect the distribution of decision-making power and the ability of women to control the reproductive process.

In this chapter I briefly examine the most salient problems faced by developing countries as they adopt cosmopolitan obstetrics.[2] Against this background I analyze some usually unexamined consequences of replacing traditional low technology with the sophisticated technology-dependent methods of cosmopolitan obstetrics. I am concerned in particular with the social distribution of knowledge inherent in different levels of technology and the attendant power to make decisions. In a concluding section I will discuss the implications of this analysis for the provision of primary health care.[3]

Generic Problems

Developing countries differ considerably in their histories, developmental resources, and development plans. Nevertheless, they face a number of common difficulties as they attempt to "upgrade" their perinatal care delivery systems in the direction of Western biomedical practice. The first of these stems from the fact that the introduction of Western obstetrics never occurs in a vacuum, but confronts pre-existing, entrenched, indigenous "ethno-obstetric" systems which are already well adapted to local conditions. An ethno-obstetric system consists of an empirically grounded and often supernaturally sanctioned repertoire of practices and a network of established practitioners who subscribe to a body of beliefs about the nature of birth which they share with childbearing women (and often men) in the communities they serve. Common knowledge within such systems includes ideas about when pregnancy and labor become problematic, what methods are to be chosen for resolving problems, and who is in charge of making decisions--notions that are not necessarily shared by the Western or Western-trained health care personnel who provide cosmopolitan obstetric services.

Difference in belief systems and in the allocation of decision-making power between the cosmopolitan and indigenous birthing systems inherently lead to conflict and often to resistance against Western-style health care, even in situations where the biomedical system would provide the better solution. In my fieldwork with Maya Indian women in Yucatan, for example, I found that they will go to a hospital only in extreme situations, and sometimes when it is too late. A major reason for their resistance is that hospital practices, such as attendance by young male physicians, genital exposure, routine episiotomies, and separation from midwife and family, violate traditional assumptions about the proper management of birth. Of course, women's resistance to hospitalization usually presents no problem at all, as normal pregnancies are effectively handled by the ethnomedical sector. However, no matter what the skill level of traditional birth attendants, there are always some conditions that fall outside their sphere of competence. Because of the efficacy of technological biomedicine in dealing with pathological cases, some accommodation between cosmopolitan obstetrics and the traditional ethno-obstetric systems should be sought.

A second difficulty which developing countries face stems from what has been called "the structural superiority"[4] of Western medicine (Lee 1982; Pfleiderer and Bichman 1985). In spite of the fact that the bulk of health care in developing countries is provided by the traditional sector, cosmopolitan medicine furnishes the accepted blueprint for health care planners and medical personnel. The unquestioned (and in some sense unquestionable) superior status of biomedicine leads to a principled, rather than reasoned, devaluation of indigenous obstetric knowledge and practitioners. Biomedicine in many developing countries has acquired a symbolic value that is independent of its use value.[5] It has come to symbolize modernization and progress and thus stands in contrast, indeed in opposition, to traditional ways of dealing with questions of well-being and disease, including childbirth and related issues of maternal and child health.

In practice, we frequently find a blanket condemnation of traditional practitioners who come to be seen as not-modern, not-progressive, and unscientific, and thus as embodying the superstition and backwardness which development programs are intended to eradicate. Within this framework, traditional methods for dealing with the dangers of childbirth are dismissed out-of-hand, without regard to any objective efficacy they might have. Thus in midwife training programs which I attended in Yucatan, useful indigenous methods such as external cephalic version for malpresentation (Jordan 1984) or the cauterizing of the umbilical stump with the flame of a candle (an effective measure against infection) were condemned. Instead, a cesarean section was advocated for malpresentation and treatment with alcohol and merthiolate (clearly inferior for antisepsis) was introduced as proper cord treatment (Jordan 1979, 1989). Such disregard for effective, empirically sanctioned local methods may lead to a greater rather than lesser mortality and morbidity.

A third ubiquitous problem for developing countries is the allocation of scarce resources. Commitment to Western-style obstetrics carries with it a requirement for trained health care personnel and for the technological instrumentation without which Western obstetrics cannot function. Without such support, the benefits provided by modern medicine are quickly swamped by the iatrogenic and nosocomial effects it generates.[6] In Third World countries, the practice of hospital-based, physician-dependent, technology-intensive perinatal management is severely hampered by realities such as inadequately trained staff, insufficient supplies of drugs, and non-repairable machinery. For example, a hospital in which I worked in Mexico had a delivery room that was built for sterile deliveries. But the hospital's autoclave had broken down, making it necessary for someone to go to the next town to have instruments sterilized after each use. Furthermore the supply of such basic items as hospital gowns was so inadequate that within any 24-hour period no more than a single birth could be accommodated; the incubators intended for premature babies were not functional and could not be repaired; the most essential medications were lacking.

The construction and maintenance of such "white elephant hospitals" consumes a tremendous amount of resources and has been decried as wasteful over and over again (e.g. WHO 1981). In Tanzania and Senegal, for example, such hospitals absorb more than half of the national health care budget, though they serve only 5% of the population (Pfleiderer and Bichman 1985) and in many developing countries up to 90% of available resources are spent on centralized curative health care services (Wilson et al. 1986). In Lesotho, one of the world's poorest countries, the capital's major hospital owns a computer (which nobody knows how to operate) but no refrigerator (Fisher 1986). To some extent, the allocation of major portions of the budget to expensive hospitals with highly sophisticated technology is part of the colonial heritage where the main concern was to service colonial administrators and urban elites. Today, the problem is compounded by the high prestige value of Western medicine and the tendency to emulate cosmopolitan health care delivery systems.[7]

In regard to MCH, the most fundamental problem lies in the fact that in Third World countries there are always two conflicting ideas about childbirth present at the same time. The traditional view sees the birth of children as a normal life-cycle event that should be handled by the family and the women's community. This contrasts with the medicalized view of birth espoused by medical personnel and development planners which focuses on the remediation of pathology and therefore sees childbirth as falling into the medical domain. Within the pathological definition of birth the goal of universal physician-attended hospital delivery is eminently reasonable. At the same time, the adoption of this framework leads to a disregard of the necessity to come to some sort of accommodation between the modern and the traditional system which would preserve the best features of both for the benefit of mothers and children.

These are problems and realities that MCH planners in all developing countries face--if not in planning, then certainly at the implementation and evaluation stages, when it becomes apparent that the uncritical imposition of technology-dependent Western obstetric practices may itself generate substantial troubles. What these planners may find is that they have inherited not only the iatrogenic problems inherent in an overly medicalized approach to birth, but also the problems inherent in practicing scientific medicine badly, that is to say, without adequate pharmacological and staff support.

Though some have suggested (e.g. Foster 1984) that Third World people recognize the superiority of Western medicine and prefer it to all other options, many more investigators recognize the limitations of cosmopolitan medicine in the developing world (WHO 1975; Velimirovic 1978; Pillsbury 1979, 1982; Sich 1982; Jordan 1983, 1989). The integration of the modern system with traditional methods of health care has repeatedly been advocated (Lee 1982; Good et al. 1979). However traditional systems have been much more eager to absorb elements of cosmopolitan medicine, such as the use of injections and antibiotics, than the other way around.

While cosmopolitan medicine monolithically claims jurisdiction over all aspects of health and illness, traditional medicines tend to be at once even more global (sometimes dealing with all misfortune) and, in some aspects, more specialized (e.g. bonesetters). Thus there may be different therapeutic traditions for different illnesses and conditions, each of which is undergoing change as a result of development. As a consequence, the population may be dealing not with a simple dual system of health care but with a multifaceted one (Lee 1982; Leslie 1980; Stoner 1986).

Explicit policies of incorporating traditional practitioners and practices into national health care systems are uncommon, except in the area of MCH where considerable attention has been paid to traditional birth attendants (TBAs). However, training is almost universally unidirectional. It does not include reciprocal teaching in which TBAs would also instruct MCH personnel in traditional practices of pregnancy and childbirth management (Jordan 1979; McClain 1981). The special attention which TBAs have enjoyed is motivated primarily by a recognition that they play a crucial role in family planning, since they have access to and enjoy the confidence of childbearing women. As far as attendance at birth is concerned, the prevalent attitude is that TBAs must be tolerated until staff and facilities can be upgraded to achieve universal hospital delivery--in spite of the fact that if this goal is desirable at all, it is unrealistic for at least the next several decades. Currently, 60 to 80% of babies in the Third World are delivered by TBAs (Population Reports 1980).

Given this constellation of common constraints and issues, it becomes particularly important to examine the role which obstetric technology plays in efforts to improve maternal and child health. There are many ways to make such assessments. My particular interest lies in scrutinizing the consequences of different levels of obstetric technology on the construction and social distribution of knowledge. This distribution has important consequences not only for medical outcome, but also for the position of women in the social structure and the control which childbearing women and their families have over the birth process. My thesis is that the importation of medical technology has sequelae which are unforeseen and not always beneficial. Beyond the possibility of dealing with problems the indigenous system is unable to handle (such as truly pathological deliveries), high technology also produces changes in the distribution of information and the power to make decisions--an epiphenomenon that has remained largely unexamined. Well-intentioned agricultural and economic development projects have often backfired to reduce women's status and range of options (Boserup 1970; Rogers 1980; Charlton 1984). The introduction of high technology in childbirth, also well-intentioned, may lead to similar results.

My analysis of obstetric technology begins with an examination of the characteristics of the artifacts of birth as they are used in traditional societies and contrasts them with the instruments of cosmopolitan Western obstetrics, the very technology which is increasingly introduced in the developing countries of the Third World. My interest lies in explicating the unexamined consequences of different levels of technology, as they are applied to managing the panhuman process of childbirth.

Obstetric Technology and Its Consequences

Levels of Technology

As far as we know, there is no contemporary or historical society where there is not some set of material objects which are routinely used at the time of birth. The complexity of such artifacts, however, varies considerably between the ethno-obstetrics of traditional societies and the technologically elaborated cosmopolitan obstetric systems of industrialized countries. One question which should be of considerable interest to development planners is: What are the consequences of replacing simple with complex technologies? To address this question I contrast obstetric settings that differ in regard to the complexity of the array of artifacts routinely used for managing normal birth.

The simplest level of technology is found in traditional societies before they are substantially influenced by Western medicine. It also prevails in many developing countries even after the introduction of cosmopolitan obstetrics, since Western methods and facilities usually cover only a segment of the population, leaving most births to be managed by the traditional, low-technology sector. Most Maya Indian women in Yucatan, for example, give birth in their own hut, attended by a village midwife, family members, and friends. The artifacts required for such births are few, simple, and mostly available in the household: a hammock or chair on which to give birth, a rope suspended from the rafters for the woman to pull on during labor, a sharp instrument to cut the cord, and similar multipurpose objects. This low level of technology is typical for the indigenous obstetric systems of most developing countries.

An intermediate level of technology is exemplified by home births in Holland or in the United States, also typically attended by a midwife, family members and friends. Here the midwife brings with her a set of tools which are somewhat specialized though still simple, such as a wooden stethoscope for listening to the fetal heart tone. In this paper I will focus primarily on the contrast between low and high technology; however, it should be noted that it is the intermediate level which might be most appropriate for maternal/child health care in developing countries.

High technology is found in the hospital obstetrics of the United States and similarly technologized societies, where attendance by medical specialists is standard and where there is a high degree of reliance on complex, specialized tools. Artifacts considered necessary for proper management of birth in high-tech situations are never supplied by the woman or her family and, as I will argue below, are in principle inaccessible and incomprehensible to nonspecialist birth participants.

Technology and Physiology

I begin my analysis by focusing on one particular artifact: the physical support used at the time the baby is born. This may be a mat on the floor, a hammock, a chair, the woman's own bed, some improvised arrangement of bolsters and pillows, or, at the upper end of the continuum, a mechanically sophisticated delivery table of the type used in high-technology hospitals.

One major change which we notice as we go from a simple object, such as a mat or a chair, to a special-purpose hospital delivery table is the diminishing degree of familiarity the woman has with the artifact. This has consequences for her experience of birth as well as for the course of labor. For example, a Maya woman who gives birth in the hammock in which she sleeps every night knows how to exploit its properties for maximum comfort. She can lie in it on her back, on her side, even on her stomach. She can use the strands of her hammock to hold onto as she pushes the baby out. Her movement is not restricted in any way, and as she senses the requirements of the descending fetus, she can adjust her body accordingly.

In general, women in developing countries, at least until Western medicine dictates otherwise, labor and give birth in upright or semi-upright positions, such as sitting, squatting, half-reclining, kneeling, or standing--often using several of these positions in sequence. The physiologic and psychological advantages of upright positions are well known and include better oxygenation, more efficient contractions, less pain and, especially for full squatting positions, an increase in the diameter of the pelvic outlet (Gold 1950; Haire 1972; Flynn et al. 1978; Williams et al. 1980; Roberts et al. 1983; McKay and Roberts 1985). Where women give birth sitting on a bed of mosses and ferns, or kneeling on a mat on the floor of their huts, they have the opportunity to listen to their bodies and take appropriate action. On a delivery table such messages cannot be followed. The woman is no longer able to move. Lying on her back on a narrow platform, with her feet in stirrups, she is effectively immobilized. Once she is arranged on the delivery table (and to some extent this is also true for the labor bed), she is not likely to get off to walk around. Nor is she likely to assume an upright position again before the birth is over.

When we observe a woman on a delivery table, it becomes apparent that the very design of the table forces her into a rigidly symmetrical body attitude. With her feet in stirrups, the table fixes her pelvis in such a way that rotating it or taking the strain off one side by tucking a leg under, for example, becomes impossible. In low-technology obstetric systems where there are no such specialized artifacts as delivery tables, women rather frequently assume asymmetrical positions (Odent 1980; Kuntner 1985), an option that generally is open to them because of the nature of the artifact on which they give birth.

The combination of upright posture and physical mobility, with frequent position changes and the assumption of asymmetrical positions, facilitates the mechanism of labor which effects the passage of the baby's body through the birth canal.[8] As a consequence, women who are free to move experience shorter and less painful labors (Caldeyro-Barcía et al. 1960; Flynn et al. 1978; Kuntner 1985; Méndez-Bauer et al. 1975; Mitre 1974; Poeschl 1985; Roberts et al. 1983). To the extent that the artifact on which the woman rests allows and encourages such mobility, the birth process is aided. Not surprisingly, complications such as changes in the fetal heart rate or dystocia (a situation where the baby gets hung up in the birth canal) can frequently be remedied by changes in position. The more sophisticated artifact, the delivery table, discourages such physiologically beneficial adjustments.

Technology and Social Interaction

Beyond their influence on the physiology of labor, artifacts also affect the nature and flow of information about the birth event. This is self-evident where highly complex technology is concerned. An electronic fetal monitor, for example, requires specialists for proper application and interpretations of output. On a more subtle level, however, even a simple innovation such as moving from a birthing chair to a hospital delivery table introduces changes in communication among birth participants which, in turn, affect social interaction.

In low-technology situations where the object on which the woman rests is a familiar one, it becomes available as a resource for joint management of labor difficulties. For example, in Yucatan the woman's attendants, most likely her husband, her mother, experienced women of the family and the community midwife, are well aware of the potential of hammocks. They may give advice about appropriate positions and they know how to arrange their own bodies around the hammock so as to provide physical and emotional assistance and guidance by talking, holding, stroking, and massaging. Facilitated by the artifact, their cumulative experiential knowledge becomes available to the woman in labor and provides a valuable resource for solving problems of comfort, lack of progress, or pain as they may arise.

Furthermore, this type of artifact makes the woman's body performance and physical state evident to all participants. As a consequence, whatever information exists within the system is available to all those present. On videotapes of Maya childbirth in

Yucatan an interesting communication system can be observed. The woman's attendants take turns holding the woman's body in their laps.[9] The woman slings her arms around her helper's neck and pulls on it whenever a contraction comes on, the strength of her pull constituting an analog to the force of her contraction. The helper, with the woman's body in her arms, is recruited into "co-laboring"--breathing with the woman and pushing with her. She acquires direct bodily knowledge of the process and its rhythm which is communicated to others by their joint bodily display.[10] The midwife, meanwhile, sits on a stool in front of the woman with a cloth-covered hand on the perineum. She feels the bulging of the advancing head and conveys the tactile information she acquires by saying such things as "Push, push now, the baby is at the door."

Within this collaborating group the woman is always central as the object of attention as well as the source of crucial information. There are no specialized tools for gathering data and no specialists to assess their significance. Rather, all parties to the event have fairly equal access to whatever information is available within the system and are competent to interpret it. The midwife may have more experience but the information she controls is not different in kind from what everyone else has access to. The overwhelming impression one gets from participating in such births is that there is a close-knit group of people who together bring all their resources to bear on getting the baby born. In such situations, attendants' behavior is characterized by a fairly high degree of active physical involvement. This involvement is facilitated by the characteristics of the physical object on which the woman rests. Birthing chairs, hammocks, mats and bean bags are accessible from all sides and allow others to get into the scene. They are thus conducive to hands-on, collaborative birthing.[11]

Contrast this sharing of information and experience with the process of giving birth on a hospital delivery table. The woman may have a support person with her--usually the father of the child in the U.S., often nobody in developing countries unless a friendly nurse takes this role upon herself. But even if there are support persons, their activity and interaction with the woman are severely restricted. The nature of the table makes it impossible to give full body support. The woman lying on it can no longer be held in anybody's arms. The lower part of her body, separated from the top by the sterile drapes over her knees, becomes inaccessible to all but the medical staff. The woman is not allowed to touch herself, she cannot see what is going on, and if she has had regional anesthesia, she cannot feel the working part of her body either. The design properties of the hospital delivery table function to reserve activity (as well as convenience) for the medical team by effectively demarcating the lower part of the woman's body as the domain of the specialist who delivers her.[12]

This kind of alienation from the activity of birthing is almost impossible where the woman is in an upright position, where she is free to see, to move, and to play an active part. A mat, a hammock, or a chair are instrumental in supporting the woman in the work of birthing. A delivery table on which she is strapped renders her passive, isolates her from interaction with her attendants, and is instrumental in processing her.

Ownership of Artifacts and Distribution of Authoritative Knowledge

I mentioned earlier that the tools required for birth in low-technology systems are few, simple, and often drawn from the general-purpose implements available in any household. Such objects, e.g. a sharp instrument to cut the cord, a basin for washing the baby, or clean, soft cloths to wrap it in, are generally supplied by the woman herself or, if brought by the midwife, carry no special mystique. Their use is transparent to all birth participants.

We have seen that in low-technology systems there is shared distribution of knowledge which is based partially on the rich store of prior experience that participants bring to a particular birth and partially on the joint access they have to the information generated during the event. What everyone knows about this birth and others like it, constitutes "authoritative knowledge" in that situation, that is, knowledge that is treated as legitimate and as consequential for the management of birth. This knowledge is horizontally and fairly uniformly distributed among participants in low-technology births. As a consequence we find that decisions about what to do when trouble arises emerge as joint decisions to which all participants contribute.

For example, even in Yucatan where there are no set expectations about how long a labor should last, there are times when it becomes clear that it is taking "too long." Remedies, e.g. that the woman should get up and walk around, that she should move from hammock to chair, that she should be given a raw egg,[13] are variously proposed, ignored, reinforced by stories of how they solved the problem in similar cases, and so on, until a (sometimes unspoken) consensus is reached and action is taken (cf. Orr 1986).

With the transformation from low to high technology a change occurs in who controls the information relevant to the management of birth. This transformation hinges on who owns the tools of reproduction. In high-technology settings, ownership of the specialized instruments and machinery without which birth cannot be accomplished lies clearly with the medical staff. Such artifacts must not be touched or handled by nonspecialists, and often are not even available for visual examination. Instrument trays, for example, are usually covered with sterile cloths. Specialized instruments provide a kind of knowledge about the state of the woman and the fetus which is not only privileged (that is to say access to which is restricted) but which also supersedes and delegitimizes any other information sources. The crucial information comes no longer from the woman's experience, the state of her body as assessed by herself and her attendants, but rather from a set of technical procedures, test results and machine output interpreted by nurse and physician specialists.

I would argue here that knowledge based on complex machinery and high technology is in principle not communicable. While even intermediate technology, such as a simple stethoscope for listening to the fetal heart, can be appreciated and used by nonspecialist birth participants, no amount of explanation can make clear to a woman hooked up to a fetal monitor why a set of squiggles on graph paper requires that she undergo a cesarean section. Yet in the hospital environment it is the machine that produces authoritative knowledge--the knowledge on the basis of which decisions about the management of labor are made.

Women, once they enter the hospital, are quickly educated about this redefinition of the situation and the reallocation of authoritative knowledge. They, too, begin to believe that the machine knows more about what their bodies are doing than they do. Behaviorally, what we observe is that birth participants, including the woman, orient to the machine for information about her current state, so that the machine becomes the attentional and interactional focus.

In the United States, attempts are often made to provide explanations, especially where pressure to attain informed consent is felt in order to avoid malpractice suits. In most Third World hospitals nobody bothers with such niceties. In any case, the information for making decisions about the management of labor is unavoidably located in the technology and its legitimate users and owners. High technology thus draws in its wake a hierarchical distribution of knowledge and social authority that reflects the equally hierarchical social position of birth participants in medicalized settings.

Use Value and Symbolic Value of Technology

One important but neglected issue in the introduction of new technology is a consideration of the symbolic value (in contrast to the use value) of artifacts and their associated procedures. Rapid diffusion and acceptance of technology often has more to do with the former than with the latter. In particular, high-tech tools and techniques may become associated with progressive medicine and, especially in developing countries, with being modern and Western rather than backward and ignorant. They may be adopted for that (unacknowledged) reason rather than because of demonstrated efficacy.

I suspect that the symbolic function of tools is at least partially responsible for the widespread uncritical acceptance of electronic fetal monitoring (EFM) in high-technology settings in the First as well as the Third World. A fetal monitor is a very expensive piece of equipment which, once present on an obstetric ward, tends to be used in an increasing number of labors, to the point that in many Western hospitals its use in even normal labor has become routine. Developing countries, where Western-trained planners tend to subscribe to the pathological model of birth and its preoccupation with "high-risk management" (Potts et al. 1983), increasingly import such machinery as well. One might imagine that such rapid adoption is based on unequivocal scientific evidence as to the instrument's efficacy, that is, a high use value. However all the available evidence indicates that EFM does not lead to improved outcomes in normal births, even in Western settings (Thacker 1987). Its ready adoption in high-technology settings in the west as well as its increasing acceptance in Third World countries can be accounted for more by its symbolic value and the fact that it reinforces technology-based control than by actual benefits for mother and child.

A similar case could be made against the routine use of ultrasound (Grant 1986) and the increasingly liberal use of cesarean section. I have myself observed massive postnatal infections in women operated on under (almost unavoidably) unsterile conditions and others have cited evidence that in many developing countries maternal mortality in cesarean section reaches 20% (Pfleiderer and Bichman 1985).

But even the advocacy of Western implements and procedures on much lower levels of technology is only rarely based on demonstrated efficacy. The use value is simply assumed. In Yucatan, for example, the indigenous low-tech procedures for cord treatment are not associated with high-prestige artifacts. Traditionally, as I noted earlier, the cord is severed with a freshly cut bamboo sliver or other sharp object, and then the stump is cauterized by slowly and carefully burning it with the flame of a candle. The rationale Maya Indians give for this procedure is that it prevents "convulsions" (neonatal tetanus) in their babies.

In training courses for indigenous midwives this simple procedure is condemned and midwives are told to cut the cord with scissors and to apply alcohol and merthiolate to the stump. This is hardly high technology but note that "obstetric scissors" cannot be treated like the household scissors the Indians are familiar with. They must be sterilized, that is, handled with specialist and therefore arcane knowledge. Unfortunately, sterilization in a hut without boiling water is well-nigh impossible and alcohol is clearly much less effective than cauterizing for killing noxious organisms. As a matter of fact, the "progressive" artifact may be instrumental in introducing those organisms. As a consequence, the adoption of what may look like advanced, scientific instruments and procedures backfires to the detriment of newborn infants.

The introduction of Western technology and instruments is always based on the assumption that they have greater use value than their indigenous low-technology counterparts. Such assumptions need to be tested, and they need to be tested under local conditions. This is rarely done. In order to understand the fundamental nature of the problems posed in the adoption of cosmopolitan technology it is important to go beyond the use value of the tools of the trade. What must as well be considered is their hidden symbolic function and their efficacy as indicators and enforcers of the social distribution of knowledge and the power to act in childbirth.[14]

The Bias Towards Upscaling

Childbirth is a process in which problems of major and minor proportions are certain to arise. To deal with these problems, every obstetric system has developed solutions appropriate to its level of technology. For example, in a low-technology system, people might deal with breech presentation by doing an external cephalic version (ECV) unaided by any tools; on an intermediate level, obstetric practitioners might do ECV supported by fetal heart auscultation; while doctors in a high-tech system might rotate the fetus in hospital, aided by drugs and monitoring equipment, and with the woman prepared for cesarean section. Or they might simply advocate routine cesarean section for such cases (Jordan 1984).

Now what is curious is that when different levels of technology are available in the same environment, the solution to problems which arise on one level is almost always sought on the next higher level and hardly ever on the next lower level. For example, if a woman's contractions slow down because she has been moved to a delivery table, she is not allowed to resume the previously effective position, but rather a remedy is sought by administering drugs that speed up labor or, in the extreme case, a section is performed. Similarly, where cosmopolitan facilities are available in developing countries, it is never the case that women are referred to the low-technology sector. Referral networks are always set up for a one-way flow of clients, from low-tech to high-tech facilities and practitioners. It may well be that this bias for upscaling rather than downscaling is a property of technological systems in general to which development planners and health care personnel might want to pay close attention.

The Diffusion of Artifacts and Procedures

One significant difference between low-tech and high-tech procedures and their associated artifacts is that they have different kinds of mobility beyond their own environment. Contrary to intuition, high-tech procedures are more easily transportable because they are not so much anchored in the thickness of daily life but rather are inherent in their artifacts. To transfer the artifact then is to transfer the procedure. Low-tech procedures, on the other hand, are embedded in a social matrix and do not move via their artifacts. They have to diffuse through social channels. While one imports a fetal monitor in order to do electronic fetal monitoring, it would not make much sense to import ropes from Africa so that women can hold on to them during labor. The knowledge of the use and benefits of such artifacts must transfuse via persons who have bodily knowledge of low-tech procedures, including the incidental use of artifacts in those procedures.[15]

Low-tech procedures, then, are only loosely connected to their artifacts, while high-tech procedures are inextricably tied to them. For example, where there is no rope to sling over the rafters, a shawl can take its place and nobody will even notice the difference. But if there is no delivery table in a hospital, there will be great disruption of the procedures normally associated with birth in that setting. Low-tech artifacts are humble, replaceable, interchangeable, and easily procurable general purpose objects with little prestige or commercial value. Hence there is no natural constituency within the development effort with a self-interest in advocating their use and thereby promoting their diffusion.

Technology and Cosmopolitics

It is clear that cosmopolitan high-technology with its associated techniques and attitudes is increasingly exported to developing countries. Few would argue that we should not make available advanced technology that promotes the health and well-being of Third World women and their children. The question is, however: Is high technology the right technology to achieve this goal?

I have suggested in the preceding pages that the health needs of women and children are not necessarily served by replacing traditional low technology with the armamentarium of cosmopolitan obstetrics. One reason is that high-technology obstetrics requires an infrastructure of resources and skills that is generically not present in developing countries. Furthermore, by the time the latest methods reach the Third World, they generally have been superseded at home--a time lag that supports the dumping of outdated artifacts and techniques. It is ironic that at a time when "natural childbirth" methods, upright birthing positions, attendance by midwives, preference for homebirths, and avoidance of high-technology gain a new ascendancy and increasing scientific support in the United States and Western Europe, the Third World is eager to introduce the most technological and biomedical model of birth. But should normal childbirth be absorbed into the medical domain as is the case in most Western countries? Are there not alternatives which Third World planners could develop if they would reassess the structural and ideological realities of cosmopolitan obstetrics? In many developing countries, indigenous ethno-obstetric systems are still intact and, if taken seriously, could provide the basis for safer, more humane, less hierarchical, and more participatory primary health care.[16]

I have also argued that the introduction of cosmopolitan obstetrics and its attendant redefinition of birth as pathology hierarchicizes decision-making under the aegis of medico-technical specialists. The domain of pregnancy and birth, previously occupied by women, is colonized by a male-identified top-down power structure. These changes are supported by the ideology of modernization and progress, an ideology that is seductive and to a large extent shared by Third World peoples themselves. High-technology cosmopolitan medicine is instrumental in establishing and maintaining hierarchical power relationships both between and within nations. For some purposes it might more appropriately be referred to as cosmopolitical medicine, a label which makes explicit its political function and efficacy.[17] Similarly I would suggest that cosmopolitan obstetrics must be seen as a cosmopolitical force that often serves the economic and social interests of First World and Third World elites, rather than those of the people for whose benefit it is ostensibly promulgated.

Conclusion

The World Health Organization, during the last decades, has identified primary health care (PHC) as the key to providing universal access to acceptable and affordable health care for people everywhere (WHO 1978, 1979, 1981). PHC de-emphasizes the sick individual, focusing instead on the social and environmental causes of illness, and relegates curative medicine to a comparatively minor role. It demands not only a redistribution of resources and social structural transformations (Heggenhougen 1984; Navarro 1984; Pfleiderer and Bichman 1985), but is also likely to stimulate political consciousness and grassroots political expertise. Indeed, the political implications of health care development at the community level have been apparent wherever the concept has been taken seriously (Werner and Bower 1982).

Under the pressure of insufficient coverage with cosmopolitan health services, the concept of primary health care has been eagerly espoused in developing countries. It has also, in many places, been co-opted by planners who ignored the necessity for social and political reforms and instead concentrated on the extension of medical coverage to rural areas, thus laying the groundwork for the biomedical colonization of communities. Technical and technological measures, such as training of village health care workers and traditional birth attendants, immunization programs, or the introduction of oral rehydration therapy, are less likely to threaten the interests of the prevailing power structure than fundamental reforms (Pfleiderer and Bichman 1985).

"Appropriate technology" is central to the ideology and implementation of PHC. However, what could be meant by that concept has not been well defined. By and large, appropriate technology seems to imply economic feasibility and, to some extent, social acceptability. What has been lacking is a radical questioning of the social costs of technologies and of their effects on the social system into which they are introduced. Under the impact of modernization and development, traditional ways of managing pregnancy, birth, and the postpartum period are in the process of undergoing major changes throughout the Third World. It has been argued that power establishes a particular regime of truth in which certain knowledges become possible and admissible (Armstrong 1983). I would suggest that technology, by determining what is to be taken as authoritative knowledge, in turn establishes a particular regime of power.

Acknowledgements

Many of the ideas expressed in this paper stem from discussions and correspondence with colleagues. I particularly want to thank Carole Browner, Rita Gallin, Robert Hahn, Susan Irwin, Willett Kempton, Ann Millard, Steven Nachman, Franca Pizzini, Madeleine Shearer, Lucy Suchman, Randy Trigg, and Mary Ann Zettelmaier for their contributions. They are, of course, somewhat responsible for the thinking expressed here.

Earlier versions of the ideas expressed in this paper have appeared as "Technology Transfer in Obstetrics: Theory and Practice in Developing Countries," WID Working Papers #126, Office of Women in International Development, Michigan State University, 1986; "The Hut and the Hospital: Information, Power and Symbolism in the Artifacts of Birth" in *Birth: Issues in Perinatal Care and Education* 14(1):36-40 (1987); and as "High Technology: The Case of Obstetrics" in *World Health Forum* 8(3):312-319 (WHO/Geneva, 1987). Further development of these ideas can be found in Jordan 1989. Fieldwork in Mexico, Europe, and the United States was supported by grant #HD MH 115711 from the National Institute for Child Health and Human Development. This support is gratefully acknowledged.

Notes

1. The World Health Organization Conference at Alma-Ata defined technology as "an association of methods, techniques, and equipment . . . together with the people using them."

2. I use the terms "Western," "modern," "scientific," "biomedical," and "cosmopolitan" medicine and obstetrics interchangeably to refer to the dominant health care beliefs and practices current in industrialized countries at the present time, though this body of knowledge and array of procedures is neither exclusively Western or modern, nor strictly scientific or biomedical, nor cosmopolitan (in the sense of "universal").

3. The data on which I draw here were collected during several periods of ethnographic fieldwork in Yucatan, Mexico, between 1972 and 1982; in the course of serving as a consultant to the Ministry of Health and the Instituto Nacional Indigenista in Yucatan for the design of training courses for traditional birth attendants in 1979; and during several periods of fieldwork in obstetric settings in Europe and the United States between 1973 and 1984.

4. "Structural superiority" of one medical system over others refers to greater control over health affairs based on greater respect in the community and preferential allocation of resources by the government (Lee 1982).

5. In this paper I employ the phrase "use value" in its common-sensical (not Marxist) meaning, i.e. as referring to the degree to which the purpose for which a tool was designed is realized.

6. Iatrogenic effects are those resulting from treatment by a physician; nosocomial effects are those originating in a hospital.

7. The underlying problem, whether due to colonialism or local history, is a hierarchical social structure which allocates resources differentially to elite and less privileged groups within society.

8. Probably because of evolutionary adaptations to bipedalism and upright posture, the human pelvis does not allow a simple passage of the baby. Rather, the fetal body must go through a series of rotations and changes in alignment which bring the head and then the shoulders into the largest diameter of the maternal pelvis. This sequence of passive fetal movements is called the "mechanism of labor" and consists of engagement, descent, flexion, internal rotation, extension, external rotation and expulsion. By contrast the births of other primates are much less problematic because their birth canal is straight and roomy in relation to the fetus (Trevathan 1987).

9. The woman lies crosswise in a hammock. Her attendant, seated on a chair at her head, pulls her body up during a contraction and gently lets it down again as the contraction fades. If the birth occurs in a chair, the helper is sitting behind her on another chair, similarly supporting the woman's body on her or his lap.

10. I use the female pronoun since most helpers are women. However, it should be noted that the husband also plays an important part and often takes a turn at "helping" the woman.

11. In many cultures comforting body contact, holding, skin stimulation and massage administered by experienced women are an integral part of labor, especially in first or difficult births. Cf. the pictures from films of births among the Zulu and in New Guinea in Kuntner (1985).

12. This conceptual and behavioral bisection of the woman's body is displayed and enforced in often subtle ways. For example, during an American hospital birth, the husband strayed towards the foot end of the delivery table to take a look, only to be gently reminded by a nurse that his wife "needed" some ice chips, a suggestion which brought him back where he belonged, namely at the woman's head. In a technologized birth the two parts of the woman's body constitute quite separate action foci and in our analyses of videotapes we have come to refer to them as "the business end" and "the interaction end," respectively.

13. The raw egg is immediately thrown up and the resulting retching almost invariably produces strong uterine contractions.

14. That the symbolic value of a tool may be greater than its use value is nicely illustrated in the history of the obstetric forceps. A crude version of this

instrument was invented in the 16th or 17th century by a family of English surgeons, but was kept a family secret for the first hundred years or so. Finally, one of the descendants sold it to a Dutch pharmaceutical college. This institution in turn marketed the invention by selling it to individual physicians who were prepared to pay a high price and who were themselves sworn to secrecy. Such physicians would appear in the birth chamber with a tool chest and operate under a sheet to deliver women who had difficulties in childbirth. They acquired the reputation of being able to deal with cases that were beyond the expertise of midwives. Their reputation, however, must have been based on something other than increased success because the "forceps" that were sold by the licensing agency consisted of only one blade and must have been totally ineffectual. Nevertheless the fact that physicians used such magical instruments and midwives did not was a factor in the transition of birth from the domain of the family and community to the domain of medical specialists.

15. An example of a low-tech procedure--which significantly quickly faded out of the American obstetric repertoire after enjoying brief popularity--is the Leboyer bath, the immersion of the newborn in warm water immediately after birth, in order to recreate for the baby an environment approximating its uterine existence. The Leboyer bath requires no arcane knowledge. Anybody who has seen it done once can improvise it any place, any time, and it matters not whether the tub for bathing the baby is round or oval, of plastic or tin.

16. In Great Britain, a well-functioning homebirth system was dismantled on the recommendation of a group of experts whose analysis turned out to be wrong (Tew 1978). Ethno-obstetric systems around the world are similarly being dismantled with little attention to the ways in which they function well.

17. See my review of Pfleiderer and Bichman (1985) in *Social Science and Medicine* 23(4):432-433, 1986.

References Cited

Armstrong, David 1983 *Political Anatomy of the Body: Medical Knowledge in Britain in the Twentieth Century*. Cambridge: Cambridge University Press.

Boserup, Esther 1970 *Woman's Role in Economic Development*. New York: St. Martins Press.

Caldeyro-Barcía, Roberto, Luis Noriega-Guerra, Luis A. Cibils, Hermógenes Alvarez, Juan J. Posuro, Serafín V. Pose, Yamandu Seca-Blanco, Carlos Méndez-Bauer, Carlos Fielitz, and Venus H. González-Panezza 1960 Effect of Position Changes on the Intensity and Frequency of Uterine Contractions during Labor. *American Journal of Obstetrics and Gynecology* 80(2):284-290.

Charlton, Sue Ellen M. 1984 *Women in Third World Development*. Boulder, CO: Westview Press.

Fisher, Anne 1986 Healing Hands. *The International Development Research Centre Reports* 15(1):16-17.

Flynn, A., J. Kelly, C. Hollins, and P. Lynch 1978 Ambulation during Labour. *British Medical Journal* 6137:591-593, August 26, 1978.

Foster, George M. 1984 Anthropological Research Perspectives on Health Problems in Developing Countries. *Social Science and Medicine* 18:847-854.

Gold, Edwin 1950 Pelvic Drive in Obstetrics: An X-Ray Study of 100 Cases. *American Journal of Obstetrics and Gynecology* 55:890-896.

Good, Charles M., John M. Hunter, Selig H. Katz, and Sydney S. Katz 1979 The Interface of Dual Systems of Health Care in the Developing World: Toward Health Policy Initiatives in Africa. *Social Science and Medicine* 13D:141-154.

Grant, Adrian 1986 Controlled Trials of Routine Ultrasound in Pregnancy. *Birth: Issues in Perinatal Care and Education* 13(1):22-28.

Haire, Doris 1972 The Cultural Warping of Childbirth. Milwaukee, *International Childbirth Education Association News*, Special Issue.

Heggenhougen, K. 1984 Will Primary Health Care Efforts be Allowed to Succeed? *Social Science and Medicine* 19:217-224.

Jordan, Brigitte 1979 *Training Courses for Traditional Midwives in Yucatan, Mexico*. Report prepared for the American Public Health Association under an agreement with USAID.

___ 1983 *Birth in Four Cultures: A Crosscultural Investigation of Childbirth in Yucatan, Holland, Sweden and the United States*. Third edition. Montreal: Eden Press.

___ 1984 External Cephalic Version as an Alternative to Breech Delivery and Cesarean Section. *Social Science and Medicine* 18(8):637-651.

___ 1989 Cosmopolitical Obstetrics: Some Insights from the Training of Traditional Midwives. *Social Science and Medicine* 28(9):925-944.

Kuntner, Liselotte 1985 *Die Gebaerhaltung der Frau: Schwangerschaft und Geburt aus geschichtlicher, voelkerkundlicher und medizinischer Sicht*. Muenchen, West Germany: Marseille Verlag.

Lee, Rance R. L. 1982 Comparative Studies of Health Care Systems. *Social Science and Medicine* 16:629-642.

Leslie, Charles 1980 Medical Pluralism in World Perspective. *Social Science and Medicine* 14B:191-195.

McClain, Carol 1981 Traditional Midwives and Family Planning: An Assessment of Programs and Suggestions for the Future. *Medical Anthropology* 5:107-136.

McKay, Susan, and Joyce Roberts 1985 Second Stage Labor: What is Normal? *Journal of Obstetric, Gynecologic and Neonatal Nunsing* (March/April): 101-106.

Méndez-Bauer, C., J. Arroyo, C. García Ramos, A. Menéndez, M. Lavilla, F. Izquierdo, I. Villa Elizaga, and J. Zamarriego 1975 Effects of Standing Position on Spontaneous Uterine Contractility and Other Aspects of Labor. *Journal of Perinatal Medicine* 3(2):89-100.

Mitre, Isaac N. 1974 The Influence of Maternal Position on the Duration of the Active Phase of Labor. *International Journal of Gynecology and Obstetrics* 12(5):181-183.

Navarro, Vicente 1984 A Critique of the Ideological and Political Positions of the Willy Brandt Report and the WHO Alma-Ata Declaration. *Social Science and Medicine* 18:467-474.

Odent, Michel 1980 *Die Geburt des Menschen: Fuer eine oekologische Wende in der Geburtshilfe*. Muenchen, West Germany: Koesel Verlag.

Orr, Julian 1986 Narratives at Work: Story Telling as Cooperative Diagnostic Activity. *Proceedings of the Conference on Computer-Supported Cooperative Work*. Austin, Texas.

Pfleiderer, Beatrix, and Wolfgang Bichman 1985 *Krankheit und Kultur: Eine Einfuehrung in die Ethnomedizin*. Berlin, West Germany: Dietrich Reimer Verlag.

Pillsbury, Barbara 1979 Reaching the Rural Poor: Indigenous Health Practitioners Are There Already. AID Program Evaluation Discussion Paper #1, Washington DC.

___ 1982 Policy and Evaluation Perspectives on Traditional Health Practitioners in National Health Care Systems. *Social Science and Medicine* 16:1825-1834.

Poeschl, Ulrike 1985 Kontroverse um die optimale Gebaerhaltung--Vertikal versus Horizontal--am Beispiel der Trobriander, Papua Neuguinea. Doctoral dissertation, Technische Universitaet, München, West Germany.

Population Reports 1980 Traditional Midwives and Family Planning. Series J, #22, May.

Potts, M., B.S. Janowitz, and J.A. Fortney, eds. 1983 *Childbirth in Developing Countries*. Boston: MTP Press Limited.

Roberts, Joyce E., Carlos Méndez-Bauer, and Deborah A. Wodell 1983 The Effects of Maternal Position on Uterine Contractility and Efficiency. *Birth: Issues in Perinatal Care and Education* 10(4):243-249.

Rogers, Barbara 1980 *The Domestication of Women*. London: Travistock Publications.

Sich, Dorothea 1982 *Mutterschaft und Geburt im Kulturwandel*. In the Series, Medizin in Entwicklungslaendern. Frankfurt, West Germany: Verlag Peter Lang.

Stoner, Bradley R. 1986 Understanding Medical Systems: Traditional, Modern and Syncretic Health Care Alternatives in Medically Pluralistic Societies. *Medical Anthropology Quarterly* 17(2):44-48.

Tew, Marjorie 1978 The Case against Hospital Deliveries: The Statistical Evidence. In *The Place of Birth*. Sheila Kitzinger and John A. Davis, eds. Oxford: Oxford University Press.

Thacker, Stephen B. 1987 The Efficacy of Intrapartum Electronic Fetal Monitoring. *American Journal of Obstetrics and Gynecology* 156: 24-30.

Trevathan, Wenda R. 1987 *Human Birth: An Evolutionary Perspective*. New York: Aldine De Gruyter.

Velimirovic, Boris ed. 1978 Modern Medicine and Medical Anthropology in the U.S.-Mexican Border Population. Scientific Publication #359. Washington, DC: Pan American Health Organization.

Werner, David, and Bill Bower 1982 *Helping Health Workers Learn*. Palo Alto, CA: Hesperian Foundation.

Williams, R.M., Margaret H. Thorn, and J.W.W. Studd 1980 A Study of the Benefits and Acceptability of Ambulation in Spontaneous Labor. *British Journal of Obstetrics and Gynaecology* 87:2(Feb):122-127.

Wilson, Ronald G., Samuel Ofusu-Amaah, and Mark Belsey, eds. 1986 Primary Health Care Technologies at the Family and Community Levels. Report of a workshop sponsored by the United Nations Children's Fund, the Aga Khan Foundation, and the World Health Organization. Geneva and New York: Aga Khan Foundation and United Nations Children's Fund.

World Health Organization 1975 Manpower Development: Training and Utilization of Traditional Healers and Their Collaboration with Health Care

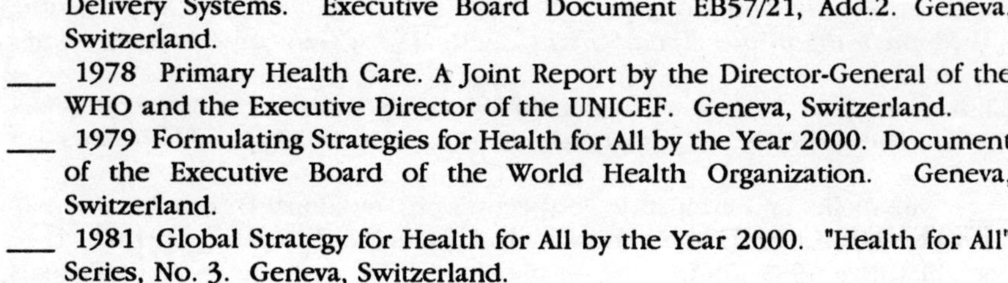

Delivery Systems. Executive Board Document EB57/21, Add.2. Geneva, Switzerland.

___ 1978 Primary Health Care. A Joint Report by the Director-General of the WHO and the Executive Director of the UNICEF. Geneva, Switzerland.

___ 1979 Formulating Strategies for Health for All by the Year 2000. Document of the Executive Board of the World Health Organization. Geneva, Switzerland.

___ 1981 Global Strategy for Health for All by the Year 2000. "Health for All" Series, No. 3. Geneva, Switzerland.

III

EXTENDING PRIMARY HEALTH CARE INTO THE COMMUNITY

Making primary health care services and health education available to rural and hard to reach populations has been one of the most difficult tasks facing developing nations. The challenge of moving health care out of urban-based hospitals and clinics and into remote communities has proved formidable, and one which has been addressed in a variety of ways with uneven success. The chapters in this section describe three commonly used but very different approaches to extending PHC into the community: the use of outreach community health workers (CHWs); compulsory medical service for newly graduated physicians; and social marketing campaigns.

The use of locally-recruited paraprofessional community health workers to deliver basic health services, like the program described in Wood's chapter on the Maori of New Zealand, has been widely used throughout the world, some places very successfully, others with mixed results. The Maori experiment illustrates one of the major strengths of such programs, that is, the benefits of enlisting individuals who know the local culture, language and social system, and can effectively bridge the gap between biomedicine and the lay community. Wood's account also highlights some of the difficulties that often emerge in such programs, such as conflicts of authority and covert competition between the professional medical community and indigenous health workers, bureaucratic constraints on the kinds of tasks that CHWs can perform, and unclear definitions of the roles and responsibilities of the workers. CHW programs in other parts of the world have also dealt with problems of morale, inadequate salaries, attrition of volunteers and conflicts with local political structures. Wood concludes that the lack of support for the Maori CHWs from officials and the medical community stems from an inadequate acceptance of the need for "developing country" style primary health care in this developed nation.

The concentration of physicians in urban areas and the corresponding shortage of doctors in rural areas is a global problem common to both developed and developing nations. Many Third World governments have resorted to compulsory medical service as a partial solution to this problem. The Mexican case study described by Rubel is typical in many ways of the kinds of difficulties encountered by physicians performing obligatory rural service. These providers are usually urban born and raised, from middle and upper class families, with little or no previous contact with country people or experience with rural medical practice. They come to their assignments inadequately prepared to deal with either the cultural background of their patients or the subtle complexities of local politics. Rubel's analysis of one young doctor's experience reveals how a local issue completely unrelated to health--the fear of depopulation and its potential threat to productive lands--had serious consequences for the physician's attempts to fulfill his bureaucratic obligations and meet patient quotas. The case study raises the question of how can medical training and a limited preparation for placement prepare these interns to cope with the sociopolitical complexities that attend the introduction of a new medical service in rural communities. At another level it raises the question whether compulsory medical service is a viable solution to the problem of uneven distribution of health care workers.

A third approach to reaching remote communities which has gained prominence in recent years is the use of social marketing strategies which rely heavily on mass media for conveying educational messages based on consumer research. As noted in the introductory chapter, anthropological methods have made a strong contribution in providing cultural insights which allow communication of new health practices in more meaningful and acceptable ways. The Indonesian nutrition education program described by Griffiths is an excellent example of a successful social marketing campaign which made extensive use of anthropological research in program design. Griffiths outlines the different phases of the intervention from formative research through strategy development and program evaluation, showing how anthropological insights were essential at each step, and concludes with valuable lessons for improving the impact of anthropological involvement on large-scale multidisciplinary projects. These lessons offer specific guidelines for avoiding some of the common pitfalls involved in collaborating with program managers and quantitatively oriented researchers.

6

Maori Community Health Workers: A Mixed Reception in New Zealand

Corinne Shear Wood

> *He aha te mea nui? He tangata, he tangata, he tangata.*
> What is the important thing in the world? It is people, people, people.
> –Maori proverb

Idealized as a way to overcome many of the limitations of clinic-based medical systems, community health workers (CHWs) were initially hailed as likely to make a major contribution to the success of primary health care initiatives. They were envisioned as being selected by their peers and perhaps even compensated by them, in money or in goods, rather than by governments or international agencies. They were to provide culturally-sensitive preventive and curative care to people--often their own friends and neighbors--who otherwise would have had no easy access to biomedical health services. Sometimes these goals have been realized, but it is also clear that in many parts of the world CHWs have not been allowed to live up to their full potential.

Thus, in a recent article reviewing the pluses and minuses of national-level CHW programs, Berman et al. (1987) state that although such programs have had considerable success, particularly in extending health care coverage to previously unserved or grossly underserved populations, in most cases it is difficult to prove that they have reduced morbidity and mortality in any substantial way. This is because even where such reductions can be documented, they may well have occurred as a result of general improvement in the standard of living rather than because of interventions by CHWs. The authors conclude that although the jury is still out, "studies suggest that existing CHW programs have low costs [but also] low effectiveness" (Berman et al. 1987: 457).

The reasons for this are multiple. First, there can be high attrition and low activity levels when CHWs work as volunteers without being paid, as is the case in Indonesia, Sri Lanka, and Thailand (Walt et al. 1989) or when, as often happens, they are not paid on a regular basis. Overburdening them with too many tasks and/or too many clients can also lead to demoralization, and these are matters in which there is wide variation from country to country. For example, in India each "health guide" covers approximately 1,000 people (Berman et al. 1987: 448), whereas the widely-praised barefoot doctors in the People's Republic of China are responsible for only 450 to 500 people each (Young 1987).

Further, it has been abundantly documented that incautious selection of CHWs can spell programmatic failure. Thus where CHWs are young males and women are excluded from program design and implementation, as in Burkina Faso, it is hardly surprising that they may not be consulted by mothers when children are sick, as has been shown in a study by Sauerborn et al. (1989). Similarly, when CHWs are seen as linked with one particular religious group, as in Oyo State of Nigeria, members of other groups may well be reluctant to use their services (Iyun 1989).

Other problems can arise when CHWs receive inadequate training. If they are unable to give appropriate answers to health questions, then, as one CHW put it, people "lose faith . . . and refuse to accept any advice" regarding other matters as well (Walt et al. 1989: 603). CHWs who lack continuous access to a stable supply of medicines--which is the case in most parts of the developing world--also lose stature in the eyes of the community. This is particularly true because in many developing countries, palliative and curative care, however simple (e.g. aspirin and first aid) is valued far more than preventive and promotive activities such as family planning and sanitation advice. Lacking both information and medicines, many CHWs are beset by insecurity and self-doubt and may find it difficult to motivate their clients.

The present account describes a small-scale but innovative Maori CHW program in New Zealand in which few or none of these problems were operative. The workers were paid, though modestly. They were female and hence had easy access to women and children. They were genuinely chosen by the community rather than being imposed on it from above, as often happens with CHWs (Walt et al. 1989: 605). They were not identified with a group foreign to any segment of the population they served; rather, they were quite literally working among their own people. They were adequately trained to perform a limited number of important health tasks that they themselves had chosen, and in the author's judgment they performed those tasks in a highly competent manner. Each had responsibility for about 300 people and therefore they were not overextended as in some CHW schemes.

Yet the health workers were burdened with opposition--not by their own clients, who by and large welcomed their efforts, but by fellow members of the medical establishment motivated by professional jealousies and fears. Occupying a novel and hence anomalous place in the New Zealand health care system, they were perceived as a threat by local practitioners, who feared loss of control if not also loss of income and who thus sought to dismiss the women as ineffectual amateurs. Further, the ambiguity of the CHWs' position made them both unsure of their proper range of authority and reluctant to try to extend its limits.

Mark Nichter (1986) has noted similar strains and insecurities among members of primary health care teams in India and Sri Lanka. The case described here is somewhat different. After an initial shakedown period in which the CHWs struggled to define and delineate their own role in relation to public health nurses, their major problem was lack of recognition and respect not from within but from physicians *outside* the team. The following is an account of these events as they took place in the Waikato region of New Zealand and as the author was privileged to witness them from the inception and planning stages onward.

Background

The Maori comprise somewhat less than 15% of New Zealand's slightly more than 3 million people. Archeological evidence indicates that they have inhabited the country for at least a thousand years (Houghton 1980). Maori legends link tribal ancestry to the occupants of an original "seven canoes" that made the hazardous journey to New Zealand from a mysterious "Havakii"; some scholars identify the latter with the Samoan Islands and others think that it was probably New Guinea.

In contrast to this ancient journey, European migration to New Zealand is quite recent: virtually all took place during the past 200 years. The advent of the European colonists was as cataclysmic for the Maori as it was for indigenous peoples elsewhere in the world (Wood 1979). Briefly put, the Maori lost most of their land holdings while being introduced to tobacco, alcohol, firearms, refined sugar, and devastating "Western" diseases such as smallpox, influenza, and typhoid (Trowell and Burkitt 1981). Denied admission to most European-run hospitals and barred from care by most European physicians, by the end of the 19th century the Maori people were on the brink of extinction (Ausubel 1965; Miller 1974; King 1977).

Even today, every epidemiological study carried out in New Zealand reveals a gross disparity between Maoris and Europeans in terms of life expectancy, infant mortality, and general morbidity (Pomare 1980). Although hospitals and most private practitioners now accept Maori patients, more subtle problems remain unaddressed. At the most basic level, economic constraints associated with inferior employment opportunities limit people's access to fee-for-service physicians. In addition, critics argue that because many physicians are insensitive to important components of Maori culture, patients are frequently alienated and health is compromised, particularly since the Maori experience high levels of long-term chronic illnesses such as diabetes, hypertension, and other cardiovascular diseases that require ongoing, lifelong medical care.

For example, one fundamental component of the Maori value system is a special reverence for the elderly, so that the ingrained European practice of having each patient wait his or her turn in the doctor's office rather than giving special consideration to older people is likely to be viewed as a serious affront. Similarly, many Maoris believe that various parts of the body--most notably the head--possess a special *mana*, or power, and standard medical procedures involving close inspection of these body parts often offend such sensibilities. The list of potential areas of conflict could be lengthened almost indefinitely, but the result can be stated with stark and somber brevity: to the extent possible, the conservative Maori avoids seeking biomedical health care until no other choice is possible. Thus, illnesses such as hypertension and diabetes that would have responded well to early and consistent treatment are all too frequently neglected, with catastrophic results.

The Genesis of a Community-Based PHC Program

In the early 1980s, the author studied certain aspects of the health status of more than 500 residents of the Waikato area on the North Island, most of whom were Maoris (Wood 1982). With full cooperation from the community, blood pressures and related anthropometric measurements were taken and information was collected on diet, perceived health concerns, and reported interactions with existing medical facilities. The health status findings were consistent with those reported elsewhere for the New Zealand Maori population (Beaglehole et al. 1978; Pomare 1980; Murchie 1984). Each of these studies documented a higher level of essential hypertension, as well as generally greater morbidity and mortality, among Maori adults than among New Zealand Europeans of similar age. In addition, however, the author's study showed that many informants were uncomfortable with certain aspects of the medical care available to them, stating that much greater recognition of Maori beliefs and customs was needed.

As a consequence of these findings, the author recommended the establishment of a culturally-sensitive health program that would be located directly on the *marae*, or traditional Maori ceremonial center (Wood 1982). Numerous meetings followed with members of the Maori community, with the District Health Office, and indirectly with the National Health Office as well. Partly because the proposal fortuitously coincided with a period of heightened Maori political and social awareness, before a year had elapsed a Maori Health Center was established on the Waahi *marae*, the *marae* where the author's study had been carried out. The government Department of Labour funded three positions for health workers to be drawn from the Maori community and the regional Public Health Department agreed to coordinate nursing services with the fledgling *marae* health organization. At the same time, improvement in Maori health was named a national priority by the National Health Office.

A facility was developed with seed money from the local hospital board and the District Health Office, augmented by modest community contributions, and an elected Waahi *Marae* Committee was established. After lengthy discussion, the committee selected three Maori women, all of whom were mothers of large families and longtime community residents, to serve as the first community health workers.

In many areas where the primary health care movement has taken root, CHWs have been called by distinctive names reflecting a special tie to their own culture. These Maori women were no exception. They chose the name *Nga Ringa Aroha* (The Loving Hands) to convey their desire to help people acquire more control over their health and take more responsibility for their own wellbeing while preserving key elements of *Maoritanga*, or the Maori way of life. The following account describes what happened when these dedicated and energetic community workers attempted to put their plans into action.

The First Years

During the first year of its existence (1983-1984), the *marae* health facility was staffed by a Maori registered nurse who was present on a part-time basis and by the three community health workers. The three women were introduced to basic health surveillance techniques by two sympathetic doctors at a nearby hospital. They were taught how to take blood pressures, how to measure glucose levels, and how to make various morphometric assessments. In addition, they received basic instruction in nutrition, family planning, and examination of children's ears. A preventive medicine (health education) component was included, and the importance of keeping accurate records was stressed. On their own initiative, the women decided to introduce a vigorous exercise component into the program. Finally, with the cooperation of obstetrical nurses and midwives, an antenatal component was incorporated into their repertoire.

The three women accepted their new roles with great enthusiasm. In a very short time, they augmented their basic training by learning to give public presentations, to locate useful audiovisual aids, to guide group exercise programs, to organize small gatherings for the dissemination of health-related material, and, perhaps most critical, to push health concerns to the forefront of people's everyday lives. As the program's reputation grew, delegations began to arrive from other Maori communities. The visitors were anxious to learn from the experiences of *Nga Ringa Aroha* so that they could initiate similar programs in their own areas. These gatherings gave people an opportunity for extensive discussion and questioning of values, goals, and concerns related to Maori and European health workers and provided a valuable forum for the exchange of ideas.

From the start, *Nga Ringa Aroha* reached out into the larger community. Because of the traditional Maori veneration of older people, they put particular emphasis on establishing contact with the *kaumatua*, or elders (in the Maori culture, the term is one that carries with it an aura of intense respect and affection). These visits included blood pressure and glucose measurements as well as transportation to a hospital or medical practitioner where needed. In keeping with tradition, the health workers arranged to provide emotional support to the *kaumatua* through such means as prayer ceremonies (*karakia*) when requested to do so. This aspect of *Nga Ringa Aroha*'s activity reflected their awareness that newly introduced European life styles had frequently disrupted family ties and roles, depriving the elders of their accustomed support mechanisms and expected high status.

In time, community members and public health nurses began to ask *Nga Ringa Aroha* to transport young children to medical facilities such as outreach "ear caravans" for examinations and treatment.

Thus the women became a common fixture at homes, schools, and *kohanga reo* (literally, "language nest": a Maori preschool program stressing maintenance of the indigenous language, tradition, and culture). By working long hours, the three women were also able to participate in numerous gatherings where many Maoris of all ages were present. These included several *poukai*, or annual ceremonial gatherings for the purpose of acknowledging the ritual and symbolic status of the Maori queen, Te Atarangikaahu, as well as many *tangi*, or funerals during which people live on the *marae* for several days. At all of these assemblies, *Nga Ringa Aroha* initiated discussions on nutrition, cigarette smoking, responsible alcohol consumption, and general physical fitness; blood pressure screening became a routine procedure. An exercise center was established on the *marae* and varied programs of Jazzercise and other age-scaled physical activities became routine events, attracting a faithful, enthusiastic following.

Less than two years after the program was begun, the Waahi "loving hands" had reached and touched well over a thousand residents of the Maori community in one way or another. Perhaps their most important contribution was an intangible one: helping people to see that they could improve their own health by taking responsibility for their own daily actions. Today, most people on the *marae* are intensely aware of the importance of high-quality nutrition and there is growing discomfort with excess body weight, smoking, and alcohol consumption, particularly during pregnancy. In sum, the beginnings of a new, healthier ideology have emerged as a direct result of *Nga Ringa Aroha* activity. A new health consciousness prevails, replacing formerly dominant attitudes of fatalistic resignation.

Interactions with Formal Health Agencies

Throughout their existence and indeed prior to their formal establishment, *Nga Ringa Aroha* have struggled to define their relationship with agencies of the New Zealand government. Because they have had to rely on various government offices--virtually all European-dominated--for their salaries and associated expenses, the women have come under pressure to modify their own cultural norms to conform to European ideas about appropriate operating procedures. Indeed, this is a problem facing emerging Maori health care movements in New Zealand as a whole. Because the institutionalized medical care system tends to view virtually all health-related activity as its own exclusive territory, parameters of responsibility and autonomy are very ill-defined.

Part of the problem is that there are no governmental categories into which groups such as *Nga Ringa Aroha* can be neatly placed. In fact, the entire concept of primary health care is foreign to most people in the country, whereas it has been widely accepted in many other parts of the world (Mahler and Labouisse 1978; Wainwright 1981; Jancloes et al. 1982; Zourai 1983; Bannerji 1984). When the term "primary health care" is used at all in New Zealand, it has been regarded as the province of the general medical practitioner. In other words, the World Health Organization concept of primary health care, with all of its broad definitional considerations, is incorrectly assumed to be equivalent to primary medical care by physicians.

Not surprisingly, this fact set the stage for conflict between *Nga Ringa Aroha* and the medical establishment as professionals attempted to block the development of paraprofessional workers. Local practitioners, who had been trained in the European tradition, had no concept of community-based primary health care as practiced by the Waahi *marae* women. Instead, they saw such programs as perhaps appropriate for a Third World country but wholly inappropriate and unneeded in New Zealand. Thus, relations between these practitioners and *Nga Ringa Aroha* have always been strained and at times almost nonexistent or frankly hostile.

A First Attempt at Control Fails

To assuage such tensions and qualms, the government public health nurses initially tried to force *Nga Ringa Aroha* into the existing bureaucratic slot of "health assistants." This move was adamantly opposed both by the women themselves and by the Waahi *Marae* Committee. For one thing, the fact that the "health assistant" job lacked any significant preventive component was highly problematic, especially in view of the newly emerging Maori health care movement. In addition, Maori health personnel saw the role of "health assistant" as one of "picking up after the public health nurses," that is, performing tasks that the nurses were either unable to accomplish because of cultural conflicts or were unwilling to perform.

Basically, being a health assistant was viewed as consisting quite literally of "nit picking," i.e. going to homes and schools to search for head lice infestations among Maori children. It was clear that for many Maori, who themselves had had to submit to such examinations during their school years, the entire subject continued to bear potent overtones of shame and embarrassment and to carry an aura of racism. Thus the role of "health assistant" implied an identity which for *Nga Ringa Aroha* was totally out of keeping with their own perceptions of their proper mission and status. Indeed, from an anthropological point of view the debate seemed to encapsulate the wide cultural chasm separating Maoris from Europeans in New Zealand, despite the fact that the government boasted and continues to boast of a high level of intercultural harmony.

Treatment of Ear Infections: A Territorial Dispute

Further attention was focused on the murky conflict between the medical establishment and the three health workers when sharp controversy arose over the proper approach to the problem of rampant ear infections among Maori children. As noted above, *Nga Ringa Aroha* had learned how to conduct rudimentary ear examinations during their period of hospital training. They knew how to recognize healthy ears, how to maintain proper ear hygiene, and how to detect which children were in need of medical intervention to avert severe pain and irreversible damage. Eager to share this knowledge, they initiated an ambitious community education program incorporating the use of colorful posters in Maori and English. They applied for a grant to enable them to develop a Maori-oriented videotape on the subject; they distributed relevant literature; and they gave "hands on" demonstrations for eager mothers using otoscopes donated on an unofficial basis by supporters in the National Health Office.

For a brief period, all was well. Soon, however, the activities of *Nga Ringa Aroha* came to the attention of the wider medical community and apparently caused great alarm. Ears, it seemed, were viewed as belonging to the exclusive domain of licensed medical doctors, and by looking into them, the health workers were overstepping their (undefined but closely watched) boundaries. The three women were instructed to give back their otoscopes and restrict themselves to transporting already-diagnosed children to appropriate practitioners or to a mobile ear caravan. Their protest that many ear problems would thus remain undiscovered until they had caused irreversible damage went unheeded. The Maori women were "put in their proper place" and ears were returned to the province of the established doctors.

The Consequences

This interaction, handled quite arbitrarily and less than diplomatically, reveals the depth and seriousness of the medical community's fears. As a result of such events, Maori primary health care workers have been virtually forced into a counterproductive adversarial stance rather than feeling confident that they can work together with Europeans in a joint struggle against disease and deprivation. Having received mixed messages of rebuke and encouragement, they are confused about what can be expected from the medical establishment. They cannot be confident about what is appropriate to request, what is likely to be denied, and what may be granted and then summarily withdrawn. The result, all too often, is an uneasy stasis.

Another disturbing consequence of the limited support hitherto extended to Maori health workers is the Maori community's growing recourse to professed "healers" who are neither scientifically-trained nor Maori. Frequently linked to the Christian evangelical movement, these untrained practitioners attract sizeable clienteles and often delay needed medical treatment. Thus, in a very complex medical landscape, dissatisfaction with existing health care as culturally insensitive plus confusing limitations on groups such as *Nga Ringa Aroha* appears to be leading to increased reliance on ineffective and potentially dangerous alternatives.

Discussion

Few informed New Zealanders today would question the need for health care programs tailored to Maori needs. The disparity between European cultural norms and the indigenous Maori value system is all too obvious (Wood and Bean 1969; Wood 1970; King 1977; Trowell and Burkitt 1981; Osuntokun 1985). It is clear that the Waahi *marae* health workers have achieved spectacular successes during their brief existence as an organized group. The crucial question is whether medical and governmental bodies will be willing to commit themselves and the resources they control to supporting such efforts and helping them to expand. As the "ear" interaction reveals, the problem is that physicians and bureaucrats often perceive community-based programs as threatening, partly because the preventive rather than curative model of health care is neither well understood nor fully appreciated within the treatment-oriented medical community.

There may be other reasons as well. One hesitates to raise the question of economic competition, but when all aspects of the situation are taken into account, this possibility cannot be ignored. With very rare exceptions, there has been no encouragement or even acknowledgement of the Waahi *marae* experiment by general medical practitioners in the area, even though two specialists on the staff of the local hospital were very supportive, as noted above, and more recently a female public health physician has cooperated with *Nga Ringa Aroha* to screen for cervical cancer. Such a phenomenon, while distressing, is far from unique on the international health scene. Throughout the world literature (cf. Newell 1975; Kasonde and Martin 1983), the same theme is repeated: in many developing countries, what should be a coalition of allies totally committed to healing is often a nonproductive stalemate instead.

In New Zealand, the dearth of medically-qualified personnel of Maori ancestry is another serious deficiency, and one that should certainly be addressed by appropriate government agencies. However, a more immediately attainable goal is that of enhancing cultural sensitivity among physicians currently in practice. These non-Maori practitioners must be encouraged to move beyond any residual tendency to patronize, belittle, or dominate in the old colonialist manner. Active cooperation with groups such as *Nga Ringa Aroha* would be a visible demonstration of their good will and good faith.

Above all, physicians need to recognize that even in the absence of such cooperation, the Maori primary health care movement will continue to gain power. Unquestionably, Maori health workers satisfy a strongly felt need by partially bridging the gap separating their people from full utilization of existing medical services. As of 1990, more than two dozen new groups similar to *Nga Ringa Aroha* had been organized in New Zealand, and the health workers involved, aware of their unique role and their distinct problems, had formed their own professional organization. Thus, for the Maori, culturally-sensitive and community-based health care is assuming its rightful place alongside other nationalist movements such as sweeping political activism, language acquisition programs, restoration of long-neglected *marae*, and renewed pride in traditional Maori art forms and legends.

Because of the enthusiastic efforts of groups such as *Nga Ringa Aroha*, dramatic changes in health-related attitudes and practices can be observed within the Maori communities of New Zealand. Attitudes are altering; new possibilities are in the air; full health and a life untrammeled by disasters formerly regarded as inevitable are beginning to emerge as reasonable expectations by and for the Maori people. One hears less and less reference to the widespread heart disease, diabetes, and gout as "Maori diseases." People are beginning to realize that many of these conditions stem from maladaptive adoption of the European life style, and that the latter can be changed.

It is clear that the Maori health workers described in the present account have achieved remarkable successes during their relatively brief period of existence. They have filled a serious void by offering culturally-sensitive health care to large numbers of their own people. Far from making cursory home visits, as was said to have occurred in a Nigerian CHW program (Iyun 1989: 937), they have dedicated themselves to the welfare of the Maori community, performing their repertoire of tasks with enthusiasm and at minimal cost.

Even more important, by linking good health status with other development issues, e.g. rejection of alcohol and tobacco, they have had an impact on Maori political consciousness far in excess of whatever they may have done to lower morbidity and mortality rates. People know that they are responsible (and responsive) to the Maori people and not to the health bureaucracy or to other commercial interests. Thus for *Nga Ringa Aroha*, the answer to David Werner's concerned question *The Village Health Worker--Lackey or Liberator*? (1977) would be unequivocally favorable.

However, the Maori women's successes have also been limited by the marginalization that has been imposed on them, i.e. by their dependence on the goodwill of a few doctors for training and support. As yet they not only lack a well-defined sphere of activity but their health care tasks have been relatively few. These tasks could well be expanded with great potential benefit to their clientele. For a start, the ear program, so popularly received and so unquestionably on target, should once again be part of *Nga Ringa Aroha*'s health repertoire.

In short, the "loving hands" movement has filled and continues to fill a serious need. It has been warmly received by the Maori people. What is called for now is a corresponding recognition on the part of the non-Maori medical establishment that dedicated workers such as *Nga Ringa Aroha* deserve their wholehearted support, their encouragement, and, if possible, their outright welcoming enthusiasm.

Acknowledgements

The author wishes to thank the many friends and board members of the Waahi *marae* who gave unstintingly of their time and energy to help advance the cause of community-based primary health care. Among them are Taitimu and Ramari Maipi, Robert and Raiha Mahuta, Tutata Matatahi, Mere Rotena, Te Puea Paulo, the late Elsie Hopa, Polly Thompson, Rick Muru, and Rick Maipi. In addition, Queen Te Atarangikaahu and her husband Whatu Paki provided invaluable support and encouragement. Many other community members also generously contributed time and energy; they are all acknowledged with profound gratitude and *aroha*. Finally, sincere appreciation is extended to Dorothy Mull for her encouragement, research assistance, and superb editing skills.

References

Ausubel, D.P. 1965 *Maori Youth: A Psychoethnological Study of Cultural Deprivation*. New York: Holt, Rinehart and Winston.

Bannerji, D. 1984 Primary Health Care: Selective or Comprehensive? *World Health Forum* 5:312-315.

Beaglehole, R., I. Prior, C. Salmond, and E. Eyles 1978 Coronary Heart Disease in Maoris: Incidence and Case Mortality. *New Zealand Medical Journal* 88:138-141.

Berman, P.A., D.R. Gwatkin, and S.E. Burger 1987 Community-Based Health Workers: Head Start or False Start Towards Health for All? *Social Science and Medicine* 25(5):443-459.

Houghton, P. 1980 *Early New Zealanders*. Auckland, New Zealand: Hodder and Stoughton, Ltd.

Iyun F. 1989 An Assessment of a Rural Health Programme on Child and Maternal Care: The Ogbomoso Community Health Care Programme (CHCP), Oyo State, Nigeria. *Social Science and Medicine* 29(8):933-938.

Jancloes, M., B. Seck, L. Van de Velden, and B. Ndiaye 1982 Primary Health Care in a Senegalese Town: How the Local People Took Part. *World Health Forum* 3(4):376-379.

Kasonde, J.M., and J.D. Martin 1983 Moving Toward Primary Health Care: The Zambian Experience. *World Health Forum* 4(1):25-30.

King, M. 1977 *Te Puea: A Biography*. Auckland, New Zealand: Hodder and Stoughton, Ltd.

Mahler, H., and H.R. Labouisse 1978 *Primary Health Care, A Joint WHO/UNICEF Report*. Geneva: WHO and New York: UNICEF.

Miller, J. 1974 *Early Victorian New Zealand: A Study of Racial Tension and Social Attitudes 1839-1852*. Wellington, New Zealand: Oxford University Press.

Murchie, E. 1984 *Rapuora: Health and Maori Women*. Wellington, New Zealand: Maori Women's Welfare League.

Newell, K.W. 1975 Health by the People. *World Health Chronicle* 29:161-167.

Nichter, M.A. 1986 The Primary Health Center as a Social System: PHC, Social Status, and the Issue of Team-Work in South Asia. *Social Science and Medicine* 23(4):347-355.

Osuntokun, B.O. 1985 The Changing Pattern of Disease in Developing Countries. *World Health Forum* 6:310-313.

Pomare, E.W. 1980 *Maori Standards of Health: A Study of the 20-Year Period 1955-1975*. Medical Research Council of New Zealand Special Report Series No. 7.

Sauerborn, R., A. Nougtara, and H.J. Diesfeld 1989 Low Utilization of Community Health Workers: Results from a Household Interview Survey in Burkina Faso. *Social Science and Medicine* 29(10):1163-1174.

Trowell, H.C., and D.P. Burkitt, eds. 1981 *Western Diseases: Their Emergence and Prevention*. Cambridge, MA: Harvard University Press.

Wainwright, R. 1981 The Licensing of Primary Health Workers. *World Health Forum* 2(1):82-84.

Walt, G., M. Perera, and K. Heggenhougen 1989 Are Large-Scale Volunteer Community Health Worker Programmes Feasible? The Case of Sri Lanka. *Social Science and Medicine* 29(5):599-608.

Werner, D. 1977 *The Village Health Worker--Lackey or Liberator?* Palo Alto, CA: The Hesperian Foundation.

Wood, C.S., and L.J. Bean 1969 The Crisis in Indian Health: A California Example. *Indian Historian* 2(3):29-32, 36.

Wood, C.S. 1970 A Multiphasic Screening Survey of Three California Indian Reservations. *Social Science and Medicine* 4:579-587.

___ 1979 *Human Sickness and Health: A Biocultural View*. Palo Alto, CA: Mayfield Publishing Company.

___ 1982 *Blood Pressure and Related Factors among the Maori and Pakeha Communities of Huntly*. Occasional Paper No. 17. Hamilton, New Zealand: Centre for Maori Studies and Research, University of Waikato.

Young, M. 1984 Study of Barefoot Doctors' Activities in China. Doctor of Public Health thesis. Baltimore, MD: The Johns Hopkins University School of Hygiene and Public Health.

Zourai, B., S. Bousnina, M. Maaleje, and T. Nacef 1983 Implementing Primary Health Programmes. *World Health Forum* 4(1):31-33.

7

Compulsory Medical Service and Primary Health Care: A Mexican Case Study

Arthur J. Rubel

The uneven distribution of professional health care providers is a worldwide problem. The distribution is skewed in favor of metropolitan urban residents, with far fewer providers available to rural populations. This disparity of physicians is especially problematic in the less developed countries, most of which have a marked rural-urban population imbalance. In such developing countries, "it is common to find four-fifths of the physicians located in a few large cities (sometimes in one metropolis) where 10 or 20% of the population live, while only one-fifth or fewer of the physicians work in rural areas, where 80 or 90% of the population live" (Fulop and Roemer 1982). In 1980 a World Health Organization survey found that "within each country the most striking feature [of health manpower development] is the divergency between town and country. In all countries without exception the rural areas are distinctly more deprived with regard to health manpower resources" (Mejía 1980: 137; see also Kindig and Taylor 1985).

Innovative efforts to attract physicians to rural areas have been attempted in many nations. As early as the 1920s, rural municipalities in Canada offered salaries to primary care practitioners, small towns in the United States offered rent-free homes, and several Australian states guaranteed rural physicians an annual minimum level of income (Roemer 1987: 326). Seventy years ago the Soviet Union began to require its physicians to perform three years of service in rural areas. In 1936 Mexico instituted its "social service obligation" by which it required medical students to complete a 6-month tour of duty in a rural, underserved area as a condition of earning a medical degree. The Soviet and Mexican experiments provided guidance to efforts by other less developed countries seeking ways to extend professional primary care services to their rural hinterlands. In fact, a number of variations on that theme have been practiced in countries as diverse as Great Britain, Tunisia, and the United States (Roemer 1987: 326-328; Mason 1971; Spencer and D'Elia 1983; Krugman, Tabak, and Fryor 1982). These and a large number of other experimental programs to extend cosmopolitan medicine to previously unserved areas or underserved areas (Ademuwagun et al. 1979; Azuni 1979; Berman, Gwatkin, and Burger 1987: 447-448; Habicht 1979; Habicht et al. 1973; Justice 1978; Kapur 1979: 30; Velimirovic and Velimirovic 1978) have received considerable attention because they promise to diminish the very high morbidity and mortality rates which are so common in less developed countries. However, evaluations of the effect of such programs (Collado-Ardón 1983: 244; Habicht 1979; Musselwhite 1981) are uncommon.

In view of Mexico's pioneering attempt to extend primary health care to undoctored rural populations through its social service requirement, and the virtual absence of evaluations of the success of this attempt, the Institute of Anthropological Investigation of the National Autonomous University (UNAM) commissioned a study of the program. Because my own experience as an anthropologist with several years' residence in rural Mexican villages indicated the problematic adaptation of the young doctors (*pasantes de medicina*) who were performing their obligatory period of social service, I initiated a one-year study of the relationship between *pasantes de medicina* and the community to which they had been assigned. The study was conducted in San Francisco,[1] a Chinantec/Spanish speaking Indian community of some 1,500 persons located on the precipitous slopes of the Sierra de Ixtlán in the State of Oaxaca. I had previously spent a year in San Francisco and was familiar with its health problems (Rubel, O'Nell, and Collado-Ardón 1984).

The Setting

The Chinantec-speaking municipality of San Francisco consists of a head-town, or *cabecera*, and a hinterland which extends down the mountainous slopes and into the tropical forest. Nestling dispersed in the hills and ridges are a number of small *rancherías*, political dependencies of the head-town. Some *rancherías* with several hundred residents have large enough populations to warrant some nominal political recognition from the state government.

These larger settlements are *agencias de policía*. The entire *municipio* territory is governed from the head-town and, traditionally, all mature males, whether resident of the head-town or of the hamlets, serve terms (*cargos*) as unsalaried officers of the municipal government. All men are expected to donate five or six years of unremunerated service to the municipal government; five if they are literate and speak Spanish adequately, six if not. In addition, all married men are obliged to contribute their labor without compensation to community projects such as constructing or maintaining a clinic, building or maintaining a school, or building and maintaining the dirt road which connects the *cabecera* to the national highway. A man who has served the stipulated number of years in unsalaried service to his *municipio* attains the status of respected elder (*anciano*) and becomes a member of the council of elders which advises the municipal authorities on matters of political, economic, and ritual importance to the community (Cancian 1965; Corbett 1974; Pérez Jiménez 1980; Rubel 1976).

From the perspective of its citizens, the single most important political concern of the citizens of San Francisco is that they be able to defend their agriculturally productive lands against interlopers from neighboring communities, many of which are more populous and wealthier. The fear of land loss is fueled by unceasing litigation and intermittent pitched battles with neighboring *municipios* over disputed plots (field notes; Browner 1986b: 716; Dennis 1987; Pérez García 1956: 155). Villagers' preoccupation with the defense of productive lands is manifested by a fear of depopulation. Many years ago *franciscanos* responded to this perceived threat by promising an annual pilgrimage to four regional churches by a delegation of *ancianos*. As one *anciano* explains, the vow was taken because "the *municipio* population did not grow. Whenever a baby was born, an adult or several adults died. These were adults who were still vigorous, young, not yet elderly. That is why we made our promise to visit the churches." Later, in the 1970s, residents sought to protect themselves from epidemics known to have decimated nearby communities by requesting the national health authorities to post *pasantes* in San Francisco.

For *franciscanos*, some of the feared consequences of depopulation are:

1) incapacity to muster forces capable of defending communal lands against stronger, more populous neighbors;
2) difficulty in finding enough men to fill all positions in the municipal government;

3) the state of Oaxaca's revocation of San Francisco's legal status as a free-standing municipality because of an unduly small population;
4) the federal agrarian authorities' settlement of outsiders on San Francisco's fallow communal lands or, worse, allocation of those plots to litigious neighboring *municipios*.

If we keep these overriding preoccupations in mind, it becomes easier to understand some of the difficulties experienced by Dr. Cruz in his effort to provide primary health care to this rural community.

Background to the Field Study

In 1980, approximately 1,900 *pasantes* were assigned to rural Mexican communities like San Francisco. These assignments were for a period of 12 months, rather than the 6 month period with which the national program had begun. Then as now, the majority of *pasantes de medicina* were posted to small rural settlements where they were responsible for an auxiliary nurse and a Class "C" clinic. A "C" clinic ordinarily consists of two or three rooms, one of which contains several hospital beds. Another room contains an examining table, a scale, a typewriter, a lamp, and a medicine cabinet. The cabinet contains a basic collection of pharmaceuticals selected by a central health authority as a primary resource for treating the diseases most common in the region. From time to time transport or other logistic problems may cause depletion of essential supplies such as medications, gauze, or adhesive tape. During such periods the physician expresses frustration with the system on which he depends, and the patients find that they have fruitlessly sought assistance.

Although *pasantes* have experienced only a brief hands-on clinical internship prior to their social service obligation, they are mandated to provide primary care to the local residents in cases of trauma and common conditions such as gastroenteritis, parasitosis, respiratory problems, and other "diseases of poverty" (Laurell 1977). More complicated problems, such as suspected tuberculosis, heart conditions and diabetes, are to be referred by a *pasante* to a larger, regional clinic or urban hospital with more sophisticated diagnostic equipment and specialty staff.

Whereas these young, newly-trained physicians are provided rich opportunities to practice primary care medicine, they receive little or no recognition from administrative superiors for their clinical competence. Unless they make a catastrophic mistake which is brought to the attention of the health authorities, the only people who will evaluate their competence as clinicians are the patients and those to whom the patient communicates dissatisfaction.

The nation's public health organization to whom they are responsible (*Servicios Coordinados de la Salud en el Estado*) is not organized to provide assistance with individual clinical cases. In the ordinary course of events, the public health supervisor of the rural zone (a physician) will rarely discuss a clinical case with a *pasante*, nor is it the supervisor's responsibility to offer advice or consultation regarding the management of cases. In fact, there is no formal mechanism by which a rural-based *pasante* can seek a more experienced clinician's counsel. In the absence of other clinicians, and with a general scarcity of telephone or radio communication in these rural areas, the young physician, in effect, practices autonomously. Whereas there is little opportunity for a *pasante* to obtain clinical counsel from more seasoned practitioners, he or she must submit reports of other professional activities for regular evaluation by the zonal supervisor and other program officials of *Servicios Coordinados*.

A few patients are referred by a *pasante* for laboratory tests. Such referrals are to a small rural hospital in the regional center of Ixtlán de Juárez. Sometimes the regional hospital is closed, other times the attending physician or laboratory staff are unavailable, and on other occasions chemicals or equipment essential to the tests have been depleted or are not in working order. Often patients who undergo tests in Ixtlán de Juárez are told to return on another day for the results. The two round-trip bus fares and the loss of productive time make such referrals problematic for patients. In addition, the Ixtlán de Juárez facility at times refers a *franciscano* patient to the large *Hospital Civil* in the state capital. Referrals to the city are even more costly for patients because the bus which leaves San Francisco's town center in the early morning does not arrive in the capital until the *Hospital Civil's* out-patient services have closed for the day. Consequently, patients must obtain overnight accommodations and food for the two day trip. Bus fares between the town center and the capital approximate a day's wages each way.

The responsibilities of the *pasante* are outlined during a five-day orientation in the state capital prior to the start of the service obligation. During this orientation week, *pasantes* attend lectures by public health program specialists seven hours a day. The lectures range from 45 minutes to two and a half hours on topics as diverse as public health policies, the organization and functions of *Servicios Coordinados*, the rights and obligations of a *pasante*, the maternal and child health program, and the role of the *pasante* during immunization campaigns. There are also lectures on specific disease control programs; notably tuberculosis, onchocerciasis, rabies, pinto, dengue, leprosy, and malaria. Only one session is devoted to the social aspects of medicine; in it *pasantes* are instructed to counsel couples on the size and spacing of their family. They are also charged with presenting public lectures on the themes of adolescent development and sexuality, venereal disease, family planning, and alcoholism.

Four hours of the *pasantes'* orientation were devoted to a lecture on customs characteristic of indigenous populations in the state of Oaxaca. The lecturer, a public health physician, began by stating his assumption that the participants had been oriented by their respective schools of medicine to the importance of understanding the social organization, culture, history, and values of communities. On being asked, everyone denied such previous training. He then asked his audience two questions: "What does the study of community mean to you?" and "Why is it important for you to understand how your community is organized?" No one responded. Although this lecture was well-prepared and delivered engagingly, the *pasantes* showed little interest in his presentation and appeared unprepared to absorb or understand its implications for them. This session closed with the admonition, "Please remember that this is very important! Don't tell us at the close of your year, 'Well, I didn't know it was my obligation [to know],' or 'I was sleeping during that session.'"

Throughout the orientation the importance of preparing and submitting one's reports to superiors was stressed. Twenty-one of thirty-two working sessions were devoted in whole or in part to the preparation and submission of weekly, monthly, and annual reports. The participants were advised that they could not expect to be freed of their service obligations at the end of the year unless all of the reports required of them were filed with the agency. The overwhelming importance attached to the many diverse reports required is wryly described in an autobiography published by one of these young physicians (Irigoyen 1974):

> I filled out the daily report, then the one on the communicables, and the monthly on tuberculosis. It is somewhat amusing to think there are some 1,500 *pasantes*, each of whom will fill out 12 monthly reports, 12 on TB, 52 on the communicables, 365 daily reports each, 4 quarterly reports, one for the year, one final and, then considering that all will include copies . . . [author's translation]

Two sets of monthly reports bear the greatest implications for the *pasante*. These constitute the *cuotas de recuperación* which inform the health authorities in Oaxaca of fees received by the *pasante* from patients. These measure the *pasante's* success in meeting patient flow expectations, or quotas. The physician's quota is calculated by averaging the number of patient visits experienced by *pasantes* who have previously served the community. Fulfillment of these quotas, and a letter from the *Presidente Municipal* which attests that the physician has served the community in a professional manner and is leaving without owing money to residents, constitute some of the grounds on which one's success as a *pasante* is evaluated. When the *cuotas de recuperación* are high, the *pasante* need have no fear. However, when they are low there is an expectation of either a corrective or sanctioning response from the zonal supervisor. This ranges from a simple admonishment to the most feared sanction: withdrawal of the physician from the community to commence the social service year again in another place. The latter may occur if the *pasante* has been absent without leave for long periods of time, has engaged in grievously disorderly conduct, or has failed to attend to patients seeking care.

Although Mexican physicians often verbally acknowledge that their formative experience as *pasantes* serving in the "front lines" of health care significantly enlarged their understanding of medicine and of themselves as human beings (see Collado-Ardón 1976), there is surprisingly little published evaluation of that experience.

The Field Study

As noted above, I spent 12 months studying the *pasante* experience. During the first nine months, I carried out participant observations and interviews of Dr. Cruz, inquiring about his clinical practice, his relationship with patients, and his interaction with the population, including the *municipio* authorities. I also conducted interviews and participant observations among his patients, their families, and the municipal authorities. In addition, I accompanied some patients who had been referred by Dr. Cruz to more clinically sophisticated centers in the district capital and to the large regional hospital in the state capital to document how the referral system functioned.

The study began when Dr. Cruz was in the third month of his social service. I observed him for nine months, i.e. until the end of his tour of duty. During Dr. Cruz's final week in San Francisco, I spent a week listening, observing, and interviewing the 1981-82 cohort of newly assigned *pasantes* during their one week of orientation in the state capital. Dr. Cruz's successor in San Francisco was a participant. I then spent three months observing the relationship between Dr. Cruz's successor and the population of San Francisco. The comments which follow are confined to observations of and interviews with Dr. Cruz, and some observations of the week-long orientation.

It is important to note that Dr. Cruz, like most *pasantes*, had always lived in a major urban center (Collado-Ardón 1976: 39-40). He had been born and raised in the city of Puebla. He was of middle-class background, his father having owned several inter-urban busses. Dr. Cruz had graduated from the national university in Mexico City, had attended medical school in the National Autonomous University of Puebla, and had completed a brief internship in a Red Cross trauma center in Mexico City. Before his assignment to San Francisco he had never heard of that municipality or, for that matter, of Chinantec Indians, and he had no familiarity with the mountainous region in which San Francisco is located. (In this respect, Dr. Cruz was not different from most of the others beginning their year of social service. They describe themselves as "parachutists" who are simply dropped into their new assignment. They are provided a sketchy orientation to the social and cultural characteristics of some of the state's indigenous groups, but none at all to those of the specific community in which they will serve.) Nevertheless, it was clear to me that Dr. Cruz arrived at his post with an idealism fed by a desire to be of service to his less fortunate countrymen. For instance, on one occasion he said: "It is good for me to be providing care for these poor peasants. It is a way for me to repay the nation for providing me my medical training. This is an important service that I provide my countrymen" (cf. Musselwhite 1981: 94-95).

The Pasante's Practice

Dr. Cruz was the tenth successive pasante serving in the government clinic in San Francisco's *cabecera*. Unlike many *pasantes*, he sought to acclimatize to village life. He was an accessible kind of physician, making house calls when necessary, affable with the townspeople, and unpretentious with his patients. During daytime hours, he attended patients or prepared reports of his activities. He attended public events such as school celebrations, holidays, and funerals. He established a sexual liaison with an unwed mother, a native-born resident with whom he spent the evenings, eating supper and sleeping in the home she shared with her parents.

I observed that Dr. Cruz and his auxiliary nurse reliably opened the clinic every day at the regulation hour of 9 A.M. and closed it for lunch, opening it again in the afternoon and closing it in early evening. The doctor spent his time seeing patients, taking the required census of the residents, offering public lectures on the topics with which he had been charged, obtaining supplies, and preparing his reports. For example, in his second month, February 1980, his log indicates four days devoted to taking a census, one day used to replenish clinical supplies in the state capital, two days of rest, and the remaining seventeen working days devoted to seeing patients. During those seventeen days he saw only thirty-one patients, averaging fewer than two per clinic day.

In his free time, Dr. Cruz prepared his obligatory reports, visited the homes of friends and acquaintances, and whiled away the daylight hours chatting with town officials. He informed me that his closest acquaintances were the President and Secretary of the municipality. Feeling bolstered by the close relationships he had established with some of the residents, Dr. Cruz commented that he was seriously contemplating establishment of a private practice in San Francisco after completing his social service obligation. His plan was to practice two days a week in the municipality and the remainder in the state capital, traveling by automobile back and forth on the new all-weather highway.

Patient attendance figures were low throughout Dr. Cruz's stay, especially in view of the documented high level of disease in San Francisco (Rubel, O'Nell, and Collado-Ardón 1984: 88-92), although not significantly below those of his predecessors.[2] In May of 1980, however, the demand for his attention fell to distressing levels and the fees he received for clinic visits, medical procedures, and medications reflected those figures. Concerned about the implications of low patient visits for his quotas and consequent evaluation, the physician responded by proposing an innovative plan of action to his zonal supervisor. He offered to add coverage to San Felipe, one of several neighboring Zapotec-speaking *municipios* litigating for San Francisco lands. Inasmuch as the two municipalities constitute a single catchment area from the point of view of the nation's health ministry and the distance between them is only five kilometers, the zonal supervisor approved the plan. Because he was required to inform the San Francisco authorities whenever he left the head-town, Dr. Cruz advised them of his plan to spend two afternoons a week providing health care in San Felipe and requested their permission to proceed. To Dr. Cruz's great surprise, they promptly refused because, explained the young doctor: "They told me, 'You are *our* physician.'"

Dr. Cruz acknowledged himself to be caught between two conflicting lines of authority: the *municipio* officials mandated to protect the socio-political interests of the community, and the program officers of the Ministry of Health charged with delivering rural health care.[3] In this dilemma, Dr. Cruz responded to what he perceived as the overwhelming pragmatic necessity of increasing his register of patient visits by extending his coverage to San Felipe. He observed:

> The community is confused as to whom I am responsible. They think of me as solely contracted to them, but that is not at all the case.

Ignoring the local authorities' prohibition, Dr. Cruz and his auxiliary nurse began walking to San Felipe two mornings a week and returning to San Francisco on the afternoon bus. After only two such efforts to extend coverage, however, they stopped in response to the sanctioning gossip to which they felt themselves subject (cf. Browner 1986a: 93-94). In the words of his nurse auxiliary:

> Here the people are egotistic. They are against one going to help other communities; one supposes other communities also have their needs, one should think about that! But what is this thing about our leaving town and why we leave, and with whom, and what time did we leave and when did we return? Authorities of these municipalities are often difficult and this particular group is even worse than others.

The doctor continued, however, to be confronted with unacceptably low numbers of patient visits. At the end of one six-day period in October without a single patient consultation, he voiced his frustration:

> Here I am nothing more than an object. I walk, I stand, I sit. I am bored with this. I am not practicing medicine. I am learning nothing. The way to learn medicine is by treating patients; from each clinical case you learn something else. If I am not treating patients here, then I must try to go somewhere else where I can treat patients. I will see whether the *rancherías* will provide me with what I need.

Dr. Cruz received permission from the zonal supervisor to test the feasibility of extending coverage from the municipal town center to residents of San Francisco's outlying lowland hamlets which front on the highway. By leaving on a morning bus Dr. Cruz could be in the lowland hamlet of El Porvenir early in the afternoon, offer primary care that afternoon and evening, and return by bus to his main clinic the following morning. His zonal supervisor supported the plan and both physicians reasoned that since the hamlets were politically and ethnically attached to the town center, the municipal authorities could not refuse a request to extend health services to their fellow citizens. In fact, the authorities *did* authorize Dr. Cruz's once a week extension of coverage to the lowland hamlets, although without enthusiasm. In mid-October Dr. Cruz left for his annual two-week vacation in a jubilant mood.

On his return his zonal supervisor confronted him with an official complaint consisting of nine formal charges brought against him by San Francisco's officials. Among those charges were malfeasance, failure to report an epidemic of communicable disease, failure to open the clinic on all working days, failure to open the clinic on time, charging excessive fees, personal misconduct, and moral turpitude. Dr. Cruz angrily denied the validity of eight of the charges, although he admitted staying with his mistress at her home every night rather than remaining accessible in the clinic building at night.

After a reprimand from his supervisor, the shocked and angry physician sought an explanation from the municipal authorities. "We don't want you to provide services to El Porvenir. It is best that you remain here," he was told. Dr. Cruz commented on that conversation as follows:

> I don't want problems. Why should I look for problems? I have three more months to serve. It's their own citizens in El Porvenir. It would mean I could provide them medical attention, but on the other hand I would have to pay bus fare. Why should I pay for transportation if I don't have to? Let it rest, why bother with it? They have serious problems with the people of the hamlets; I don't want to become involved in them. I'm happy here, I don't want to allow things to bother me. I'll be leaving soon, with my letter from the *Presidente Municipal*.
>
> Suppose the community or the [Municipal] President don't like the way I work? That's without significance! However, if my supervisor or somebody higher in the hierarchy of the Ministry thinks badly of me and my work, that, then, is what matters to me! Hell, I can be pulled out just like that [snap of fingers] and sent to another community.

Were that to happen, Dr. Cruz would lose the months of service he had spent in San Francisco and would have to begin his social service obligations anew. Consequently, his dominant thought during his remaining three months' service was how to prevent being removed from San Francisco to begin an additional twelve months of social service in a different municipality. His social service had turned sour; it had become an onerous tour of duty.

His entire attitude over the remaining three months was formed by the desire to satisfactorily complete his service, to "*librarme*" (free myself). During the remaining months he appeared to be merely "marking time," simply meeting his obligations and preparing his required reports:

> Now, when people come for services, they will have to look at a schedule posted on the wall, and if that's the way that they want it, that's what they will have! I told the authorities, "If that's what you want from me, O.K. That's what you will get." I'll be just another bureaucrat, and it won't be me that loses, but you and the community. Anyone who has to come to the clinic and is unable to pay in full, must come with an authorization (*oficio*) from the [municipal] authorities. I will not attend them unless they have such an authorization. I will no longer give people credit or a discount on my own. Those unable to pay for services or medication must come with an authorization. I don't like to be this way, but you asked for it! I feel particularly hurt and resentful because it was my buddies (*cuates*) who went behind my back and complained to my supervisor.

In one conversation with him during this period, I asked why he did not take a medical history from his patients. He responded:

> *Here* what does it matter? It is just a waste of materials, of time, and of energy. People don't answer your questions, they usually don't come back when you tell them to return. What does it matter? When you are in your private practice, ah! That's different. You take a very careful history, you ask the right questions. You ask about any other problems that the patient has, other than the complaint; you do a careful examination. You know what they say? That the more careful you are with a patient, and the more you ask about their problems, the more likely they are to return. Ah, that is something different. [In my private practice] I will treat patients like human beings (*gente*), like *seres humanos* because they will come back to you, and they are *your* patients. Now [here] those records would just become another file, pure paper, more of the paper with which we are engulfed.

His earlier career strategy to establish a private practice in the state capital and another in San Francisco was no longer mentioned; in fact, he informed several of us, "I will never set foot in San Francisco again in the role of physician." Further, the estrangement was reciprocated by the authorities and other townspeople. No longer did the President and Secretary seek Dr. Cruz out for casual conversation, and the number of patient visits dropped further still.

Indeed, during this period his patient registry showed no patients for a full week.

Analysis

To explain the estrangement and the formal charges against Dr. Cruz, one needs to return to the fundamental concerns of this community, those which led to its request for a physician in the first place. As was noted earlier, the issues which most preoccupy San Francisco's authorities are protection of the productive communal lands and ensuring a sufficient number of able-bodied males to perform *corvée* labor and fill positions in the system of *cargos*. The request for a physician was premised on the importance of strengthening local manpower by diminishing socially debilitating sickness, disability caused by accidents, and premature death. Bordered by larger and richer communities, *franciscanos* were constantly tormented by the fear that their able-bodied adult male population would shrink to the point that either they would prove unable to successfully defend their lands from outsiders or the state of Oaxaca would declare it insufficiently large to maintain its legal status as a separate municipality (*municipio libre*). Examples of other *municipios libres* which have lost their autonomous status and been reduced to *agencias*, dependencies of larger neighbors, are well known to *franciscanos*.

When Dr. Cruz proposed to extend medical coverage to San Felipe, he unwittingly raised the specter of strengthening that *municipio's* hand in the land conflict. The negative response to his proposal by the San Francisco authorities was neither capricious nor malicious; it was founded on the realistic fear that improvement in the health of San Felipe's citizens increased the threat to San Francisco's lands.

Opposition to Dr. Cruz's second proposal to extend medical care to San Francisco's own hamlets is somewhat more difficult to comprehend, but it, too, becomes more clear when seen contextually. The *municipio* of San Francisco is made up of the head town and all its outlying hamlets. Residents of the outlying settlements have traditionally served in public office and contributed *corvée* labor in the same way as the residents of the *cabecera* (Pérez Jiménez 1980). In recent years, however, some hamlets, in particular El Porvenir, have negotiated directly with state and federal agencies, obtaining improvements such as potable water, a primary school, boarding facilities for pupils and the loan of heavy land-moving machinery with which to open a road. Each of these successful negotiations has eroded the central authority of the head-town and increased the likelihood of hamlet secession, a realistic problem with many historical precedents (Bevan 1930: 20). The *municipio* authorities feared secession because it would mean not only the loss of productive agricultural lands but also the loss of a portion of the male adults desperately needed for *corvée* labor and for manning unsalaried municipal offices. The loss of these two assets would threaten the very viability of this community as a politically autonomous *municipio libre*.

Clearly, Dr. Cruz's ability to meet his quotas by extending his coverage of medical care in this severely underserved region was hampered by the socio-political problems of which he remained quite unaware. Caught between the often conflicting demands of his health service obligations and the political aspirations of San Francisco, his capacity to provide the level of care he had originally intended was severely diminished. His innovative efforts to increase the number of patients served, initially supported by his zonal supervisor, were made in isolation from the context in which the responses of the municipal leadership were deliberated and delivered. Greater understanding of how the townspeople weighed health care decisions among their other pressing concerns would have avoided Dr. Cruz's isolation and might have improved his quotas. In addition, it would have increased the likelihood of his establishing his own practice to provide additional health care to this underserved hinterland (cf. Habicht 1979: 70; Collado-Ardón 1983: 244), an uncommonly achieved goal of the *pasante* system.

This case study illustrates some unanticipated difficulties which affected a pasante's effort to provide primary care in a rural community. Those difficulties were socio-political in nature. Neither Dr. Cruz's personal background nor his medical education prepared him for these disruptive events. Moreover, the lecture material presented during the single orientation session which had been devoted to the history and customs of the indigenous communities of the region was insufficiently specific to prepare him for this experience. As Habicht has commented, based on his experience in rural Guatemala, "a curriculum to train community physicians would place more stress on socio-anthropology and community development than on cystic fibrosis and heart surgery" (Habicht 1979: 75). Certainly, if Dr. Cruz had been sensitized in medical school to how sociocultural factors could affect his clinical practice, and if his initial orientation as a *pasante* had provided information specific to San Francisco, his year of social service might have been less problematic.

Acknowledgements

This research was generously supported by the Instituto de Investigaciones Antropológicas, Universidad Nacional Autónoma de Mexico during my appointment as a Distinguished Visiting Researcher. I am indebted to Carole Browner for her constant, enthusiastic encouragement and help during the field work in San Francisco and in the preparation of this analysis from start to finish. I am happy to acknowledge my indebtedness to Frank Cancian, Rolando Collado-Ardón, Linda Hunt, Raymond Murray, Luis Alberto Vargas, and Dorothy Mull for many constructive comments and suggestions on several drafts of this paper. Remaining defects are solely the responsibility of the author.

Notes

1. Pseudonyms are provided communities and individuals to protect their privacy.

2. Indeed, these low figures from San Francisco are quite consonant with attendance reported from other rural *municipios* in Mexico. Tsu (1980: 146) reports her observations of rural health care in the state of Durango: "It appears that the central component of the rural health system, the village (or C-level) health centers, are being used only minimally by local residents, despite the presence of serious health problems . . . physicians sit idly much of the day in empty centers, few women seek regular prenatal or postpartum care, deliveries are rarely performed (although the centers have two or three beds for this purpose), and a relatively small proportion of eligible couples use any kind of contraception."

Similar observations are reported of rural primary care facilities in the states of Yucatan (Menéndez 1981: 290), and Michoacán (Wiest 1983: 178).

3. *Servicios Coordinados* has since been decentralized and is now a state, not a federal entity.

References

Ademuwagun, Z.A., J.A.A. Ayoade, D.M. Warren, and I. Harrison, eds. 1979. *African Therapeutic Systems*. Waltham, MA: Crossroads Press.

Azuni, T. 1979. The Dilemma of Traditional Healing with Special Reference to Nigeria. *Social Science and Medicine* 13:33-41.

Berman, P.A., D.R. Gwatkin, and S.E. Burger. 1987. Community-based Health Workers: Head Start or False Start Toward Health for All? *Social Science and Medicine* 25:443-459.

Bevan, Bernard. 1930. *The Chinantec: Report on the Central and South-eastern Chinantec Region*. Mexico City: Instituto Panamericano de Geografía e Historia.

Browner, C.H. 1986a. Gender Roles and Social Change: A Mexican Case Study. *Ethnology* XXV(2):89-106.

___. 1986b. The Politics of Reproduction in a Mexican Village. *Signs* 11:710-724.

Cancian, F. 1965. *Economics and Prestige in a Maya Community: The Religious Cargo System in Zinacantan*. Stanford: Stanford University Press.

Collado-Ardón, R. 1976. *Médicos y Estructura Social*. Archivo del Fondo #70. Mexico City: Fondo de Cultura Económica.

___. 1983. Perfil y Arraigo del Médico en el Medio Rural en México. *Educación Médica y Salud* 17(3):243-262.

Corbett, J.G. 1974. *The Context of Politics in a Mexican Community: A Study of Constraints on System Capacity*. Unpublished Ph.D. dissertation, Stanford University.

Dennis, P.A. 1987 *Intervillage Conflict in Oaxaca*. New Brunswick and London: Rutgers University Press.

Fulop, T., and M.I. Roemer. 1982. *International Development of Health Manpower*. WHO Offset Publication 61, Geneva.

Habicht, J-P. 1979. Assurance of Quality of the Provision of Primary Medical Care by Non-Professionals. *Social Science and Medicine* 13B(1):67-75.

Habicht, J-P, and Working Group on Rural Medical Care. 1973. *Delivery of Primary Care by Medical Auxiliaries: Techniques of Use and Analysis of Benefits Achieved in Some Rural Villages in Guatemala*. Pp. 96-108. Medical Care Auxiliaries (Scientific Publication #278). Washington, DC: Pan American Health Organization.

Irigoyen, R.F. 1974. *Cerocahui: Una Comunidad en la Tarahumara*. Mexico City: Universidad Nacional Autónoma de México.

Justice, J.W. 1978. Training Across Cultural Barriers: The Experience of the Indian Health Service with the Community Health Medic Training Program. In *Modern Medicine and Medical Anthropology in the United States-Mexico Border*. Boris Velimirovic, ed. (Scientific Publication #359) Washington, DC: Pan American Health Organization.

Kapur, R.L. 1979. The Role of Traditional Healers in Mental Health Care in Rural India. *Social Science and Medicine* 13B:27-31.

Kindig, D.A., and C.M. Taylor 1985. Growth in the International Physician Supply. *Journal of the American Medical Association* 253(21):3129-3132.

Krugman, R.D., E. Tabak, and G.E. Fryor, Jr. 1982. Effectiveness of the AHEC Concept in Colorado. *Journal of Medical Education* 57:87-90.

Laurell, A.C. 1977. Disease and Rural Development: A Sociological Analysis of Morbidity in Two Mexican Villages. *International Journal of Health Services* 7:401-423.

Mason, L. 1971. Effectiveness of Student Aid Programs Tied to a Service Commitment. *Journal of Medical Education* 46:575-583.

Mejía, A. 1980. World Trends in Health Manpower Development: A Review. *World Health Statistics Quarterly* 33:137.

Menéndez, E.L. 1981. *Poder, Estratificación y Salud*. Mexico City: Ediciones de la Casa Chata.

Musselwhite, J.C. 1981. *Public Policy, Development, and the Poor: Health Policy in Mexico*. Ann Arbor: University Microfilms International.

Pérez García, R. 1956. *La Sierra Juarez (Libro Segundo)*. Mexico City: Private edition.

Pérez Jiménez, G. 1980. *La Institución del Municipio Libre en México*. Mexico City: author's publication.

Roemer, M.I. 1987. Rural Healthcare: A Worldwide Issue. *Bulletin of the Pan American Health Organization* 21(3):326-333.

Rubel, A.J. 1976. Micropolitics in Oaxaca, Mexico. *Anthropological Quarterly* (Special Issue) 48(3):153.

Rubel, A.J., C.W. O'Nell, and R. Collado-Ardón. 1984. *Susto, A Folk Illness*. Berkeley and Los Angeles: University of California Press.

Spencer, D.L., and G. D'Elia. 1983. The Effect of Regional Medical Education on Physician Distribution in Illinois. *Journal of Medical Education* 58:309-315.

Tsu, V.D. 1980. Underutilization of Health Centers in Rural Mexico: A Qualitative Approach to Evaluation and Planning. *Studies in Family Planning* 11:145-153.

Velimirovic, B., and H. Velimirovic. 1978. The Utilization of Traditional Medicine and its Practitioners in Health Services: A Global Overview. In *Modern Medicine and Medical Anthropology in the United States-Mexico Border*. Boris Velimirovic, ed. (Scientific Publication #359) Pp. 172-185. Washington, DC: Pan American Health Organization.

Wiest, R.E. 1983. Male Migration, Machismo, and Conjugal Roles: Implications for Fertility Control in a Mexican Municipio. *Journal of Comparative Family Studies* XIV(2):167-181.

8

Using Anthropological Techniques in Program Design: Successful Nutrition Education in Indonesia

Marcia Griffiths

> I know what we should teach. The women need to know about balanced diets, and including nutrient-rich foods in their families' meals. They don't do this now because they say it's not their custom: if they only knew how important it is . . .

The attitude expressed in the above quotation continues to be espoused by many nutrition educators despite overwhelming evidence that merely giving people scientifically "correct" information is unlikely to influence their actual behavior (Zeitlin and Formación 1981; Berg 1987). Few would deny that changing feeding practices should be an important part of primary health care programming, given that: 1) infections associated with malnutrition are the main cause of child death in the developing world (Tomkins and Watson 1989) and 2) in most settings malnutrition is brought on by poor feeding practices as well as by limited resources. However, the tendency is for nutrition educators to continue to teach what they themselves were taught rather than to meld scientific principles with local perceptions and practices. Further, when educators do consult the intended audience (i.e. the people), they often rely on traditional KAP (knowledge, attitudes, and practices) interview techniques. The latter carry the interviewers' biases and usually yield only superficial data on beliefs, resources, and the actual reactions of families to changing their food habits. There are abundant examples of such inadequate research leading to inappropriate program decisions and ineffective nutritional intervention programs (Zeitlin and Formación 1981).

On the other hand, tremendous benefits can be realized by adopting an anthropological perspective and using social science research techniques during the different phases of a primary health care program (Salmen 1987). This is especially true for initial planning of primary health care programs and for deciding which media and messages to use in communications programs (Griffiths et al. 1981; Nichter and Nichter 1981; Booth and O'Gara 1985). However, some agencies have become disillusioned with anthropological research, viewing it as ethnographic research that requires an extensive time commitment and is too comprehensive to allow salient features to emerge that could easily be applied to program design. Of late, however, more and more anthropologists have been adapting and streamlining techniques to make them more useful and manageable for program development work (Scrimshaw and Hurtado 1987; Brown and Bentley 1988; Griffiths 1988; Griffiths et al. 1988). Some of these efforts draw on lessons learned during the project described below.

A nutrition education pilot project in Indonesia (1977-1982) demonstrated that when the intended beneficiaries are consulted using methods that emanate from anthropology, they themselves can make a major positive contribution to educational messages and strategies (Griffiths et al. 1980; Griffiths and Manoff 1980; Griffiths, Grady, and Cook 1980; Griffiths and Zeitlin 1983; Zeitlin et al. 1984). This reinforces the primary health care tenet that people can create their own programs. The Indonesia project's objective was to demonstrate that changes in nutritional status could result from education alone. The challenge was to produce messages that would address the most pressing nutrition problems facing rural people and would effectively motivate them to modify their food habits as often as three or four times a day. For this to happen, local perceptions, beliefs, and customs had to be well understood.

Project Background

In 1977, the project was begun in five subdistricts of three provinces: the Special Territory of Yogjakarta, Central Java, and South Sumatra. The total population of the area was about 225,000 living in 40,500 households. The project, directed by the head of the Ministry of Health's (MOH's) Center for Community Health Education, was one component of the Indonesian Nutrition Improvement Program funded with assistance from The World Bank.

The project developed in four stages. In the first, efforts focused on building an intersectoral team at each administrative level to ensure a common understanding of problems and approach and to define a specific function and role for each sector representative. The local teams had supervisory responsibilities and the authority to make implementation decisions. The project, preferring a community to a top-down orientation, adopted this structure to demonstrate that the role of the health service providers was to assist communities in discovering their *own* problems and then to help them obtain the tools to deal with them.

In the second stage, a community infrastructure was developed mirroring that of the national nutrition program simultaneously being put in place by the MOH Nutrition Directorate. About 2,000 volunteer nutrition workers, or ***kaders***, were selected by their communities, trained, and provided with equipment to begin a monthly weighing program that covered more than 52,000 children. The ***kaders*** were expected, eventually, to be responsible for much of the community education effort. Although they received no personal remuneration, each village had a small ***kader*** fund which they collectively decided how to spend. In some instances they bought bicycles for their work or purchased rabbits for a community project.

During the second phase, great attention was given to building a spirit of cooperation, to keeping the teams at each administrative level abreast of program decisions in the communities, and to ensuring that everyone was motivated and knew the goals of the project.

The third stage saw the development of the communications strategy. This included extensive research involving participation of families in the project areas, actual production of the materials, and finally, their dissemination.

The fourth stage was a time of continued project implementation and evaluation. The following pages focus on the third and fourth phases and describe in more detail how anthropological research techniques were used.

Developing the Communications Strategy

A review of available literature on nutrition practices in Indonesia indicated that while many beneficial and detrimental practices had been identified, little was known about the reasoning underlying those practices and how resistant the mothers were to change. Thus, from the outset, priority was given to anthropological research aimed at understanding mothers' thinking and motivation.

Before a research protocol was designed, a project advisory group helped to identify major nutrition problems and a potential communications infrastructure for message delivery. Problems included:

- protein-energy malnutrition in children zero to four months old (mothers' lactation practices);
- protein-energy malnutrition in children five to eight months old (introduction of solid food);
- protein-energy malnutrition in children nine to 24 months old (total food quantity);
- infant diarrhea;
- undernutrition of pregnant women;
- undernutrition of lactating women; and
- vitamin A deficiency in young children.

The advisory board felt that both interpersonal and mass media might be used. Nutrition volunteers were working in all project villages and might become strong face-to-face communicators. At the time, however, they were poorly trained and inclined to drop out of nutrition programs at a high rate. Radio was also promising. Most people owned radios, and coverage by the government-owned stations was good, although some communities did not receive strong signals. Privately owned stations did not reach far into the rural areas but were popular in communities closest to the town from which they transmitted.

Consumer Research

Methodology

Faced with a variety of nutrition problems and having little information on practices and virtually none on attitudes, the project team developed a highly qualitative, program-oriented, and inexpensive research methodology designed to identify the perceptions and expectations of mothers with well-nourished and malnourished infants. The goal was to identify positive changes mothers might make in feeding practices, to analyze mothers' possible resistance to making these changes, and to highlight their motivations for changing.

The investigation plan called for intensive work with a small sample of the project's intended beneficiaries. In each of the 5 subdistricts, 2 villages were selected, so that a total of 10 villages out of 60 in the project participated in designing the program. The steps in the investigative process were these:

1. The community conducted a "self-survey" (a technique taken from the pre-existing Indonesian primary health care program), which consisted of weighing all children and charting their weights on a single community graph. Children with signs of vitamin A deficiency and women with anemia were also identified.

2. A community meeting was held to discuss the self-survey results and to allow mothers and village leaders to suggest solutions to problems that had been identified. The meeting was also the forum to announce a plan for followup household investigations and to obtain the village leader's endorsement.

3. Central-level staff met and developed question guides for a variety of health problems based on the solutions that mothers and others had proposed to address each problem. Each question guide (not a questionnaire with precoded responses) was structured to stimulate discussion and to explore in great depth the experiences of mothers. It contained suggested lines of questioning and items for the investigators to probe. For example, the guide that focused on weaning included suggestions for probing about cooked and uncooked foods available in the home, food preparation techniques, availability and acceptability of suitable weaning foods that had been proposed at the community meeting, and feeding frequency and quantities.

4. In each of the three project provinces, a small investigation team was hired and trained in interview, participant-observation and structured observation techniques. All of the team members were women, and they all lived in the villages where they worked. They included social science and nursing students, midwives, and nutritionists; all could speak the local language. Those who completed the work most satisfactorily had high school training in home economics, worked in a provincial-level community program, and had children of their own.

5. In each village, the families for the investigation were selected to include a pregnant women, a nursing mother, a malnourished child, or a child with diarrhea, preferably under the age of two. (Village midwives, shopkeepers, health workers and officials also contributed their insights.)

6. Village volunteers helped the team to locate appropriate families. Once in the home, the investigator carried out the following procedures:

a) To double check the child's nutritional status, she weighed the infants to confirm that their classification from previous monthly weighing records was correct.

b) She used the question guide to cover one or two topics with the mother in an informal, leisurely manner, and she observed such things as the condition of the kitchen and water storage facilities. Whenever possible, the entire discussion was taped to spare the investigator extensive note-taking and to document the local language.

c) She spent part of the interview making an assessment of what the mother or baby had eaten in the previous 24 hours. (Using a precoded dietary recall sheet that had been designed by project leaders, investigators were quickly able to calculate whether the infant's or the mother's diet was deficient in protein, calories, or vitamin A.)

d) At this point, the interview departed significantly from the conventional household survey. Based on the age of the child and the outcome of the dietary recall for mother and child, the investigator worked out particular dietary changes with the mother that would improve her own or the child's nutrient intake. For example, the mother of a 6-month-old with an inadequate intake of major nutrients might be asked to suggest what she could add to her child's porridge that would be good for the baby's health and what she thought about several predetermined alternatives.

The investigator and the mother then worked together to develop a recipe for an enriched weaning food. Since team members did not follow a rigid format, they were able to start with the ingredients that the mother already had in the house, her methods for preparing foods, and her recipes, and then suggest that critical ingredients such as oil be added.

The mother fed the new food to her child while the investigator was there and she and the investigator discussed what she liked or disliked about the food.

e) Before leaving, the investigator promised to return in three or four days and asked the mother to continue to try whatever nutritional activity they had agreed upon. In the case of a weaning food, this involved giving the food to her child several times every day. In the case of iron supplements it meant taking the pills daily.

f) When the investigator returned, the mother usually had modified the activity or intervention (e.g. the weaning food recipe) to suit her own needs and had some comments or questions.

This opportunity for "product development"--for trial, adaptation, and retrial--in the mothers' homes was one of the most important elements of the methodology.

Insights from the Research Translate to Project Objectives

The interview data was analyzed by the field team as the study progressed so that the question guides could be adapted to probe new hypotheses and ideas. It was a dynamic, not a static process. At the end of the study, project personnel had a comprehensive picture of current attitudes and practices and of rural mothers' openness to altering them. Thus qualitative research provided the substance of the program. It drew on the trials of new practices for the behavior change objectives and on the mothers' remarks for the motivation elements in the messages.

It is this link between research and program that is so often missing. The valuable insights that anthropological research can offer primary health care programming are lost because the insights are not clearly and continuously stated for the program manager or because the researcher leaves the project before the activities are planned.

The Indonesia research offered many different kinds of insights important to planners. One type was the practices susceptible to change. For example, women routinely discarded colostrum because they thought it was dirty. This had been shown in other studies. The investigation made a novel finding, however: the belief was not firmly held. Many women thought the custom was old-fashioned and had heard of other women giving colostrum to their infants with no harmful effect. Modifying this behavior became a priority because it appeared so feasible.

A second type of insight was the need to alter a message thought of as "standard." For example, the breastfeeding message was changed from one stressing breastfeeding duration to one about using both breasts. In the rural areas of Indonesia where the project took place, almost all mothers breastfed through at least the child's first two years. Thus breastfeeding practices initially appeared to conform to medical guidelines and did not seem to merit special attention in the education campaign. However, after discussions with many mothers, it became clear that there was a problem because they complained that their infants cried often and that their hunger could not be satisfied with breastmilk. As a result, mothers felt compelled to feed the babies other liquids and solid foods such as banana soon after birth, with attendant contamination and nutrition problems. Further observation and discussion led to the finding that women in Java were primarily using the left breast to feed their infants and women in South Sumatra were primarily using the right breast. By the time the child was three or four months old, mothers complained that they had no milk in the unused breast. This practice, and brief feedings, seemed plausible explanations for the infants' apparent hunger.

Project staff advanced many hypotheses to account for the breast preferences, such as the way a woman's blouse (*kebaya*) unbuttoned and the taboo against using the left hand. Another explanation came from some Javanese health workers during a group interview: the left breast contained "food" and the right breast "water"; mothers offered the "food" before the "water." A baby who seemed content after being suckled at one breast was never offered the other. South Sumatran health workers reasoned along similar lines to explain why women there favored the right breast. The more abundant milk in the favored breast could have given rise to the mothers' belief that it was the more substantial nourishment ("food"); meanwhile, the lower milk output from the unused breast was to "finish" the feeding.

While this did not explain what originally prompted the favoring of one breast, it did explain why the mothers believed thcy should feed their infants in this way. The breastfeeding message subsequently developed focused on mothers' concern for their infants' satisfaction as a means of changing this undesirable practice: "Each time you breastfeed, use both the right and left breasts: be sure your child is satisfied."

The existing message about oral rehydration also proved inadequate in light of what was learned in the investigation. When mothers tried to make oral rehydration solution in their homes by following the nationally disseminated recipe, they were unable to do so correctly because they did not have the teaspoons the recipe called for to measure the ingredients. The mothers helped modify the mixing instructions so that they called for a tablespoon (which everyone had) to measure the sugar and a two-finger pinch to measure the salt.

A third type of insight gained from the research was the need for local adaptations of some of the recommended practices. Numerous trials showed that women in all subdistricts prepared weaning foods made of a remarkably similar combination of local ingredients. However, there was substantial regional variation in preparation methods, e.g. the way in which fats were incorporated in the weaning food. For example, in one area, oil was added to the porridge by frying *tahu* or *tempe* (fermented soybean foods) before they were mashed in the porridge; in another area, a few drops of coconut oil were added to cooked rice; and in another, the weaning food was cooked in coconut milk. Thus, messages on weaning were developed that reflected regional preferences in preparation techniques, not just ingredients.

Behavioral Objectives

Each of the behavioral objectives for the project reflected what was learned from the mothers during the initial research. After planners became aware of the mothers' practices vs. "ideal" practices, they then could recommend feasible but improved practices. The key project behaviors were:

Pregnant women:	Each day eat four plates of food, eat green vegetables four times, take an iron pill.
Lactating women:	Same as above, plus drink eight glasses of liquid per day.
Mothers of infants 0-4 months:	Breastfeed only, and use both breasts at each feeding.
Mothers of infants 5-8 months:	Breastfeed, using both breasts. Feed the baby *bubur campur* (enriched rice porridge) four times per day. Introduce this supplementary food patiently. (Recipes for *bubur campur* vary by region.)

Mothers of infants 9-24 months:	Give the child adult food four times per day, including *tahu*, *tempe*, or fish and green vegetables. Offer snacks between meals. Continue to breastfeed.
Mothers of children with diarrhea:	Give the child an oral rehydration mixture made with a two-finger pinch of salt, a tablespoon of sugar, and a glass of water. Continue to feed the child soft foods. (This message has special versions for cholera and non-cholera areas.)
All mothers of children under 5 years old:	Take the child for weighing every month. If the weight does not increase, s/he is not healthy, so seek advice and give her/him more food. Ask your *kader*, midwife, or the health center staff for nutrition advice.

Designing Media Strategy and Materials Based on Research Results

The first decision taken in planning the media strategy was that the principal audience for the messages, mothers, would be segmented according to their particular circumstance--the age of their child or their physiological state (see objectives above). This segmentation was done to avoid the common error of many educational primary health care programs in assuming that the audience is monolithic--that, for instance, all mothers are alike. The research clearly indicated that they were not. The mother of a 24-month old did not have the same concerns as a mother of a 4-month old. Why then, project designers reasoned, should the mother of a 4-month old be confused with information important to a mother of a 24-month old?

The challenge in designing the media strategy became how to deliver an audience-specific messages to each audience. Because so many *kaders* were deployed throughout the project area, they clearly had the potential to give the appropriate messages to each mother. Radio was also desirable because it was popular and because it could support the messages delivered by the *kaders* while encouraging people to seek advice from them and from health center staff. Thus, short radio dramas were written for the priority messages listed above, emphasizing how children of particular ages should be fed. The taped interviews with village women were consulted throughout the creation of the scripts, and the concerns, questions, and language of the women were used to explain the advice that was offered. The script on *bubur campur* (enriched rice porridge) illustrates the format. It emphasizes how to make *bubur campur* and addresses an often mentioned concern of mothers--the food's digestibility--as well as other "resistance points" encountered in the homes.

Spot #4: *Bubur Campur* -- Javanese Version

TUNE:	In, up.
SLOGAN:	Good Nutrition -- Healthy Child.
TUNE:	Up, out.
MOTHER I:	Hi, Bu. What's that you're making?
MOTHER II:	I'm making ***bubur campur*** for my child, Atik. She is 5 months old now. [Identification of child's age attracts attention of mothers with a child of similar age.]
MOTHER I:	That looks like a strange combination and a bother besides. [Resistance point.]
MOTHER II:	No, it's easy and cheap. [These characteristics are important to mothers.] Rice, green vegetables, *tahu* or *tempe*, and coconut milk.
MOTHER I:	But why?
MOTHER II:	To help my baby grow to be healthy and strong. [Benefit.]
MOTHER I:	A 5-month-old can digest these foods? [Resistance point.]
MOTHER II:	Yes, ask Bu Kader. [Reinforces *kader* prestige and builds morale.] The ingredients are well cooked and soft. The vegetables and *tahu* or *tempe* are mashed and cooked with the rice in coconut milk. [One of the alternative preparation methods.]
MOTHER I:	That's a lot together with breastfeeding.
MOTHER II:	Oh no. A 5-month-old needs this much food. And the breastfeeding should be from both breasts each time: not only from one. Breastmilk as before, and ***bubur campur*** four times a day. Otherwise, our children will not grow enough . . . but you are not listening.
MOTHER I:	I'm thinking. Breastfeeding from both breasts and ***bubur campur***--rice with well-cooked, mashed green vegetables and *tahu* or *tempe*, cooked with coconut milk. Are you sure of this? [Repeats principal points.]

MOTHER II:	Ask Bu Kader. She told me when I weighed my child at the weighing post. You should do that, too. If you need more information, you can ask the kader, the midwife, or the Health Center staff. [Reinforces authority of health personnel.]
MOTHER I:	Always new ideas these days.
MOTHER II:	Not always good ones like *bubur campur*!
SLOGAN:	Good Nutrition -- Healthy Child.
TUNE:	Up, out.

It was a challenge finding a material that could be used by the *kaders*, who were the mainstay of the communications effort. The material had to help ensure message consistency and also engage the families in the education. Again, insights gained from the anthropological research proved helpful. All the participants in the investigations had expressed enthusiasm for having something to display in their homes. Posters seemed the natural solution, but it was felt that they were too passive.

Finally, an experimental material called an "action poster" was developed. A poster was designed for each audience segment that depicted pictorially the action to be undertaken. Under the picture were boxes--one for each day of the month and one for each time of day the action was to be performed. At monthly growth monitoring sessions held in the villages, mothers were given these posters to take home to remind them what they would try to do for their child. The boxes were to serve as their own inventory of compliance. No one expected that mothers would mark the boxes every day. But each time a mother passed the poster with its empty spaces, she was prompted to think about the recommended practice and of her commitment to try it. Even if the boxes were only marked twice, that was proof that she had tried the practices since her contact with the *kader*.

Project Evaluation

After a year and a half of full project implementation, an evaluation was carried out. "Project" or nutrition education (NE) areas were compared to socioeconomically matched sub-districts and villages outside the project areas. It was found that, first, NE *kaders* scored higher in knowledge of nutrition and in their level of nutrition activity than the ***kaders*** they were compared to. Second, the project favorably influenced the *families*' nutrition-related knowledge, attitudes, and practices, and these changes in practices appeared to have resulted in improvements in nutritional status. The positive results of both the ***kader*** and the household evaluations indicated that the NE communications strategy could make other Indonesian community nutrition programs more effective.

A total of 1,000 households with either a nursing mother or a child less than 24 months old were involved in the evaluation: 600 in the project areas and 400 in the comparison areas. Evaluators looked at the mothers' participation in nutrition activities, their nutrition knowledge scores, the mothers' and children's consumption of key foods, their dietary intake of calories and protein, and the infants' nutritional status as measured by weight-for-age, height-for-age, and weight-for-height. NE household scores for each of these indicators were significantly better than those of comparison households.

To highlight the nature of the results, a few key indicators are summarized below:

1. Key Foods. Correlations between knowledge of nutritional messages and improved practices were high in the NE sample. The latter were measured through dietary recalls, which indicated that NE project children received more of the foods identified in the messages than comparison children.

2. Nutrient Intake. Mothers who were breastfeeding and children in the NE villages had higher protein and calorie intakes than comparison mothers and children. It was clear that the practices recommended in the messages had been implemented and had improved nutrient intake.

3. Nutritional Status. Children in the NE sample grew significantly better after five months of age than children in the comparison sample. The growth curve for infants in the NE sample flattened at seven months, while the curve for the comparison group infants flattened at five months. The mean weights for NE infants never fell below the normal zone, whereas the mean weights for infants in the comparison group dropped below the normal zone at the thirteenth month. The differences between the samples were significant ($p<.05$) at two and three months, at seven and eight months, and from 14 months onwards.

The average difference in weight between the NE and the comparison infants 17 through 24 months of age was slightly more than half a standard deviation. In other words, during the second half of the second year of life, about 20 percent more children in the NE sample had normal weight for their age. Furthermore, about 20 percent of the children whose growth was within the normal range had better growth status than comparison children whose growth was normal. Thus, 40 percent of the NE children had improved nutritional status. These differences were validated in each of the five areas evaluation was carried out.

4. Program Effect. Generally, the samples were similar on all measured socioeconomic indicators (e.g., occupation, education, mother's age, radio ownership, and money spent on food). Thus program participation explained most of the difference between groups. The project's effect was particularly pronounced in families where the mother had one to five years of education. In the comparison group, women with less formal schooling tended to know fewer nutrition facts and have a higher rate of malnutrition among their children than those with more schooling, but in the NE sample, these differences were virtually erased.

Implications for Anthropological Research

For social scientists involved in this type of work, there are several lessons to keep in mind:

- Be involved from the beginning of the program and try to stay involved when reports are written and research results are built into the program design. Otherwise, late in the design process a false interpretation of the data may lead to bad decisions that later may be blamed on the research.
- Do not let qualitative work that answers the question "why?" be lost to quantitative results or to people's desire to have numbers to describe the population. Literature reviews summarizing quantitative information are useful preludes to establishing qualitative research questions but are not sufficient in and of themselves.

- Listen carefully to the needs of the program managers so the research product will meet those needs. Limit the research scope to priority areas. Complete ethnographies, while interesting, are seldom useful in program planning. If, for example, kinship patterns could influence certain health care utilization patterns, explore these, but do not give a general description of the kinship patterns--give only their influence on utilization.

- Include a participatory phase in the research protocol. It is clear that in the research reported on here, the household trials were essential. Without them, hypotheses could not have been refined. In this project, the depth interviews, structured observations, and trials were done during the same visit to the household. In subsequent projects these activities were divided into two phases. First the depth interview and structured observations were done and later the household trials. Methodologically, this is neater and the interviewers have more time to plan appropriate and useful trials.

- Package results of the research in a way that is ready for program planners to pick out what they need. Listing the results under pertinent headings rather than writing out full paragraphs makes reading easier and quicker. At the end of each section of results there should be a "therefore" statement that shows the pertinence of the results to the program.

The success of this project demonstrates the value of properly researched and executed communications messages in nutrition education programs. It also underlines the importance of anthropological research methods in program design.

References

Berg, A. 1987 *Malnutrition: What Can Be Done?* Baltimore: The Johns Hopkins University Press.

Booth, E.M., and C. O'Gara 1985 Field Note 10: Percentages or Perspective: A Comparison of Quantitative and Qualitative Research. In *Field Notes*. Washington, DC: Agency for International Development.

Brown, K.H., and M.E. Bentley 1988 *Improved Nutritional Therapy of Diarrhea: A Guide for Planners and Decision Makers involved in CDD Programs*. Arlington, VA: PRITECH.

Griffiths, M. 1988 Improving Infant Feeding Practices by Social Marketing Methods. A paper prepared for the World Health Organization Ad Hoc

Scientific meeting, Improving Infant Feeding Practices to Prevent Diarrhea or Reduce Its Severity -- Research Issues at Johns Hopkins University, April 25-28.

Griffiths, M., T. Cook, R.K. Manoff, and M. Zeitlin 1981 A Case for an Anthropological Perspective in Nutrition Education Materials Design. Presented at the International Congress of Nutrition, San Diego, August.

Griffiths, M., E. Piwoz, M. Favin, and J. Del Rosso 1988 *Improving Young Child Feeding During Diarrhea: A Guide For Investigators and Program Managers*. Arlington, VA: PRITECH.

Griffiths, M., T. Cook, M. Zeitlin, and R. Manoff 1980 *Nutrition Communication and Behavior Change Component, Indonesian Nutrition Development Program: Volume I. Concept Testing*. Washington, DC: Manoff International.

Griffiths, M., and R. Manoff 1980 *Nutrition Communication and Behavior Change Component, Indonesian Nutrition Development Program: Volume II. Communications Strategy*. Washington, DC: Manoff International.

Griffiths, M., R. Grady, and T. Cook 1980 *Nutrition Communication and Behavior Change Component, Indonesian Nutrition Development Program: Volume III. Materials Pretesting*. Washington, DC: Manoff International.

Griffiths, M., and M. Zeitlin 1983 *Nutrition Communication and Behavior Change Component, Indonesian Nutrition Development Program: Volume V. Kader Evaluation*. Washington, DC: Manoff International.

Nichter, M., and M. Nichter 1981 *An Anthropological Approach to Nutrition Education*. Newton, MA: Educational Development Center.

Salmen, L.F. 1987 *Listen To The People*. New York: Oxford University Press.

Scrimshaw, S., and E. Hurtado 1987 *Rapid Assessment Procedures for Nutrition and Primary Health Care*. Los Angeles: UCLA Latin American Center and United Nations University.

Tomkins, A., and F. Watson 1989 *Malnutrition and Infection*. Lavenham, Suffolk: Lavenham Press Ltd.

Zeitlin, M.F., and C.S. Formación 1981 Study II: Nutrition Education. In *Nutrition Interventions in Developing Countries*. Cambridge: Oelgeschlager, Gunn and Hain.

Zeitlin, M., M. Griffiths, and R. Manoff 1984 *Nutrition Communication and Behavior Change Component, Indonesian Nutrition Development Program: Volume IV. Household Evaluation*. Washington, DC: Manoff International.

IV

ETHNOMEDICAL MODELS

One of the important consequences of anthropological research on primary health care has been the recognition of the value of ethnomedical studies focused on particular health problems. By structuring research around a defined illness, health practice or set of related problems, ethnographic research can reveal important relationships between cultural belief systems and health behavior which often have significant implications for program planning and patient care. While anthropological interest in popular models of illness is not new, what sets apart recent research in this area is the ability to move directly from a set of findings into specific, pragmatic applications that command the attention of decision-makers and sometimes redirect health policy. Moreover, large numbers of studies are increasingly being conducted on a single health problem in different societies. This makes cross-cultural comparisons possible and reveals general patterns of belief and behavior from which new theoretical insights can be drawn.

A good example of these developments is furnished by the large number of anthropological studies on diarrheal illness that have been carried out in recent years. We now know a great deal about how people construct and label illness associated with excessive stool loss, how they conceive its causes and physiology, and how they arrive at decisions about diagnosing and treating it. Probably more than for any other health problem, anthropologists have documented for diarrhea that one cannot equate biomedical notions of illness with folk concepts, and that failure to take account of ethnomedical context can devastate an otherwise well-planned intervention. Kendall's chapter synthesizes this diverse literature by examining components of diarrheal disease explanatory models and aspects of the help-seeking process. His review highlights recurrent patterns in the cultural construction of a set of related illnesses. Going a step further, Kendall shows how the study of home management of diarrhea enlarges our understanding of the domestic (as opposed to public) domain of health care, an insight that will undoubtedly stimulate further discussion.

In Nichter's chapter, the focus is on a particular health intervention, immunization programs in India and Sri Lanka, and the main argument centers on the inappropriateness of the currently dominant military metaphor of vaccination campaigns in light of popular conceptions about how vaccines work. Not only does the military metaphor create unnecessary mystification and false expectations, which can negatively impact program goals for utilization and coverage, it subtly reinforces the social control and unequal power relations based on uneven distribution of knowledge, a problem the author terms "communication underdevelopment." A better approach, Nichter argues, would be one based on a convergence model of negotiated meaning, shared understandings, and communication processes adapted to local belief structures.

The third chapter in this section is distinct in being the only one in this volume dealing with an industrialized nation in the western hemisphere. Heurtin-Roberts and Reisin examine patients' explanatory models of hypertension in a southern U.S. city, showing how the lack of congruence with providers' biomedical model of the disease has significant repercussions for treatment outcome. Although the disease in question is a chronic disorder more closely associated with the health problems of industrialized countries, many of the same issues regarding delivery of primary health care in less developed countries are relevant in this context as well. The authors present data which demonstrate that patients who hold explanatory models of hypertension that are very different from the biomedical view are significantly less likely to follow prescribed therapeutic regimens and maintain their blood pressure under control when compared with patients whose beliefs are more similar to those held by physicians.

Taken together, these three chapters suggest that whether the problem is diarrhea, immunizations, or hypertension, understanding of ethnomedical models is vital to the success of primary health care.

9

Public Health and the Domestic Domain: Lessons from Anthropological Research on Diarrheal Diseases

Carl Kendall

Introduction

The relationship between the biological substratum and the social and cultural milieu has long been a central focus of anthropology. Medical anthropology has focused on a portion of this relationship, the relationship between disease and the cultural construction and treatment of illness. Medical anthropologists have, for the most part, focused on the diversity of responses to generic disease and the definitions of health and illness. When generalizations are drawn from different cultures, they usually identify similarities in human approaches to organizing ill health, such as the sick role, the identification of therapy managing units, the search for appreciable causes, and other features irrespective of specific disease. Rarely has the opportunity presented itself to focus on one unique disease in different cultural contexts.

Our ability to attempt comparative analyses has been limited by the quality of information available on disease in different societies and by problems in defining similar disease categories for valid comparison. On the one hand, when the medical community focused on diseases of the tropics, it targeted diseases relatively uncommon in Europe and North America at that time--e.g. yellow fever, malaria, onchocerciasis--that threatened visitors to tropical areas and constituted new disease entities for cosmopolitan medicine. On the other hand, ethnographers, perhaps in an effort to elevate their subjects in the eyes of their readers, tended to gloss over the common infectious diseases and high mortality of the societies they studied and focused on the intricacies of kinship, social organization, and ritual.

Increasing interest in international health and primary health care over the past twenty years, reflected in the programs of the World Health Organization and international development agencies, however, coupled with a growing interest in applied and collaborative anthropology, provide a valuable opportunity to make systematic cross-cultural comparisons of at least diarrheal disease. The significance of comparative research in this area is twofold. First, a major multinational effort, coordinated by the Diarrheal Diseases Control Programme, World Health Organization, UNICEF, USAID and other donors, is currently underway to reach underserved populations with ORS and diarrheal prevention strategies such as breastfeeding and improved weaning foods, providing an opportunity for the application of anthropological research in this effort to improve health in the developing world. Secondly, the number of anthropologists engaged in studying health is growing.

A growing literature documents that the study of diarrheal diseases does offer important insights into the organization of health, community, and culture. But the long preamble that constitutes the introduction to this chapter is a way of recognizing the discomfort felt by researchers in both public health and anthropology with the limitations of this approach. Some feel that providing documentation of successful integration of anthropology in public health programs, or ethnographic accounts of program failure, does not resolve the inherent difficulties facing public health programs, on the one hand, or contribute significantly to anthropological theory, on the other. This chapter is an effort to address both of these concerns.

Diarrheal diseases along with a small number of other diseases, such as the group of diseases glossed as acute respiratory infection, present exceptional opportunities for comparative research. Diarrheal diseases are extremely common in the young in households, and are so closely related to living conditions that their severity and incidence constitute a physical marker of the social and economic status of the household.

Diarrheal Disease

Acute diarrhea is the leading cause of death worldwide in children under the age of four (Snyder 1982; Puffer and Serrano 1973) and is a major factor in undernutrition (Scrimshaw et al.

1968). The Diarrheal Diseases Control (CDD) Program of the World Health Organization, in an exercise designed to identify treatable episodes of diarrhea, estimates that there are 1.8 billion episodes of diarrheal disease in the world (excluding China) in children less than five years of age each year.

The association between faltering growth and diarrheal episodes has been well established (Behar 1975; Black et al. 1984; Condon-Paoloni et al. 1977; Martorell et al. 1975). Nutritional consequences of diarrheal episodes are due to a number of factors: food withholding (Scrimshaw and Hurtado 1988); anorexia (Martorell et al. 1980) and vomiting during episodes; metabolic costs of infection; and other factors. Faltering growth follows reduced consumption and malabsorption during and after the diarrheal episode. This or any malnutrition, acute or even marginal, may increase the likelihood of reinfection, thus perpetuating the disease cycle. Although early in the development of programs to control diarrheal disease it was felt that acute dehydrating watery diarrheas were responsible for the majority of deaths, it is increasingly recognized that many children who die suffer repeated episodes of diarrhea over a prolonged period and suffer profound malnutrition.

The environmental conditions prevalent in most developing countries facilitate the transmission of diarrheal pathogens. Although improvements in many of these conditions must await substantial investment in the health sector and general socioeconomic growth, advances in medicine, health behavior research, and public health communications make possible the development of specific interventions to reduce the diarrheal disease burden now--particularly in children for whom diarrheal episodes have very serious consequences.

Deaths due to dehydration resulting from diarrhea can be controlled by administering a special oral rehydration solution and a massive worldwide program has been undertaken by UNICEF, WHO, AID, and other donors to provide this solution to children. As some have noted (Nations and Rebhun 1988), however, a certain commodity fetishism characterizes donor emphasis on this solution. ORS must be complemented by nutrition enhancement and disease prevention activities. A recent review of preventive interventions by the Diarrheal Diseases Control Program of the WHO identified four such interventions that are likely to be cost-effective: promoting breastfeeding, improving weaning practices, improving water supply and sanitation, and promoting personal hygiene.

The etiologies of diarrheal diseases are now fairly well known. Although as recently as 20 years ago only 30% of diarrheal pathogens could be identified, today, nearly 80% of diarrheal episodes can be associated with a pathogen. Although there are outbreaks of diarrheal diseases caused by uncommon agents, the majority of diarrheal diseases can be attributed to just a few--principally rotavirus and enterotoxigenic *E. coli.* The course of illness is, of course, affected by more than the agent. Previous condition of the child, parental financial and health-seeking resources, and concurrent illness all play a role. The relationship of the social and cultural response to the cause and the course of this illness constitutes an important question for the methods of cross-cultural research, i.e., a plausible argument can now be made for certain cross-cultural generalizations, at least for the simplest episodes.

A major impetus for this research has been the commitment to primary health care of the World Health Organization and the Declaration of Alma-Ata. This commitment involves a distinctly interdisciplinary and intersectoral approach to "health." On the one hand, the declaration calls for economic and social development to achieve improved health and on the other it calls for "essential health care based on practical, scientifically sound, and socially acceptable methods and technology made universally accessible to individuals and families in the community through their full participation" (World Health Organization 1978: Section VI). The former concern arises from critiques of the impact of curative medicine, exemplified in works such as Djurfeldt and Lindberg's sharply critical study of the opening of a rural health clinic in Thaiyur Panchayat, Tamil Nadu, India (Djurfeldt et al. 1975), in the Rockefeller Foundation Conference Report "Good Health at Low Cost" (Halstead et al. 1985), and in dissatisfaction with Walsh and Warren's Selective Primary Health Care (Berman 1986; Briscoe et al. 1985; Kendall 1988; Rifkin and Walt 1986).[1] Anthropologists would appear to play an important role in this debate, since they usually present a community-level perspective and address the many interests that need "integrating."

A Brief History of Anthropological Interest

Anthropological participation in this applied program marks a welcome development, one in which anthropologists participate as members of multidisciplinary research teams. At the same time, efforts to describe local responses to one of the world's most common diseases offer a challenge to anthropological and other social science theory.

Diarrheal diseases and other common maladies are found mentioned in the monographs and field notes of anthropologists everywhere, but they did not become a focus of research until water and sanitation and other health programs gained prominence after World War II.

Paul's *Health, Culture and Community* contains articles, such as Edward Wellin's "Water Boiling in a Peruvian Town" (Wellin 1955b) that are classics of applied anthropology. Erasmus (Erasmus 1952) is another precursor. Early nutrition surveys and reports such as Wellin's "Maternal and Infant Feeding Practices in a Peruvian Village" (Wellin 1955a), R.N. Adams' work with INCAP (Adams 1957), Nancy Solien Gonzalez's work in Guatemala (Gonzalez 1963), and Cosminsky and Scrimshaw's work on medical pluralism (Cosminsky and Scrimshaw 1975) are precursors of much of this research. The nutritional anthropology literature has played a seminal role in this involvement. Since 1979 and the development of the Diarrheal Diseases Control Programme, anthropologists such as Bentley (Bentley et al. 1988), Coreil (Coreil and Genece 1988; Coreil and Mull 1988; Coreil 1988), Nations (Nations et al. 1984), Nichter (Nichter 1988, 1989), Scrimshaw (Scrimshaw and Hurtado 1987, 1988), myself (Kendall et al. 1984; Kendall 1985, 1988, 1989), and others (Baer and Ackerman 1988; Early 1983; Green 1986; Green and Mokhubu 1984; Trotter 1985, for example) have contributed to this literature.

Categorizing the Literature

The largest group of articles are those produced by public health scientists about "beliefs and practices" related to diarrheal disease. This information is drawn from anecdotal sources occasionally provided by a developing country author or from surveys that have incorporated items about beliefs and practices. (Bersh 1985; Bertrand and Walmus 1983; Brieseman 1984; Chen 1971; Epling and Siliga 1967; Faruque et al. 1985; Holdsworth 1975; Imperato 1974; Johnson 1979; Kielmann and McCord 1977; Maina-Ahlberg 1979; Shahid et al. 1983) A second set of analyses are the product of anthropological investigations directed toward diarrheal disease (Nations 1982; Kendall 1985; Bentley 1985) based on relatively lengthy fieldwork. These works focus primarily on the delivery of health services. Finally, a third set of studies are reports produced by medical scientists using anthropological methods that are the product of relatively short-term research for applied purposes (Escobar et al. 1983; Hurtado 1979; Lozoff et al. 1975; Yusuf et al. 1984; de Zoysa et al. 1984b) and by anthropologists using "rapid assessment techniques" (Scrimshaw and Hurtado 1987; Sachar et al.

1985; Bentley et al. 1988). A larger and growing literature in this area remains mostly unpublished (e.g. Vandale, 1978; Vielman and Hurtado 1985; Vielman 1986; Villatoro and Hurtado 1986). Several excellent reviews have also appeared (Weiss 1988; Levine 1990).

An interesting characteristic of many of these articles is the fact that little in the way of substantial theory, whether in anthropology or in related social sciences such as demography and economics, has been tapped. This article will demonstrate the relevance of theories in medical anthropology to the study of diarrheal diseases. In addition, these studies are subject to a number of specific criticisms. The knowledge, attitudes, and practices (KAP) approach embodied in many of the first set of surveys has been well criticized from different perspectives.[2] In addition, these articles, for the most part, accept an implicit biomedical definition of diarrheal disease. Anthropological studies reviewed here have been criticized for an overly narrow focus, and rapid assessment techniques have been faulted for poor execution and for generating apparently anomalous findings. Given these caveats, a review of current knowledge and issues follows.

Findings

Recognition and Labeling: Simple and Complicated Episodes

An early discovery was the existence of local differentiation of diarrheal episodes into simple and complicated categories of illness. Lozoff (Lozoff et al. 1975) anticipates much of the interest in this area. In India, *behdi*, or diarrhea which is treated through "dietary manipulation" and cosmopolitan medicine, is differentiated from *dosham*, a named syndrome associated with diarrhea, vomiting, sunken eyes, and sunken fontanelles. Lozoff realizes that these named illness complexes have determined courses of treatment, and that diagnosis and treatment of *dosham* entail a complex elaborated folk etiology and course of therapy. Lozoff also notes that simple diarrhea is explained by non-cosmopolitan means, even if cosmopolitan therapy is utilized.

The specifics of local systems of labeling diarrheal illness are reported in other sources. For example, de Zoysa and her colleagues (de Zoysa et al. 1984a, 1984b), utilizing a KAP approach in a study of diarrheal diseases in Zimbabwe, found a distinction between "physical" causes and "spiritual" causes of disease, and the same willingness to utilize cosmopolitan resources for diarrhea produced by physical causes. A review of notes from household interviews showed that a total of forty-five events or conditions were named as causes of diarrhea. These responses are recorded into two categories, "physical" and "spiritual." The authors note that "perceived cause was the only significant predictor for the utilization of the formal health services" (de Zoysa et al. 1984b: 733).

The finding that diarrhea is often compartmentalized into secular or "physical" causes and "spiritual" ones is repeated throughout the literature. In Honduras simple uncomplicated episodes of disease (perceived as disease or signs) are differentiated from complicated episodes. The former are amenable to home, pharmacy, and clinic therapy. This finding will probably be repeated for all common diseases and may be a uniform pragmatic response to illness.

Scrimshaw and Hurtado's (1987, 1988) studies in Central America used an anthropological rapid assessment technique, providing a uniform set of research guides and training to non-professional research staff. These investigations confirmed a distinction between simple and complicated episodes of diarrheal diseases. For example, four studies in El Salvador (Bonilla et al. 1987a-d) revealed a common distinction between "light" diarrhea and serious diarrhea (*diarrea suave o pasajera / diarrea grave o peligrosa*). In Yuscarán, Honduras, country people differentiated simple episodes of diarrhea from a group of named diarrheal diseases considered more serious (Kendall 1985; Kendall et al. 1984; Kendall 1988). Similar results are reported from India and Bangladesh (Bentley 1985; Green 1986). In Honduras, cases attributed to one illness involving diarrhea--*empacho*--were not treated with ORS at all (Kendall 1985).

A second issue is the differentiation of a normal state from an illness episode. Numerous accounts report the presence of loose stools in children without a corresponding diagnosis of diarrhea by the community. Especially when diarrhea accompanies significant life events in children, illness may not be diagnosed (Kendall 1985; Kendall et al. 1984).

The importance of the categorization into simple and complicated episodes arises because complicated episodes are often not treated with cosmopolitan interventions (cf. Kendall et al. 1984). As is the case in much public health literature, these categories are not indigenous ones but those imposed by researchers. The risk here is that researchers will now "find" this distinction elsewhere. The new "folk etic" created in these studies often threatens to distort local variation. Furthermore, more in-depth analysis might permit relating many of these named causes. De Zoyza et al. note these difficulties:

> Clearly, the information reported here needs to be validated by in-depth studies using more rigorous techniques: classic anthropological methods for the study of belief systems on health and disease and quantified epidemiological surveys for the collection of health service utilization data (de Zoysa et al. 1984b: 733).

Etiologic Concepts

The articles cited in the section above also demonstrate that diarrheal disease is identified at the local level as a number of named entities. In Honduras, diarrheal diseases included evil eye (*ojo*), fallen fontanelle (*caída de mollera*), indigestion (*empacho*), and worms (*lombrices*) (Kendall et al. 1984). In El Salvador investigators reported *ojo, susto, empacho, infeccion, lombrices, colerín* (excess of choleric humor), *disintería*, and *mollera caída* (Bonilla et al. 1987a-d). Coreil (Coreil 1988) reports worms (*ve*), indigestion or swelling (*gonfleman*), fallen fontanelles (*tet fann*), and evil eye (*maldyok*) as named illness categories in Montrouis, Haiti. Coreil also notes that several ethnophysiological processes are attributed as causes of diarrheal episodes, such as spoiled mother's milk (*let gate*), and teething (*dentisyon*). Allman and Allman note for Port-au-Prince:

> In Haitian Creole the words *vant lib, vant mennen, dyare, vant kondwi*, and *vant pase* are used to refer to liquid stools. When stools contain blood, the condition is referred to as *kolorin* and when vomiting (*vomisman*) occurs it is called *anterit* (1986: 14).

These researchers also list sex while breastfeeding, breastfeeding during pregnancy, fontanelle disease (*tet ouve*), evil eye (*maldyok*), contact between a newborn and a menstruating woman, and bad air (*move se*) as causes of diarrhea. But the names used to describe diarrhea or its causes can at times refer to a named illness, at times to a symptom. As Allman and Allman perceptively note:

> Diarrhea is not always viewed as a disease itself, but can be considered a symptom of another disease. For example it is seen as accompanying stomach aches, swelling (*gonfleman*) and *tet ouve* or fontanelle disease. This was learned in studying the most common infant and child illnesses, and was not referred to often when questions on diarrhea were asked directly. . . . Similarly, evoking supernatural causes for a diarrhea episode was rare and generally came up in regard to cases where the disease was not treated adequately and the child died (1986: 15).

The difficulty demonstrated exists here at two levels. First, *diarrhea* as a cosmopolitan portmanteau word used in clinics worldwide is not well defined, but is widely used. Epidemiologic research has often adopted an arbitrary definition, such as three or more loose stools a day, but a normal breastfed infant without disease may have even more than that. Other studies beg the question and adopt mothers' definitions, although they do not spell out what those definitions are. At the second level, the issue is the definition of a folk illness. Rarely have the appropriate analyses been conducted to carefully distinguish named illnesses, symptoms and signs. This is of great importance for survey research, both for designing a questionnaire and for the coding of responses. If *gonfleman* is a kind of diarrhea, as that term is used in the medical community, but one not elicited when asking about diarrhea as that term is used in the vernacular, it is easy to see why the disease and its treatment are might be underreported. Biomedical researchers and anthropologists have committed this nominalist fallacy in pursuit of cross-cultural research. This error has consequences for therapy, since as Allman and others have noted, these "non-diarrhea" diarrheal diseases may be the most serious.

Green (1986) illustrates another problem of the use of survey research. When Green inquired about the types of diarrhea in a purposive sample of 240 rural and urban Bangladeshi households, he found that

> 74% of respondents mentioned general, plain, ordinary or simple diarrhea: 63% mentioned diarrhea accompanied by continuous vomiting and weakness (5% of this group used the English term 'cholera' for this type); 30% mentioned bloody diarrhea or bloody dysentery (*amashaya* in Bangla); and 28% mentioned greenish or yellowish diarrhea or diarrhea with mucus (sometimes called *buniaga*). (Multiple responses were allowed for all questions in which response categories were not mutually exclusive.) Less frequently cited were diarrhea with weakness (but no mention of vomiting) (12%); stomach ache (8%); diarrhea with fever (4%); diarrhea with worms (3%); and diarrhea associated with teething in young children (1%) (Green 1986: 359).

Green had conducted research funded by a USAID social marketing project, and had followed accepted practice in survey research for marketing and health communications. This survey item was used to confirm results of earlier in-depth interviews. Although one may find significance in the fact that 16% of informants did not consider loose stools as diarrhea, it is difficult to imagine how to interpret the distribution of these numbers, and Green liberally includes caveats in his report such as the following:

> It should be kept in mind that respondents may feel constrained to mention mystical causes to better educated strangers in the context of an impersonal interview and that villagers tend to tell interviewers what they think the interviewers want to hear. . . . Answers to a single direct question on diarrhea treatment can be misleading. (1986: 359)

The clash of scientific cultures here is obvious, as is the argument concerning quantitative and qualitative research, although it bears repeating. Surveys are not an appropriate research tool for the analysis of semantic domains. To establish the provenance of these diarrheal illnesses, and the use of the word "diarrhea," anthropological methods and a range of other grounded research techniques are needed.[3]

Despite the diversity of local terminology related to diarrheal disease, comparative analysis reveals important commonalities across cultures. Among the reasons for this are the shared regional systems of health care such as the Galenic, Ayurvedic and Unani.

Regional Health Systems and Their Impact on Diarrheal Disease

Many studies cite the importance of the hot-cold distinction used in India and Latin America (Coreil and Genece 1988; Escobar et al. 1983; Kendall 1985; Kendall et al. 1984; Kumar et al. 1985; Lozoff et al. 1975; Vielman 1986; Kielmann and McCord 1977), the ethnophysiology of digestion (Bonilla et al. 1987a-d); Kendall 1985; Vandale 1978; Vielman and Hurtado 1985; Escobar et al. 1983), and common therapeutic measures such as purgatives (Escobar et al. 1983; Kendall et al. 1984; Trotter 1985) and fasting (Kendall 1985).

The hot-cold distinction refers to a classification of matter and energy, including humans. Kumar and associates (1981, 1985) note that, in India, excessive heat in the body is thought to produce diarrhea, and in many parts of the world, diarrhea accompanied by blood is attributed to heat. [See Mull and Mull, Chapter 14--Eds.]Coreil and Genece (1988) identify heat as a perceived cause of diarrhea in Haiti. On the other hand, other studies report that excessive cold can cause diarrhea. Such cultural variation has led many health authorities to be skeptical of this information, assuming that there is great local and individual variation as well as condemning such "unscientific" beliefs as irrational (Kumar 1984; Kumar et al. 1981, 1985). Here, of course, researchers may be conjoining or confusing different illnesses when discussing "diarrhea." In addition, knowledge of regional medical systems and their common elements provides much of the information needed to resolve apparent conflicts. Many of these regional medical systems have fallen into disuse and may be incompletely known, and limited knowledge of, for example, the hot-cold system may generate false classifications of hot-cold diseases (see Tedlock 1987). Much of this confusion can be resolved by recourse to an underlying explanatory model (Kleinman 1980) of the illness episode.

Commonly, a distinction is made between folk, traditional and cosmopolitan medical systems. Differentiation of these systems is often difficult. Working in a small community, different health system practices become part of the local explanatory model. However, many of these explanatory models partake of archaic regional systems. This is the case in Honduras. The foundation of many beliefs is humoral physiopathology or humoral medicine, which can be traced from the traditions reported by Galen, through Arabic Unani medicine to Spain, and from there to the New World.

Humors, hypothesized as essential components of the body, are based on four elements--earth, air, fire, and water--thought to be the essential components of matter. The four elements can be arranged in a two-by-two table to demonstrate their essential properties of relative moistness and relative heat. The four humors that constitute the body share these properties, as do all material objects. Local conditions such as temperature or dampness give to each person a specific preponderance of a single humor, which accounts for their personality.

These formulaic recipes for explaining misfortune are readily adaptable to new situations and many of the varieties of diarrhea disease reported in the literature can be linked through application of these underlying models. Regional and local variations exist, of course, and these beliefs are now syncretic with contemporary medical beliefs. However, since many of these beliefs aptly describe symptoms, concern social, especially household, regulation, and are closely linked to other beliefs within the culture, they are unlikely to disappear. The following sections explore these models as an example of how ethnographic research can resolve these apparent contradictions.

Ethnophysiology of Digestion

In El Salvador rapid ethnographic assessment provided the following model of digestion (freely translated):

> In the stomach, food is cooked (*se cuecen los alimentos*) and therefore the stomach has to stay warm. When the climate turns cool, the stomach

> gets cold, letting food leave the stomach undigested. If you eat food with cold properties during the cold season you can also get stomach problems. Food which is considered cold, even though heated in the fire, always maintains this property. Tamales, beef or pork consommé and chicken soup are all considered cold food. In addition to these foods cucumbers and tomatoes are cool. The outside surface of the bean sticks in the stomach and for this reason it is not recommended to give children beans at nighttime, because the night is cold and the food is cold, thereby making the child sick (Bonilla et al 1987a: 12).

Both excess cold and excess heat can upset this system, and specific diseases and specific therapies have different properties. The question, "Is diarrhea a hot or a cold disease?" therefore is meaningless.

In addition to hot and cold, diarrhea caused by worms has been reported in several geographic areas. In Honduras, worms were considered an essential part of digestion, living as symbiotes in a sac just under the stomach. Worms are thought to aid the digestive process but could become dangerous if not fed regularly and appropriately or if mechanically disturbed (cf. Nichter 1988). Maina-Ahlberg (1979) discusses belief in a "big worm" in the belly which, if disturbed, causes diarrhea.

However, although few biomedical practitioners doubt their clients when they report worm-caused diarrhea, the multiple explanatory models are quite diverse. In Honduras, the worms are symbiotes of the gut living in a compartmentalized stomach (q.v. Kendall et al. 1984). They are associated by Hondurans with roundworms. The "big worm" may be associated in Africa with a belief in a spiritual serpent in the abdomen that is the seat of personal power. Finally, "worms," in a biomedical sense, are not a significant cause of diarrhea.

Of course, both intracommunity and intercommunity knowledge of these causes and processes varies. However, what is essential is not the fact that the statement "an apple is a cold food" can be applied everywhere, but rather that (1) this classification system has significance for diarrheal disease etiology in many parts of the world, and (2) the process of discovering and deciphering these attributes can be uniformly applied in societies which recognize these regional systems. Additional research needs to be conducted on alternate and regional health systems in order to guide the extension of primary health care coverage activities. This research will help resolve much of the apparent heterogeneity of responses.

Treatment

Almost all articles in the literature reviewed have comments on treatment, since the introduction of a new therapy, ORS, was the impetus for research. Deciphering information here is difficult, since researchers seldom take pains to describe the sequence of recourse to cure, the multiple therapies, and the diarrheal disease being treated. My review of the literature here is illustrative rather than exhaustive.

Nations (1982) provides a compact account of recourse to care from her work in Fortaleza, Brazil. Home remedies, store-bought remedies, traditional healers, and pharmacists were all considered appropriate. After eight days of illness, community health leaders, rehydration centers, doctors, and the hospital were deemed appropriate. In other areas, reported sources of care included midwives, herbalists, masseurs, injectionists, shamans, shopkeepers, pharmacists, nurses, and doctors.

Medicines used for diarrhea include a wide number of herbs. Mint tea is widely used throughout Latin America, as are *ruda*, tobacco, and other plants (see Bonilla et al 1987). Coreil (1988) reports the common use of guava leaves in Haiti, along with numerous other kinds of herbal teas. Medicines are often taken as infusions, which provides health workers with an opportunity to promote the use of these remedies in the home as adjunct therapies with ORS.

Local treatment often entails dietary manipulation, and foods ingested are carefully controlled. In Lima, for example, mothers report withholding solid food from evening meals when diarrhea strikes or as a prophylactic measure to prevent diarrhea.

A subset of articles deal with potentially dangerous therapies (Ackerman 1983; Ackerman et al. 1982; Trotter 1985) such as *azarcón* and *greta*, poisons used as purgatives. The use of purgatives in general is widespread, since it is felt that many diarrheal episodes may be caused by ingested food, and therefore cleaning the gut of these foods would speed healing. In fact, a parallel is sometimes made in Honduras and elsewhere in Central America between superficial infections and gastrointestinal infections. Just as skin wounds need to be kept clean and dry, and treated with topical antibiotics and harsh fluids, so too, should the gut be treated. Purgatives, of course, present a danger for children, because they can induce dehydration.

Explanatory Models

Although much of this information is common knowledge to health practitioners working in diarrheal disease control, these models leave many health professionals unsettled. Are they still applicable? Are they changing? How varied is knowledge of these systems? Kleinman provides a response to this concern through his use of explanatory models.

> Explanatory models are the notions about an episode of sickness and its treatment that are employed by all those engaged in the clinical process. The interaction between the explanatory models of patients and explanatory models of practitioners is a central component of health care. The study of practitioner explanatory models tells us something about how practitioners understand and treat sickness. The study of patient and family explanatory models tells us how sufferers make sense of given episodes of illness, and how they choose and evaluate particular treatments. The study of the interaction between practitioner explanatory models and patient explanatory models offers a more precise analysis of problems in clinical communications. Most importantly, investigating explanatory models in relation to the sectors and subsectors of health care systems discloses one of the chief mechanisms by which cultural and social structural context affects patient-practitioner and other health care relationships (Kleinman 1980: 105).

Kleinman differentiates explanatory models from beliefs about sickness and health which he attributes to the health ideology of each sector:

> Explanatory models, even though they draw upon these belief systems, are marshalled in response to particular illness episodes. They are formed and employed to cope with a specific health problem, and consequently they need to be analyzed in that concrete setting (Kleinman 1980: 106).

Explanatory models are not easily elicited:

> An explanatory model is partly conscious and partly outside of awareness. It is based on a cognitive system that directs reasoning along certain lines. Since explanatory models involve tacit knowledge, they are not coherent and unambiguous. In responding to an illness episode, individuals strain to integrate views in part idiosyncratic and in part acquired from the health ideology of the popular culture. Hence, it is characteristic of explanatory models that they undergo change fairly frequently. Popular explanatory models often use symbols whose referents the individual may not be aware of and whose treatment options he may not fully understand. The "diffused" nature of popular

> medical knowledge contrasts to the "institutionalized" nature of professional and specialized folk medical knowledge. For this reason popular explanatory models are rarely invalidated by experience (Kleinman 1980: 109).

Much of what goes under the rubric of knowledge in KAP studies of health beliefs reflects both health ideology and popular explanatory models, as defined by Kleinman, while much of what is recorded as self-report of practices reflects patients' explanatory models. This makes interpretation of survey items difficult. Explanatory models are constructed by the researcher with information collected about cases and episodes of real illness, usually from home interviews, in response to open-ended questions about illness. Weiss (1988) provides a discussion of explanatory models in diarrheal disease in his excellent review of the cultural construction of diarrheal disease.

Health-Seeking Behavior

Several other key concepts in medical anthropology such as folk illness and explanatory models have proved important in describing the order underlying the range of facts provided by the literature and in pointing a direction for future research. An additional key concept that needs to be considered in the context of diarrheal disease is "health-seeking behavior." Conceptualizing illness in terms of health-seeking behavior addresses the illness episode as a complex treatment path. Multistage recourse to cure is usually divided into sequences such as onset, recognition, diagnosis and treatment, and outcome. Each of these will be separately discussed below.

Onset

The onset of disease refers to the initiation of a pathological process. In the case of diarrheal disease, onset may be difficult to determine. Mothers' first signs of diarrhea in toddlers or older children are often not loose stools, but children's complaints, lack of appetite, or irritability. Mothers may not respond initially to these signs, waiting to determine if this is a discrete transient event or an episode of illness. Onset is a biological process, and takes place in the household, but recognition is not.

Public health studies of diarrheal disease often note the social preconditions of ill health--poor water storage or availability, dirt floors, lack of separate utensils and cooking vessels, shortage of firewood--as confounders of major hypothesized biological relationships. These studies come closer to defining the domestic circumstances of onset, but again the items and issues discussed are those of the biomedical idiom. Studies are designed, furthermore, to "control" for these circumstances through design, so that they are not the object of the study. But although onset takes place in a biologically envisioned environment, recognition takes place in a socially constructed one. The domestic environment in a fuller sense is a field or locale where biological, social, cultural, economic, and political institutions play out their impact on the child. The status and role of women, migration, daily routines, normal eating habits, market prices, and competition for resources are all important for understanding recognition. Recognition entails the definition of altered circumstances in the household, an unusual decline of appetite, an unusual stool (but not necessarily a loose stool). Researchers must be familiar with these normal circumstances in order to deal with the emergency of diarrheal disease.

Recognition

Recognizing an illness involves two phases. Initially home remedies, modification of diet, or other simple interventions may be adopted, and no other sources may be contacted. The episode is treated within the framework of the household (see Berman et al. 1989) and is treated as a minor change in a normal pattern of defecation. Caretakers will often comment that three days of loose stools is not sufficient to warrant a trip to the clinic, or that diarrhea that accompanies teething is normal. Caretakers are unsure whether a particular episode provides important information about a child's personality, response to certain kinds of foods, or chance for long-term survival, on the one hand, or constitutes a cause for alarm, on the other. If the episode continues, however, a transition is made from an occurrence which exists within the domestic environment, controlled by parents and caretakers, to an episode which becomes public. These public episodes entail named diarrheal diseases, proper courses of therapy, and sanctions--of sorts--for parents or caretakers who inappropriately treat these episodes. One reason parents postpone visits to clinics or healers is that the visit is an admission of this public concern for domestic matters. Current commercial or pharmaceutical interventions, such as ORS, appear to be treated as part of this public domain of illness.

The argument here is simply that programs designed to promote ORS or other treatment and preventive behaviors in the home must deal with a boundary that is not necessarily personal or psychological but one that is also social in nature. Within the domestic domain numerous public characteristics come into play: women hold more equal status with their spouses, or in the absence of spouses hold sole authority; intimate knowledge of their children and the environment constitutes their basis for care and decision-making about health and illness. Women are the principal mediators of health in this domain, but their concerns are little dealt with in programs [see Mull, Chapter 2--Eds]. In contrast, in the public domain, women must often defer to men and relinquish authority, especially in cosmopolitan medical therapy. Their specific knowledge about their children is little valued, and they are heavily sanctioned by the public and the medical system for their child's ill health. Recognition of illness constitutes an admission of failure, and this has prompted some resistance to the adoption of cosmopolitan paradigms of diarrhea and treatment.

Conclusion

This chapter began by identifying concerns of two fields with applied ethnographic research on health programs. It has outlined some of the limitations of research to date (overly limited research focus and reliance on survey research methods) and has focused on a variety of anthropologically-based studies on diarrhea. It has argued for the importance of defining the episode through local language, through local and regional health systems and symptoms, and by recognizing the social nature of illness and the transition across domains manifested in the terms "public" and "private," "folk" and "cosmopolitan." Theory exists in medical anthropology that can explain much of the "disturbing" variation in findings remarked on by public health research.

Recognizing the multistage nature of illness episodes, this chapter has attempted to demonstrate that the puzzles presented to health professionals in using ethnographic data are better resolved through further ethnographic research, not by rejecting this research. Ethnographic concepts such as the ones presented in this article offer an opportunity to link public health efforts with advances in the social sciences. The relationship between the biological substratum and the cultural and social milieu may be two aspects of a dualism, and not the duality presented in the introduction to this paper. Public health needs to support research in this area, and the social sciences in turn will be invigorated by the opportunity to participate in applied multidisciplinary research.

Notes

1. The needs of the Diarrheal Diseases Control Program are instructive in demonstrating the ways in which applied anthropology has been shaped by donors. A feature of these technical primary health care programs is that they attempt to apply health planning models consistently within the narrow focus of the intervention. For example, the primary training course of the Diarrheal Diseases Control Program includes modules that establish priorities for interventions using available epidemiological data, set reasonable targets and objectives, and detail many aspects of delivery such as how to write a task and job description for the service provider, how to establish supervision and monitoring schemes, and how to resolve problems in delivery (WHO Training Course for National CDD Programme Managers 1981).

One key component of this program is the case management strategy of diarrheal diseases with oral rehydration therapy, described in clinical terms. Thus a child is examined and weighed to determine water and electrolyte deficit, a quantity of solution is calculated, and the child is administered solution. The intervention is designed to appeal to medical practitioners who are familiar with intravenous therapy and its calculations, the mastery of which constitutes an important part of medical training. This training takes as a given the control of the clinical setting and the control of patients and parents within it. It then is translated into the normative training modules. At the same time, it is realized that the largest proportion of cases of diarrhea in children are never treated in hospitals or clinics. The CDD program estimates a total of three diarrheal episodes per child per year, but few if any clinics report this level of treatment; and in fact surveillance activities have demonstrated many more than three episodes.

The realization that the program to be successful must not be clinic-based is the reason behind the support for research into home-based therapy. But whereas the clinic can be normatively constructed by a service provider, treatment in the home, implying unfamiliar and diverse circumstances and loss of practitioner control, constitutes a new level of concern for health professionals, and thus the call for social science assistance.

2. Cf. Cleland (1973) and Iverson (1977). Rogers and Kincaid (1981) have aptly characterized the fit between a linear model of communications and social science survey methodology. The linear model, with an hypothesized source and receiver, lent itself to top-down development projects and a rigid survey methodology to allow the use of minimally trained fieldworkers. In addition, the use of detailed, closed-ended survey instruments is limited in new locales, especially because of their insensitivity to language. Often these studies are conducted as part of a program evaluation, so that change in response is more important than the actual response. Little attention is paid to the external validity of the item.

3. Also of concern is the debate about the ontological status of folk illnesses, their translation, and concern about biological reductionism (Hahn 1985). These are not yet research issues in international public health.

References

Ackerman, A. 1983 Lead Oxides Used in the Treatment of Empacho. Presented at US/Mexico Cross-Border Health Association Meeting. Mimeograph.

Ackerman, A., E. Cronin, D. Rodman, K. Horan, K. Hammond, L. Aldaz, R. Kellner, D. Ouimette, W. Dunn, S.L. Fannin, A. Martinez, and J. Chin 1982 Lead Poisoning from Lead Tetroxide Used as a Folk Remedy--Colorado. *Morbidity and Mortality Weekly Report* 30(52):647-648.

Adams, R.N. 1957 Cultural Surveys of Panama, Nicaragua, El Salvador and Honduras. Pan American Sanitary Bureau Scientific Publication No. 33.

Allman, J., and S. Allman 1986 *Treatment of Childhood Diarrhea in Rural and Urban Haiti*. Pan American Health Organization.

Baer, R., and A. Ackerman 1988 Mineral Folk Remedies in Latin America: The Use of Arsenic, Lead and Bismuth. Mimeograph.

Behar, M. 1975 The Role of Feeding and Nutrition in the Pathogeny and Prevention of Diarrheic Processes. *Pan American Health Organization Bulletin* 9(1):1-9.

Bentley, M.E. 1985 The Household Management of Child Diarrhea in Rural North India. Paper presented at the Third Asian Conference on Diarrhoeal Diseases. Bangkok, Thailand.

Bentley, M.E., G.H. Pelto, W.L. Straus, D.A. Schumann, C. Adegbola, E. de la Pena, G.A. Oni, K.H. Brown, and S. Huffman 1988 Rapid Ethnographic Assessment: Application in a Diarrhea Management Program. *Social Science and Medicine* 27(1):107-116.

Berman, P., C. Kendall, and K. Bhattacharyya 1989 The Household Production of Health: Putting People at the Center of Health Improvement. In *Towards More Efficacy in Child Survival Strategies*. I. Sirageldin, W.H. Mosley, et al., eds. Baltimore: Johns Hopkins University, Department of Population Dynamics.

Berman, P. 1986 Service Use and the Performance of Rural Health Services: What are the Issues? Regional Seminar on the Use of Rural Health Services. Manila: Asian Development Bank, January 20-25.

Bersh, D. 1985 Estudios de Diarrea en el Quindio: Aspectos epidemiologicos y de comportamiento. Unpublished.

Bertrand, W.E., and B.F. Walmus 1983 Maternal Knowledge, Attitudes and Practice as Predictors of Diarrheal Disease in Young Children. *International Journal of Epidemiology* 12(2):205-210.

Black, R.E., K.H. Brown, and S. Becker 1984 Effects of Diarrhoea Associated with Specific Enteropathogens on the Growth of Children in Rural Bangladesh. *Pediatrics* 73(6):799-805.

Bonilla, D.E., M. Alferez de Castillo, and F. Piñeda 1987a-d a. Informe Final de la Investigación Antropológica Realizada en el Cantón Chanmico, San Juan Opica, La Libertad. b. Informe Final de la Investigación Antropológica Realizada en el Municipio de Quelepa, San Miguel. c. Informe Final de la

Investigación Antropológica Realizada en el Cantón El Zapote, San Francisco Menéndez, Ahuachapán. d. Informe Final de la Investigación Antropológica Realizada en el Municipio de San Cristóbal, Cuscatlán. Ministerio de Salud Pública y Asistencia Social de El Salvador, Instituto de Nutrición de Centro América y Panamá (INCAP).

Brieseman, M.A. 1984 Child Health: Knowledge and Practice of New Zealand Mothers in the Treatment of Infantile Diarrhoea. *New Zealand Medical Journal* 97:39-42.

Briscoe, J., R.G. Feachem, and M.M. Rahman 1985 Measuring the Impact of Water Supply and Sanitation Facilities on Diarrhoea Morbidity: Prospects for Case-control Methods. WHO unpublished document WHO/CWS/85.3-CDD/OPrR/85.1. Geneva: WHO.

Chen, P.C.Y. 1971 Socio-Cultural Aspects of a Cholera Epidemic in Trengganu, Malaysia. *Tropical and Geographical Medicine* 23:296-303.

Cleland, J. 1973 A Critique of KAP Studies and Some Suggestions for their Improvement. *Studies in Family Planning* 4(2):42-47.

Condon-Paoloni, D., J. Cravioto, F.E. Johnston, E.R. De Licardie, and T.O. Scholl 1977 Morbidity and Growth of Infants and Young Children in a Rural Mexican Village. *American Journal of Public Health* 67(7):651-656.

Coreil, J., and E. Genece 1988 Adoption of Oral Rehydration Therapy Among Haitian Mothers. *Social Science and Medicine* 27(1):87-96.

Coreil, J., and J.D. Mull, eds. 1988 Anthropological Studies of Diarrheal Illness. *Social Science and Medicine*, Special Issue 27(1).

Coreil, J. 1988 Innovation Among Haitian Healers: The Adoption of Oral Rehydration Therapy. *Human Organization* 47(1):48-57.

Cosminsky, S., and M. Scrimshaw 1975 Medical Pluralism on a Guatemalan Plantation. *Social Science and Medicine* 14:267-278.

de Zoysa, I., D. Carson, R. Feachem, B. Kirkwood, E. Lindsay-Smith, and R. Loewenson 1984a Home-based Oral Rehydration Therapy in Rural Zimbabwe. *Transactions of the Royal Society of Tropical Medicine and Hygiene* 78:102-105.

___ 1984b Perceptions of Childhood Diarrhoea and its Treatment in Rural Zimbabwe. *Social Science and Medicine* 19:727-734.

Djurfeldt, G., and S. Lindberg 1975 Pills Against Poverty: A Study of the Introduction of Western Medicine in a Tamil Village. Scandinavian Institute of Asian Studies. Monograph Series No. 23.

Early, E.A. 1983 National Control of Diarrheal Diseases Project, Cairo, Egypt: Country Trip Report. The John Snow Public Health Group, Boston.

Epling, P.J., and N. Siliga 1967 Notes on Infantile Diarrhoea in American Samoa (A Sketch of Indigenous Theory). *Journal of Tropical Pediatrics* 13(13):139-149.

Erasmus, C.J. 1952 Changing Folk Beliefs and the Relativity of Empirical Knowledge. *Southwest Journal of Anthropology* 8:411.

Escobar, G., E. Salazar, and M. Chuy 1983 Beliefs Regarding the Etiology and Treatment of Infantile Diarrhoea in Lima, Peru. *Social Science and Medicine* 17(17):1257-1269.

Faruque A.S.G., A.S.M.M. Rahman, and K. Zaman 1985 Childhood Diarrhoea Management by Mothers and Village Practitioners in Rural Bangladesh. *Tropical and Geographical Medicine* 37(3):223-226.

Gonzalez, N.S. 1963 Some Aspects of Child-bearing and Child-rearing in a Guatemalan Ladino Community. *Southwest Journal of Anthropology* 19:411.

Green, E.C. 1986 Diarrhea and the Social Marketing of Oral Rehydration Salts in Bangladesh. *Social Science and Medicine* 23(4):357-366.

Green E.C., and L. Mokhubu 1984 Traditional Healers in Swaziland: Toward Improved Cooperation Between the Traditional and Modern Health Sectors. *Social Science and Medicine* 18(12):1071-1079.

Hahn, R.A. 1985 Culture-bound Syndromes Unbound. *Social Science and Medicine* 21(2):165-171.

Halstead, S.B., J. Walsh, and K.S. Warren 1985 Good Health at Low Cost: Proceedings of a Conference held at the Bellagio Conference Center in Bellagio, Italy. New York: The Rockefeller Foundation.

Holdsworth, D. 1975 Traditional Medicinal Plants used in the Treatment of Gastric Ailments. *Papua New Guinea Medical Journal* 21(2):175-182.

Hurtado, J. 1979 La "Mollera Caida": Una Subcategoria Cognitiva de las Enfermedades Producidas por la Ruptura del Equilibrio Mecánico del Cuerpo. *Boletín Bibliográfico de Antropología Americana* 50:11-20.

Imperato, P.J. 1974 Cholera in Mali and Popular Reaction to Its First Appearance. *Journal of Tropical Medicine and Hygiene* 77:290-296.

Iverson, D.C. 1977 Reassessment of the Knowledge/Attitude/Behavior Triad. *Health Education* 8(6):31-34

Johnson, C.A. 1979 Infant Diarrhea and Folk Medicine in South Texas. *Texas Medicine* 75:69-73.

Kendall, C. 1985 *Explanatory Models of Diarrheal Diagnosis and Treatment: An Ethnographic Evaluation of the Mass Media and Health Practices Project in Honduras. 1980-1983*. Menlo Park, CA: Applied Communications Technology.

___ 1988 The Implementation of a Diarrheal Disease Control Program in Honduras: Is it 'Selective Primary Health Care' or 'Integrated Primary Health Care'? *Social Science and Medicine* 27(1):17-23.

___ 1989 The Use and Non-use of Anthropology: The Diarrheal Disease Control Program in Honduras. In *Making Our Research Useful: Case Studies in the Utilization of Anthropological Knowledge*. B. Rylko-Bauer, A. McElroy, and J. van Willigan, eds. Boulder, CO: Westview Press.

Kendall, C., D. Foote, and R. Martorell 1984 Ethnomedicine and Oral Rehydration Therapy: A Case Study of Ethnomedical Investigation and Program Planning. *Social Science and Medicine* 19(3):253-260.

Kielmann, A.A., and C. McCord 1977 Home Treatment of Childhood Diarrhea in Punjab Villages. *Journal of Tropical Paediatrics and Environmental Child Health* 23(4):197-201.

Kleinman, A. 1980 *Patients and Healers in the Context of Culture*. Berkeley: University of California Press.

Kumar, V. 1984 Community Implementation of Oral Rehydration Therapy. *Indian Journal of Paediatrics* 51:1-6.

Kumar, V., C. Clements, K. Marwah, and P. Diwedi 1981 Maternal Beliefs Regarding Diet During Acute Diarrhea. *Indian Journal of Paediatrics* 48:599-603.

___ 1985 Beliefs and Therapeutic Preferences of Mothers in Management of Acute Diarrheal Disease in Children. *Journal of Tropical Pediatrics* 31(2):109-112.

Levine, N. 1990 The Determinants of Appropriate Utilization of Home-Based ORT: A Critical Review of the Literature. Prepared for the Diarrhoeal Diseases Control Programme of the World Health Organization. Unpublished.

Lozoff, B., K.R. Kamath, and R.A. Feldman 1975 Infection and Disease in South Indian Families: Beliefs about Childhood Diarrhea. *Human Organization* 34(Winter):353-358.

Maina-Ahlberg, B. 1979 Belief and Practices Concerning Treatment of Measles and Acute Diarrhoea Among the Akamba. *Tropical and Geographical Medicine* 31:139-148.

Martorell, R., J.P. Habicht, C. Yarbrough, A. Lechtig, R. Klein, and K. Western 1975 Acute Morbidity and Physical Growth in Rural Guatemalan Children. *American Journal of Diseases of Children* 129:1296-1301.

Martorell, R.C., C. Yarbrough, S. Yarbrough, and R.E. Klein 1980 The Impact of Ordinary Illnesses on the Dietary Intakes of Malnourished Children. *American Journal of Clinical Nutrition* 33:345.

Nations, M. 1982 Illness of the Child: The Cultural Context of Child Diarrhoea. Ann Arbor, MI: University Microfilms International.

Nations, M.K., D.S. Shields, J.G. Aranjo, and R.L. Guerrant 1984 Care Within Reach: Appropriate Health-Care Delivery in the Developing World. *The New England Journal of Medicine* 310(24):1612.

Nations, M.K., and L.A. Rebhun 1988 Mystification of a Simple Solution: Oral Dehydration Therapy in Northeast Brazil. *Social Science and Medicine* 27(1):25-38.

Nichter, M. 1988 From Aralu to ORS: Sinhalese Perceptions of Digestion, Diarrhoea and Dehydration. *Social Science and Medicine* 27(1):35-52.

___ 1989 *Anthropology and International Health: South Asian Case Studies.* Boston: Kluwer Academic Publishers.

Puffer, R.R., and C.V. Serrano 1973 Patterns of Mortality in Childhood. Report of the Inter-American Investigation of Mortality in Childhood. PAHO Scientific Publication #262.

Rifkin, S., and G. Walt. 1986 Why Health Improves: Defining the Issues Concerning 'Comprehensive Primary Health Care' and 'Selective Primary Health Care.' *Social Science and Medicine* 23(6):359-566.

Rogers, E.M., and D.L. Kincaid 1981 *Communication Networks: Toward a New Paradigm for Research*. New York: The Free Press.

Sachar, R.J., G.S. Javal, B. Cowan, and H.N.S. Grewal 1985 Home-based Education of Mothers in Treatment of Diarrhoea with Oral Rehydration Solution. *Journal of Diarrhoeal Diseases Research* 3(1):29-31.

Scrimshaw N.S., C.E. Taylor, and J.E. Gordon 1968 Interactions of Nutrition and Infection. WHO Monograph No. 57. Geneva: WHO.

Scrimshaw, S.C.M., and E. Hurtado 1987 *Rapid Assessment Procedures for Nutrition and Primary Healthy Care*. Tokyo: The United Nations University.

___ 1988 Anthropologists' Involvement in the Central American Diarrhoeal Disease Control Project. *Social Science and Medicine* 27(1):97-106.

Shahid, N.S., A.S.M.M. Rahman, K.M.A. Aziz, A.S.G. Faruque, and M.A. Bari 1983 Beliefs and Treatment Related to Diarrheal Episodes Reported in Association with Measles. *Tropical and Geographical Medicine* 35(1)51-156.

Snyder, J. 1982 The Magnitude of the Global Problem of Acute Diarrhoeal Disease: A Review of Active Surveillance Data. *WHO Bulletin* 60:605.

Tedlock, Barbara 1987 An Interpretive Solution to the Problem of Humoral Medicine in Latin America. *Social Science and Medicine* 24(12):1069-1083.

Trotter, R.T. 1985 "Azarcón" and "Greta": A Survey of Episodic Lead Poisoning From a Folk Remedy. *Human Organization* 44(1):64-72.

Vandale, S. 1978 Factores Sociales y Culturales que Influyen en la Alimentación del Lactante Menor en el Medio Urbano. *Salud Pública de México* 20(2):215-230.

Vielman, L. 1986 Estudio Antropológico Sobre Supervivencia Infantil y Comunicación en Cuatro Comunidades de El Salvador (Componente Diarrhea). Instituto de Nutrición de Centro América y Panamá (INCAP).

Vielman, L., and E. Hurtado 1985 Informe Final de la Investigación Etnográfica Sobre Algunos Aspectos de Salud y Nutrición Realizada en la Colonia Juárez Guanagazapa. Instituto de Nutrición de Centro América y Panamá (INCAP).

Villatoro, E., and E. Hurtado 1986 Informe Final de la Investigación Etnográfica Sobre Algunos Aspectos de Salud y Nutrición en una Comunidad de Huehuetenango. Ministry of Health and Social Assistance of Guatemala.

Weiss, M. 1988 Cultural Models of Diarrheal Illness: Conceptual Framework and Review. *Social Science and Medicine* 27(1):5-16.

Wellin, E. 1955a Maternal and Infant Feeding Practices in a Peruvian Village. *Journal of the American Dietetic Association* 31(9):889-894.

___ 1955b Water Boiling in a Peruvian Town. In *Health, Culture and Community: Case Studies of Public Reactions to Health Programs.* B.D. Paul, ed. Pp. 71-103. New York: Russell Sage Foundation.

World Health Organization 1978 The Declaration of Alma-Ata, The International Conference on Primary Health Care, Alma-Ata, USSR.

___ 1981 Training Course for National CDD Programme Managers.

Yusuf, H.I., A.S. Adan, K.A. Egal, A.H. Omer, M.M. Ibrahim, and A.S. Elmi 1984 Traditional Medical Practices in Some Somali Communities. *Journal of Tropical Pediatrics* 30(2):87-92.

10

Vaccinations in South Asia: False Expectations and Commanding Metaphors

Mark Nichter

> Medical scientists are acutely aware of biological factors affecting deterioration of vaccines due to poor storage and lack of an adequate immune response in children because of malnutrition. Far less attention is given to the social constraints to effective vaccine use (Mosley 1984: 7).

In a recent article reviewing advances in vaccine development and supply, Warren (1986) describes what amounts to a biotechnological revolution in the brewing. At present fewer than ten vaccines are in general use in the Third World, but it is predicted that twenty new ones will be available within the next two decades. These will probably include vaccines against diarrheal and respiratory diseases, the two main causes of child morbidity and mortality in the developing world. At this moment of rapid biotechnological advancement, it is timely and somewhat sobering to examine the contrast between primary health care providers' perceptions of vaccinations and lay perceptions, and the implications of each view. In describing this contrast, I will draw on data from my own fieldwork in South India and Sri Lanka, regions having relatively low and relatively high rates of immunization coverage, respectively.

Vaccinations: A View from the Top Down

When I discussed vaccination programs with mid-level health personnel and their superiors in South Asia, it was clear that their frame of reference was that of a military campaign. It did not matter what people knew or did not know about vaccines, they said. The success of an immunization effort depended almost exclusively on (1) a reliable supply of the vaccine, (2) enough manpower to vaccinate, (3) the following of a schedule, and (4) compliance as guaged by people's uncritical acceptance of immunization. The candid comment of one South Asian health planner, reproduced below, echoes the opinion of several informants interviewed in India and Sri Lanka:

> The beauty of vaccination programs is that they require little from the community beyond lining up and holding out their arm at the proper time. The health worker needs only to tell them when to come to the clinic. The technology is relatively simple and mobilizing the community may be done through the influence of village leaders like the schoolmaster.
>
> It matters little whether a soldier understands the principles of how the rifle he uses works as long as he knows how to aim, load, and shoot. It is the same with vaccinations. All of this talk of community health efforts is good for speeches only. To get vaccination programs done, targets must be set and field staff must be closely supervised as was done during the smallpox campaign. It is like the military.
>
> We face three major problems. First, there are pockets of resistance against vaccinations resulting from superstition. Second, we face problems organizing camps, and third, we have a morale problem among the troops. In a war, you see results when you are winning; you see bodies. In this war, the bodies saved look the same as the ones that are walking around. People think that death rates are lower because of curative not preventive measures like vaccinations.

Certainly there are parallels between war and immunization campaigns in terms of the maintenance of supply chains and the coordination and deployment of a large number of hierarchically-arranged people. However, extension of the military metaphor as a cognitive model (Lakoff 1987) underscores certain features of vaccinations while obscuring others. Vaccines are not bullets, and syringes, despite their physical contours, are not weapons. Vaccines do not "destroy," as such, but instead help the body build an early warning system of antibodies. These antibodies in turn identify sources of danger so that the body can mobilize preexisting resources and manipulate its internal environment.[1]

If a military model is to be applied, it may be more exact, then, to identify the *body*, rather than the primary health care worker, as the soldier in an immunization campaign. A "Vaccination Commando" campaign in Burkina Faso sponsored by the incoming revolutionary government popularized the image that "diseases wage war and vaccinations make children 'as strong as commandos'" (UNICEF 1985).

In a post-revolution context conducive to a cultural model organized around war (Quinn and Holland 1987), a military model of vaccination may hail strongly felt values about liberation and the need for community action. As Fillmore (1977) and Quinn (1982) have noted, key words index scenarios, categories of experience, and associated emotions. In other contexts, however, popularization of a military model may yield quite a different set of associations which are centered on the individual, antithetical to the mobilization of community action, and insensitive to the people's perspective on the meaning of immunization.

Why is the military model of vaccination so popular in the Third World? In large part, thinking about immunization programs has been influenced by the highly successful smallpox campaign which demonstrated the importance of disease surveillance in managing immunization programs. While surveillance is essential to any immunization program, it is misguided to model other vaccination programs on smallpox and its vaccine, since the latter are unusual in a number of ways (Wehrle and Wilkins 1981).

First of all, smallpox spreads slowly and one must have contact with an infected person to get it; there are no extrahuman reservoirs. Further, all those infected are symptomatic with visible lesions, which makes tracing of contacts and selective containment procedures possible and universal immunization unnecessary. Moreover, the smallpox vaccine is highly stable; it does not need refrigeration; and it can be administered by the simple technology of the bifurcated needle. Finally, the worldwide smallpox campaign gained momentum both from a fear that the disease might be used in germ warfare (Sidel 1986) and from a recognition of the high recurrent cost of maintaining quarantine facilities (see Ebrahim 1987).

Currently "targeted" immunizable diseases such as pertussis, diphtheria, tetanus, and measles are very different from smallpox in one or more of these respects. Thus a "search and destroy" model is much less appropriate for such diseases than it was for smallpox. In addition, such a model fosters a "technical fix" mentality which is inconsistent with the primary health care ideology set forth at Alma-Ata. It leads health workers to give high priority to meeting "coverage quotas" and low priority to providing community education, so that meaningful community involvement in vaccination programs is lacking.

Further, when limited information is presented to a community, misconceptions about the power of immunizations abound, and false expectations and fears then influence people's perceptions of vaccination efficacy and appropriateness. Compliance from one immunization to the next is then gained more by appeal, endorsement, and power relationships than by any true understanding of how vaccinations work and the reasons they are given.[2]

It must be acknowledged that local understanding of immunization is not the only and often not the most immediate factor influencing immunization acceptance rates.[3] Other important factors are vaccine supply, clinic timing and accessibility, client identification and followup, vaccine administration policy during minor illness, opportunity costs and indirect costs incurred in vaccination attainment, and the nature of the relations between health staff and community. Also significant is the role played by powerful and esteemed community leaders (Henderson et al. 1973; Singarimbun et al. 1986; Mull et al. 1990) and the ability of social networks to facilitate information flow and thus enhance immunization coverage (Hanks and Hanks 1955). In some contexts, where immediate action must be taken to control an epidemic, these factors take precedence. However, in contexts where long-term adherence, rather than short-term compliance, to vaccination programs is the objective, "knowledge about" vaccinations is important. Studies in Gambia (Hanlon and Byass 1988), Indonesia (Streatfield and Singarimbun 1988), the Philippines (Friede et al. 1985), Honduras (Bonilla et al. 1985), and Haiti (Coreil et al. 1989) suggest that maternal knowledge about immunizations is a significant predictor of a child's vaccination status.

Health service research focusing on logistical aspects of vaccination needs to be accompanied by careful ethnographic studies aimed at identifying lay perceptions of immunization and at developing sensitive educational approaches that can enhance community involvement.[4] A recent comprehensive review of the social science literature indicates that there is a paucity of such studies (Heggenhougen and Clements 1987). Reports of "coverage rates," in contrast, are abundant, but I will argue that in the areas of South Asia described below, coverage does not index either lay knowledge about immunizations or a desire for them. Rather, it reflects public health policing efforts based on a quasi-military model. These efforts are laudable in purpose but questionable in principle if informed community participation is truly an objective of primary health care.

Lay Perceptions of Vaccinations in South India

> An awareness that immunizations protected against some diseases existed in all villages sampled. The disturbing aspect of the "knowledge" regarding protection from diseases was that there was a spillover effect whereby respondents expected protection from a wider range of diseases than was feasible. Thus, respondents across various groups mentioned that immunization injections protected the child from diarrhea, dysentery, vomiting, fever, pneumonia, malaria, and even the lowly cough and cold. The danger of such expectations was that disillusionment could set in very rapidly . . . a large population of skeptical mothers are watching from the wings! (Indian Marketing Research Bureau 1987)

> While talking with mothers, the investigator asked them why they had their children immunized. The general response was, "We heard that the injection prevents sickness." When asked which diseases were prevented by these "injections," the mothers were at a loss for an answer. One lady eventually ventured a reply. "I'm not sure but I think it prevents polio." "And what is this polio?" "I don't know, ***behenji***; we are illiterate people, what do we know of such things?" (UNICEF 1984)

Between 1974 and 1980 I conducted ethnographic research on health-related behavior in two districts of Karnataka State in southern India. Over a ten-month period in 1979-80, two samples of households were visited four to five times either by myself or by an Indian anthropologist, Dr. K.H. Bhat, accompanied by a local member of a community diagnosis team (Nichter 1984). As part of this research, household members were questioned about the vaccinations they had received. Their ideas about the purpose of vaccinations and how vaccinations worked were also investigated. In the first field area (North Kanara district), members of 200 lower-class to lower-middle-class multicaste households were interviewed. In the second field area (South Kanara district), members of 82 rural and 30 urban households (lower-class, multicaste) were interviewed.

Communication Underdevelopment

Let us first consider what informants had been told by health workers about immunizations. In more than three-quarters of the households surveyed in each district, at least one household member had received what was believed to be a vaccination. Our operational definition of vaccinations was "free injections that pregnant women or children were asked to receive by government health workers." Informants were not always sure what kind of injection had been administered, a point which will be elaborated below.

Villagers believed that health staff were very anxious to vaccinate mothers and children because they derived some cash benefit from the government for each case just as they did for family planning interventions. They were aware that health staff were scolded if their case numbers were too low. Awareness was fostered by health workers themselves, since the latter often pleaded with people to accept immunizations. Several village informants complained that health staff were so concerned about winning favor with their superiors that they asked children to receive vaccinations at inappropriate times, e.g. during times of "weakness" (see below) when receiving a vaccination was dangerous. Pressures to meet targets took precedence over the welfare of the people.

Discounting smallpox, in only 11% of the households in North Kanara and in only 28% of the households of South Kanara had a family member been informed as to the illness prevented by the vaccination a member had received. Villagers in both districts were familiar with tetanus and whooping cough, and, although the correspondences are not exact, local illness categories exist which encompass each of these diseases. Yet when health workers were observed administering vaccinations and asking people to attend a vaccination clinic, it was noted that very few such workers used either a local or a formal illness term.

In North Kanara, community members became irate when they were told that the "triple" vaccination (DPT: diphtheria, pertussis, tetanus) was a medicine that protected against whooping cough, not malaria as they had assumed--a misperception allegedly fostered by a nurse-midwife. Living in a nucleated settlement, they knew only too well the strained cries of children coughing night after night with *nayi kemmu*, "dog cough." At a village meeting, several people expressed the suspicion that they had been deliberately misled by doctors who wanted to make money from treating this illness privately. Several stated that had they known that immunization protected against *nayi kemmu*, they would have demanded it. On the other hand, they had little concern about malaria.

Health staff, for their part, said that the people were uneducated and could not understand vaccinations, and, in any case, they had not been instructed to use local terms and give details. It was rather the people's "duty" to receive vaccinations because the government wanted it. These health workers emphasized vaccination timing and little more. Indeed, when we asked thirty field staff to name the diseases covered by the state program for immunization in 1979 (tuberculosis, diphtheria, pertussis, tetanus, and poliomyelitis), fewer than half could name all five diseases and five of the thirty could not name three.[5]

Further, when I asked informants from 30 households in Mangalore city what they had been told about vaccinations, people in 24 of the households said that health workers had simply stated, "Vaccinations are good for health and they prevent disease." In only 9 households could a person correctly name one illness other than smallpox that was prevented by a vaccination; in 6 of these cases, a local term encompassing whooping cough was mentioned, and in the remaining 3, a term associated with tetanus was given. Other informants, however, stated incorrectly that vaccinations prevented rashes, coughs, fevers, and diarrhea. Rural informants gave similar responses.

With respect to vaccinations received, it appeared that fewer than one-third of school-aged children in the samples from North and South Kanara had received more than one dose of the DPT vaccine[6]--a vaccine which several informants knew by name, although they did not know its purpose. Mothers were also asked about vaccinations that they had received during their two most recent pregnancies. About one-third of the mothers said that they had had a government health injection at that time. Presumably the injection was tetanus toxoid, but this is hard to determine because in some cases a doctor had told the women that it was a vitamin or tonic injection.

Stated willingness to accept vaccinations during pregnancy ranged from 17% to 60% according to the caste of the informant. Members of a few castes were particularly vocal in speaking out against such vaccinations, associating them with hospital births and/or with covert government attempts to introduce family planning. Several women expressed fear that these "tonic injections" would cause them to have big babies and therefore difficult deliveries (Nichter and Nichter 1983). Their concern was based on the fact that health workers who administered vitamin and mineral tablets had told them that they would produce a big healthy baby.

Women from both North and South Kanara said that if they did not accept vaccinations, they might be offered poor government health service should they require it. Indeed, several women viewed relationships with government midwives as entailing reciprocity. If the auxiliary nurse-midwife (ANM) assisted a woman during delivery, then the woman's family would be in the midwife's debt. Family members would be asked to go for family planning or to receive vaccinations to fill the nurse-midwife's quota. I was told by one woman in no uncertain terms that this was why she had delivered alone rather than calling in a midwife, although the latter lived only three kilometers away.

Ideas about how Vaccinations Functioned

Many people accepted what they had been told by health workers: that vaccinations were powerful "health injections." Although seemingly harmless, one problem with this formulation is that powerful medicines, like strength-producing foods, are not always thought suitable for the body when it is in a weakened state or during an unhealthful season. Thus some people spoke of children suffering from general ill health and weakness as "unable to stand the shock" of a health injection.[7] Their perceptions were in part supported by the actions of local practitioners. Eight out of ten who were observed would not vaccinate a child ill with mild fever, productive cough, or diarrhea.

Some villagers who associated vaccinations with shock regarded this in a positive light. They were more willing to vaccinate "weak" (but not "ill") children, terms which have relative meaning. One Harijan woman compared vaccination to the practice of branding, which was common in South Kanara a few decades ago. She said that young children were branded at the joints or sternum to stimulate the flow of blood, strengthen the body *narambu* (nerve) channels, and insure the proper movement of limbs. Bluish-looking blood in the veins on the side of a baby's head was viewed as a sign that blood flow was not correct. Branding of the sternum was thought to make the lungs expand and was done when a baby exhibited shallow breathing or cried excessively after birth. In the past, among some castes, branding was performed on all babies on the fifth day after birth as a promotive health practice. Like branding, the informant noted, vaccinations shocked the body to insure health later on.

On a similar note, another informant compared vaccination to the ritual practice of ear piercing, saying that both practices improved strength and helped the body ward off illness. (He drew further parallels between ear piercing, the slashing of the ear of a young calf when it would not suckle, and the pounding of a spike into a tree when it would not bear fruit.) When asked whether the medicine in the vaccination was important or just the prick, he said that the medicine was also important and that it warded off fits. He compared it to *chinne* medicine, a local preparation thought to prevent fits which villagers administer periodically to their children, especially during times of risk, e.g. at transitional times such as "no moon" days (Nichter 1989a: Chapter 5).

Several semi-educated informants believed that vaccinations protected against all serious infectious illnesses (*antu roga*). Others spoke of vaccinations being similar to bitter tonics which one took now and then to protect against illness associated with impurity as well as against *krimi*, a local term conveying the notion of tiny wormlike germs. Several informants perceived *krimi* as attracted to impurity (Nichter 1989a: Chapter 4).

We explored this perception that vaccinations removed toxins as a possible way to enhance acceptance of tetanus toxoid immunizations in South Kanara District. The vaccinations were described as reducing the "toxicity" (*nanju*) associated with pregnancy and wounds. In South Kanara, pregnancy is considered a time of heightened toxicity because when menstrual blood is no longer expelled, the impurities that it carries are thought to remain inside the body. Similarly, wound infections exuding pus are associated with blood impurities rising to the body surface. This is one reason that folk dietetics involving *nanju* foods are strictly adhered to when wounds are healing although little attention may be paid to the cleanliness of the wound itself.

Our message that tetanus vaccinations were *nanju*-removing injections may well have contributed to the increased acceptability of such vaccinations in the region. During a return visit to South Kanara in 1984, I found that an increasing number of agricultural workers in the area were requesting anti-*nanju* injections after injuries.[8]

A few semi-educated informants compared vaccinations to penicillin, saying that vaccinations were long-lasting doses of antibiotic that travelled all over the body to prevent illness. In some cases, injections were deemed necessary for good health as well as to prevent disease. During a short visit to South Kanara in 1987, I was told by a literate petty shopkeeper that her 10-year-old son was ill with pneumonia because the government could not afford to give free vaccinations to children past the age of five or six. She believed that promotive health injections needed to be given for the first 16 years of life. She imagined that the wealthy purchased such injections and that their children were therefore healthier. As distinct from a military metaphor organizing her thoughts about immunizations, she had developed a commodification of health model wherein she believed health could be obtained from vaccinations themselves (Nichter 1989a: Chapter 9).

A few informants thought that vaccinations were given to small children to help them "become accustomed" to allopathic medicines. Once three doses were administered, a child would be capable of benefitting from allopathic medicine when it was received later in life (Nichter and Nordstrom 1989). Vaccination reactions were interpreted as evidence that the body does not easily become accustomed to such a powerful medicine. One informant, a long-time friend, compared the side effects of vaccinations to the problems that I as a foreigner had experienced when consuming new foods in India:

> When you first came here you could not digest the meals we placed in front of you. We offered you our most tasty curries and you ate. Your eyes watered, your mouth burned, you drank an abundance of water, and your anus burned as you squatted soon afterward. Our small green chili peppers are like your vaccinations. They are also good for health. You suffered from what we relish and in time, after many meals, you now relish as we do. My son, after suffering from two vaccinations, is now able to take the power of English medicines with only minor side effects. Others who are not habituated to English medicines have serious side effects. Last year a man from Bantwal side had fits and died after being given his first injection because his body could not take to this foreign medicine at a time when he was weak.

Although side effects following vaccinations were generally regarded negatively, a few informants like the one quoted above perceived them as an unfortunate but necessary set of responses manifested by the body as it became habituated to medicine. Other people perceived side effects such as fever to be signs of a vaccination's strength. This accords with the popular notion that injections which burn are more powerful than ones which do not, a notion that has led to the misuse of calcium gluconate by some doctors wishing to please clients by producing a burning sensation (Nichter 1989a: Chapter 7). In exploratory health education efforts we incorporated these notions and found it useful to suggest to people that after-effects were signs of the vaccination's worth.

Trust and Vaccination Acceptance

Some informants associated vaccination programs with being asked to accept family planning. While in some contexts this association involved the social relations of receiving assistance and notions of reciprocity, in others it involved the very purpose of vaccinations. A number of villagers suspected that vaccinations were offered to children to both enhance their health, and to reduce their capacity to have more than one or two children when they matured. Immediate health was gained at the price of fertility. Indeed, on one uncomfortable occasion I was accused of being a CIA agent investigating how well this American-inspired scheme was progressing!

A trust issue also arose with respect to vaccination administration. More than 40% of informants (in a composite of the North and South Kanara sample) noted that they did not trust PHC staff to administer injections. Because of traditional concepts of purity and pollution, I had anticipated some intercaste concern about needles that had entered the bodies of multicaste persons polluting higher-caste persons. Such a concern was rarely voiced. Instead, people were worried about the technical competence of the person administering the vaccination and the care which that person might choose to exercise.

Many informants cited cases of paralysis following vaccination, although I was able to trace only one such case--a child who had developed polio after being immunized.[9] People also spoke of the possibility of the vaccinator hitting a nerve (*nara*) and thereby causing irreparable damage. If vaccinators were really well trained, informants asked, why were they not routinely allowed to administer *all* injections, including antibiotics? Some said that vaccinators had "uncertain aim" and that for that reason, they only administered free medicine, not costly medicine for fear that they might waste it.

"Aim" proved to be an important health concern. "After all, why do some people respond to the same type of injection faster than others?" I was asked. While some people claimed that it depended on the constitution, strength, or habituation of the body, others said that it was because the doctor had taken better aim. If the injection allowed the medicine to enter the mainstream of the blood, then it moved quickly through the body. That was why an injection given on one side of the body could cure a symptom on the opposite side. If the aim was bad, however, and the medicine did not enter the mainstream of the blood but some small tributary, then its effect would be delayed, just as if it had been a tablet rather than an injection.

Villagers spoke of private doctors being careful to take good aim because their popularity and thus their fees were determined by their good reputation. Government vaccinations, however, did not involve fees and therefore little care was exercised. Moreover, the vaccinators were often outsiders who were not accountable to the community, and there was little or no follow-up. As one person put it,

> Strangers come and give injections to our children without first doing *tapas* (diagnoses of their state of health). Can we trust that their aim is good with so many children to see? And then they disappear and we are left with children having fever. These people do not inquire about the

health of our children on the days following the vaccination nor do they give medicines!

Later the government sends people to ask if our children have taken vaccinations two times or three times. Our son has taken them once and was ill for three days. This is a sign that the medicine was not good for his body, but for my sister's son two injections were taken with only slight fever. For him the injections took and may have some benefit. The same medicine does not work well for all people. So when these government people come I say, "Yes, my son has taken three government injections, two here and one at the village of my mother last year."

Another informant compared vaccination to DDT spraying programs. He said that whenever his house was sprayed, the DDT killed the mosquitoes but his family was then plagued with bedbugs (DDT kills cockroaches, which keep the bedbug population in check). Bedbugs kept his family from sleeping and were more of a problem than mosquitoes or malaria. For malaria one had pills and just a few days of suffering each month, but for bedbugs!

In any case, he felt that one became ill with malaria not only because of mosquitoes but because of one's particular blood quality. The same was true of tetanus. He supported his opinion with a bit of folk wisdom about ants:

There are ants everywhere. On that tree ants crawl without doing any harm. Only that tree over there they have decided to eat. They are destroying the tree leaf by leaf. Why that tree? It is because the conditions of the tree are attractive to them. One must look to see why the ants are hungry and why they choose a particular tree. The *krimi* (germ-like creatures) the health workers talk of are like the ants.

I am bitten by a mosquito, but not as often as the next person who has malaria. It is not just the mosquito; it is the blood of the person that matters. If you give that person an injection [vaccination] to prevent malaria; is the man now healthy? No, his blood is still impure and attractive to other *krimi*.

Now if you come and spray that man's house with DDT, and remove one problem only to bring another problem! The health workers do not listen to our complaints about bedbugs. When we complain, they say having our house sprayed is our duty. I have sprayed my house twice out of duty. Next time let the man who sprays come and sleep in this house when the bedbugs want blood.

People were also concerned about the potency of government-supplied vaccines. If the curative medicine administered by the government was of questionable quality, they said, why should they believe that preventive vaccines were any more effective? Even the aftereffects could have been caused by adulteration.

Two points may be raised here. First, government doctors concurrently engaged in private practice often downplay the quality of government medicine, asking patients to either see them privately for better medicines or to bring medicines from a chemist's shop. This fostered an already existing idea that anything free (government medicine) is of dubious quality. Second, given the "communication underdevelopment" described above--where health workers claimed that vaccinations were "good for general health"--it is not surprising that their efficacy was questioned.

Illness Classification and Perceptions of Vaccine Efficacy

Vaccinations may be directly or indirectly associated with local illness categories that are much broader than the biomedically-defined diseases for which the vaccine was intended.[10] For example, in South India neonatal tetanus is often designated by the same illness term as other conditions involving fits and inability to suck milk. When the immunization is found not to prevent such conditions, it may be judged ineffective.

Chen (1986) has noted this as a problem in Bangladesh. He states that three local Bengali terms for tetanus--*dhanostinkar*, *alga*, and *takuria*--were also applied to neonatal syndromes that resemble tetanus. As a result, people came to believe that tetanus toxoid vaccine was only 50% effective. Similarly, Brown (1983) reports that in Cameroon, stories about unsuccessful measles vaccines may be traceable to people's using a native term inclusive of measles for illness episodes that were not clinically measles. (Rubella, scarlet fever, and a range of viral rashes may mimic some of the features of measles.) I identified a similar problem on the island of Mindoro in the Philippines (Nichter 1989b) where the term *sikal* indexed measles as well as chicken pox and other children's rashes, thus reducing perceptions of the vaccine's efficacy.

Although biomedical disease categories do not map onto indigenous categories with a perfect fit, it still may be advantageous for primary health care workers to identify a vaccine by the name of an illness to which people are familiar. In cases where confusion is likely, a hybrid name specifying a subtype of a known illness may be worth coining. Native healers commonly specify subtypes of illness categories for which they do and do not claim expertise (Nichter 1989a: Chapter 4). Specifying the illness for which a vaccine provides protection will prove more challenging for diseases involving symptoms like a rash than for diseases like pertussis having more distinctive features. Future studies designed to test the significance of improved vaccination knowledge on acceptance rates will need to carefully study the specificity and sensitivity of terms used.

Lay Perceptions of Vaccinations in Sri Lanka

Thus far, I have considered informants' perceptions and misperceptions about vaccinations in South India, an area with relatively low immunization rates. Yet misperceptions are a problem even in Sri Lanka, a highly literate nation ranking as one of the best-immunized in the developing world, with coverage approximating 90% in some parts of the country.[11] In many cases, people have little idea what illnesses are prevented by the vaccinations they are asked to accept.

For example, a Sinhalese master's degree student whose field study I helped supervise (Ratnayake 1985) surveyed knowledge of immunizations in a small rural village in Matara district in southern Sri Lanka. He found that of 110 lower-middle-class mothers with children under 5 years of age, 42% did not know what illnesses were prevented by the two tetanus toxoid vaccinations they had been asked to take. Forty-five percent did not know the illnesses prevented by the triple (DPT) vaccine, and 43% did not associate BCG (a vaccine for tuberculosis) with any particular illness. Even among those mothers who had between six and ten years of schooling (N = 65), a third had low levels of knowledge about the illnesses associated with specific immunizations.

In my own medical anthropological fieldwork in rural areas of central and southern Sri Lanka in 1984-85, I asked 20 literate women about the purpose of tetanus toxoid, a vaccine referred to in Sinhala as *behet dehkana denna* (the two-time-given medicine). Among their answers were: "to prevent heavy bleeding," "to reduce pain during delivery," "to make delivery easier," "to make the baby grow better," "to purify the blood," "to cure vitamin deficiency," "to prevent something bad from happening," and "to repel germs (*visabija*) attracted to the afterbirth." Some women commented simply that tetanus immunizations were "good for the body."

Eleven of the 20 women reported having received a vaccination during one of their last two pregnancies. Although *pittagasma* is a local word used for tetanus, only 6 of the 11 women had been told that the vaccination was for *pittagasma*. The other 5 had been told only that it was "good for health." The lay model of *pittagasma* was quite different from the biomedical model of tetanus in any case. While many informants had gleaned from newspapers and radio programs the idea that *pittagasma* was caused by germs (*visabija*), visualized as small wormlike creatures, few understood that there were different types of germs associated with specific illnesses. Most women interpreted the term "germ" used in health messages as a single malevolent agent causing many kinds of illnesses. In the present case, *visabija* were deemed to invade the body at a time of shock (*gasma*) related to blood loss.

Thus, as I have pointed out elsewhere (Nichter 1989a: Chapter 4), apparent community acceptance of germs as a cause of illness (in this case, *pittagasma*) must be interpreted with care. It must not be assumed that germs have replaced other agents of malevolence or that a doctrine of specific etiology has been understood. In such a setting, it is hazardous to tell people that a vaccine prevents or fights germs, as has sometimes been done in Sri Lanka, for such a claim leads to false expectations that the vaccine will have broad powers.

False Expectations

As in India, many Sinhalese women thought that vaccinations were "good for general health"--having been told this by health staff--and that they protected against cough, colds, fever, skin ailments, and diarrhea. Given these unreasonable expectations, it is not surprising that in Sri Lanka as in South India, many people who have received vaccinations do not perceive them as having "worked." Several Sinhalese informants told me that children who had been immunized were no healthier than children who had not been, as they still had fevers, colds, and diarrhea.

Such thinking illustrates the point that the seeming success of an immunization program, as evidenced by an increase in coverage, may paradoxically lead to long-term ambivalence about vaccination and other public health programs if immunization is not accompanied by meaningful consumer education.[12] In Sri Lanka, in India, and in the United States as well (cf. Chaiken et al. 1987), many people receive vaccinations not because they actively desire them but because of coercion and prodding. Health workers pressure households to accept immunizations because the government requires them. To a much lesser extent do citizens actively seek immunizations because they understand what illnesses they prevent.

An immunization program may achieve high coverage rates in this way, but at a cost. Where households and the community assume little responsibility for immunization, health workers come to be viewed as agents of social control, unmet expectations lead to disillusionment, and, inevitably, immunization histories may be falsified.

Nonacceptors

Despite high rates of coverage in Sri Lanka, a segment of the population remains unvaccinated and some people default even when vaccines are readily and freely available. Earlier, I highlighted three reasons for nonacceptance of vaccinations in India: suspicion that they were a covert form of family planning, mistrust of the skill of government vaccinators, and fear that some people were too weak or too ill to withstand the shock of the vaccination. In Sri Lanka I rarely encountered the first two concerns, but the third one was quite prominent. In fact, in 11 of 15 cases of immunization nonacceptance that I investigated, the parents said that their child was too weak or too ill to be vaccinated when scheduled to do so. In seven of these cases, parents were unclear as to whether a vaccination should be made up at a future time.

In a parallel finding, Ratnayake (1985) notes that 57% of the 110 mothers that he interviewed believed that a child suffering from weakness, recurring cough, or diarrhea should not be vaccinated. Thirty-two percent of his informants also thought that immunization was unwise for a child with poor digestion or *mandama dosha*, a folk illness associated with protein-calorie malnutrition (cf. Nichter 1989a: Chapter 5). Thus the malnourished child--the child at greatest risk from a cycle of infections--was one of the children least likely to be vaccinated.

Such ideas underline the need for a merging of curative and preventive health services. Considering the fact that in the developing world, children of the rural poor may be ill for one-third of the year up to age three (McAuliffe et al. 1985; Rao et al. 1971), it is likely that many will be deemed unfit to receive immunizations at scheduled clinic times. If a "catch them while you can" approach is nevertheless taken, then followup curative care is crucial. Without such care, mothers may come to view attendance at clinics as placing their children at increased risk at a time of pre-existing vulnerability.

Further, ideas about vulnerability are not limited to mothers. When I interviewed ten primary health care workers and ten private practitioners (allopaths) in Sri Lanka, I found that a majority of health care providers advised against a child receiving vaccinations while ill, weak, or in a state of malnutrition such as *mandama*. In some cases, this advice was clearly defensive. Health providers wanted to dissociate their immunization from the course of an illness. In other cases, providers spoke of the vaccination as dangerous because it might trigger illness and/or shock the body. It was evident that the populace was being offered a mix of messages about vaccination protocol during illness. (This problem was even more prominent in India.)

I also found that when people gave as a reason for vaccine nonacceptance the fact that immunization services were offered at "inconvenient times," this complaint often masked health concerns connected with traditional notions about weather. Besides worrying about "weakness," in both India and Sri Lanka people may weigh the appropriateness of receiving a vaccination against ideas about the "qualities" of the prevailing weather or season. For example, rainy days, which are associated with the exacerbation of illness and sluggish digestion, are considered inappropriate times to vaccinate and place the body at immediate risk.

In Sri Lanka, I found that summer season (*Vesak*) was deemed a bad time of year for immunizing pregnant women and children because it was associated with a proliferation of sour fruits such as mango, durian, mangostein, and cashew fruit. Some informants explained that sour fruit heated the body and caused bile (*pitta*) to rise, while others said that the fruit's acidic quality caused the blood to become humorally imbalanced. Summer is also a time of year associated with outbreaks of boils and sores, and some people said that it was inadvisable to receive a vaccination at a time when the blood was already imperfect. The vaccination might either aggravate the blood condition or interfere with heat leaving the body, which could cause serious problems.

Curiously, vaccinations were not considered *as* heating to the body as curative injections, yet the latter were accepted by vaccination abstainers during summer months. On this point, informants noted that when an injection is required for an immediate cure, one must accept its heating side effects and take cooling medicines to counterbalance them. Injections cured symptoms, while immunizations would not "answer" (be efficacious) if the body were in a state of humoral discord.

Ideas about proper diet after receiving a vaccination also emerged. After being vaccinated, it is customary in South Asia to avoid foods believed to harm the blood or to create humoral imbalance. For example, in South Kanara, people avoid foods such as brinjal and popular fish like Indian mackerel which are thought to heighten blood toxins (Nichter 1986). Similarly, in Sri Lanka manioc and jackfruit are not eaten after one is vaccinated. Since these foods are seasonal staples for some people, vaccinations may be postponed.

Discussion

> The medical establishment is in real trouble. Not only is it caught in the worries of rising costs versus finite budgets but it has the problem of defining its own image and philosophy. It makes good social, economic and professional sense to take the choice of intervention options nearer to the consumer whenever they have the chance. This is what is meant by "demystification" of medical technology (Mahler 1975).

It is apparent from the above summary that vaccinations have been interpreted in a variety of ways within South Asian popular health cultures and that vaccination-related behavior is influenced by indigenous health concerns. It is also evident that these concerns are not addressed when health educators work with a "persuasion" model of communication that engenders compliance rather than with a "convergence" model of communication (see Kincaid 1979) facilitating comprehension and adherence.

Employing a convergence model involving negotiated meaning and mutual understanding leads to a set of health imperatives shared by health workers and the community. In South Asia, however, little attempt has been made to explain what vaccinations are, how they function, which illnesses they protect against, and for whom they are and are not intended. Instead, short-term compliance has been gained through personal relationships established between health staff and the public, through appeal by community leaders, and through coercion by those in positions of power.

I do not mean to minimize the importance of routinization in vaccination schedules nor the need for a well-developed health infrastructure to achieve adequate immunization coverage. However, routines without community comprehension are in danger of becoming nothing more than a technical fix approach to health. Equity demands that knowledge about vaccinations be fairly distributed. Community participation demands informed, motivated response.

I contend that "communication underdevelopment" in health education and paternalistic approaches to immunization that rely on social control lead to the propagation of false expectations which may in turn undermine confidence in public health programs. There is a need to move beyond processes fostering compliance and client identification (e.g. surveillance and appeals by communicators) to processes that establish credibility and relevance for immunization programs themselves. *Demand* for vaccinations, as distinct from passive *acceptance*, requires appropriate conceptualization (cf. Kelman 1969; Fugelsang 1977) of what immunizations are and what they are not and what Mahler (1975) has referred to as demystification. This entails the negotiation of cultural models (Quinn 1982) which frame key concepts within a "taken for granted" world through a complex of images which index experience.

Health workers may facilitate conceptual accommodation by helping local people locate the new in relation to the known. Given the richly pluralistic South Asian health tradition, much potential exists for explaining vaccinations through existing preventive health concepts and the experiential lifeworld of indigenous populations.[13] Toward this end, a contextual mode of "education by appropriate analogy" has been proposed by several researchers (Flavier 1975; Maglalang 1976; Nichter 1989a: Chapter 10, and 1986; Were 1985) as one way to provide the community with a grassroots sense of modern health recommendations. This mode of education is not intended as a replacement for formal science teaching, but rather as a first step in the process of education. Cultural models organized around central metaphors influence and direct action.

As I have attempted to show earlier in this paper, the military metaphor as it is applied to vaccines compels health personnel to think of vaccines as "weapons" in the fight against disease. Along with that metaphor comes a certain posture toward health care provision--a posture of command. The image of doctors and public health workers producing health and holding off disease with powerful tonics and fixes is misleading if not dangerous. When such thinking is operationalized, medicines become necessary for health and vaccinations become loosely associated with endless rounds of magic bullets fired at disease targets, targets that are often moved to hit the bullet so that higher rates of immunization coverage can be shown.

A "commando" mentality has also led to the practice of intensifying vaccination efforts during epidemics, with a resultant blurring of boundaries between the preventive and the curative in people's minds. When cholera vaccinations have been deployed in this way in India, for example, many in the lay population have concluded that the vaccinations control early symptoms of cholera that they believe can progress into the illness. As an indirect result of such practices, some have demanded vaccines during health crises while questioning their value during times of relative wellness.

In reality, the aggressive use of vaccines during epidemics is first and foremost an attempt to reduce panic and provide a sense that something is being done.[14] The seemingly insignificant monetary cost of such practices must be measured against the undesirable ramifications of the false sense of security that is created. One problem is that people may incorrectly conclude that vaccinations cure almost everything and thus undervalue the need to engage in community-based health efforts. Where the vaccination is perceived as a magic bullet, it is all too easy to neglect such efforts in the belief that as long as individuals "get their shots," all will be well.

Alternative, non-military metaphors might lead to quite different images of vaccines and quite different action plans. For example, one might employ information theory to explain vaccines as encoded information which, once incorporated, enables the body to recognize danger in the form of harmful external forces. When elaborated (e.g. by an analogy between antigens and factories emitting toxic waste), this image could link immunology to environmental and occupational health as well as to political-economic models of exploitative underdevelopment. Vaccines would then be presented as sources of long-term instruction leading to collective self-empowerment rather than as commodified "quick-fix" solutions to problems.

Over the past few years there has been debate between those advocating selective disease interventions and those advocating community process models of primary health care (Walsh and Warren 1979; Rifkin and Walt 1986). The gap between these two approaches may be narrowed if informed communities come to play an active role in the management of "their," as opposed to "government," health services. Vaccinations, if explained through familiar images and analogies, can become community resources which are actively desired and understood rather than just passively accepted. This in turn may lead to demand for improvements in the distribution and administration of vaccines, e.g. enhanced sterile techniques.

Thus, although some critics have claimed that vaccines are fetishes of industrialization and biotechnology, they can be presented in such a way as to stimulate ideas about community development. I have suggested, for example, how antigens could be compared to factories spewing forth toxins and how vaccines could be compared to forces able to recognize such hazards and to mobilize the (social and collective) body against them. For this to happen, health education must embrace consumer education, combatting the false expectations attendant on simplistic models of magic bullets and the like. In short, it is time for primary health care workers to not only inject vaccines into physical bodies but, equally important, to raise the resistance of the communities they serve to larger invasive pathogens and the false consciousness of commodified health.

Acknowledgements

An Indo-U.S. Subcommission on Education and Culture grant facilitated data collection for this paper during 1979-80. The Sri Lanka data was collected while I was a Fulbright lecturer attached to the Postgraduate Institute of Medicine, Colombo (1982-83), and a WHO consultant to the Bureau of Health Education (1983). I would like to acknowledge the assistance of Bureau members in helping me to conduct interviews and validate findings. I would also like to thank Susan McCombie for her constructive criticism of an earlier version of this paper and Dorothy Mull for editorial assistance based on a keen understanding of the issues.

Notes

1. From a bioscience standpoint, the military analogy may fit some features of the immune response such as the antibody's interaction with phagocytic cells and reactive "killer T" cells' destructive response to virus infected hosts as a means of removing a site for virus breeding. Other central features of the immune response, however, may just as readily be represented by images leading to a different set of perceptions about vaccinations.

2. Much of this scenario is as characteristic of the First World as it is of the Third World. Even in the United States, few mothers know exactly what kinds of diseases "baby shots" are for; many think that immunizations offer general protection against disease, a notion perpetuated by poster advertisements; and people have misgivings about pregnant women receiving vaccines. Thus Fulginiti (1984) has argued, in the U.S. context, that parents need to be educated about the nature, prevalence, and risks of the *diseases* against which children are vaccinated as well as the benefits, risks, and side effects of *vaccines*. He has emphasized that health care providers must move beyond an "it's time for baby shots" mode of communication if the public is to play a responsible part in immunization programs.

3. A wide range of predisposing, enabling, and service related factors have been found to influence health behavior (see Bartlett 1984 and Population Reports 1986 for useful reviews). Several studies have suggested that health beliefs are of only minor importance in influencing vaccination acceptance. For example, Morgan (1969) found in Nigeria that although only 20% of one community knew how smallpox was transmitted and only 70% thought it could be prevented, 90% accepted vaccination. In this case, endorsement by respected leaders appeared to be key.

4. Research stating the importance of people's ideas about health is often associated with the "health belief model." One problem with this model is that often, little attention is paid to the metamedical and political-economic context in which such ideas are embedded. Moreover, the data presented as indicating health beliefs are often an artifact of structured surveys that simplistically pose indigenous (often supernatural or fatalistic) notions of etiology against modern

ideas, whereas in reality, both types of notions often exist in the mind of a single individual. Ethnographic research on lay perceptions of illness and vaccinations needs to be viewed separately from such studies.

5. More recent surveys have produced similar findings. In a Karnataka-based study carried out by the Population Centre, Bangalore (1984), the following results were obtained when health workers were asked to name the six immunizations covered by the Expanded Programme for Immunization (EPI) program:

Cadre of field staff	Number of immunizable diseases named				
	6	5	4	<4	N.A.
Male health worker (N = 111)	5%	29%	22%	11%	35%
Female health worker (N = 89)	2%	36%	28%	13%	21%
Block health educator (N = 6)	17%	33%	33%	--	20%

Knowledge about immunizations among Indian physicians working in rural areas has been found to be similarly sketchy. Of 48 doctors interviewed by Maheshvari et al. (1987) in Rajasthan, only 29% could name all six diseases covered by the EPI program. While most knew when to administer DPT, few knew its composition. Sixteen doctors (33%) did not know that OPV (oral polio vaccine) was a live vaccine. Interestingly, 42% of practitioners said that reading newspapers, not medical journals, was the main way they updated their medical knowledge.

6. Immunization statistics are very unreliable in India (Basu 1985). In the study area, the coverage rates reported by health center staff were up to double those reported by villagers. This was probably due both to inflated figures and to mothers' lack of awareness that an immunization had been received.

7. A recent study in Kerala, India, produced similar findings (Premita et al. 1987). The researchers interviewed mothers of children admitted to the Trivandrum Medical College Hospital with vaccine-preventable diseases. (In 1984 this group constituted 10.4% of all admissions and in 1986 2.9% of admissions, showing probable increases in immunization coverage.) The child's "illness" was the main reason given for both nonimmunization with DPT (40% of cases) and for booster default (50% of cases).

8. This view of tetanus vaccinations as combatting *nanju* was not generalized to every type of immunization. For example, some villagers said that the DPT vaccine itself had *nanju* qualities. Indeed, I observed dried cow dung and turmeric paste placed on the arms of children to remove *nanju* after they had received DPT injections. Both substances are frequently used for ritual purification. Cow dung, for example, is used to clean the floor after delivery, it is put on a newborn's cradle, and it is sometimes applied to the umbilical cord after birth. In more modern families, commercial preparations believed to have the same anti-*nanju* properties are often used rather than cow dung and turmeric.

9. This may have been a case of provocation polio. Wyatt (1984) has observed that paralysis caused by poliomyelitis often follows the injection of the limb. In the United States, vaccinations were at one time advised against in summer (a peak time of enterovirus infections) due to a concern about provocation polio. This raises the issues of vaccines being a catalyst for manifestation of subclinical infections. For example, measles depresses cellular immunity allowing T.B. to activate. Evidence does not presently implicate live measles vaccine in the activation of T.B., but this remains a possibility. In the United States, some doctors recommend that a child receive a skin test for T.B. prior to receiving a measles vaccine.

10. Overexpectation from vaccines is not confined to developing countries. While working at a county health department in the southwestern United States, McCombie found that every year the department would get several complaints from people who had received the "flu" vaccine and hence expected to experience no flu-like symptoms--not even diarrhea (personal communication, 1987). On the wide range of meanings associated with the term "flu," see McCombie 1987a.

11. By 1985, 94% of pregnant women in Sri Lanka were reported to have been immunized with two doses of tetanus toxoid. Between 1978 and 1984, improved immunization coverage resulted in a reported reduction of cases of diphtheria from 216 cases to 17, of pertussis from 703 to 201, of neonatal tetanus from 874 to 84, and of polio from 153 to 16.

12. The same criticism may be made of social marketing campaigns that measure success by the number of items sold or by the percentage of people who indicate familiarity with the product when surveyed. We need studies that measure people's behavior and their ideas about health innovations over time. Only such studies will give us insights into the effect of expectations on behavior. For example, the social marketing of ORS as a product for *diarrhea*, not dehydration, led many people in developing countries to interpret it as a new medicine that would stop diarrhea and to lose faith in it when that expectation proved false. We need not just social marketing of *products* such as ORS (or immunizations) but marketing of *knowledge* about products, as well as careful longitudinal research to assess the results of such efforts.

13. Ideas about the multiple causality of illness are commonplace in Asia, so that pre-existing notions about health need not be discounted in order to introduce something new. For example, Luschinsky (1963) notes that in one region of India, villagers believed tetanus to be caused by an invisible flying insect called Jam. Midwives successfully linked this idea with the need for better hygiene by telling people that the insect might light on dirty places such as unsterilized sickles and knives.

14. One is reminded here of Hsu's classic study (1955) of a Chinese cholera epidemic in which he describes the Chinese use of spirit water and the government's use of cholera vaccine at such times as complementary magical practices. My study of Kyasanur Forest Disease (Nichter 1987) shows how officials tried to pacify the community with a promise of vaccines after this disease of development raged out of control and a community action group began linking it to deforestation. In the West we make similar use of inexpensive vaccinations at times when the public demands action (McCombie 1987b).

References

Bartlett, E.B. 1984. The Contribution of Behavioral Science to Patient Education Practice: A Review. In *Advances in Medical Social Science*, Vol. 2. J. Ruffini, ed. Pp. 1-43. London: Gordon Beach.

Basu, R.N. 1985. India's Immunization Programme. *World Health Forum* 6:35-38.

Bonilla, J., J. Gamarra, and E. Booth. 1985. Bridging the Communication Gap: How Mothers in Honduras Perceive Immunization. *Assignment Children* 69(72):443-454.

Brown, J.E. 1983. Low Immunization Coverage in Yaounde, Cameroon: Finding the Problems. *Medical Anthropology* 7(2):9-18.

Chaiken, B., N.M. Williams, S.R. Preblud, W. Parkin, and R. Altman. 1987. The Effect of a School Entry Law on Mumps Activity in a School District. *Journal of the American Medical Association* 257(18):2455-2458.

Chen, L. 1986. Primary Health Care in Developing Countries: Overcoming Operational, Technical and Social Barriers. *Lancet* November 29:1260-1265.

Coreil, J., A. Augustin, E. Holt, and N. Halsey. 1989. Use of Ethnographic Research for Instrument Development in a Case-Control Study of Immunization Use in Haiti. *Int. J. Epidemiology* 18(4):901-905.

Ebrahim, G. 1987. Immunization in Childhood--Current Trends and New Developments. *Pediatrics* 33:66-67.

Fillmore, C. 1977. Frame Semantics and the Nature of Language. In *Origin and Evolution of Language and Speech*. S. Harnad, H. Lancaster, and J. Steckles, eds. New York Academy of Sciences.

Flavier, J. 1975. The Agricultural Approach to Teaching Family Planning in the Philippines. Paper presented at the meeting of the International Women's Year Tribune, Mexico City. June.

Friede, A., C. Waternaux, et al. 1985. An Epidemiological Assessment of Immunization Programme Participation in the Philippines. *International Journal of Epidemiology* 14(1):135-142.

Fugelsang, A. 1977. Doing Things Together: A Report on an Experience in Communicating Appropriate Technology. Upplasa, Sweden: Dag Hammarskjold Foundation.

Fulginiti, V.A. 1984. Patient Education for Immunizations. *Pediatrics* 74(Supplement):961-963. American Academy of Pediatrics.

Hanks, L.M., and J.R. Hanks. 1955. Diphtheria Immunization in a Thai Community. In *Health, Culture and Community*. B. Paul, ed. Pp. 155-185. New York: Sage.

Hanlon, P., and P. Byass. 1988. Factors Influencing Vaccination Compliance in Peri-urban Gambian Children. *Journal of Tropical Medicine and Hygiene* 91:29-33.

Heggenhougen, K., and J. Clements. 1987. *Acceptability of Childhood Immunization: Social Science Perspectives*. EPC Publication No. 14. London: London School of Hygiene and Tropical Medicine.

Henderson, R.H., H. Davis, D.L. Eddins, and W.H. Foege. 1973. Assessment of Vaccination Coverage, Vaccination Scar Rates and Smallpox Scarring in Five Areas of West Africa. *Bulletin of the World Health Organization* 48:183-194.

Hsu, F. 1955. A Cholera Epidemic in a Chinese Town. In *Health, Culture and Community*. B. Paul, ed. Pp. 135-154. London: Russell Sage.

Indian Market Research Bureau. 1987. *Immunization: A Summary Report on Knowledge, Attitudes and Practices--Mothers*. New Delhi: UNICEF. November.

Kelman, H.C. 1969. Processes of Opinion Change. In *The Planning of Change*. W. Bennis, ed. Pp. 470-496. New York: Holt, Rinehart and Winston.

Kincaid, D.L. 1979. *The Convergence Model of Communication*. Paper 18. Honolulu: East-West Center Communication Institute.

Lakoff, G. 1987. *Women, Fire and Dangerous Things*. Chicago: University of Chicago Press.

Luschinsky, M.S. 1963. Problems of Culture Change in the Indian Village. *Human Organization* 22:66-74.

Maglalang, D. 1976. *Agricultural Approach to Family Planning*. Manila: Communication Foundation for Asia.

Maheshwari, R.K., B.D. Gupta, and S. Karunkaran. 1987. Knowledge and Attitude of Rural Doctors Regarding Immunization. Paper presented at the annual conference of the Indian Academy of Pediatrics, Madras, India, October 9-11.

Mahler, H. 1975. Health: A Demystification of Medical Technology. *Lancet*, November 1:829-833.

McAuliffe, J., M.A. de Souza, M. Nations, D.S. Shields, I.L. Tavares, J. Leslie, J.G. Araujo, and R.L. Geurrant. 1985. Prospective Studies of the Illness Burden in a Rural Community of Northeast Brazil. *PAHO Bulletin* 19(2):139-146.

McCombie, S.C. 1987a. Folk Flu and Viral Syndrome: An Epidemiological Perspective. *Social Science and Medicine* 25(9):987-993.

___ 1987b. "Shoot 'Em or You're Dead": The Politics of Intervention in Public Health. Paper presented at the American Anthropological Association annual meeting, Chicago, November 18-22.

Morgan, R. 1969. Attitudes toward Smallpox and Measles in Nigeria. *International Journal of Health Education* 12:77-85.

Mosley, W.H. 1984. Child Survival: Research and Policy. *Population and Development Review 10* (Supplement):3-23.

Mull, D.S., J.W. Anderson, and J.D. Mull. 1990. Cow Dung, Rock Salt, and Medical Innovation in the Hindu Kush of Pakistan: The Cultural Transformation of Neonatal Tetanus and Iodine Deficiency Disease. *Social Science and Medicine* 30(6):675-691.

Nichter, M. 1984. Project Community Diagnosis: Participatory Research as a First Step Toward Community Involvement in Primary Health Care. *Social Science and Medicine* 19(3):237-252.

___ 1986. Modes of Food Classification and the Diet-Health Contingency: A South Indian Case Study. In *Aspects of Food Systems in South Asia*. R. Khare and K. Ishvaran, eds. Pp. 185-222. Durham, NC: Carolina Academic Press.

___ 1987. Kyanasur Forest Disease: An Ethnography of a Disease of Development. *Medical Anthropology Quarterly* 1(4):406-423

___ 1989a. *Anthropology and International Health: South Asian Case Studies*. Norwell, MA: Kluwer Academic Publishers.

___ 1989b. Acute Respiratory Illness, Recognition and Behavior Study: Mindoro Philippines. WHO Report to the Programme for Control of Acute Respiratory Infections, Geneva, Switzerland.

Nichter, M., and M. Nichter. 1983. The Ethnophysiology and Folk Dietetics of Pregnancy. *Human Organization* 42(93):235-246.

Nichter, M., and C. Nordstrom. 1989. The Question of Medicine Answering: Health Commodification and the Social Relations of Healing in Sri Lanka. *Culture, Medicine and Psychiatry* 13:367-390.

Population Centre. 1984. *Gaps in Knowledge, Skills and Practices of Health and Family Planning Personnel*. Bangalore, India.

Population Reports. 1986. *Immunizing the World's Children*. Johns Hopkins University Population Program Publication 14(1):153-192.

Premita, D.P., N.S. Karunakaran, and S. Bai. 1987. Vaccine Preventable Diseases: Remediable Failures in Immunization Strategy. Paper presented at the annual meeting of the British Paediatric Association, York, England.

Quinn, N. 1982. Commitment in American Marriage: A Cultural Analysis. *American Ethnologist* 3(3):775-798.

Quinn, N., and D. Holland. 1987. Culture and Cognition. In *Culture Models in Language and Thought*. D. Holland and N. Quinn, eds. Pp. 3-41. New York: Cambridge University Press.

Rao, P.S., V. Benjamin, and J. Richard. 1971. Specific Morbidity Rates in a Rural Area. *Indian Journal of Medical Research* 59(6):965-973.

Ratnayake, L. 1985. *Lay Perceptions of Immunization and the Immunization Behavior of Mothers*. Field project report. Colombo, Sri Lanka: Post Graduate Institute of Medicine.

Rifkin, S., and G. Walt. 1986. Why Health Improves: Defining the Issues Concerning "Comprehensive Primary Health Care." *Social Science and Medicine* 23(6):559-566.

Sidel, V. 1986. War and Peace: Smallpox and the Use and Abuse of Public Health. *American Journal of Public Health* 76(10):1189-1190.

Singarimbun, M., K. Streatfield, and I. Singarimbun. 1986. *Some Factors Affecting Use of Childhood Immunization*. Research Note No. 7CS. Canberra: Australian National University, Research School of Social Sciences.

Streatfield, K., and M. Singarimbun. 1988. Social Factors Affecting Use of Immunization in Indonesia. *Social Science and Medicine* 27(11):1237-1245.

UNICEF. 1984. *Immunizing More Children: Towards Greater Community Participation*. New Delhi, India.

___. 1985. Vaccination Commando in Burkina Faso. *Assignment Children* 69/72:301-327

Walsh, J., and K. Warren. 1979. Selective Primary Health Care: An Interim Strategy for Disease Control in Developing Countries. *New England Journal of Medicine* 301(18):967-974.

Warren, K. 1986. New Scientific Opportunities and Old Obstacles in Vaccine Development. *Proceedings of the National Academy of Science* 83:9275-9277.

Wehrle, P., and J. Wilkins. 1981. Immunizing Agents: Potential for Controlling or Eradicating Infectious Diseases. *Annual Review of Public Health* 2:363-395.

Were, M.K. 1985. Communicating on Immunization to Mothers and Community Groups. *Assignment Children* 69/72:429-442.

Wyatt, H. V. 1984. The Popularity of Injections in the Third World: Origins and Consequences for Poliomyelitis. *Social Science and Medicine* 19(9):911-915.

11

Folk Models of Hypertension among Black Women: Problems in Illness Management

Suzanne Heurtin-Roberts and Efrain Reisin

Introduction

This paper discusses hypertension control in New Orleans as a problem in anthropology and primary health care, where difficulties in the management of hypertension in a largely Black population are related to folk illness models and health beliefs. Findings from research investigating these folk models and their relationship to illness management, specifically compliance with biomedical treatment, are reported. It is argued that many of the problems of primary health care delivery in the United States are similar to those in developing nations and that anthropology can make a significant contribution to primary health care in developed nations as well.

Primary Health Care in an "Affluent" Society

The discussion of primary health care has traditionally taken place in the context of developing and Third World nations. Recently the concept has been applied to public health programs in the fourth world and the "welfare state" (O'Neil 1986; Hessler and Twaddle 1986). Yet throughout this discussion, anthropologists in Western industrialized nations have shown a tendency to focus on "them" and not "us." This is in part due to the past general tendency of anthropologists to look askance at home-based research, deeming it more appropriate for sociologists (Cassel 1977; Hughes 1974). For American anthropologists, at least, it may also be related to a peculiarly American "missionary" urge to help the "poor of the world" while neglecting serious problems at home.

Two often-stated goals of primary health care should be noted. One goal is the delivery of basic health services to everyone in a community at a price the community can afford (see Gish 1979 and Mull [Chapter 2] for a historical discussion of primary health care). That an affluent and technologically advanced nation such as the U.S. should fall short of this basic goal raises serious questions about our system of health care. American affluence is not equitably distributed nor are basic health services. New and Donahue (1986) point out that primary health care problems generally are a function of the political economy at the national and international levels. In addition to these broad parameters, however, problems in primary health care delivery can traced to local and regional economic history.

The late anthropologist Marian Pearsall argued that the American South has much in common with Third World post-colonial nations (1966). Its former plantation economy has left it with a large, extremely poor underclass that is racially and culturally distinct from a still formidable ruling elite. This distinctiveness not only poses problems in designing health care both suitable and acceptable to a large Black population, but also makes it more difficult to convince the elite of the necessity to do so.

Much of the contemporary South remains a single-commodity economy producing raw materials whose price is controlled by the industrialized world. In Louisiana, efforts at industrialization have concentrated on oil and gas production. The recent drop of oil prices has caused Louisiana's oil-dependent economy to all but collapse.[1] Faced with critical budget deficits, the state government has threatened the public health care system with draconian budget cuts (Times-Picayune 1987a). At the time of this writing, Louisiana is only with great difficulty providing basic health care to its population (Times-Picayune 1986a, 1988).

A second goal of primary health care is to promote self-determination, that is, to enhance indigenous elements in health care delivery and to foster the use of local resources. A basic premise of the effort is to provide health care from the "bottom-up" rather than the "top down" (New and Donahue 1986) and to involve full community participation. In New Orleans, "indigenous forces" and local resources include biomedical professionals as well as a large, culturally distinct population.

As Welsch (1986) noted, the concern for self-determination and "scientifically sound" technology in primary health care is inherently contradictory. This contradiction often takes the form of an intrinsic tension between local autonomy and external professional authority. In a setting involving local biomedical professionals as well as patients with a distinctive culture, there exist two markedly different symbolic worlds within one local system of action. Tension, conflict, and resulting problems are then placed within the indigenous system itself rather than on a local/external axis. This problem must be addressed if there is to be an effective primary health care program.

Our purpose here is to examine the problem of hypertension control in a New Orleans clinic as a case study of such a disjunction between professional and popular health concepts. In short, we present an anthropological analysis of a primary health care problem in a First World situation focusing on the interaction between culture and delivery of basic health care in a U.S. community.

Hypertension, Compliance, and Health Beliefs

Hypertension and Compliance

In the normal vascular system, the ratio between cardiac output and total peripheral resistance of the vascular system is constantly regulated. Blood pressure in the systemic circulation is kept within certain limits both at rest and during periods of stress. When hypertension is present, this ratio is disturbed (Lund-Johansen 1983). Over time this can cause damage to the vessel walls and organ damage. Possible sequelae of this condition include heart disease, kidney disease, stroke, and blindness (Williams, Jagger, and Braunwald 1980).

According to general biomedical thought, hypertension is normally asymptomatic and can be determined only by medically detected signs, such as measures of blood pressure, although symptoms are known to occur infrequently (Williams, Jagger, and Braunwald 1980). Control of hypertension requires blood pressure monitoring at regular intervals. The poorer the control, the greater the frequency of monitoring required, with weekly measurement not being uncommon. It is thus important to keep hypertension controlled for two reasons: (1) uncontrolled hypertension results in disease and death; and (2) related morbidity and more frequent medical visits tax the health care system.

The prevalence of hypertension in Black Americans is considerably higher than that of the White population and hypertension-related deaths are disproportionately higher among

Black persons (Joint National Committee 1984). Control of hypertension in this population is thus particularly important.

Contemporary biomedicine provides numerous treatment possibilities to aid in the control of hypertension. These include various pharmacological strategies designed to dilate vessels, reduce cardiac output, and decrease blood volume, all with the end purpose of reducing the pressure at which the cardiovascular system operates. Dietary restriction of sodium and weight reduction are also used (Williams, Jagger, and Braunwald 1980). These treatments cannot be effective, however, if they are not used correctly by the patient population. To a great extent, they are not.

According to a report of the Joint National Committee on High Blood Pressure, compliance is the crucial missing link in hypertension control (1984). A widely accepted estimate of the magnitude of noncompliance in the general population is that, of those hypertensives under biomedical treatment, about one-half adhere to their regimens (Kirscht and Rosenstock 1977; Dressler 1980; Taylor et al. 1978; Hershey et al. 1980).

Research on compliance with biomedical treatment is represented by a vast literature which spans several decades (see Leventhal, Zimmerman, and Gutman 1984 for a general review). Factors investigated include sociodemographic patient characteristics, the patient-practitioner relationship, aspects of the therapeutic regimen, and the organization of health care. Demographic, socioeconomic and organizational correlates, although providing a basis for policy and planning, offer little insight into patient behavior and have limited clinical utility.

Health Beliefs

A large body of research has accumulated which indicates that cognitive factors including health beliefs are important factors in illness behaviors such as compliance. Much of this research has been based on the Health Belief Model, derived from cognitive psychology, which relates patient beliefs, attitudes, and motivations to illness behavior (Maiman and Becker 1974). First used to predict preventive health behavior, the model's use has been successfully extended to research on compliance with antihypertensive treatment (Hershey et al. 1980; Nelson et al. 1978; Kirscht and Rosenstock 1977). Although there has been some question about their importance relative to each other, patient perceptions generally found to be significantly associated with compliance include severity of disease, locus of control over treatment, and efficacy of treatment. In these studies, approximately 15% of the variance was explained.

While this type of quantitative, theoretically derived research has proved useful, it has some limitations. The Health Belief Model has been deductively derived from theory in cognitive psychology, generating research on beliefs that are theoretically significant (Maiman and Becker 1974). Sole reliance on theoretically generated survey questions can mean that entire domains of health cognition may not be tapped. This is especially problematic where culturally distinctive beliefs may be involved.

Blumhagen makes this point in his discussion of Health Belief Model applications to compliance in hypertension (1982), noting the fallacy of depending too much on what theory deems important and not on what the "people" think is important. Certainly, a more empirically grounded approach is appropriate (Glaser and Strauss 1967). Inductive, ethnographic research, as reported in the present study, can provide a social and cultural context to elucidate the relationship of cognition to illness behavior.

Yet, the difficulties lie not only in the research approach, but also in the manner in which the problem is formulated. It may be advisable to rethink the concept of compliance, which is usually defined as the extent to which a patient's behavior coincides with that prescribed by a physician for treatment of a disease (Sackett 1976). Trostle and associates demonstrated in a study of epileptics that behavior often labelled "noncompliant" by the medical profession can be viewed as a reasonable effort at illness management (Trostle, Hauser, and Susser 1983). Strict adherence to the traditional conceptualization of compliance focuses attention on a narrowly defined behavior which ultimately addresses only the issue of obedience to medical authority.

By employing a holistic, ethnographic perspective, the focus on compliance can be reconceptualized as a problem in illness management. This allows a shift from issues of obedience/disobedience to the contextual and personal phenomena coming to bear on an individual's actions. Not only does this permit a patient to be viewed as a cognizant, rational person making choices, but it allows a deeper understanding of these choices.

Still, the concept of compliance cannot be discarded completely, even if only because so much medical research has been phrased this way in the past. It does refer to the problem of acting inappropriately according to what is biomedically perceived as therapeutic. As a part of biomedicine's symbolic world, the compliance concept reflects the reality of biomedicine as it is currently practiced, and as encountered by the patient. Nonetheless, compliance must be recognized as only one of the behaviors which comprise an individual's total effort at illness management.

The concept of explanatory models offers another useful perspective on compliance. As developed and used by Kleinman (1980), explanatory models of illness are conceptual models constructed and used by individuals to explain particular illness episodes. Details and refinements of the concept have been discussed elsewhere (Blumhagen 1981; Kleinman 1981; Young 1982).

For our purposes it is necessary to remember that the concept's utility derives from its individuality, the explanation of a particular illness episode by a particular individual. In gathering explanatory models of more than one individual we may attempt to consolidate and formulate them as representative illness models held by a group. In doing so, however we no longer have an "explanatory model" as used by Kleinman but a folk model of illness, a useful symbolic construct summing and expressing more diverse, individually held beliefs. It would be a mistake to expect individual explanatory models to be identical to more general folk models of illness (Pelto and Pelto 1975).

Folk Health Beliefs and Hypertension

In a classic review, Snow summarized the health beliefs of a number of U.S. Black populations including Blacks in the U.S. Southwest and in Michigan (1974). Regarding hypertension, Snow found that the term "high blood pressure," or simply "high blood," did not refer to the biomedically recognized condition (1974, 1976). Rather, "high blood" is a condition where the blood was too rich, thick and hot, and total blood volume was excessive. The blood was thought to rise up toward the head and remain there, with negative health consequences.

The Miami Health Ecology Report describes the health culture of several ethnic populations in Miami (Weidman 1978). Among U.S. Southern Blacks and Bahamians in Miami, Weidman and her associates found beliefs concerning "high blood" similar to those described by Snow (1974, 1976). Southern Blacks used the term "pressure" rather than "high blood" more frequently than did Bahamians, but both terms were found to have the same meaning (Weidman 1978: 542). Southern Blacks, Bahamians, and Haitians in Miami all were concerned with blood conditions relating to blood volume, temperature, thickness, and level and movement in the body (Weidman 1978).

In a study in Washington State, Blumhagen investigated health beliefs and high blood pressure in a primarily Anglo-American, middle-class sample (1980, 1982). He found that his informants tended to implicate emotional factors and psychological stress with the etiology of a condition called "hypertension" rather than with that of high blood pressure. Blumhagen described hypertension (as opposed to high blood pressure) as a folk illness which he characterized as "hyper-tension." Blumhagen concluded that, in his study population, "hyper-tension" represented a state of increased emotional tension and psychological stress, whereas "high blood pressure" referred to the biomedically defined condition.

Although there has been some ethnomedical research on Blacks in the South (Weidman 1978, 1979; Hill 1976; Nations et al. 1985; Snow 1974), there is a conspicuous paucity of such work in New Orleans and in Louisiana in general. Furthermore, such ethnomedical research as has been done has generally focused on the simple cataloguing of ethnomedical beliefs as folklore (Webb 1971; Hurston 1931), with little concern for their implications for illness behavior or treatment.

The present study investigated the explanatory models of hypertension held by Black patients being treated for hypertension at Charity Hospital in New Orleans, and compared these models with those of the physicians on the clinic staff. Since older Black women constitute the majority of patients treated for hypertension in the hospital's ambulatory clinics, and since resources for the research were limited, we decided to focus on females. The nature of both patient and practitioner illness models were formulated and their implications for compliance and illness management were determined.

The Setting

Unlike most U.S. cities, New Orleans has a population in which Blacks make up the majority (55%). Although New Orleans Blacks share with other U.S. Blacks an overrepresentation among the poor and disadvantaged (Times-Picayune 1987b), to cast them in the role of a ghetto minority would seriously misrepresent the situation. The problem of primary care in New Orleans is not to provide basic health care to Blacks but to Orleanians in general, most of whom happen to be Black. The difference is significant.

The Health Care System

The Charity Hospital System of Louisiana is a state owned and operated system of hospitals and clinics mandated to provide quality health care services to all residents of the state, with emphasis on services to the medically indigent (Storer et al. 1986). Most public hospitals in the United States are under the aegis of local governments. Louisiana is unique in that it is the only state in the nation which supports a statewide hospital system for the needy (Dubos 1985). In essence the Charity Hospital System is Louisiana's primary health care program.

Much of Louisiana's public health care, however, is centralized at Charity Hospital in New Orleans (hereafter CHNO; popularly called simply "Charity") (Storer et al. 1986). In 1984-85 it accounted for over 34% of total outpatient visits in the system and provided 64% of all outpatient services public or private in Orleans Parish.

Forty percent of all patient care at CHNO is provided free of charge. Only 5% of all patients treated have private insurance. (Because of high unemployment rates in the state, few persons carry medical insurance.) Thus, following trends in recent years, the demand for services at CHNO is likely to increase in the future (CHNO Financial Office 1987).[2] This comes at the same time that massive budget cuts are threatened by the state (Times-Picayune 1987a). City and parish governments face budgetary problems similar to those faced by the state, and therefore are in no position to provide financial support. Faced with increasing demand and dwindling resources, the system's prospects for continued delivery of basic health care are bleak.

One solution to this dilemma is to reduce demand for services. At CHNO especially this may be possible if chronic illnesses like hypertension can be better controlled. This would decrease demand for both outpatient and inpatient services.

At CHNO, by far the majority of hypertensive outpatients are treated in the General Medicine Clinics by residents from two local medical schools, supervised by the faculty of these schools. On a typical day, from 200 to more than 300 patients attend those clinics. A smaller, weekly Special Hypertension Clinic staffed by one of the medical schools treats 10 to 15 patients per week.

The Patient Population

The Black population of New Orleans is disproportionately represented in Medicine and Special Hypertension Clinics. For the last six months of 1986, of the 13,690 patients seen in Medicine Clinic, 77% (10,606) were Black, 22% (3,002) were White, and 1% (82) were listed as "Other." For the same period in Special Hypertension Clinic, of 316 patients, 90% (285) were Black and 10% (30) were White (CHNO Financial Office 1987, personal communication).

Statistics on diseases treated in outpatient clinics are not available. A simple tally of 112 patients for a single day of one school's Medicine Clinic showed that 69 (62%) were treated for hypertension (although not hypertension alone). Although Black males are at highest risk for hypertension (Joint National Committee 1984), of the hypertensives seen, 43 (62%) were Black females, 38% of the total day's patients. The administration of CHNO estimates that a diagnosis of hypertension is related to 30% of Charity's hospitalizations.

This presents a problem for CHNO, whose task it is to control the blood pressure of a significant part of the population. With over 70% of its patients being Black, CHNO's patient population is that part of the general population most at risk for hypertension and tending to suffer from the most severe sequelae. It is apparent from its heavy patient load and the large number of hypertension-related hospitalizations that the institution is faced with serious problems in hypertension control. It is also apparent that control is greatly important to the patients' health and also to the health care system.

Methods

The patient sample consisted of 60 Black female hypertensives aged 45-70 drawn at random from patients of Medicine and Special Hypertension Clinics at CHNO between May 1985 and August 1986. The patient sample was limited to females, who make up the majority of hypertensives at CHNO, to allow the use of a smaller sample. This decision was made due to limited resources for research. Clinic charts were reviewed, those meeting selection criteria were flagged, and patients were asked to participate in the research upon arriving for their regularly scheduled clinic appointments. Twenty per cent of selected patients refused to participate because of conflicts with employment or family disruptions and obligations. These were replaced by additional randomly selected patients to complete the sample. Thus study participants were those whose employment was minimal or flexible enough to allow participation, who were otherwise unemployed, and whose personal and social situations were stable enough to permit participation.

Illness models, health beliefs, and attitudes were elicited in two formal interviews. The first interview focused on the individual's explanatory model of hypertension (Kleinman 1980). The second interview included general questions related to health beliefs and attitudes and personal health status. All interviews were topically standardized and semi-structured, yet open-ended to allow for volunteering of information not directly requested by the interviewer. In addition, conversations held throughout the followup period were used as supplementary data.

Participants were each followed for approximately two months and were usually interviewed in their homes rather than in the clinic, depending on the informant's preference. The followup was designed to obtain data on compliance with prescribed treatment and to monitor blood pressure.

Six case studies are presented in this report. These were not elicited as formal case histories, but were selected from interviews with the sixty respondents because they represent particularly articulate individuals, and because they illustrate common themes and problems in hypertension management in this sample.

Compliance was measured by monthly pill counts to determine the ratio of pills actually taken to those prescribed. In addition, self-reports were used in the form of daily medication diaries. Data from these two sources were used to rank the informants from one to four on a scale of poor to good compliance. In cases where the correct ranking was uncertain, field notes were checked for additional information. Ten cases were selected at random and ranked by an independent rater. There was interrater concordance in all but one of the cases, thereby demonstrating acceptable reliability for the rating method.

A second sample was composed of 15 resident physicians staffing the clinics. This sample can be characterized as "opportunistic" in that informants were selected in terms of who was available and willing to be interviewed on a given day. The residents' interview protocol followed closely that of the patients, with the addition of questions on the physician's perceptions of the patient population.

Results

The Patients' Illness Models

Participants described their illness in terms of "pressure" or "pressure trouble." When asked for more specific terms, the response was usually "high blood pressure," "high blood," or "hypertension." Many informants discriminated between "high blood" (or "high blood pressure"), and hypertension. They considered "high blood" simply a shortened version of the term "high blood pressure" ("I just say 'high blood'"), but hypertension was considered "something else again." Over half said that these two illnesses were different but related. Fifty-three per cent differentiated between high blood and hypertension, 37% said there was no difference, and 10% said they did not know or were uncertain of the distinction. Of those who did not recognize a difference, 6 said they were aware that some people differentiate between the two. This suggests that the recognition of two separate illnesses related to blood pressure is widely shared in this population.

Despite individual variation in explanatory models, two basic folk illness models were evident from the interviews: "high blood/high blood pressure" (which will simply be called "high blood") and "high-pertension."[3] It is these two folk illnesses which will be discussed. See Table 11.1 for patients' characterizations of these two illnesses.

One can have both folk illnesses at the same time, although they do not have to begin at the same time. Furthermore, one illness can go away and the other begin. Each illness requires its own management strategy, even when concurrent with the other.

The pathophysiologies of both folk illnesses seem to work on what can be called a "thermometer" model. Participants describe normal blood as being "at rest" or "quiet," with the blood being lower in the body. When "pressure trouble" occurs, the blood rises in the body toward the head.

The pathophysiologies of these two illnesses differ markedly in other respects. In general, "high blood" is said to be a "disease of the blood" wherein excessively "hot," "thick" or "rich" blood rises up in the body, clogs, and tends to remain there (it is said to be "elevated"). Participants say their blood can be elevated for months at a time ("it stays high"). The illness is said to "work on the heart too hard."

In "high-pertension," the blood is usually "at rest." At times of sudden intense emotion, it shoots up suddenly to the head, but then goes back down. This sudden rise can cause instant death. "High-pertension" is said to be a "disease of the nerves." In "high-pertension," the blood tends to go up higher, all the way to the head, and more rapidly than in "high blood." It is said to "accelerate" in "high-pertension," whereas in "high blood" it only "elevates." One informant said that it "shoots up to my head and rings like a bell."

This dichotomy is similar to that described by Blumhagen (1980, 1982). His predominantly White middle-class sample considered hypertension (Blumhagen called it "hyper-tension") to mean that an individual was very nervous and under a good deal of stress. "High blood pressure" denoted the biomedically recognized illness involving impaired cardiovascular functioning. Elements of New Orleans "high-blood" and, to a lesser extent, "high-pertension," also resemble the folk illness "high blood" described by Snow (1974, 1976) and Weidman (1978). Both "high blood" and "high-pertension" involve excessive thick, hot blood which rises in the body.

The course of "high blood" is said to be predictable and often related to diet. Eating restricted foods was frequently noted as a trigger. For example, respondents made such statements as "I know if I eat a little piece of pork it'll go up and stay up for weeks" and "I knew if I ate that gumbo it would run my blood up but I did it anyway."

"High-pertension" is thought to be extremely unpredictable since the blood only goes up when someone is very upset emotionally, and this is not easily foreseen. Because it is unpredictable, sudden, and the blood goes up higher than in "high blood," "high-pertension" is thought to be more dangerous.

The two diseases differ in perceived etiology. "High blood" is generally thought to be caused by heredity ("it's in the family") or by eating the "wrong food." Participants considered the most harmful foods to be pork (fresh or salt), salt, "seasoning" (defined as added garlic, onion, bay leaf, thyme, celery, bell pepper, salt and pepper), and "grease." "High-pertension" is caused by "bad nerves," stress, worry and anger. Food is not a causal factor in "high-pertension."

An important aspect of this emotional causation was the belief that an individual has "high-pertension" because she has a nervous, excitable temperament and is prone to worrying. Some women thought "high-pertension" could be inherited in association with an excitable, tense personality.

Various exacerbating factors can aggravate the pre-existing conditions. Factors in "high blood" are "wrong foods," stress, and heat (weather or body temperature, which make the blood hotter and thicker). Worry and anger did not figure as important problems, and "nerves" were not thought to exacerbate "high blood." However, the most important exacerbating factor in "high-pertension" is "nerves," followed by stress, worry, anger, financial problems, and children. Only two persons mentioned diet as a problem. Again the etiological dichotomy between diet and heredity in "high blood" and emotion in "high-pertension" is apparent.

Hysterectomy and menopause were considered by some women to exacerbate both "high blood" and "high-pertension." According to patients, when the menstrual flow is stopped, excess blood goes up to the head, aggravating one's "pressure troubles." As one woman phrased it "There's no place for all that waste blood to go so it backs up into your head."

Appropriate management of the two folk illnesses differs accordingly. The majority of women thought appropriate treatment for "high blood" included medically prescribed antihypertensive drugs, dietary control, and, less importantly, weight loss. This is in direct contrast to the management of "high-pertension," for which medication was not thought particularly useful. Of those who thought medications might help, some women said these should be "nerve pills" or some other medication to cause relaxation and sleep. Neither dietary control nor weight loss were considered effective in "high-pertension" management. Most important in the management of "high-pertension" was for the individual to avoid worrying, relax, rest, stay quiet, and get away from people. Although rest was important for the treatment of "high blood," these other factors were much less important.

A number of home remedies such as garlic, vinegar or lemon juice in various combinations to "thin" and "cool" the blood and "draw it away from the head" were considered useful for both illnesses but were seen as supplements to biomedical care rather than substitutes.

It is interesting to note that, although essential hypertension is generally considered asymptomatic except for times of severe crisis, only four individuals said they absolutely never experienced symptoms. Twenty-three (72%) said those with "high blood" would ordinarily experience symptoms and 24 (75%) said the same for "high-pertension."

The array of symptoms experienced was long and varied; it included headaches, weakness and dizziness, blurred vision, seeing spots or glitter, nosebleeds, "glarey" eyes, the "blind staggers," blacking out and "falling out" (see Weidman 1979), chest pains, drowsiness, red eyes, smelling fresh blood in the nose, tasting fresh blood, and having one's breath smell like blood. The sensation of having blood in one's mouth and nose, along with reddened eyes, was said to indicate the presence of blood at a dangerously high level in the body; one's blood has "gone up."[4]

With the exception of disorientation, fewer individuals listed symptoms for "high-pertension" than for "high blood." There is not enough difference between symptoms mentioned for "high blood" and those mentioned for "high-pertension" to truly suggest separate symptomatologies, with the exception of disorientation. Only two people mentioned this as a symptom of "high blood" while 13 mentioned it for "high-pertension."

The Resident Physicians' Models

Illness models expressed by the residents staffing the clinics were quite different from those expressed by the patients (see Table 11.2). Most notable is the small amount of variation in the residents' models. This is, of course, to be expected since standardization is a goal of medical education.

All residents recognized only a single disease entity which could be called either hypertension or high blood pressure. Two, however, did think that "hypertension" was more appropriate as a disease name since "high blood pressure" could imply only a measure of blood pressure.

The residents described the pathophysiology as a process wherein peripheral vascular constriction resulted in peripheral resistance against too great a blood volume for the system's capacity. The end effect was a cardiovascular system operating at excessively high pressure with possible damage to the system and other organs.

While all residents agreed that the cause of essential hypertension is basically unknown, five thought heredity was implicated, one also blamed obesity, and two said the etiology was multifactorial. Exacerbating factors were thought to relate to general lifestyle including poor diet (high in sodium, fat, and calories), obesity, and smoking. Only three mentioned stress as aggravating the condition.

Appropriate treatment was unanimously thought to be medication, but only three residents felt that medication alone would normally be adequate. Dietary control was considered important, weight loss was mentioned by several, but only two noted that relaxation or stress management might be useful.

Only two residents felt that hypertension was completely asymptomatic. While five residents thought that symptoms were experienced only in times of severe hypertensive crisis, six said symptoms were possible at other times and two felt sure their patients experienced symptoms during the regular course of their illness. Remember that only four patients experienced no symptoms and most experienced a wide variety.

It is noteworthy that both patients and medical residents acknowledged the presence of symptoms in hypertension although hypertension is considered asymptomatic by much of the medical profession and for this reason is called the "silent killer" by the American Heart Association. This represents a disjunction between the general biomedical description and illness as experienced in real life by the patient and practitioner.

It is medically acknowledged that symptoms can be experienced in *malignant* hypertension (a crisis state of severely high blood pressure requiring immediate emergency treatment) and infrequently in a small percentage of hypertensives. In the general population of mild and moderate hypertensives, symptoms are considered rare (Robertson 1983). However, the majority of women in the patient sample experienced numerous symptoms with great frequency. Patient and practitioner responses suggest that biomedical disease theory inadequately reflects what actually occurs in experience and practice.

Furthermore, although residents concurred that the duration of the illness was lifelong, five then volunteered that, in their experience, they had actually seen it "go away," i.e. the patient's blood pressure was controlled to the point that medication was no longer required, the blood pressure remained controlled, and the patient was "cured." As one resident phrased it "I know it's not supposed to happen, but I've seen it happen."[5]

The physician sample is too small to draw any real conclusions, but it does call to mind the often-cited distinction between overt culture (what people say they do and think) and covert culture (what they really do and think), i.e. the difference between idea and practice. The question of overt and covert culture in medicine has scarcely been addressed and certainly could be investigated for its influence on practice, treatment, and illness management.

Certainly the greater incongruence occurs between the patients' and practitioners' illness models. The fundamental difference is that patients recognize two illness entities whereas professionals recognize only one. This means that, unknowingly, patients and practitioners are often not even discussing the same illness.

Although all but three of the 15 residents were aware of folk terms for hypertension, only three of these doctors knew something about the recognition of different illnesses by the patients they treated. One resident said "high blood" meant having a high hematocrit (perhaps indicating his awareness of the folk belief in excessively "rich" blood). Another said "high blood" referred to the period before menses and "low blood" after menses. A third said "high-pertension" meant that the patient was too tense.

Influence on Compliance

The rate of noncompliance with prescribed antihypertensive medication was found to be 52%, a finding which is consistent with the 50% generally found in compliance research on hypertension.

The patient's illness model (whether or not "high blood" and "high-pertension" were considered different illnesses) was significantly related to compliance (See Table 11.3). Of those patients who were noncompliant, 20 (65%) persons believed the illness to be different, whereas only 6 (19%) persons thought they were same. For those who were compliant, 12 (41%) thought there were two different illnesses while 16 (55%) thought they were the same. The Lambda test showed that 34% of the error in predicting compliance could be explained by patient's illness model. In other words, those who subscribed to the idea of separate illnesses were disproportionately represented among the noncompliant patients.

Although "high-pertension" is considered a more serious illness than "high blood," medical treatment is not considered useful and it is thought to be difficult to control the environmental factors that trigger emotional upsets. Health Belief Model research suggests that compliance would be lower among individuals self-diagnosed with "high-pertension" since these individuals perceive low treatment efficacy. This was found to be the case in our sample.

The nature of the self-diagnosis was significantly related to compliance (see Table 11.4). Those persons who labeled themselves as having "high-pertension" were by far the least compliant with treatment. Those with "high blood" alone exhibited greater compliance, while those who did not differentiate between the two illnesses showed compliance levels similar to those of the general population (Joint National Committee 1984). Lambda showed that 52% of the error in predicting compliance could be explained by patient self-diagnosis.

In order to better understand the behavioral environment in which compliance and noncompliance take place, we now turn to selected case studies of hypertension management. The illness histories and personal explanatory models of six women are presented to provide the social context and cultural meaning of the relationship between folk beliefs and response to hypertension.

Cases

The first case illustrates the relatively simple, direct efforts that patients felt were necessary to manage "high blood."

Case 1: Althea Bernard[6] is a 61-year-old widow with five grown children who aid her financially. She also derives a small income from selling pralines (pecan candies) and "cold cups" of frozen Kool-Aid to neighborhood children.

Ms. Bernard has had "high blood" for 30 years, since the birth of her last daughter. When Ms. Bernard's blood goes up it stays up, so, she says "You got to take your medicine all the time," unlike in "high-pertension," which, according to Ms. Bernard, "shoots up but comes down." She says all you can do for "high blood" is take your medicine, watch what you eat, rest, and pray. During the winter she ate some pork roast and she got terrible headaches. "It must have done something to my blood and it went up real high. The doctor at Charity Hospital said it might be that." This would not have influenced "high-pertension," she says, because "food and pork aren't bad for high-pertension." She does take a "nerve pill" but it doesn't do anything to her blood because she doesn't have "high-pertension." Ms. Bernard says she always takes her medicine, unless she forgets, which happens only occasionally. Ms. Bernard's compliance was, in fact, excellent and her blood pressure was well-controlled during her participation in the research.

Since medication and dietary control are thought to be effective, illness management for Ms. Bernard is fairly straightforward. Ms. Bernard's life can be characterized as stable and quiet, and while she is certainly not well off, she does not lack the basic necessities of food and shelter. This stability, without doubt, supports her efforts to manage her "high blood."

Compliance, however, may not be so simple a matter for those with "high-pertension." Since "high-pertension" is a disease of the nerves, medication is not thought to be an important element of treatment. Rather, relaxation, rest, and, occasionally, tranquilizers are considered appropriate.

Case 2: Rosie Mae Batiste is a 64-year-old woman who has had "high-pertension" for forty years, ever since the birth of her first child. She said she had "high-pertension" because she worries too much, "My children say 'Mama, you worry too much,' and I guess I do have my share. The doctor thinks I'm real worried or upset about something. . . . Is it somebody I'm living with or something, . . . my children? They ask me that a lot."

During the interview a bill collector came to the door. When Ms. Batiste came back she said "You see this works on my nerves too, this is why my pressure goes up." Her medication caused no side effects she was concerned with. "It [the medicine] don't bother me, it don't cause me any hardship." She did admit, "I skip the pills some of the time. . . . When my blood goes up, I don't think it [medication] really does me any good, and I don't want any of it on the other days. I just try to stay relaxed and get rest. I think the Lasix [a diuretic] is just for fluid, I don't know if it really does anything for your pressure." Ms. Batiste used to take a tranquilizer and she now takes an antihistamine for an allergic rash, and believes they both helped her "high-pertension" since they make her relaxed and drowsy.

Ms. Batiste took only about 40% of her medication and her blood pressure was poorly controlled. Even where medication is considered possibly effective, other aspects of the illness "high-pertension" make it difficult to control. In the next case, the episodic, unpredictable nature of "high-pertension" is significant.

Case 3: Florida Joseph is a 54-year-old widow. Ms. Joseph receives S.S.I. (Supplementary Social Income), a disability-related Federal assistance, and her eight children aid her financially. Her medication is paid for by Medicaid. Ms. Joseph attributes her "high-pertension" to a particularly stressful job she held for 20 years. "At work you had to keep your anger in. . . . And that kind of stuff builds up in you and makes your blood go up. . . . With high-pertension, you don't know when your blood's gonna go up so you can't treat it like high blood." With "high blood," "you know the blood's always up so you can do what's necessary to keep it down, . . . [you can] work on it all the time. . . . [With high-pertension], it could be down, and all of a sudden your blood goes up so high it could kill you. That's the trouble, no warning; you don't never know when to take your medicine." When asked why she did not take it all the time, just to be sure, she said taking "all that medicine when you don't need it, that works your system too hard. Besides that's not the main thing. As long as I'm calm, I'm all right."

Ms. Joseph said she hadn't been taking her pills because her "blood's been okay." Her blood pressure was never controlled during the time she participated in the study. When we went to see her for her last blood pressure measurement no one was home. Later in the day we learned she had been taken to the emergency room because she was feeling sick and her blood pressure was dangerously high. When we last spoke to her she said "Well, with that high-pertension you never can tell."

Unlike Ms. Batiste, Ms. Joseph believed that medication could possibly help her "high-pertension." Since the illness is episodic and unpredictable, however, she did not know when to take it, and disapproved of taking medication at times when it was not needed. Consequently, Ms. Joseph's compliance was poor.

The interaction of folk beliefs with side effects of certain blood pressure medications can be influential in different ways depending upon the individual's assessment of the situation. The next two cases illustrate this.

Case 4: Lillie Dubose is a 70-year-old spinster who lives alone and was told by her doctor to stop working due to her blood pressure. She is experiencing severe financial difficulties but receives free medication through Medicaid.

Ms. Dubose says she has "low blood"[7] and "high-pertension." She says she knows she has "low blood" because her mother had it and because she is very pale and has small veins like her mother. [In fact, Ms. Dubose is a very dark-skinned woman.] She is not sure when her "high-pertension" started because she went to the doctor only this year at the urging of her brother. She has "high-pertension" because "I'm poor and worn out and there's a lot of pressure on me." She said "high-pertension" means you have too much "pertension," i.e. you are too tense, and the only treatment for that is "not to get mad, for your life to change or to die. It will knock you out, much quicker than high blood pressure."

At first the doctor prescribed Aldomet but that made Ms. Dubose feel "very, very sick." The doctor then changed her to Minipress, which, like Aldomet, can cause weakness, dizziness, and drowsiness, although usually only initially. She said the doctor was experimenting on her with a strange drug and she did not want to take it. It made her feel ill as well. Ms. Dubose said people have a big vein in their heads where the blood collects, and the medicine was pulling the blood down too hard, all the way down to her feet. "I can feel it going past my knees, they ache and feel weak. She's [the doctor] pulling all the strength out of my body." Ms. Dubose took no more medicine.

Ms. Dubose interpreted the side effects of dizziness, drowsiness, and weakness to indicate that the medication was pulling her blood down too far. In combination with her condition of "low blood," the medication was drawing the blood dangerously low and sapping the strength from her, resulting in her refusal to take the medication. Experiences with the same medication can be interpreted differently, however, as the next case demonstrates.

Case 5: Odile Porche is a 66-year-old woman with "high-pertension." Ms. Porche says it runs in her family, and people get it from being nervous, worried and upset. She says she gets "pertension attacks" wherein she yells and screams and gets mad. Her attacks are unpredictable. "With high blood you know it's up but the pertension can hit you at any time. . . . The pressure pill helps. You have to take all that medicine. It all has a drug in it. It makes you quiet and calm and that's what they want you to be. I take it and it puts you right to sleep, you can't stand up. I think it really works."

Ms. Porche is taking Aldomet, the same medication which Ms. Dubose first took and which she felt made her sick, yet Ms. Porche interprets her experiences differently, perceiving the drug to act as a sedative and therefore of use in the treatment of a nervous disease like "high-pertension." However, since Ms. Porche, like Ms. Joseph, feels she needs to take her medication only when she "has an attack," she is medically noncompliant and her blood pressure is poorly controlled.

The situation becomes more complex when "high blood" and "high-pertension" are both involved and are complicated by financial contingencies.

Case 6: Doretha Jackson is a 60-year-old divorced woman. She has had both "high blood" and "high-pertension" since her husband started "acting ugly" about 20 years ago. She has serious financial difficulties, having raised three children alone, cared for her dying mother, and twice lost all her possessions, once in a hurricane and two years later in a fire. When first seen she was taking prescribed antihypertensive medication for her "high blood," watching her diet, and drinking white vinegar. She said the pills "thin and draw water off your blood; I think they cool your blood." For "high-pertension," she said, she was trying to control her mind. "I've always had a bad temper, you know; if you can control your mind, you can control your blood. But that mind makes your blood start to boiling like in a pot. The pills ain't gonna stop it, you're gonna have high-pertension no matter what, there's no one who can stop it except yourself."

At the time of the next visit, Ms. Jackson was extremely short of funds and had run out of medication. As an alternative she was watching her diet and continued to drink vinegar. "I had me some little expenses I had to take care of and I just didn't have the money. Besides, I'm watching what I eat for high blood, I'm real good about that. . . . I wouldn't mind buying the medicine if I had the money, but I'm careful of what I eat and it won't help the high-pertension anyway. You have to think positive, not negative 'cause if you think negative that will hit you and make your pertension build up and that will be something else." When last seen, Ms. Jackson had been off of medication almost two months but had managed to have her prescription refilled by one-half.

In this instance a patient was willing to take her medicine, but since she needed to spend her money on other things, she felt she had acceptable alternative strategies to manage her health. Her beliefs supported taking medicine for only one of her "pressure troubles"--"high blood," but not "high-pertension." She was noncompliant in the sense of obeying her doctor's orders, but from her own perspective she was adequately managing her illness.

Unlike Ms. Jackson, Ms. Dubose and Ms.Porche had no financial obstacles to taking medication, yet their assessment of the nature of their illnesses and medications precluded their complying with their prescribed drug regimens. Ms. Jackson would have complied had she been financially able. Each of the six women thought they were taking appropriate steps to manage their illness and support their health, yet only one, Ms. Bernard, could be described as compliant from the strictly biomedical viewpoint.

Discussion

It must be remembered that folk illness models and self-diagnoses are abstractions representing more complex and fluid realities. Folk beliefs must be considered in conjunction with the contingencies of everyday life to understand efforts at illness management. The preceding cases illustrate the complexity of these efforts and of the behavioral environments in which they are embedded.

It cannot be argued that folk beliefs alone are sufficient to explain behavior. Rather, this study demonstrates how the patient's cognitive world provides meaning, organization, and understanding of illness phenomena such as symptoms, treatment, and interaction with health professionals.

Similarly, the physician's cognitive world influences not only his or her comprehension of the patient's illness, but action towards that illness's construction and treatment.

When these two worlds meet in everyday medical practice, the result can be the creation of new symbolic forms and areas of congruence where at first there was disparity. This was apparent in the case of some residents coming to accept their patients' reporting of symptoms as characteristic of high blood pressure, contrary to official medical teaching. In this sense, health education can be mutual.

Conclusion

It may seem that the reader has been led rather far afield from the initial discussion of a primary health care problem in New Orleans. The problem was formulated as one of increasing demand for services in the face of diminishing resources. Inadequate hypertension control in the patient population was seen as a significant factor in that demand, one which could be improved if patient compliance with treatment could be increased.

Our study of medication adherence among Black women demonstrated the influence of cultural beliefs and illness models on compliance. These factors have broader implications for general illness management and health care delivery.

Diagnostic labels used by a practitioner may differentially influence compliance in persons subscribing to different nosologies, and this may provide a key to explaining problems in illness management. If medical intervention is to be effective, health professionals must be aware of the cultural world of their patients and be prepared to accommodate it.

The introductory statement expressed the intent of demonstrating anthropology's utility in primary health care in a technologically sophisticated, complex society. This paper demonstrated the contributions of the anthropologist as ethnographer. Further contributions must come from the anthropologist as "culture broker," negotiating between the "soft" realities of culture for change in the hard realities of illness behavior, primary health care, and human well-being.

Acknowledgements

This research was supported in part by a grant from the University of California, San Francisco. This is a substantially revised version of a paper given at the Association for Social Sciences in Health session, 115th Annual Meeting of American Public Health Association, New Orleans, Louisiana, October 21, 1987.

Notes

1. The state of Louisiana and the metropolitan area of New Orleans are presently experiencing a grave financial crisis brought on by plummeting oil prices worldwide, an oil-dependent economy, and a singular lack of foresight and leadership by past elected officials. (Times-Picayune 1986b, 1987a)

2. This information was provided by a CHNO administrator who requested anonymity. Projections and estimates are his, based on information from hospital records. Since CHNO is a recipient of Federal funds these figures are not privileged information but are part of the public record.

3. Eight informants explicitly used the term "high-pertension." They explained it to mean one had too much "pertension," a general term to describe stress, "nerves," or worry. This term will be used to distinguish it from the biomedical "hypertension," and Blumhagen's "hyper-tension" (1980). "High blood pressure" will be considered an informal term referring to both the folk illness "high blood" and the biomedical "hypertension," but not the folk "high-pertension." It will take a folk or biomedical meaning from the context of its use. "High blood" will denote the folk illness contrasted to "high-pertension" in New Orleans. There are, then, three main illness categories being discussed regarding this research. Two are folk illnesses, "high blood" and "high-pertension," and one is a biomedical disease "hypertension."

4. The source of these symptoms is unclear. It is possible for antihypertensive medications to cause many of these symptoms as side effects, yet many women experienced these symptoms before undergoing treatment. Some of these symptoms can be attributed to severely high blood pressure not being treated,

while nosebleed can occur in even moderate hypertension. Also, many of these symptoms are nonspecific to hypertension. It is possible that some persons aware of cultural illness models interpret nonspecific complaints such as headaches and dizziness as part of the experience of "high blood" and "high-pertension."

5. Recent research suggests that "cures" of mild hypertension can occur. Clinical trials of 184 mild hypertensives showed that sodium-restricted diets and weight loss allowed approximately 70% of the sample to maintain blood pressure control for five years after withdrawal of prolonged drug therapy (Langford et al. 1985)

6. All names used in the case studies are pseudonyms.

7. "Low blood" is the reverse of "high blood." One's blood is too thin and cool, and is situated too low in the body. This results in weakness and lack of vitality.

TABLE 11.1

Salient Characteristics of "High Blood" and "High-Pertension" According to Patients (elicited from the 32 recognizing two folk illnesses)

	"High Blood"	"High-Pertension"
Pathophysiology		
hot, rich blood	18 (56%)	3 (9%)
thick blood	19 (59%)	0
blood moves up	27 (84%)	16 (50%)
blood moves up suddenly	3 (9%)	30 (94%)
blood moves to head	14 (44%)	30 (94%)
blood stays up	28 (88%)	0
blood clogs	19 (59%)	2 (6%)
Course		
predictable	29 (91%)	4 (13%)
unpredictable	1 (3%)	24 (75%)
episodic	3 (9%)	27 (84%)
symptoms present	23 (72%)	24 (75%)
can be controlled	23 (72%)	12 (38%)
Cause		
heredity of illness	19 (54%)	1 (3%)
heredity of personality	0	11 (34%)
personality (not inherited)	1 (3%)	9 (28%)
diet	26 (81%)	0
"bad nerves"	0	30 (94%)
stress	10 (31%)	14 (44%)
money	5 (16%)	13 (41%)
anger	0	12 (38%)
Exacerbating Factors		
"bad nerves"	18 (56%)	3 (9%)
stress	10 (31%)	26 (81%)
worry	5 (16%)	25 (81%)
anger	0	19 (59%)
money	1 (3%)	11 (34%)
children	2 (6%)	11 (34%)
diet	24 (73%)	2 (6%)
heat (body/environment)	8 (25%)	2 (6%)
hysterectomy/menopause	7 (22%)	7 (22%)
Treatment		
prescribed drugs	24 (75%)	10 (31%)
diet	29 (91%)	1 (3%)
weight loss	11 (34%)	1 (3%)
"nerve pills"	0	9 (28%)
not worrying	2 (6%)	31 (97%)
relaxation	9 (28%)	30 (94%)
rest	22 (67%)	24 (75%)
stay quiet	4 (13%)	18 (56%)
stay away from people	0	10 (31%)

TABLE 11.2

Salient Characteristics of Hypertension
(elicited from 15 physicians)

	Hypertension
Pathophysiology	
vascular constriction	15 (100%)
excessive blood volume	15 (100%)
system functioning at an excessively high pressure	15 (100%)
Course	
symptoms only in sever crisis	5 (33%)
symptoms possible anytime	6 (40%)
symptoms probable	2 (13%)
completely asymptomatic	2 (13%)
Cause	
unknown	15 (100%)
heredity	5 (33%)
obesity	1 (7%)
multifactorial	2 (13%)
Exacerbating factors	
diet	9 (60%)
obesity	5 (33%)
salt	4 (27%)
stress	3 (20%)
smoking	2 (13%)
Treatment	
medication	15 (100%)
medication alone	3 (20%)
weight loss	4 (27%)
relaxation	2 (13%)
diet	9 (60%)
personality change	1 (7%)

TABLE 11.3

Patients' Belief That "High Blood" and "High-Pertension" Are Different Illnesses Compared with Compliance

$\underline{n} = 60$

"High Blood" and "High-Pertension" are Different Illnesses	Poor Compliance	Good Compliance
Yes	20 (33%)	12 (20%)
No	6 (10%)	16 (27%)
Don't know	5 (8%)	1 (2%)

Chi-square: 9.1556 $\underline{P} < 0.0103$

Lambda, with compliance dependent: 0.3448

TABLE 11.4

Patients' Self-Diagnosis Compared with Their Compliance

$\underline{n} = 60$

Self-Diagnosis	Poor Compliance	Good Compliance
"High Blood"	1 (2%)	6 (10%)
"High-Pertension"	10 (17%)	1 (2%)
Both	9 (15%)	5 (8%)
Not Sure	5 (8%)	1 (2%)
Not Applicable*	6 (10%)	16 (26%)

Chi-square: 19.2448 $\underline{P} < 0.0007$

Lambda, with compliance dependent: 0.5172

* Respondents thought that "high blood" and "high-pertension" were the same.

References

Blumhagen, Dan 1980 Hypertension: A Folk Illness With a Medical Name. *Culture, Medicine and Psychiatry* 4:197-227.

___ 1981 On the Nature of Explanatory Models. *Culture, Medicine, and Psychiatry* 5:337-340.

___ 1982 The Meaning of Hyper-tension. In *Clinically Applied Anthropology*. N.J. Chrisman and T.W. Maretzki, eds. Pp. 297-323. Dordrecht, Holland: D. Reidel.

Cassel, Joan 1977 The Relationship of Observer to Observed in Peer Group Research. *Human Organization* 36:412-416.

Dressler, William W. 1980 Ethnomedical Beliefs and Patient Adherence to a Treatment Regimen: A St. Lucian Example. *Human Organization* 39:88-91.

Dubos, Clancy 1985 The Battle of Big Charity. *Gambit*, June 8. New Orleans, Louisiana.

Gish, Oscar 1979 The Political Economy of Primary Care and "Health by the People": An Historical Exploration. *Social Science and Medicine* 19:217-224.

Glaser, Barney G., and Anselm Strauss 1967 *The Discovery of Grounded Theory*. Chicago: Aldine.

Hershey, J.C., B.G. Morton, J.B. Davis, and M.J. Reichgott 1980 Patient Compliance with Antihypertensive Medication. *American Journal of Public Health* 70:1081-1089.

Hessler, Richard M., and Andrew C. Twaddle 1986 Power and Change: Primary Health Care at the Crossroads in Sweden. *Human Organization* 45:134-147.

Hill, Carol 1976 A Folk Medical Belief System in the American South: Some Practical Considerations. *Southern Medical Journal* 64:11-17.

Hughes, E. Charles 1974 Who Studies Whom? Plenary Address of the 33rd Annual Meeting of the Society for Applied Anthropology. *Human Organization* 33:327-334.

Hurston, Zora Neale 1931 Hoodoo in America. *Journal of American Folklore* 44:317-417.

Joint National Committee on Detection, Evaluation and Treatment of High Blood Pressure. 1984 The 1984 Report of the Joint National Committee on Detection, Evaluation and Treatment of High Blood Pressure. *Archives of Internal Medicine* 144:1045-1057.

Kirscht, J.P., and I.M. Rosenstock. 1977 Patient Adherence to Antihypertensive Regimens. *Journal of Community Health* 3:115-124.

Kleinman, Arthur 1980 *Patients and Healers in the Context of Culture*. Berkeley: University of California Press.

___ 1981 On Illness Meanings and Clinical Interpretation: Not 'Rational Man,' But a Rational Approach to Man the Sufferer/Man the Healer. *Culture, Medicine and Psychiatry* 5:373-378.

Langford, H.G., Donald Blaufox, Albert Overman, Moten Hawkins, J. David Curb, Gary R. Cutter, Sylvia Wassertheirt-Smoller, Sarah Pressel, Connie Babcock, J.D. Abernathy, Jeanne Hotchkiss, and Myra Tyler 1985 Dietary Therapy Slows Return of Hypertension after Stopping Prolonged Medication. *Journal of the American Medical Association* 253:657-664.

Leventhal, Howard, Rick Zimmerman, and Mary Gutman 1984 Compliance: A Self Regulation Perspective. In *Handbook of Behavioral Medicine*. W. Doyle Gentry, ed. Pp. 369-436. New York: Guilford Press.

Lund-Johansen, Per 1983 The Hemodynamics of Essential Hypertension. In *The Handbook of Hypertension*, Vol. 1. Jis Robertson, ed. Pp. 151-173 Amsterdam: Elsevier Science Publishers.

Maiman, Lois A., and M. Howard Becker 1974 The Health Belief Model: Origins and Correlates In Psychological Theory. *Health Education Monographs* 2:336-353.

Nations, Marilyn, Linda A. Camino, and Frederic B. Walker 1985 "Hidden" Popular Illnesses in Primary Care: Residents' Recognition and Clinical Implications. *Culture, Medicine and Psychiatry* 9:223-240.

Nelson, Eugene C., William B. Stason, Raymond R. Neutra, Harold S. Solomon, and Patricia McArdle 1978 Impact of Patient Perceptions on Compliance with Treatment for Hypertension. *Medical Care* 16:893-906.

New, Peter Kong-ming, and John M. Donahue 1986 Strategies for Primary Health Care by the Year 2000: A Political Economic Perspective. *Human Organization* 45:95-96.

O'Neil, John D. 1986 The Politics of Health in the Fourth World: A Northern Canadian Example. *Human Organization* 45:119-128.

Pearsall, Marion 1966 Cultures of the American South. *Anthropological Quarterly* 39:128-141.

Pelto, Pertti J., and Gretel H. Pelto 1975 Intra-Cultural Diversity: Some Theoretical Issues. *American Ethnologist* 2:1-18.

Robertson, Jis, ed. 1983 *The Handbook of Hypertension*, Vol. 1. Amsterdam: Elsevier Science Publishers.

Sackett, D.L. 1976 Introduction. In *Compliance with Therapeutic Regimens*. D.L. Sackett and R.B. Haynes, eds. Pp. 1-6. Baltimore: Johns Hopkins University Press.

Snow, Loudell F. 1974 Folk Medical Beliefs and Their Implications for Care of Patients. *Annals of Internal Medicine* 81:82-96.

___ 1976 High Blood is Not High Blood Pressure. *Urban Health* June:54-55.

Storer, James, Barry Singleton, Robert Marier, Becky Manuel, Marilyn Chutz, and Elliott C. Roberts 1986 Charity: Urban Hospital's Local and Statewide Significance. *Journal of the Louisiana State Medical Society* 138:51-57.

Taylor, D. Wayne, David L. Sackett, and R. Brian Haynes 1978 Compliance with Antihypertensive Drug Therapy. *Annals of the New York Academy of Sciences* 304:390-403.

The Times-Picayune 1986a Charity: An Ailing System. Six-day Special Report. Jason deParle, Staffwriter. *The Times-Picayune* (April 20-25). New Orleans, LA.

___ 1986b State's Jobless Rate Hits 13.4%. *The Times-Picayune* (December 30):A1, A4. New Orleans, LA.

___ 1987a Colleges Top Roemer's List of $66 Million in Cuts. *The Times-Picayune* (December 2). New Orleans, LA.

___ 1987b Blacks: Poverty Rate High in New Orleans. *The Times-Picayune* (April 10). New Orleans, LA.

___ 1988 Charity to Close 135 Beds, State Says. Jack Wardlaw. *The Times-Picayune* (January 13). New Orleans, LA.

Trostle, James A., W. Allen Hauser, and Ida S. Susser. 1983 The Logic of Noncompliance: Management of Epilepsy from the Patient's Point of View. *Culture, Medicine and Psychiatry* 7:35-56.

Webb, Julie Yvonne. 1971 Superstitious Influences, Voodoo in Particular, Affecting Health Practices in a Selected Population in Southern Louisiana. Master's Thesis. Tulane University, School of Public Health. New Orleans, LA.

Weidman, Hazel H. 1978 Miami Health Ecology Report: A Statement on Ethnicity and Health, Vol. 1. Department of Psychiatry, University of Miami School of Medicine.

___ 1979 Falling Out: A Diagnostic and Treatment Problem Viewed from a Transcultural Perspective. *Social Science and Medicine* 13:95-112.

Welsch, Robert L. 1986 Primary Health Care and Local Self Determination: Policy Implications from Rural Papua New Guinea. *Human Organization* 45:103-112.

Williams, Gordon H., Paul I. Jagger, and Eugene Braunwald 1980 Hypertensive Vascular Disease. In *Harrison's Principles of Internal Medicine*, 9th ed. T.R. Harrison, ed. Pp. 1167-1178. New York: McGraw-Hill.

Young, Allan 1982 Rational Men and the Explanatory Model Approach. *Culture, Medicine and Psychiatry* 6:57-71.

V

ISSUES AND METHODS IN APPLIED RESEARCH

Anthropological research methods were greatly refined and developed during the 1980s. Data-gathering techniques became more diversified and rigorous, issues of reliability and validity were taken more seriously, and analysis of findings became more sophisticated. In applied fields, anthropologists became increasingly involved in multidisciplinary collaborative research that required at least a basic familiarity with quantitative methods, and sometimes to use such method themselves. As a result of such developments, issues such as how anthropologists should go about doing applied research and the uses and limitations of different methods are now widely discussed. The chapters in this section address many of these issues, each from a very different perspective.

The Pelto, Bentley, and Pelto chapter reviews current theoretical perspectives, elements of research design, and techniques for data collection and analysis commonly used in anthropological research on primary health care. Although the review has general applicability, the authors illustrate key points by showing how they could be applied to studies of child diarrhea in the developing world. They also provide useful guidelines for applying specific methods to answer different kinds of research questions, noting the strengths and weaknesses of each technique and discussing ways in which qualitative and quantitative methods can be articulated. Both the novice and experienced field researcher will find helpful clarification of important methodologic issues in this chapter.

In the next chapter, Ramakrishna, Brieger, and Adeniyi present an excellent case study of the application of anthropological research at each phase of a health intervention, a guineaworm control program in Nigeria. The reader follows the project through all its stages: problem diagnosis, team building, objective setting, collection of baseline data, implementation of program interventions, evaluation of results, and finally institution-building via development of a professional association of community health workers. This study is particularly useful in its focus on anthropological collaboration with people from other disciplines such as health educators and in its detailed description of genuine participatory research involving representatives of the communities.

Reflecting on their field experiences since 1965, Dorothy and Dennis Mull conclude the volume with a personal account of lessons they learned while carrying out health research in various parts of the world. They address some of the central issues in anthropology and primary health care, such as the bias within anthropology against applied work, the problems frequently encountered in conducting field research in developing countries when resources are scant and time is limited. Their case study from rural Pakistan illustrates a number of these issues as well as some solutions that they arrived at in the course of the project. The authors make a strong case for continued anthropological involvement in primary health care research, arguing that such involvement is essential if the health needs of Third World communities are to be adequately met.

12

Applied Anthropological Research Methods: Diarrhea Studies as an Example

Pertti J. Pelto, Margaret E. Bentley, and Gretel H. Pelto

Introduction

The purpose of this paper is to review the basic elements of research methodology that characterize applied medical anthropology in the area of primary health care, using studies of diarrhea as the basis for discussion. This disease is an excellent focus for such a review because of its importance for health problems in Third World countries and its central place in the "child survival" strategies of national and international health agencies. Also, diarrhea is a relatively easily identified illness, of worldwide distribution, in which culturally patterned beliefs and practices play an exceedingly important role.

In most of the developing world, traditional practices for the home management of diarrhea interface with cosmopolitan treatments, sometimes with negative consequences (Bentley 1985, 1987; Nations 1982; Nations and Rebhun 1988). In particular the misuse of cosmopolitan medications in the treatment of diarrhea is a serious and increasingly recognized problem.

Frequently medical anthropologists have found it useful to structure their research on a particular illness or symptom cluster. Sometimes the focus on a specific disease is selected for theoretical and methodological reasons; at other times it is required because of the emphasis in an applied program in which the anthropologist is working. The focus on a particular disease helps to sharpen hypotheses and keep structured data-gathering within manageable limits. Research that seeks to encompass a wide array of different illnesses must often sacrifice depth for breadth, and statistical analysis is constrained by the small number of cases of each illness.

Moreover, research on a specific problem, such as diarrhea, permits the anthropologist to identify a coherent body of biomedical knowledge and practice, as well as appropriate research sites.

In this paper we will first review the kinds of theoretical approaches current in one sector of medical anthropology, and then examine main elements of methodology used in recent anthropological research on diarrhea and similar areas of investigation. General guidelines for development of research strategies will also be outlined.

Theoretical Frameworks

Most medical anthropologists working in the field of primary health care in developing countries utilize a framework of implicit or explicit cultural ecological theory. This requires the use of concepts and terminology derived from medical (especially epidemiological) and biological research, nutritional science, human ecology, and cultural anthropology. Drawing from different disciplines provides a broad, eclectic framework. Alland (1970), McElroy and Townsend (1989), and others have described essential elements of the approach. To the traditional anthropological concern with cultural beliefs, the key elements that are added include a strong emphasis on features of the local/regional environment, with special attention to relevant pathogens, water and sanitation facilities, local economic resources, and other factors that affect living conditions and patterns of disease. Seasonal variations in rainfall, ambient temperatures, and other contributors to disease incidence are also relevant to the framework.

Medical anthropologists, like epidemiologists, focus attention on economic conditions and social stratification as they affect the dietary patterns and health behaviors of local populations. Anthropological research is increasingly "epidemiological" in its focus on discrete predictors and risk factors. The inclusion of ecological and epidemiological components in the explanatory matrix produces an updated version of the traditional "holistic orientation" that has been an enduring aspect of anthropological field work.

The concept of "adaptation" is usually a central element of the theoretical structure guiding research in medical anthropology. In some well-known studies, "adaptation" is used in the genetic, biological sense with reference to long-term biocultural evolution, as in the study of sickle-cell anemia and lactose intolerance (Livingstone 1958; McCracken 1971; McElroy and Townsend 1989). However, in community health studies the concept of "adaptation" is usually applied to the processes of choice and decision-making by individuals and households in relation to health practices.

The concept of adaptation, applied to health care decision making, contrasts sharply with the acculturation model that characterized much of earlier anthropological work. In the latter perspective, people in non-modern societies were generally seen as relatively passive followers of "traditional cultural practices," in health care as in other behaviors. When "acculturation" or "modernization" took place, some people--the "innovators"--were thought to change their cultural beliefs, hence the "acceptance" of new modes of health care and medications required a change in belief structures. There was also the assumption that openness to a particular form of behavioral change reflected a general receptivity to "modernization."

In contrast, contemporary medical anthropologists use the concept of adaptation to focus attention on people as active, rational decision-makers who select from among a range of alternative behaviors or "solutions," depending on their knowledge, resources, and other factors. Innovators, or "acceptors" of newly introduced practices do not necessarily have to radically change their belief systems. Some researchers have studied the actual decision-making process (Young 1981), but more usually the research is directed to identifying the various "constraints" and "facilitators" that explain variations among individuals and households in their health-seeking behaviors. This research paradigm also includes the recognition that decisions are not "all or nothing," as recurrent choices may take different shapes in response to shifting conditions.

The focus on the micro-level factors that affect household decision-making leads to consideration of intra-cultural and intra-community diversity. Even within the smallest communities one can expect to find differences in the patterns of environmental constraints and facilitators. Households vary with respect to economic resources, social contacts, access to new information, and other ecological factors. Short-term situational factors can also play a role in shaping choices of action.

Although a general ecological framework informs much of the work in medical anthropology, there is, nonetheless, a wide range in theoretical perspectives along the continuum between "materialist/economic orientation" and "cultural beliefs/symbolic patterns" views of behavioral causality (Young 1981). Some researchers, such as Woods and Graves (1973), have presented evidence for the central importance of economic/material factors in health behaviors. In contrast, Fabrega (1974), Kleinman (1980) and others have emphasized the importance of cultural "explanatory models" and related beliefs as powerful influences on behavior.

In the past the predominant view among anthropologists was that cultural belief systems were the prime activators (or suppressors) of health-seeking behaviors. It was generally assumed that people would not utilize health services or participate in health-seeking actions unless these were congruent with their cultural beliefs concerning the nature and causes of illness. This "culturological" view often led to fairly conservative statements concerning peoples' reasons for choosing not to go to "modern" health facilities. For example, it was commonly assumed that medical recommendations in Latin American communities would never be followed unless they were fully attuned to "hot/cold" balances derived from humoral theory. Also, it was generally thought that people would not use cosmopolitan or "Western" medical treatment for illnesses believed to be caused by culturally specific agents (e.g., supernatural actions) not understood by cosmopolitan medical people. This view of health practices was expressed by Saunders in relation to Mexican-Americans in the Southwestern United States:

> Physicians, it is felt, understand 'natural' diseases and are able to do something about them. But if the disease is thought to be of magical or psychological origin, assistance is more likely to be sought from a *curandera*, a *bruja*, or some other type of folk specialist, since they are assumed to be more familiar with and, hence, better able to treat such disease. A complaint of *susto* or *mal ojo* will be listened to understandingly by a folk specialist (Saunders 1954: 150).

Saunders added that

> sickness, particularly if it be serious, is likely to be viewed as a crisis, and in situations of crisis people of all cultures tend to resort to those patterns of thinking and acting that have been most deeply ingrained in them as a result of their cultural experiences (Saunders 1954: 160).

These assumptions about peoples' health-seeking behaviors are based on the widely-held notion that "a person's view or theory of disease naturally determines what he will do in order to get well" (Fabrega 1974: 245). However, recent research, including data concerning the extremely rapid spread of commercial pharmaceuticals, suggests that many people accept a very wide range of "foreign" medical interventions, particularly injections and pills, even for illnesses such as *susto*, evil eye, and other "culturally defined" complaints (Bentley 1987; Foster 1978; Hunte 1987; Pelto 1987).

Current thinking in medical anthropology centers on the exploration of "medical pluralism," which is found in most populations. Usually there are complex "patterns of resort" that are only partly related to discernible local cultural theories about disease causation (Scrimshaw and Scrimshaw, in press). Rather than focussing chiefly on cultural definitions of illness and causation, anthropologists have turned increasing attention to the analysis of how people manage multiple (alternative) health services in relation to their beliefs about the respective merits and shortcomings of the alternatives (Janzen 1978; Press 1971). For example, in research in rural Mexico, Young (1981) demonstrated that peoples' perceptions about the *gravity of particular illness episodes* interacted with their assessment of economic costs and likelihood of cure. These factors, Young felt, were more important than traditional beliefs about "hot and cold" in explaining health-seeking behaviors. Recent research has also indicated that people will at times seek cosmopolitan medical attention even for supposedly "cultural" illnesses, such as *susto*, "evil eye," and other illnesses in Latin American communities (D. Parrella, personal communication; Trotter and Chavira 1981). The widely reported adoption of cosmopolitan medications by indigenous healers is a further manifestation of eclectic "opportunism" in health care behaviors (cf. Coreil 1988; Hunte 1987).

While there is now substantial evidence that acceptance of newly introduced health practices does not necessarily require a change in general cultural belief systems, it is also recognized that cultural beliefs about causes and types of illnesses play a significant role in health-seeking behaviors, in interaction with other variables. For example, Bentley (1985, 1987), Scrimshaw and Hurtado (1988), Kendall and associates (1983), and others have described the importance of cultural taxonomies of diarrhea and variations in treatments indicated in relation to the typologies. Thus ecological theory in medical anthropology includes careful attention to cultural, ideational factors in the explanatory models.

Key Research Questions

Most of the research on diarrhea by anthropologists is intended to answer practical, applied questions. At the same time, the studies expand our conceptual frameworks in the realm of theory in medical anthropology. Some of the main questions addressed in this research sector include the following:

1. What environmental, economic, behavioral, and cultural factors account for differences in incidence and severity of diarrhea in different families or different children?
2. What are the *emic*, culturally specific *explanatory models*, including taxonomies, of childhood diarrhea; and how do these affect peoples' choices of diarrhea management?
3. What environmental, economic, behavioral, and cultural (and other) factors account for the different patterns of diarrhea management in different households, communities, and cultures?
4. What factors influence the acceptance or nonacceptance of oral rehydration therapy (ORT), and effective, appropriate use of ORT in management of childhood diarrheal illness?
5. To what extent do people within a cultural setting share a single *explanatory model* of diarrhea, from which situational, non-cultural factors cause variations in actual behaviors and outcomes?
6. What can the study of diarrhea management teach us about the household dynamics underlying peoples' coping with acute, life-threatening illness?

Basic Elements of Research Design in Medical Anthropology

Focus on the "Dependent Variable"

Many research projects in medical anthropology are designed to focus on particular illnesses or pathological conditions, which are conceptualized as the *dependent variables*, to be predicted or "explained" by multiple independent variables. Usually it is important to measure a number of aspects of the disease and its management. With respect to diarrhea the relevant variables may include, in addition to occurrence and indicators of type and severity, "management strategies for diarrhea," "acceptance" or use of various treatments or health care alternatives (including oral rehydration therapy, or ORT), and feeding practices. For example, Bentley (1985, 1987) gathered data in a North Indian community on acceptance of ORT, dietary changes, types and amounts of fluids given, types of health care sought, and medications given. Coreil (1988) examined people's knowledge and use of ORT in a coastal area of Haiti, and also included "choice of packet over home recipe" and "delay in starting ORT" among the dependent variables. In Zimbabwe, de Zoysa and associates (1984) examined a range of different treatment actions utilized for diarrhea, and found that the only consistent predictor of use of the formal health services was the *perceived cause* of the illness:

> illness ascribed to 'physical' causes, or to a combination of 'physical' and 'social and spiritual' causes, were brought to the attention of . . . formal health services more often than illness ascribed to 'social or spiritual' causes only (de Zoysa et al. 1984).

Multiple Independent Variables

Cultural ecology as a theoretical framework requires researchers to consider the additive and interactive effects of multiple independent variables--the various constraints and facilitators that operate at the household level of decision-making and selection of behavioral alternatives. The holistic nature of cultural ecological theory draws attention to the importance of several sectors of independent variables, including economic-material resources, micro-environmental features (such as water and sanitation conditions), household composition, ethnicity, access to primary health care facilities, and various aspects of cultural beliefs and attitudes. These are viewed as parts of the system of interacting factors affecting the dependent variables. Regardless of a researcher's tendency to emphasize or de-emphasize cultural belief systems, or "explanatory models," the economic resources (socio-economic status) of households should always be part of the selection of independent variables (cf. Woods and Graves 1973). Proximity to cosmopolitan health care facilities may be a key variable (cf. de Zoysa et al. 1984), and urban versus rural residence is important in many research designs (e.g. Coreil and Genece 1988). Eisemon and associates (1987) found strong effects of formal education in their study of mothers' comprehension of ORT instructions in Kenya.

Folk Taxonomies of Diarrhea

Cultural beliefs and explanatory models of diarrhea are often highly elaborated. Anthropological research from diverse cultures shows that most cultural groups recognize (and name) several different varieties of childhood diarrhea, as the following examples illustrate.

Green (1985) found that healers and lay people among the Swazi identified three major types of diarrhea, two of which were felt to be due to "unnatural causes." *Kuhabula*, a very serious type of diarrhea in which the child's sunken fontanelle is a primary symptom, is believed to be caused by the accidental or perpetrated inhaling of smoke from therapeutic fumigations. "Greenish diarrhea that may later become yellowish," accompanied by other serious symptoms, is a sign of *umphezulu*, which is believed to be caused *in utero* by the actions of the mother. Both of these types of diarrhea call for enemas and other traditional treatments, and are usually taken to traditional healers if home remedies fail (Green 1985: 281-283).

In South India, Lozoff and colleagues (1975) found that diarrhea identified as *dosham*--characterized by loose stools, vomiting, sunken eyes and fontanelle (the classical symptoms of dehydration)--usually went untreated. *Dosham* was not considered to be a "normal" diarrhea type, but rather a separate disease requiring treatment that was not directed to the diarrhea as such.

Bentley (1987) found that women in a North Indian rural area recognized five common types of diarrhea (*dust*)--*khooni dust* (bloody), *pani dust* (watery), *phate-phate* (bits and pieces), *hare dust* (green diarrhea, often attributed to evil influences), and *pila dust* (yellow, or summer, diarrhea). Although the choice of treatment for all diarrhea types was cosmopolitan medical care (with the exception of some cases of "green" diarrhea, which were treated by exorcism), bloody diarrhea was considered to be particularly worrisome and dangerous. Its appearance led to rapid behavioral responses.

In Lima, Peru, Escobar and associates (1983) reported six categories of diarrhea recognized by their informants. These were not necessarily the "indigenous categories," but those of the investigators. Escobar's results point out the importance of preliminary ethnographic research to identify emic taxonomic categories, before quantitative data collection is begun.

In practically all communities where ethnographic research has been carried out the influence of diarrhea taxonomies on therapeutic choices emerges. Anthropological researchers have found that diarrhea typologies are closely intertwined with beliefs concerning the etiologies of childhood diarrhea, which, in turn, influence household decisions about how to manage the problem.

In northeast Brazil, Nations (1982, 1983) found that rural mothers consider diarrhea and dehydration to be "symptoms of a number of folk-defined illnesses including evil eye, . . . fright disease (*susto*), spirit intrusion, . . . intestinal heat, . . . and fallen fontanelle (*caída de mollera*)" (1983: 4). Kendall and associates found that "four major etiologies are often ascribed to diarrhea by rural Honduran informants: (1) worms (*lombrices*); (2) evil eye (*ojo* or *mal ojo*); (3) sunken fontanelles; and (4) indigestion (*empacho*)

(Kendall et al. 1983: 355). In North India, Bentley found that mothers identified a number of seemingly "naturalistic" causes of diarrhea, including

> hot weather (66%), bad food (36%), overeating (30%), teething (24%), cold weather (23%), 'hot' food (16%), 'hot breastmilk' (after a mother works in the sun or consumes a 'hot' food) (15%), evil eye (12%), and dirty water or germs (4%).

Lists of causes of diarrhea reported in Niger (Hogle 1985) also appeared to favor "naturalistic" causes, including food-related ones (spoiled or rotten food, various types of foods such as peanuts, beans, badly cooked broths, bad quality of breastmilk, excess of milk, rotten fruit, some traditional foods); and then behaviors (giving broth at too early an age, staying too long in the sun); and finally conditions such as teething, weaning, sunken fontanelle, upset stomach, anorexia of the mother, fevers, and the "stress of the hot season."

Concerning the Assumption of Homogeneous Belief Systems

It is very important to avoid the assumption that all the people in a community or cultural group share a common set of beliefs about any particular illness. There *may be* an underlying pattern of homogeneous beliefs--a single "explanatory model" of diarrheal disease in a given community--but such uniformity must be demonstrated from individual data rather than assumed at the outset. If a single cultural pattern can be demonstrated, then only a small number of key informants may be needed to delineate the cultural model. Recently Romney and associates (1986) have presented a methodology for testing the presumption of a single underlying cultural pattern in a given domain of local health beliefs. They have also shown that, in the presence of an underlying homogeneous cultural pattern or "cognitive map," individuals will vary in degree of expertise or knowledge of the cultural pattern. Similarly, Garro (1986) demonstrated that in a Mexican community there was a coherent set of cultural beliefs about illness, and the people who were more specialized in traditional treatments--the indigenous healers, or "experts"--showed greater coherence and agreement than ordinary "laypersons."

Behaviors versus Beliefs

In community health research it has been productive to devote considerable attention to observed and reported *behaviors*, even when part of the design calls for delineation of "cognitive maps" concerning diarrheal illness and treatment. A study that deals only with peoples' opinions and attitudes, or hypothetical choices of health care alternatives, would not be able to address the extent to which the particular cognitive dimensions or belief systems directly affect behavioral patterns of diarrhea management or other health behavior, for several reasons. In the first place, questions of attitudes and hypothetical choices are often too abstract and unrelated to everyday experience. Second, recent research has shown that any given responses to particular illness episodes are only partly determined by attitudes and beliefs, because situational constraints and "facilitators" usually play major roles in affecting individual decisions. Third, people may report "ideal patterns"--what they think the interviewer wants to hear--rather than what they actually do.

The Household as the Unit of Analysis

Medical anthropologists as well as many field epidemiologists and other community-based researchers are in general agreement that the prime unit for gathering data about health behaviors is the household. Households are the visible, functioning social/economic systems within which care and feeding takes place, economic resources are marshalled, and decisions about health care behaviors are commonly made. It is hard to find exceptions to this general rule.

The *household interview* has become a core element of much work in medical anthropology--even in studies in which research is initiated in a clinic or hospital. In the latter case the informants, although recruited from a clinic-based patient population, should be "contextualized" in terms of the household decision-making systems from which they come to the clinic.

In practically every society, households vary in composition, economic assets, and other characteristics that are highly relevant for understanding health-seeking behaviors, including diarrhea management. The education level of the adults in a household is another variable of interest in many parts of the world as formal schooling is becoming more available. Other household characteristics of importance include wage-labor migration, women's work patterns, sources of water and fuel supplies, sanitation-hygiene practices, and many others.

Macrolevel Influences on Community Health Issues

Recent research on ORT programs and other aspects of diarrheal disease provides some guidelines for assessment of the linkages between microlevel and macrolevel processes (cf. DeWalt and Pelto 1985). Most anthropological research on diarrheal disease has been directly related to ORT programs, which are particularly clear instances of macrolevel (national and international) projects intended to influence behaviors of individuals at community and household levels. In the research of Kendall and associates in Honduras, the macrolevel program included a mass media campaign to promote public acceptance and use of ORT, coupled with dissemination of the actual materials (facilitated by attractive packaging) (Kendall, Foote, and Martorell 1983: 357). In most diarrhea research anthropologists have included direct questions about *knowledge* of ORT, as well as attitudes toward use of the materials. Thus, evidence of an identifiable impact from the macrolevel system was sought at the household level.

In addition, community level research often focuses attention on the discrepancies or "miscommunications" between macrolevel and microlevel entities. Nichter, for example, reported that the term for "dehydration" used on Sri Lankan ORT packages was not understood by the majority of rural people, despite the high rates of literacy in practically all sectors of the population (Nichter 1988). In Nicaragua, Hudelson found that medical personnel explained ORT to mothers as "good for cleaning the stomach" because they knew that this concept was seen as important for treatment of diarrhea among the local people. Unfortunately the health providers were unaware that "cleaning the stomach" also entailed withholding food from the child (Hudelson 1989). In a similar vein, the previously cited studies by Bentley, Coreil, and others have all noted the difficulties of transmitting the concepts of "dehydration" and "rehydration" to rural people, particularly in areas with low literacy.

A substantial component of anthropological research on diarrhea can be seen as the study of macrolevel to microlevel communications. On the other hand, the explicit intent of many anthropological research projects is to communicate microlevel understandings and cultural concepts to policymakers. Research thus far reveals that ORT interventions have varied considerably in the degree to which they attempt to develop useful knowledge of microlevel beliefs and practices. Many programs are primarily "top down," in which the communications model in ORT interventions is generally quite linear and program failures can result from the hierarchical structure (Kendall, Foote, and Martorell 1983: 358). On the other hand, during the 1980s there has been increasing interest in utilizing local-level ethnographic information to improve macrolevel policy-formation.

Anthropological studies have also documented the presence and use of modern pharmaceuticals for treatment of diarrhea. In North India, Bentley (1987) found that antibiotic medications were used in more than 80% of the diarrhea episodes she recorded, although medical researchers estimate that fewer than 10% of diarrhea episodes require pharmaceutical treatment. Much more research is needed on the factors influencing peoples' use (and overuse) of drugs for diarrhea.

Some studies have included information about the types of persons and facilities that serve as the distributors of drugs. For example, Coreil (1988) reported on the role of traditional healers in promoting ORT in Haiti. However, most studies have not taken advantage of the opportunity to examine the commercial channels of distribution through which the pharmaceuticals and other cosmopolitan medical materials reach the local areas. Tracing the distribution networks could provide better understanding of an increasingly important aspect of macro-microlevel interactions in the health field.

Basic Elements of Research Strategy in Medical Anthropology

The Importance of Ethnographic Data

Perhaps the most striking characteristic of research in medical anthropology, as contrasted with other disciplines involved in international health research, is the insistence on qualitative ethnographic data-gathering as an essential first stage to any quantitative data collection. The importance of the qualitative-descriptive phase is based on the premise that quantified, structured data-gathering can succeed only if it is carefully attuned to specific local cultural and environmental conditions, local language nuances, and other cultural-ecological features that must be *discovered* through key informant interviewing and direct observation. In the terminology of contemporary anthropology, the initial ethnographic phase of research is essential for developing an *emic* perspective--the insider's viewpoint and definitions of realities.

The initial ethnographic component of research does not necessarily require large investments of time (cf. Scrimshaw and Hurtado 1987; Pelto and Pelto 1978; Bentley et al. 1988). Anthropologists have generally emphasized the importance of long-term immersion in the local culture(s) before structured interviewing is initiated, but applied anthropologists frequently find it necessary to produce preliminary descriptive data in short periods of time. This is particularly the case when the data are urgently needed for program planning [cf. Mull and Mull, Chapter 14--Eds]. Some researchers have found that important descriptive data can be collected in relatively short-term field work, especially if the anthropologist is already familiar with the particular cultural setting. A few weeks of intensive field work *may* be adequate preparation for designing the instruments to be used in structured data-gathering. Of course, the initiation of quantitative interviews with detailed interview schedules does not terminate qualitative data-gathering (Bentley et al. 1988). Structured survey techniques are often carried out concurrently with continued ethnographic (qualitative) observations.

Although most anthropological research in community health includes quantified information, the numerical data alone are grossly insufficient for an effective analysis. Numerical data require "contextualization" with descriptive, qualitative materials. Such data may include case materials--vignettes of particular individuals and their practices with regard to diarrhea management and other health care behaviors--as well as primary descriptions of the variables that have been selected for numerical treatment. Folk taxonomies are part of the descriptive materials. The recent history of cosmopolitan health care resources, including ORT efforts, also makes up part of the ethnography.

Relatively Small Samples and In-Depth Data

The eclectic, ecological approach in medical anthropology often includes the use of very detailed structured interviews. It is not uncommon to encounter interview protocols of 18 to 25 pages, requiring one or two hours (or more) per interview. Such time-consuming data-gathering generally means that samples must be small in order to keep down the costs of interview personnel and to permit data-gathering within a reasonable period of time. Although samples of 100 to 150 households are considered desirable for this type of study, researchers must often settle for smaller numbers, particularly when they have few assistants and slim financial resources. In some cases, however, resources permit a dual strategy, in which a large-scale survey of several hundred households is used to gather data on certain key variables and in-depth data are collected from a subsample drawn from the larger survey.

Clinical versus Community-Based Data

To an increasing extent anthropologists carry out research in cooperation with local primary health care personnel. Such cooperative arrangements may come about in connection with specific community health projects. For example, Bentley carried out her research as part of an ORT intervention study undertaken by the All-India Institute of Medical Sciences. Similarly, ethnographic research on diarrhea was carried out in Nigeria and Peru as part of a series of intervention projects involving dietary management of diarrhea (Bentley et al. 1988).

In some situations anthropologists begin their studies of diarrhea by gathering data from records at a clinic or health center and by observing patients in a clinical setting. However, it is important to recognize that the patients who come to a clinic are always a non-random sample of the community, so that generalizations can only be made to the population of clinic users. In studies of diarrhea management it must be assumed at the outset that many cases of diarrhea will not be brought to the attention of clinic personnel; therefore at least a portion of the sampling in such studies should be based on the universe of households in the community, rather than on clinic-based sampling. In some cases it is useful to follow up a portion of the community-based cases when they appear at the clinic or other primary health facility. This sort of follow-through can provide valuable information concerning the relationships of different sectors of the community to available health centers and other resources.

Designs for Hypothesis Testing

Given the types of research questions and the elements of research strategy outlined above, several different research designs are common in fieldwork.

Representative Sample of a Local Population

Perhaps the most common research design in medical anthropology is the study of a representative sample of households in a delimited community or local region. In some cases the sample is actually "all eligible households"; for example, "all households with small children." In larger communities, the population of all eligible households is first defined by means of a census, and then a random sampling technique is used to select the cases for research.

When the local population is composed of several sub-communities, distinct sub-groups or social strata, *stratification* of the sample may be advisable, in which case the distinct sub-communities or social strata are each sampled separately, in order to insure adequate numbers of cases from each category. For example, in Coreil's research in Haiti random samples were drawn in each of 14 "program sectors" (Coreil 1985: 3). In some cases where a representative sample of an entire region is desirable, it may be necessary to devise a two-stage process: (1) selection of a random sample of communities from the region followed by (2) selection of a random sample in each of the designated communities. This *cluster sampling* technique is useful in situations where the research population is fairly large and the researchers wish to concentrate resources in selected sub-communities (Bernard 1988; Pelto and Pelto 1978).

Intervention Group/Control Group Model

Bentley's research in North India was closely linked to an ORT intervention program, and thus involved a component of "evaluation" of the effects of that ORT campaign. As a consequence, the design was based on a sample in a "project village" plus households in two "control villages" in which the ORT project was not active (Bentley 1987, 1988). In this design a portion of the hypothesis-testing takes the form of statistical comparisons between Group I and Group II, testing for the effects of the intervention program. In most studies of this sort, the testing of group differences forms only one part of the data analysis, as many hypothesized relationships do not specifically involve the intervention as an explanatory variable.

Case-Controlled Comparison

In many epidemiological studies, particularly those structured around clinic or hospital populations, a sample is first drawn from among "cases" of the illness, and a matched sample is selected from the same community. Selection criteria for the matched cases serve to control for extraneous, confounding variables (Susser 1973: 76-77). In their study of malnutrition in children in Baluchistan, Hunte and Sultana (in press) used a somewhat similar research strategy. They had a sample of 25 malnourished children, matched with 25 well-nourished children of the same age. This design permitted the investigators to make comparisons between the two groups in order to identify differences in independent variables that might account for the occurrence of malnutrition.

A case-control methodology was undertaken by Clemens and Stanton (1987) in Bangladesh, as part of the development of an intervention program to modify behavioral factors associated with the incidence of diarrhea. Structured observations within two groups of households identified respectively as having "high" and "low" incidence of diarrhea were carried out to identify behaviors possibly contributing to differential rates of diarrhea. Fieldworkers were assigned to observe behavior in the households without being told whether a household was "low" or "high" in diarrhea incidence. The authors describe how their findings provided the basis for an intervention strategy:

> Three practices differentiated the two groups: more control (82%) than case (53%) mothers who were observed to prepare food washed their hands before beginning the preparation ($p < .01$); fewer control families (33%) than case families (80%) had ambulatory children who, when observed to defecate, did so in the family's living area ($p < .01$); and fewer control than case families had children who were observed to place garbage or waste products in their mouth. Focus on these three empiric associations enabled the design of a community-specific educational intervention which is simple in construction and based upon naturally occurring, financially feasible, salutary practices (Clemens and Stanton 1987: 288.

It should be noted that the case-control design is a means of manipulating the dependent variable, which is usually an illness or pathological condition. The design is less well suited to sorting on an independent variable. Since we normally expect to encounter multiple explanatory (independent) variables in relation to diarrhea or any other pathological condition, we would not usually wish to select a sample in terms of a particular independent variable unless a clear-cut experimental program was involved. In the case of an evaluation, the focus on a particular independent variable is, of course, fully justified.

Prospective Cohort Study

Anthropologists have not generally recognized the potential usefulness of prospective cohort studies. A *cohort* is any sample of individuals or households that is chosen at a given point in time, in terms of some control criteria, and then monitored in the following weeks and months for incidence of an illness, or other variable of interest.

The prospective case-following method has become common in studies of diarrhea, usually in studies of treatment patterns and feeding practices rather than in measurement of incidence or analysis of antecedents of the illness. The prospective cohort design is not generally useful for studies of infrequent sicknesses, unless one has a large population and a long research period. (To study an infrequent disease such as cancer or heart disease one needs a cohort of thousands, studied over a number of years.)

Data-Gathering Methods

As outlined above, the specific data-gathering methods of medical anthropologists include a mixture of quantitative and qualitative procedures. General descriptions of anthropological research procedures are available in a variety of publications, including Bernard 1988; Epstein 1967; Johnson 1978; Naroll and Cohen 1973; Pelto and Pelto 1978; and others. The discussion here will highlight some techniques of data-gathering that are especially applicable to field research on diarrheal disease and ORT intervention programs.

Use of Focused Ethnographic Field Guides

It is highly recommended that researchers prepare a field guide to specify the research techniques that will be used in their specific project. An excellent field manual for the collection of data on health-seeking behavior has been developed by Scrimshaw and Hurtado (1987). This manual can be adapted to fit specific culture contexts and project goals. An outline of key features to include in studies of feeding practices, often an important component of diarrhea research, has been suggested by Pelto (1984).

A guide for "Rapid Ethnographic Assessment of Dietary Management of Diarrhea Practices" has been developed by researchers from Johns Hopkins University (Bentley 1986; cf. Bentley et al. 1988; Brown and Bentley 1989). The manual was designed for use in Peru and Nigeria, for the preliminary ethnographic phase of the Dietary Management of Diarrhea Project. It was used in training the anthropologists prior to fieldwork and for collecting data required for subsequent phases of research. The guide covered all phases of the research, including information on entering the research communities, sample selection, investigation of cognitive taxonomic models of diarrhea, the collection of dietary intake data, data management and analysis, and report-writing. The guide enabled the anthropologists to collect data in multiple study sites in conformity with the project goals, and to complete field work and prepare a detailed report within a limited time period (six weeks). The ethnographic data from the first phase were then used to design the advanced phase of the research in Peru and Nigeria, including a sample survey and longitudinal study (Bentley et al. 1988).

Key Informant Interviewing for Exploration of Belief Structures

One of the first tasks in diarrheal research is to discover the emic (cultural) taxonomies people use to categorize diarrhea. Spradley (1979) has described a number of different approaches to "domain analysis," in which the interviewer explores in depth the categories people use in a particular topical area. This task may require a number of hours of informal openended interviewing with a few key informants, in order to obtain an exhaustive list of, for example, "types of diarrhea" and the specific diagnostic features of each. From such a list the key informant interviewing can be expanded to explore the entire *explanatory model* concerning etiologies of different types, associated symptoms, treatment, prognosis, and other features. Once the descriptive features of the diarrhea taxonomy, and other relevant elements of the cultural belief system have been identified, certain key features can be imbedded in a structured interview schedule in order to examine intrapopulation variations and to analyze relationships of the belief system to actual behaviors in concrete cases of illness. Techniques for systematic qualitative research on cultural domains are presented by Werner and Schoepfle (1987) and Weller and Romney (1988).

When lists of categories (e.g. types and causes of diarrhea) have been identified, the pile sort and triad sort techniques can be used to discover the ways in which the categories are interrelated, as well as the key attributes or qualities used to distinguish them. These research techniques work best with literate informants, though in some nonliterate populations the sorting of pictures (drawings) has worked successfully.

The data from pile sorts and triad sorts and similar structured interviewing can be analyzed using various techniques of cluster analysis and multidimensional scaling. Weller and Romney describe data-gathering and subsequent analytic procedures in their handbook on *Systematic Data Collection* (1988). The analysis of the various sorting techniques can be conducted in field sites using microcomputers, e.g. with the ANTHROPAC computer program developed by Borgatti (1989, 1990).

The cognitive mapping methods and analytic techniques described here are designed to study cultural belief systems. In applied programs these cultural data are usually combined with behavioral data in order to examine the interactions of cultural, social, ecological, and other factors that affect people's management of their children's diarrhea.

Monitoring Illness Episodes

To undertake a detailed study of actual behaviors in cases of diarrheal illness, the crucial research component is the identification and monitoring of diarrheal episodes. First a study population is defined and eligible households for the sample, or "cohort," are identified. Households with children under 30 months of age are often selected, as the incidence of diarrhea is much higher in the first two or three years, after which surviving children have increasing immunity to infections.

The most difficult task in illness monitoring is to devise a surveillance system whereby children with diarrhea are identified as soon as possible after onset. In some instances the researcher makes a tour of all cohort households at least once a week. Village health workers or "health volunteers" can also be recruited and trained to monitor the cohort households. In other studies anthropologists have "piggy-backed" onto larger epidemiological studies, and followed the cases identified by their surveillance teams (Bentley 1987).

When children with diarrhea are reported, the research staff must visit the household as soon as possible to carry out a semi-structured interview plus direct observations. They should observe the sick child directly, and should inspect any medications or other materials that are used by the household to treat the illness. Data collectors must be trained in the clinical signs of dehydration, dysentery, and malnutrition so that complications can be identified in a timely manner, and an effective referral system must be in place so that children with any of these clinical signs can be referred quickly for medical services.

Interviewing mothers of children with diarrhea is usually quite openended, and includes queries about feeding patterns (what foods and fluids are given, which are withheld or reduced, etc.), use of home remedies, and expectations concerning next phases of treatment. Other features of the "explanatory model" can be explored, particularly views about the causation of this particular episode. The chronological sequence of the illness, treatments, and other features should be recorded as fully as possible, in order to permit reconstruction of the "patterns of resort" and other key aspects of illness management.

In her North Indian research, Bentley followed fifty cases of diarrhea, making home visits throughout the duration of the episodes and for a time afterward in order to make comparisons of feeding patterns during and after diarrhea. The home visits lasted from one to two hours per day, and included the collection of both quantitative and qualitative data. Some of the diarrhea episodes were protracted, yielding a thick file of data for individual cases. The episodes ranged from 2 to 60 days in duration.

When episodes of diarrhea are studied, the unit of analysis becomes the individual episode, and special statistical techniques are required to adjust for the fact that some households will appear more than once in the data set. A cohort of 100 households with small children may produce a sample ranging from 50 to 200 episodes, depending on the length of the research period and the incidence rates of diarrhea in the local area.

In principle the researcher should visit the household of each "case" every day during the diarrheal episode, to record in detail all stages of the illness, feeding patterns, treatment, and related features. However, during times of increased diarrheal incidence in a community, the researcher may find it impossible to follow all cases. In that situation some system of case selection is necessary, perhaps with a randomizing method to insure that a representative sample of cases (episodes) is obtained. In their research in northern Peru, Bentley and Brown (1986) developed a systematic protocol for assigning diarrhea cases to observers for monitoring.

Monitoring and careful observation of illness episodes is undoubtedly the best method for obtaining data concerning the actual behaviors of people in cases of childhood diarrhea. The ability to accurately recall information about diarrheal episodes seriously deteriorates within a short time after the illness. Hence recall data about diarrheal illness in past months is not considered reliable for intensive data analysis. The "decay rate of informant recall" is one of the most serious problems affecting the reliability of data gathered in survey interviewing (cf. Bernard et al. 1986).

Informants' responses in interviews are also affected by the tendency to report "ideal behavior" instead of actual behavior. For example, in North India mothers stated that the staple food, *chapati* (a flat wheat bread), was harmful for children during diarrhea because it was "heavy" and "difficult to digest." Therefore, they said, it should be withheld. Removal of *chapati* from the diets of children during diarrheal episodes could have serious nutritional consequences, as it is the major source of non-breastmilk calories. During actual diarrhea episodes, however, it was found that more than 80% of the children continued to consume this staple food (Bentley 1987). This example underscores the need to complement statements about reported behavior with direct observation.

Other types of data in addition to the cognitive "explanatory model" interviews and behavioral observations can be collected during the monitoring of diarrheal episodes. Although some baseline data on the cohort households is important before case-monitoring, it is possible to "fill in the blanks" concerning household variables in the course of following the case. Data on household composition, economic conditions and other characteristics can be gathered, in part, from direct observation, and then checked by means of a structured protocol.

Data Analysis

Testing specific hypotheses in anthropological research on diarrhea generally involves three phases of quantitative analysis. First the researcher produces a full "profile" of the data set in terms of frequencies of categories, central tendencies (e.g. median and mode), missing data, and other descriptive features. The profile may include the tabulation of temporal fluctuations in numbers of cases, thus producing data on seasonality of illness. Other frequencies and percentages may be sufficient to document some key questions raised at the outset of the study.

The second phase of quantitative analysis generally involves constructing key variables, such as "household type," "material style of life," and other background variables, as well as categorizing and grouping "types of diarrheal illness," "types of treatments," and other intervening and dependent variables. These are analyzed in bivariate form, often by means of nonparametric statistics, such as Chi-square, Mann-Whitney U, and the nonparametric correlation techniques (Kendall tau; Spearman rho, and others).

The third phase of statistical analysis often takes the form of a multivariate analysis (multiple regression, logistic regression, discriminant analysis), in which the effects of several independent variables are examined in relation to one or more key *dependent* variables. This should be done with small sets of carefully selected independent variables, particularly since the total number of cases is often less than 100. Logistic regression is particularly suitable when analyzing small samples and (primarily) nonparametric data. Recently medical anthropologists have shown greater interest in the use of multivariate statistical methods, in part because of the increased accessibility of statistical programs for both microcomputers and mainframe computer systems.

Summary and Conclusions

Qualitative and quantitative approaches to the study of diarrheal illness have been the focus of this paper as a way of illustrating certain broad trends of investigation in medical anthropology. Diarrhea is an important research topic, and provides a useful example for illustrating the mixture of applied and theoretical features that are increasingly incorporated in anthropological research designs. The examples of research mentioned in this review are not exhaustive of the topical domain, nor have we touched on all the research in diarrhea carried out by non-anthropologists.

Methodological sophistication is essential if anthropologists are to realize their potential for contributing to improved health care systems in developing countries and underserved populations in the industrialized nations. Increasingly, anthropologists have been able to communicate effectively with researchers in other disciplines because of the methodological and theoretical linkages provided by the ecological frame of reference, which links the work of various types of researchers. We feel that increased precision in quantitative data-gathering, coupled with further development of techniques in qualitative ethnographic research, can lead to greater usefulness of applied medical anthropology and make important contributions to theory and practice in community health research.

References

Alland, A. 1970 *Adaptation in Cultural Evolution: An Approach to Medical Anthropology*. New York: Columbia University Press.

Bentley, M. 1985 The Household Management of Child Diarrhea in Rural North India. Paper presented at the Third Asian Conference on Diarrhoeal Diseases. Bangkok. November.

___ 1986 *Ethnographic Guide for Dietary Management of Diarrhea Fieldwork, Peru and Nigeria*. Unpublished. The Johns Hopkins University, Department of International Health.

___ 1987 *The Household Management of Child Diarrhea in Rural North India*. Doctoral dissertation, University of Connecticut.

___ 1988 The Household Management of Child Diarrhea in Rural North India. *Social Science and Medicine* 27(1):75-86.

Bentley, M., and K. Brown 1986 *Research Protocol, Longitudinal Study, Ancash, Peru*. Unpublished. The Johns Hopkins University. Department of International Health.

Bentley, M., G.H. Pelto, W. Straus, D. Schumann, C. Adegbola, E. de la Pena, G. Oni, K. Brown, and S. Huffman 1988 Rapid Ethnographic Assessment: Applications in a Diarrhea Management Program. *Social Science and Medicine* 27(1):107-116.

Bernard, H.R. 1988 *Research Methods in Cultural Anthropology*. Beverly Hills: Sage Publications.

Bernard, H.R., P.J. Pelto, O. Werner, J. Boster, A.K. Romney, A. Johnson, C. Ember, and A. Kasakoff 1986 The Construction of Primary Data in Cultural Anthropology. *Current Anthropology* 27(4):382-396.

Borgatti, S. 1989, 1990 ANTHROPAC (software program).

Brown, K.H., and M.E. Bentley 1989 *Improved Nutritional Therapy of Diarrhea: A Guide for Program Planners and Decision Makers*. Arlington, VA: PRITECH.

Clemens, J.D., and B.F. Stanton 1987 An Educational Intervention for Altering Water Sanitation Behaviors to Reduce Childhood Diarrhea in Urban Bangladesh. *American Journal of Epidemiology* 125(2):284-291.

Coreil, J. 1985 Acceptance of Oral Rehydration Therapy in Haiti. Report to the Pan American Health Organization. Washington, DC.

___ 1988 Innovation among Haitian Healers: The Adoption of Oral Rehydration Therapy. *Human Organization* 47(1):48-57.

Coreil, J., and E. Genece 1988 Adoption of Oral Rehydration Therapy among Haitian Mothers. *Social Science and Medicine* 27:87-96.

de Zoysa, I., D. Carson, R. Feachem, B. Kirkwood, E. Lindsay-Smith, and R. Loewenson 1984 Perceptions of Childhood Diarrhoea and its Treatment in Rural Zimbabwe. *Social Science and Medicine* 19(7):727-734.

DeWalt, B.R., and P.J. Pelto 1985 *Micro and Macro Levels of Analysis in Anthropology: Issues in Theory and Research*. Boulder, CO: Westview Press.

Eisemon, T.O., V.L. Patel, and S.O. Sena 1987 Uses of Formal and Informal Knowledge in the Comprehension of Instructions for Oral Rehydration Therapy in Kenya. *Social Science and Medicine* 25:1225-1234.

Epstein, A.L. 1967 *The Craft of Social Anthropology*. London: Social Science Paperbacks.

Escobar, G., E. Salazar, and M. Chuy 1983 Beliefs Regarding the Etiology and Treatment of Infantile Diarrhea in Lima, Peru. *Social Science and Medicine* 17(17):1257-1269

Fabrega, H. 1974 *Disease and Social Behavior: An Interdisciplinary Perspective*. Cambridge, MA: MIT Press.

Foster, G.M. 1978 The Role of Medical Anthropology in Primary Health Care. *Bulletin of the Pan American Health Organization* 12(4):335-340

Garro, L. 1986 Intracultural Variation in Folk Medical Knowledge: A Comparison of Curers and Noncurers. *American Anthropologist* 88:351-370.

Green, E.C. 1985 Traditional Healers, Mothers and Childhood Diarrheal Disease in Swaziland: The Interface of Anthropology and Education. *Social Science and Medicine* 20:277-285.

Hogle, J. 1985 Promotion of Oral Rehydration Therapy in Niger. Paper presented at annual meeting of American Anthropological Association. Washington, DC.

Hudelson, P. 1989 Management of Diarrhea in Managua, Nicaragua. Unpublished doctoral dissertation. University of Connecticut

Hunte, P. 1987 Intermediate Healers in Baluchistan, Pakistan. Paper presented at annual meeting of Society for Applied Anthropology. Oaxaca, Mexico.

Hunte, P., and F. Sultana Health-Seeking Behavior at the Household Level in Rural Baluchistan, Pakistan. In *Primary Health Care and Nutrition in Developing Countries*. S. Scrimshaw and N. Scrimshaw, eds. Tokyo: United Nations University Press. In press.

Janzen, J.M. 1978 *The Quest for Therapy in Lower Zaire*. Berkeley and Los Angeles: University of California Press.

Johnson, A. 1978 *Quantification in Cultural Anthropology*. Stanford: Stanford University Press.

Kendall, C., D. Foote, and R. Martorell 1983 Anthropology, Communications, and Health: The Mass Media and Health Practices Program in Honduras. *Human Organization* 42(4):353-360.

Kleinman, A. 1980 *Patients and Healers in the Context of Culture*. Berkeley: University of California Press.

Livingston, F.B. 1958 Anthropological Implications of Sickle Cell Gene Distribution in West Africa. *American Anthropologist* 60:533-562.

Lozoff, B., K.R. Kamath, and R.A. Feldman 1975 Infection and Disease in South Indian Families: Beliefs about Childhood Diarrhea. *Human Organization* 34(4):353-359.

McCracken, R.D. 1971 Lactase Deficiency: An Example of Dietary Evolution. *Current Anthropology* 12:479-517.

McElroy, A., and P.K. Townsend 1989 *Medical Anthropology: An Ecological Perspective*. Boulder, CO: Westview Press.

Naroll, R., and R. Cohen 1973 *A Handbook of Method in Cultural Anthropology*. New York: Columbia University Press.

Nations, M. 1982 Illness of the Child: The Cultural Context of Diarrhea in Northeast Brazil. Doctoral dissertation. University of California, Berkeley.

___ 1983 Spirit Possession to Enteric Pathogens: The Role of Traditional Healing in Diarrheal Disease Control. *Proceedings of the International Conference on Oral Rehydration Therapy*. U.S. Agency for International Development. Washington, DC. June.

Nations, M., and L.A. Rebhun 1988 Mystification of a Simple Solution: Oral Rehydration in Northeast Brazil. *Social Science and Medicine* 27(1):25-38

Nichter, M. 1988 From Aralu to ORS: Singhalese Perceptions of Digestion, Diarrhea, and Dehydration. *Social Science and Medicine* 27(1):39-52.

Pelto, G.H. 1984 Ethnographic Studies of the Effects of Food Availability and Feeding Practices. *Food and Nutrition Bulletin* 6(1):33-43.

Pelto, P.J. 1987 Indigenous, Cosmopolitan and Intermediate Healers. Paper presented at annual meeting of Society for Applied Anthropology. Oaxaca, Mexico.

Pelto, P.J., and G.H. Pelto 1978 *Anthropological Research: The Structure of Inquiry*. New York and London: Cambridge University Press.

Press, I. 1971 The Urban Curandero. *American Anthropology* 71:741-756.

Romney, A.K., S.C. Weller, and W.H. Batchelder 1986 Culture as Consensus: A Theory of Culture and Informant Accuracy. *American Anthropologist* 88(2):313-338.

Saunders, L. 1954 *Cultural Difference and Medical Care: The Case of Spanish-Speaking People of the Southwest*. New York: Russell Sage Foundation.

Scrimshaw, S., and E. Hurtado 1987 *Rapid Assessment Procedures for Nutrition and Primary Health Care: Anthropological Approaches for Improving Programme Effectiveness*. Tokyo: United Nations University Press.

___ 1988 Anthropologists' Involvment in the Central American Diarrheal Disease Control Project. *Social Science and Medicine* 27(1):97-106.

Scrimshaw, S., and N. Scrimshaw, eds. *Primary Health Care and Nutrition in Developing Countries*. Tokyo: United Nations University Press. In press.

Spradley, J. 1979 *The Ethnographic Interview*. New York: Holt, Rinehart and Winston.

Susser, M. 1973 *Causal Thinking in the Health Sciences*. New York and London: Oxford University Press.

Trotter, R.T., and J.A. Chavira 1981 *Curanderismo: Mexican American Folk Healing*. Athens, GA: University of Georgia Press.

Weller, S.C., and A.K. Romney 1988 *Systematic Data Collection*. Beverly Hills: Sage Publications.

Werner, O., and G.M. Schoepfle 1987 *Systematic Fieldwork*. 2 volumes. Beverly Hills: Sage Publications.

Woods, C., and T. Graves 1973 *The Process of Medical Change in a Highland Guatemalan Town*. Los Angeles: UCLA Latin American Center.

Young, J. 1981 *Medical Choice in a Mexican Village*. New Brunswick: Rutgers University Press.

13

Anthropology, Health Education, and the Evolution of Community Control in Primary Health Care

Jayashree Ramakrishna, William R. Brieger, and Joshua D. Adeniyi

Introduction

The concept of primary health care (PHC) encompasses a comprehensive, holistic view of health, a philosophy of self-reliance, and an emphasis on community involvement to develop culturally relevant and locally controlled services (WHO/UNICEF 1978). Health education, the first among eight essential PHC services, consists of a variety of learning activities that promote voluntary adaptations in health and related behavior (Green et al. 1980). Learning activities include interpersonal and mass communication, training professional and volunteer staff, community organization, and fostering social support networks. These activities are crucial for eliciting community involvement and promoting self-reliance. Designing health education programs requires a thorough diagnosis of the social, cultural, economic and political factors that influence health behavior, thus affording health planners the understanding needed to make services culturally and economically appropriate.

It is no longer adequate to talk of health education in abstract or philosophical terms. If health education is to make its intended impact on primary health care, a thorough and scientific documentation process is necessary from the diagnostic through the evaluative stages of program development.

Situation-specific operational research is an ideal approach to this process, hence the need for incorporating anthropological methods into health education planning and programming. Ethnographic data provide health educators with valuable insights into community life, highlighting important lessons on how and why educational interventions work or fail. Field-based data collection yields many opportunities for community involvement and ownership of programs. Qualitative research using grounded theory (Glaser and Strauss 1967) enables health education programs to build on existing community health patterns instead of imposing ready-made solutions.

This chapter describes the complementary relationship between health education interventions and the anthropological research methods that help plan, implement, and evaluate those interventions. Of focal importance is the growth of a short-term disease-specific research project into a community controlled primary health care system. The political neglect, poverty, and geographical dispersion of the study community as described herein made program growth a slow but challenging process requiring all the theoretical and practical resources of health education and anthropology.

Description of the Study Community: Idere, Nigeria

On the surface it would appear that the town of Idere has basic health services. Like the other six towns in the Ibarapa Local Government, Oyo State, Idere has a maternity center and dispensary. A public health inspector is assigned to the town, and the Igbo-Ora Rural Health Centre is only seven kilometers to the southeast.

A closer look shows that these facilities do not meet community needs. Not all of Idere's 10,000 residents have equal access geographically to the services. Like other communities in the predominantly Yoruba area of southwestern Nigeria, Idere consists of a main settlement and many satellite farming hamlets. Approximately 8,000 people live in town while the remainder are dispersed among 40 surrounding hamlets.

The closest hamlet is five kilometers from town, the farthest more than thirty. Farm residents maintain links with their extended family compounds in town and visit home on weekends and holidays. Because of relatively expensive and infrequent transportation, farm dwellers are effectively isolated from the town and its amenities. Daily health care depends on home remedies and itinerant medicine peddlers.

Even in town, services do not meet local expectations. The government maternity center and dispensary lack basic supplies and often run out of medicines. Adults who have time and money travel to the Igbo-Ora Health Centre, leaving the Idere dispensary to provide palliative treatment for school children.

Consequently, medicine selling has become a lucrative business in town. The five major medicine shops are accessible at almost any hour, unlike the dispensary that opens for only eight hours a day, six days a week. The town also boasts 33 traditional healers, ranging from basic herbalists to diviners. Both syncretic Christian churches and traditional Moslem sects offer healing and health guidance.

Idere residents have a wide variety of choices in health care, but this array of services can scarcely be called a comprehensive health system. There are many gaps, such that easily preventable diseases persist and simple illnesses develop to a crisis stage before effective treatment can be obtained. It was a preventable water-borne condition, dracunculiasis (guineaworm) that helped draw attention to Idere's poor state of health care.

The Igbo-Ora Health Centre, while being an Oyo State Ministry of Health facility, is also the base of the University of Ibadan's Ibarapa Community Health Program. Since 1963, health science students and faculty from the main campus (110 kilometers to the east) have delivered services, conducted research, and provided training in this district of 150,000 people. In March 1978 a medical student research project documented guineaworm prevalence of 18% in Idere's main town. This was a perplexing finding because Idere had supposedly enjoyed piped water since 1967.

Closer investigation revealed that the piped water system had been faltering since 1975. The overextended system experienced frequent burst pipes during road construction and difficulty in finding spare parts for worn-out equipment. Many weeks usually passed before Idere taps discharged water.

Idere's dispersed settlement pattern of town and hamlets, with constant movement among them, was in large part responsible for the resurgence of the waterborne helminthic disease.[1] Farm residents who never had access to tap water reintroduced guineaworm to the ponds surrounding the main town during weekend visits. Following breakdown of the taps, these ponds were the only options available to most residents.

Concerned about the state of affairs in a community so near, staff of the Ibarapa Program, assisted by student interns and faculty from the African Regional Health Education Center (ARHEC) at the University, met with Idere's leaders to discuss options for controlling guineaworm and filling the general gap in health care. A decision was made to introduce PHC using volunteer primary health workers (PHWs). In November 1978, a three-month pilot training program began for PHWs chosen by the residents of ten farm hamlets.

Relying mainly on health education, the PHWs were able to increase local knowledge that guineaworm is acquired through drinking pond water, organize villagers to provide safe water supplies, and mobilize donations to stock village drug kits. Prevalence of guineaworm decreased in most of the ten villages, but the long-term goal of PHC for the whole community was still not within reach (Akpovi et al. 1981).

Efforts to involve local government health staff (midwife, pharmacy assistant, sanitarian) to provide supervision, continuity, and expansion proved futile as administrative and logistical bottlenecks kept them from functioning beyond their stationary facilities. University staff provided services mainly in the context of teaching and therefore lacked the resources to furnish broad-based coverage of the district.

Fortunately the pilot efforts in Idere had attracted attention both within the University and beyond. In 1981 the UNDP/World Bank/WHO Special Programme of Training and Research in Tropical Diseases (TDR), through its Social and Economic Scientific Working Group, funded a three-year project in Idere to examine the potential for control of four endemic diseases (guineaworm, malaria, onchocerciasis, and schistosomiasis) in the context of PHC. The grant was coordinated from ARHEC, which drew upon the talents of people from many disciplines within and outside the University of Ibadan.

The timing of the project was fortuitous because its baseline survey documented that the prevalence of guineaworm in the 1980-81 dry season had climbed to over 40%. By this time, tap water supply to Idere had diminished to only a trickle once or twice a month. The three other tropical diseases were also found to pose major health threats. Under the philosophy of PHC, control of all of these endemic problems would be part of a larger network of promotive, preventive, and curative services.

Research Program Processes

The research on the social and behavioral aspects of tropical disease control evolved through six major overlapping phases including team building, objective setting, baseline data gathering/problem diagnosis, intervention planning, monitoring and evaluation, and finally institutionalization. The latter phase extended well beyond the three-year time span provided by the funding agency, but PHC must proceed at the convenience of the community.

The interdisciplinary and intersectoral nature of PHC was reflected in the range of backgrounds of research team members. The principal investigator, a health educator, and health education colleagues formed the core of the team. Also involved were experts in the areas of epidemiology, health management, maternal and child health, environmental health, health statistics, adult education, school health, medical anthropology, medical geography, economics, geology, hydrology, and entomology.

The first task of the team at a special workshop in July, 1980, was to draft a research proposal with two major objectives:

1. To develop and demonstrate an interdisciplinary approach to tropical disease control.
2. To identify the social and economic factors that influence the human behaviors associated with the transmission of the four target diseases in order to recommend appropriate educational interventions for controlling the diseases in the context of PHC.

Inherent in these objectives was a need for two broad types of study: (1) survey and in-depth research on the nature of the four common diseases and the social, cultural and behavioral factors that influence them; and (2) intervention or operational research.

The "team" nature of the project had a noticeable effect on the development of baseline data-gathering tools. The questionnaire survey was a common methodological denominator of all the disciplines and so it was adopted for initial study. All team members contributed questions which were translated into the Yoruba language. In all, 1,935 interviews were conducted with Idere heads of household in both town and surrounding villages.

Computer analysis was planned for the complex data set. Due to mechanical and personnel problems not uncommon in developing countries [cf. Mull and Mull, Chapter 14--Eds.], only frequency data emerged from the process. Codified results were not always consistent with the experiences of team members in the field, a problem that often occurs when data is analyzed far from the study area by personnel unfamiliar with the community.

To improve data quality, the health educators reanalyzed smaller portions of the survey by hand. Interviewers' idiosyncrasies (e.g. writing "destination" for "destiny" as a disease cause) were identified. Reanalysis yielded rich information on traditional medications which were previously coded as a "traditional" versus "modern" dichotomy. The large number of "don't know" answers, possibly a polite form of non-response to a tedious questionnaire, also became apparent, necessitating the development of qualitative field work.

An example of the above problem is the question of guineaworm treatment, which 36% of respondents said was best done in hospital. A review of clinic records showed that fewer than 4% of guineaworm victims actually used the clinic. In-depth interviews gave Idere people's full perspective on the disease, i.e. that it is a natural part of the body like a tendon. It comes out when a person's blood is weak or at the instance of a local divinity. The disease has no traditional cure, only palliative therapy. Idere people believe that there is no Western medicine for guineaworm (Ramakrishna et al. 1985-86).

The various data collected were not ends unto themselves, but stimuli for intervention by team members. A subteam might develop a project, but was expected to draw on the skills of other team members. Four major interventions were developed: (1) community health education through trained volunteer primary health workers; (2) improved community water supply; (3) school health education; and (4) adult education.

The first two interventions were interrelated, in that one of the main jobs of the PHW was community mobilization to improve water quality and thereby prevent guineaworm. These first two interventions are fully described herein. Two strong subteams formed around these interventions and were active throughout the life of the project. The first subteam consisted of three health educators, one with a background in medical anthropology. The second subteam was environmentally oriented and consisted of a microbiologist, a hydrologist, and a geologist.

Experience dictated that the size of the entire research team was unwieldy for specific intervention. At the same time the goals of PHC would be thwarted if each subteam worked in isolation. Coordination therefore evolved through the core of health educators, who drew on the skills and expertise of other members in a contractual manner (Brieger and Ramakrishna 1986-87). The core team concept was also applied in the field in Idere. The health educators, as the core, drew on the talents of relevant local staff--general practitioner, medical records clerk, midwife, sanitarian, community nurse, laboratory technician, school teacher, and others--to carry out training and provide service.

Subsequent sections describe the intervention, followup, and institutionalization processes. Relevant baseline data for the PHW training program are woven into a discussion of theoretical models and training design development. The intervention processes also provided an opportunity for continuous qualitative data collection which was invaluable for adjusting the project to local realities.

Planning Models for Intervention

Intervention design relied on four conceptual frameworks. First, overall planning was done in the context of the PHC paradigm emphasizing cultural relevance, community involvement, and a holistic perspective on health care. Intervention was based on the eight essential services as enumerated in the Alma-Ata Declaration (WHO/UNICEF 1978). [See also Mull, Chapter 2--Eds.]

Two other models were used to determine the technical and social feasibility of specific services which PHWs might deliver. Clark and Leavell's (1958: 14-38) "Levels of Prevention" was used to review technological alternatives. Green's Behavioral Antecedents Model (or PRECEDE) aided in an educational or social diagnosis (Green et al. 1980). The fourth model assisted in the development of culturally relevant education and communication through a process known as Health Belief Synthesis, a concept developed by the authors especially for this project (Brieger et al. 1988). These models are described below.

In designing PHC interventions, apart from considering community interests and needs, one must identify the different levels where intervention might take place (Clark and Leavell 1958: 14-38). The first of five levels in the continuum is HEALTH PROMOTION, which includes good water, nutrition, and environmental sanitation, factors that contribute to overall wellness. The second level, SPECIFIC PROTECTION, consists of techniques such as immunization and chemoprophylaxis directed at specific diseases. In the absence of such technologies, EARLY DETECTION can identify certain diseases in an asymptomatic stage when treatment is more effective. The fourth level, prompt treatment and LIMITATION OF DISABILITY, involves timely action once symptoms are manifest. REHABILITATION, at level five, attempts to restore function and maintain health status by preventing further deterioration.

Ideally, in PHC, health promotion should be stressed in preference to disease treatment. Practically, it may be difficult to intervene at the promotive level for all diseases. In some cases health technology is not effective or affordable, and in others seemingly simple options may not be socially or culturally acceptable. Hence for each disease, actions at each level of prevention were evaluated on the basis of: (1) technical feasibility, including effectiveness, availability, and side effects; and (2) sociocultural factors including perceived efficacy, cost, convenience, durability, maintenance, political climate, and level of organizational development within the community (Brieger, Ramakrishna, and

Adeniyi 1987). Guineaworm control provides a good example of this evaluative process.

Options for Guineaworm Control

At the level of health promotion two broad groups of technologies were considered for guineaworm control: improvement of water supply and treatment of water from existing sources. The former, long-term strategy, included shallow dug wells, borehole wells, and reactivation of the damaged piped water system. Short-term choices included boiling, filtering through a clean cloth, and adding a pesticide to pond water to kill cyclops. Options were considered in the context of PHC--that is, what can be accomplished through local initiative, self-reliance, and available resources.

Educational diagnosis showed that a direct approach to prevention could be thwarted by the common belief that guineaworm, as a natural part of everyone's body, cannot be prevented. Two other attitudes also posed a problem. Most Idere residents were of the opinion that large projects, such as water supply, were the government's responsibility. Politicians reinforced this view of government as giver. Many people were willing to wait to see if the government would actually resuscitate the failed piped water system. Another common attitude held by hamlet residents was that these were "temporary" settlements, and so they preferred to make major investments and improvements in the family compounds in town where they would eventually retire.

Economic constraints inhibited reactivation of the piped water system or drilling a borehole (per capita income in Idere is only N500 annually and the value of the Naira declined steadily throughout the planning and intervention period from being at par with the U.S. dollar in the early 1980s to N7.50 per dollar by the end of the decade). Geographical dispersion of the farm population made these options less desirable. Finally the team's geologist found that borehole yield would be too small.[2]

The short-term measures were then analyzed. Boiling would not be acceptable because Idere people believe "water has no enemy" and see no need to "cook" it before consumption, a situation documented by many health workers over the years (Wellin 1955). Firewood is becoming scarce. In Idere, allowing water to settle or adding alum to precipitate particulate matter is believed to produce clean water (but this has no effect on disease organisms).

Filtration of pond water through a clean cloth was initially seen as an inconvenience. It takes two people, one to hold the cloth and the other to pour. Fibers in regular cotton cloth trap dirt, so the cloth must be kept clean or filtration time increases. The team therefore began a search for alternative filter material (Brieger, Ramakrishna, and Adeniyi 1986-87).

The option of using the relatively safe pesticide Abate (temephos) to kill cyclops in local ponds would face logistical problems in maintaining regular supplies. Many ponds over a wide area would need treatment every six weeks, but health workers usually have no transportation. Those applying the chemical must be able to calculate water volume. Some ponds have religious significance which might make treatment objectionable.

No specific protection or early diagnostic technologies have been perfected for guineaworm. Rehabilitation, which may involve surgical removal of an embedded worm, physical therapy, and expensive antibiotic treatment for secondary infection, are beyond the resources of a village PHC program.

Treatment to limit disability is constrained by lack of an effective drug to cure guineaworm and the correct belief that Western medicine is ineffective. Traditional herb and oil mixtures smell strongly and are thought to make the worm come out and soothe the painful area, but do not cure. Idere people do not try to remove the worm by winding it out on a stick as is done in many countries since people fear that it might break and cause more misery.

The need to prevent disabling secondary infection is seen in the local proverb *Ti sobia yoo ba di egbo, oluganbe ni a a ranse si*, (before guineaworm [*sobia*] becomes a sore, it is *oluganbe* leaves we call for). While people are willing to dress the ulcer with boiled *oluganbe* leaves (*Ipomoea asatifolia*) after the worm is expelled, they believe that covering the site before the worm is out will anger *sobia*, which will fight the body and try to emerge elsewhere (Ramakrishna et al. 1985-86). Bandaging done at the clinic is quickly removed once patients reach home.

Inexpensive antiseptic lotions are available locally, however, and some people use these in bath water to prevent or treat skin diseases. It may be feasible to use these to clean the active ulcer site daily. Then after the worm emerged, local dressing practices with boiled leaves could continue.

Based on this social and technological diagnosis, one long-range and two-short term interventions were chosen to comprise a multi-strategy approach to the problem (Brieger et al. 1984-85). Filters at the health promotion level and ulcer cleaning for limiting disability were selected. Hand-dug, cement ring wells were targeted for long-term health promotion. These issues were thoroughly debated among the local volunteer PHWs.

Health Belief Synthesis helped explain these interventions to the PHC trainees and later to the community. The bridge between scientific thought and local beliefs began by looking at notions of causation. Both traditional and modern ideas focus on the dry season as the time of greatest guineaworm activity. As observed scientifically, the dry season is the time when pond water levels are lower and the concentration of cyclops higher. Culturally, the dry season is the time when the Yoruba divinity *Soponna*, who represents the wrath of the Supreme Being, is most active, inflicting rash-like illnesses including measles, boils, and (formerly) smallpox. The initial symptoms of guineaworm--fever, rash, and itching at the site, especially the week before the worm emerges--place *sobia* within *Soponna's* realm.

The conceptual bridge is built by postulating that when *Soponna* makes the earth hot and the streams dry, the quality of water in ponds becomes visibly poor. Since people also believe that "weak blood," as representing general poor health, causes the worms to emerge, the connection between weak blood and water quality is made. This leads to the need for filters and wells. In fact, this synthesis was first made by one elderly man from a village that had participated in the pilot program and had been enjoying the benefits of well water.

Synthesis of traditional and modern beliefs concerning treatment starts from a common recognition that there is no cure for the disease, acknowledges the traditional proverb about *oluganbe* that encourages prevention of disability, and then emphasizes that care and cleaning of the ulcer can begin even earlier. Ultimately since there is no cure, the final emphasis must be on the need to improve water supply.[3]

Health Education Strategies

Health education strategies were chosen to complement and promote the technical interventions described above. Priority was given to the recruitment and training of volunteer PHWs. This decision was based on both managerial and communication issues (Brieger and Akpovi 1982-83). The PHC goal of providing regular and easy access to care can only be met if skilled people are available right in the community.

The dispersion of hamlets, with difficult access during the rains, makes it desirable to have PHC skills vested in at least one person per hamlet, or a total of 40 individuals. To cover the whole district, this number would be multiplied tenfold. No district health agency can afford to employ so many PHWs, even part-time. Since the workload in a typical hamlet of 50 people does not require a full-time health worker, the logical management approach is to recruit local volunteers.

From the communication perspective, local volunteers provide the basis for a more efficient and effective transfer of health ideas and skills than do visiting health staff. In turn, a local person can provide more detailed and accurate information about the community, its needs, and its progress to program coordinators. The PHW, then, is a strategic link between the village and outside resources.

Primary Health Worker Training Process

There are four major components of the PHW training process: (1) basic community organization to mobilize interest and support; (2) recruitment of suitable trainees; (3) identification of relevant content (knowledge, attitudes, and skills); and (4) selection of appropriate training methods and materials.

Community organization requires a thorough knowledge of local settlement patterns, leadership structures, male and female roles, the organization and acceptability of local health system(s), and people's attitudes toward and norms concerning participation in self-help projects. This information was obtained through mapping, in-depth interviews, participant observation, and review of case study materials from previous interventions.

On the basis of the above information, visits were made to all Idere hamlets in late 1982 and early 1983 to discuss with residents and leaders the potential of PHC, the nature of the program (especially its self-help focus), and the ways in which villagers could become involved. This led easily into the recruitment phase of the program.

The organizers let villagers know that it was their own responsibility to select PHW trainees. They were to decide who was capable, who would do the work, and who would be respected. The organizers stated that hamlets could select more than one trainee, that both males and females would be welcome, and that literacy, though helpful, was not an absolute requirement.

Repeat visits were made to confirm trainee selection and to announce the time and place of the training sessions. In the dry season of early 1983 (a time when farmers are relatively free) the first training sessions were held, once a week for twelve weeks, at three strategic locations. A second round took place at two other sites in late 1983.

In order to retain trainees, team members tried to make the sessions accessible and convenient. This required a good understanding of the community and of local work patterns. Training took place in three schools, a tobacco warehouse, and a local government dispensary, all of which were centrally located within clusters of villages. This variety of sites also guaranteed that the number of participants at any one site would be small (around 20), thus enabling the trainers to cater to individual competency development (Davies 1973). Evening time was chosen because the bulk of the day's work would be completed. The two-hour sessions began around 4:00 p.m. and ended before sunset. Lessons were held only once a week in order not to burden the volunteers. This gave opportunity to practice the new skills between lessons.

A total of 106 volunteers were trained--38 from the main town and 68 from the hamlets. Trainees included both men and women; farmers, traders, tailors, secondary school students, and others; educated and illiterate individuals; and Moslems, Christians, and traditionalists. The proportion of women (10%), though small, was an accomplishment since traditionally Yoruba women have no accepted role in matters involving medicine.

Training objectives, content, and skills were developed by considering the expressed needs of the community, survey results, team member observations, clinic records, and requests by the PHWs themselves. Lessons that dealt with specific disease conditions were organized under the following broad headings: (1) recognition (to ensure that everyone was talking about the same disease entity); (2) notions of causality; (3) preventive measures; and (4) treatment options. Other topics such as the role of the PHW, nutrition, and village sanitation were also addressed.

Training Methods

Previous experience with health education in Ibarapa had shown that direct translation of Western health concepts into the local language is a poor form of communication as these ideas may be either incomprehensible or at variance with local perceptions (Brieger 1985). Using a local trainer should make messages more acceptable, but if what he or she says is strange and confusing, comprehension will not take place. Therefore a two-way flow between trainer and trainee that synthesizes scientific and community beliefs is desirable. This approach was used in the introductory aspect of each PHC lesson.

In addition, local methods of communication and instruction such as proverbs, stories, songs, and poems were used to communicate significant messages and to entertain, functioning as memory aids in a community with low literacy levels. Not only did the trainer use these methods, but he also enlisted the trainees in creating new poems, songs, and stories. This made sessions fun, for the Yoruba delight in elegant turns of phrase and apt expressions. The trainers emphasized that the process and methods used in training should be emulated by the PHWs in their own teaching of villagers. Thus the trainer served as role model.

Organization of the Lessons

Lessons usually began by: (1) reviewing existing beliefs and perceptions on the day's topic; (2) involving trainees in sharing information and clarifying local concepts; (3) highlighting those ideas that bridge traditional and Western concepts; and (4) providing opportunities to demonstrate and practice skills.

The interactional, participatory nature of this introductory (or diagnostic) stage of the session was also intended to bring forth relevant local practices and ideas that could actually enhance disease control, complementing the available Western health technologies. Ideas obtained from the trainees were examined carefully and attempts were made to relate them to modern notions of causation, prevention, and treatment. For example, concerning recognition, Idere trainees were familiar with most of the classic clinical symptoms of onchocerciasis (itching, visual deterioration) and added several of their own (body aches, infertility). Team members took these ideas seriously and through further study were able to link musculo-skeletal pain to onchocerciasis (Pearson et al. 1985), and have begun to explore the issue of infertility (Brieger et al. 1987).

Modern and traditional ideas about the causes of onchocerciasis were also linked. Idere people believe that small organisms, *kokoro*, exist naturally in the body and can cause disease if they are "too much." This idea can be used to explain the presence of subcutaneous microfilariae in onchocerciasis, a sample of which was taken from a volunteer trainee and examined by all under a microscope brought to the training site. Seeing the tiny wriggling worms helped participants understand why the disease causes so much itching and why the medicine (diethylcarbamazine-citrate) initially increases the itching as the little worms fight it.

After explaining that small biting black flies carry the tiny worms from person to person, trainees are encouraged to think of ways to repel the flies. Examples of local repellents include citrus fruit peels, *efinrin* leaves (in the mint family), and spring onion leaves. Trainees joked that while these substances drive away flies, they might also repel one's spouse. These natural repellents are also mentioned during the malaria lesson.

Much was also learned about how to communicate more effectively about malaria, known as *iba* in Yoruba. Local people link malaria with yellow fever and jaundice, known as *iba ponju* (fever with yellow eyes). Since the word fever is tied closely to malaria, it was necessary to find an appropriate term for the symptom of high body temperature, *ara gbigbona*. With this knowledge it was possible for the trainers make distinctions among different diseases that cause fever.

Idere people believe that hard work in the hot sun can result in *iba*. As Lucas and Gilles (1973: 76-77) point out, in malaria-endemic countries immunity levels are high (among adults) and disease only occurs when immune status is low due to stress or other factors. Synthesizing the two ideas, the trainer first commended people's astute observation that malaria attacks those who are tired from overwork and emphasized the need for adequate rest and nutrition. Yet since malaria does not affect *all* people when they are tired, the trainer guided the discussion to consider how malaria might enter the body in the first place.

For treating malaria, people like to make a bitter-tasting *agbo* (traditional herbal tea), for which each family usually has a recipe. Samples of the bitter herbs and chloroquine were brought to the lesson. Trainees tasted both and noted their similar bitter taste. Explanation was given that the important difference between the two is that the dose can be measured more accurately with chloroquine tablets. Although chloroquine is recommended, people are not discouraged from taking *agbo* as this might be clinically beneficial (Ajose 1957: 269), and fluids aid in preventing dehydration.

There are some gaps that are difficult to bridge. It is commonly believed that malaria is not a serious disease, while febrile convulsions are considered life-threatening. Using anthropological techniques such as in-depth interviews and observations of mothers with sick children, team members learned that febrile convulsions are defined as another disease, *ile tutu*, literally "cold earth," which is caused by cold entering the child's body. Malaria, as noted earlier, is supposedly caused by heat. The convulsions are seen as an advanced stage of shivering. Ironically, the shivering noticed in some children with malaria was traditionally perceived as the onset of *ile tutu*, and the child was immediately bundled up to keep warm, which may worsen the very condition it is meant to avoid.

A pragmatic approach to such situations was needed as it would have been fruitless to confront a set of beliefs that were so diametrically opposed to Western thought. Opportunities were found during training and followup visits to villages to demonstrate the speedy benefits of tepid sponging. Having accepted PHC, the trainees were receptive to new ideas presented empirically.

Supervision, Monitoring, and Evaluation

Supervision is essential for several reasons. First, the initial training must be short because volunteers cannot afford to be away from work and home for long. Supervision is needed to help PHWs remember what they have learned, give them feedback as they put it into practice, and thereby ensure that skills are developed.

A second aspect of supervision is role building. PHWs who a few months ago were farmers, traders, and craftsmen like other villagers now claim to have new capabilities and duties. They need encouragement from their trainers to carry out the new role. The trainers may need to intercede with villagers to lend legitimacy to the PHWs, to help them gain respect, to instill leadership skills and to provide technical and emotional support.

The third supervisory need relates to resources. The program organizers have a responsibility to help PHWs and the community identify outside resources to meet their needs. For example, when medicines run low, PHWs need to know how to get new stock at a reasonable price and how to anticipate the quantity and cost of each medicine needed for the future. Other kinds of external assistance needed include guidance on selecting a well site and sources of care for handicapped children.

Finally, supervision of PHWs is an essential part of program monitoring and evaluation, providing timely feedback that can be incorporated into ongoing management (WHO 1969: 30; WHO 1981). Qualitative evaluation is most appropriate here because it gives the supervisor flexibility to see and act upon the unintended consequences of the program (Trice and Roman 1974; Weiss and Rein 1972; Patton 1980).

Supervision met with numerous practical constraints. To guarantee transportation, team members developed a supervisory schedule as part of the medical students' teaching program. Thus each of the 13 villages with PHWs clustered to the northeast of Idere received an average of four supervisory visits per year. Logistical and time constraints precluded a similar arrangement for the western sector. Visits had to be arranged in the late afternoon when farmers were free, although this was outside the official working hours of University drivers.[4]

Learning from Case Studies

Involvement of the medical students enhanced their own learning about PHC (Brieger, Ramakrishna, and Adeniyi 1984). After the weekly visit, each member of a student group (5-10 members) wrote a case study report of the village based on observations and interviews. Issues covered included PHW knowledge and performance, program successes and limitations, villager knowledge, opinions and participation, and general observations about the hamlet including sanitation and water supply. The team member(s) who led the students in the field stressed the use of multiple methods to cross-check data and the need for research methods that did not alienate the "clients" (Argyris 1968).

These individual reports, together with observations by the team members, were compiled into composite case studies of each village. A series of case studies over time helped identify trends in a particular village and provided a comparison among villages. Several lessons learned from the case studies are presented below.

Students learned the value of multiple data-gathering methods when responses to interviews that water was being filtered did not match observations of untreated water. Open-ended discussion of the matter revealed that people found the purchase, use, and cleaning of a cotton filter cloth to be inconvenient (until 1985 when a new type of cloth filter was introduced).

Interviews and group discussions revealed that PHW and community perceptions about PHC were at some variance with the purposes outlined at the beginning of the program. Rumor held that training was a precursor to building a clinic in the village and hiring the PHW as a government employee. Some villagers had hidden agendas when selecting PHWs. While most PHWs had the ideal characteristics of permanent residence, respect, and basic literacy, choice was not based on these factors alone. A few PHWs had not been successful in other ventures. Villagers felt that PHC would provide them an opportunity for advancement, especially in light of rumors about jobs. Not surprisingly, PHWs chosen with this misplaced sense of charity did not perform well. Discovery of these problems enabled team members to counsel individual PHWs and to clarify rumors at village meetings.

Another trend seen in the case studies was a misconception about the revolving funds used to stock village medicine kits. These were supposed to be started through donations and maintained when villagers purchased the medicines at near cost. Because the state government was offering free medical care, villagers were reluctant to pay for drugs. Through village meetings, the realities of "free" care were discussed and resolved. Villagers came to realize that transportation to a government clinic cost more than drugs from a revolving fund. Even, after reaching the clinic, patients might find no stock, since the government never properly forecast the tremendous cost of its policy. By acting on the findings of the case studies, team members were able to catch problems like this in time and keep the program running.

Useful patterns concerning program outcome were observed. Larger villages (50 residents or more) tended to participate more actively than smaller ones. Two major indicators of such activity were identified as (1) contributing money for village drug kits; and (2) digging wells. Also, hamlets where there was a central tree for communal gathering and relaxation on hot afternoons were more active than those without a shade tree. In line with grounded theory, these insights gained through participant observation form the basis of hypotheses that can be tested in future research.

The case studies clearly showed that preventive aspects of health cannot be separated from the curative. Most PHWs established credibility by providing relief to a needy person. Someone with malaria does not want to hear how to prevent mosquito bites. Rather, she wants to know how to get better. At the same time, if she is helped when she is sick, she may be more favorably inclined to listen to the PHW talk about prevention (cf. Wood, Chapter 6). PHWs who maintained a village medicine kit did show confidence in tackling both preventive and curative problems.

In the absence of a drug kit, PHWs were reluctant to employ even the non-drug therapies they had been taught (tepid sponging for fevers, immersing burns in cold water, mixing salt-sugar solution for diarrhea), let alone engage the community in preventive action. Villagers expected medicine for illness and considered alternatives as inferior. As seen above, this problem stemmed in part from false expectations for free medicines. Once this was resolved, villagers provided their PHW with resources to meet their perceived health care needs.

Finally, the case studies showed how ideal health technologies measured up in village reality. Salt-sugar solution for preventing dehydration in diarrhea was a prime example. Interviews indicated that people could memorize the ingredients, but in-depth discussion revealed that they believed sugar could cause piles and dysentery, which were thought to lead to impotence and infertility. Secondly, it was difficult to find sugar in remote hamlets. With this insight, team members were able to calm fears about "too much" sugar. Demonstrations and taste tests in the villages conducted by PHWs and medical students solved part of the problem. Sugar availability was addressed by including it in the village drug kit.

Organizational Growth and Development

Although training attempted to foster the growth of a social system among the PHWs (Havelock and Havelock 1973: 51), and supervision tried to develop individual role identity, the PHWs did not coalesce as a group until some months after training. Experience has shown that while supervisors can guide, progress will not be made until villagers take responsibility for their own program (Werner and Bower 1982: Chapter 10, 14-18). Local action was crucial in the case of Idere since the government health system did not have the resources to establish formal ties with the PHWs. Eventually the Idere PHWs came to the conclusion that group action was necessary. Participant observation enabled team members to understand and facilitate this process.

Not until two months after the June 1983 graduation of the first set of trainees did a small group gather for professional reasons. They had realized that it would be cheaper to buy medicines in bulk, and pooled their money to purchase from a local medicine shop. In the process they concluded that regular meetings of this kind would be beneficial. They communicated this idea to the team members, who began sharing it with other PHWs during supervisory visits.

The inaugural meeting for a PHW Association took place in October 1983 with 35 trainees attending. Officers were elected, and the group decided to levy members N.50 dues at each fortnightly meeting. As it was guineaworm season, initial meetings focused on how to encourage preventive action.

The group decided that the association should have the following functions: (1) continuing education; (2) maintenance of high performance standards; (3) community service projects; and (4) group acquisition and sharing of resources. Over the next six years these functions have been carried out by establishing a revolving fund for drugs, constructing two community wells, producing and distributing special nylon cloth water filters, organizing community cleanup activities, delivering a community education campaign on yellow fever, planning new lessons (on physical therapy, acute respiratory diseases, anemia, and prescribing practices), revising past lessons fortnightly, reviewing members' performance and problems at each meeting, and organizing three rounds of new PHW training.

The association was not without its ups and downs. From these experiences the team members as participant observers learned much about local politics, social interaction, and group processes, and used this information to keep the association on course. The subsurface divisions between East and West Idere, with overtones of Christian and Moslem differences respectively, became evident after the first few meetings. The initial location was under a tree in front of a local staff member's house in the east end of town. When Moslem participation was observed to dwindle, officers met with the prominent Moslem PHWs. Ironically, the solution was simple--move the venue across the street to the veranda of the central mosque.

It was also observed that some members would float in and out of the meeting, often staying just long enough to pay their dues. Team members were curious whether this was normal behavior. Ojo (1966: 58-61) has described various forms of social organization among the Yoruba, including age group associations, social clubs, and farm work groups. Social interaction, including parties, is sponsored by such groups, in addition to work and community projects. Not only did such events often conflict with the Sunday evening gatherings of the PHWs, but the obvious social benefits of these other organizations were also more attractive to some PHWs.

PHW attendance did increase during special meetings such as when new medicine supplies were distributed, new lessons were delivered, by-laws were debated, officers were elected, or new project plans were unveiled. Team members learned that the meetings must be perceived as valuable to the individual member, not just beneficial to the community. Therefore more attention was placed on ensuring that the association addressed the personal needs of members, including feelings of accomplishment and increased self-esteem. Access to the drug revolving fund, supplies of cloth water filters, and new knowledge through continuing education have been among the factors that have attracted and sustained a regular dues-paying membership of 30.

Important lessons were learned about of local leadership styles. To an outsider, the decision making process at association meetings would appear circuitous and slow. What was being practiced was a local form of consensual decision making. Traditionally, leaders allow group members to voice their views and debate among themselves. Discussion continues until the leader senses a major direction emerging. When he feels that the group is ready, the leader announces the decision. A visitor might think that the leader is shirking his duties initially and then finally dictating to the group.

In Yoruba this consensual statement is called *alase*, and the person who states the final conclusion is known as *apase*. The group is bound by social convention to accept the statement, but if the statement is premature or against the will of the group, it will backfire on the leader (Hare 1969: 25-41). Making a consensual statement is a learned skill. This became obvious whenever the association's elderly chairman was absent and the "younger" vice-chairman, a man in his 50s, presided. Members became more cautious in their comments, and the vice-chairman was visibly uncomfortable when stating a decision. Because the organizers, using a participant-observer approach, were able to recognize these issues, they could facilitate local control.

By the time monofilament nylon water filters were introduced (August 1985) the group felt confident enough to make all the necessary decisions about selecting local tailors to produce the filters, decide on a fair price, organize themselves to educate the community, and sell the filters. Strong feelings were expressed that while profit was acceptable, it should be standard and minimal (only N.20 on a base price of N1.25, 1.50, and 2.50 for the various sizes of filters) to reflect the PHWs' community service orientation (Brieger, Ramakrishna, and Adeniyi 1986-87).

Conclusion

The Idere case shows how anthropology and health education can make a potent combination for developing appropriate PHC strategies. These strategies are in keeping with the local culture and resources, and encourage community participation in planning, maintenance, and evaluation. Anthropology and health education have an important commonality: both disciplines are predicated on a thorough understanding of the client community from that community's point of view. Both also agree that the definition of "client" includes various groups and neighborhoods within the community as well as the formal health care providers and the organizations for which they work. The two disciplines work synergistically. Anthropology complements health education with systematic and appropriate diagnostic tools. Health education provides the means for carrying theory into action. The benefit of this interaction accrues to the PHC planning, implementation and evaluation processes.

Sometimes the present state of national PHC programs does not always encourage this synergy to take place. Policies change frequently to reflect the latest vogue--PHC last year, child survival today, and cost recovery tomorrow. Because of these ever changing attitudes, official government-sponsored community development efforts have been called "grass without roots" (Jain, Krishnamurthy, and Tripathi 1985).

In spite of these problems, anthropological methodology and health education strategies can be used to translate the goals of Alma-Ata into community action. Perseverance is necessary because community-based PHC is time and energy intensive. Change may be slow when the community is enabled to develop at its own natural pace. Anthropology and health education can help locate and strengthen traditional networks and resources resulting in a healthy local greening--a greening that will be sustained in time because this grass will have roots.

Acknowledgements

This work was sponsored by a grant from the Social and Economic Scientific Working Group of the UNDP/World Bank/WHO Special Program of Research and Training in Tropical Diseases, and was based at the African Regional Health Education Centre, University of Ibadan, Nigeria.

Notes

1. Guineaworm is a meter-long threadlike subcutaneous parasite. When it is ready to expel its larvae into pond water, it forms a painful blister on the host's skin, usually in the lower limbs. When the host wades into ponds, the larvae are liberated and subsequently swallowed by minute crustaceans of the cyclops species. When water containing infected cyclops is drunk, the larvae are freed in the stomach of the next victim, pass through the stomach wall, and begin the nine- to twelve-month process of maturation and migration to subcutaneous tissues. The new worms emerge in the dry season (in western Nigeria) when lower pond water levels provide an ideal concentration of cyclops to facilitate transmission. The key transmission behaviors are wading in pond water by individuals with open guineaworm ulcers and drinking of untreated pond water by others.

2. Although traditional hand-dug wells are cheaper (N200-N300), they usually collapse due to the nature of the soil. A higher grade of dug well lined with cement rings costs about N1,500 and is a more feasible and immediate alternative in the main town, though still costly for small hamlets.

3. Briefly, the process described above found that early detection was the most appropriate level to intervene against onchocerciasis (Brieger et al. 1988). Prompt treatment was most feasible for malaria, and the same long-term promotive measure for guineaworm control, improved water supply, was deemed beneficial for schistosomiasis control.

4. Fortunately, one of the drivers was a resident of Idere and enrolled in PHC lessons. Afterwards he enthusiastically assumed responsibility for driving the recalcitrant vehicles through bush paths late into the evening. He actively participated in orienting the medical students, serving as interpreter, guide, resource person, and teacher. In the process he became sensitive to PHC implementation problems in each village and evolved into an effective supervisor of his fellow PHWs. As in many local development projects, time and budget were not adequate for ongoing action after the initial research funds expired. Therefore continuation of the program hinged on the personal interest and dedication of people like the driver.

References

Ajose, O.A. 1954 Preventive Medicine and Superstition in Nigeria. *Africa* 37:269.

Akpovi, S.U., D.C. Johnson, and W.R. Brieger 1981 Guineaworm Control: Testing the Efficacy of the Health Education Approach to Primary Health Care. *International Journal of Health Education* 24(4):229-237.

Argyris, C. 1968 Some Unintended Consequences of Rigorous Research. *Psychological Bulletin* 70(3):185-197.

Brieger, W.R. 1985 Food Groups in Cultural Perspective. *Tropical Doctor* 15(1):42-43.

Brieger, W.R., and S.U. Akpovi 1982-83 Health Education Approach to Training Village Health Workers. *International Quarterly of Community Health Education* 3(2):145-152.

Brieger, W.R., and J. Ramakrishna, 1986-87 The Health Educator as a Team Leader in Primary Health Care. *International Quarterly of Community Health Education* 7(3):259-267

Brieger, W.R., J. Ramakrishna, and J.D. Adeniyi 1984 A PHC Approach to Medical Education. *Africa Health* 6(5):22-23.

___ 1986-87 Community Involvement in Social Marketing: Guinea-worm Control. *International Quarterly of Community Health Education* 7(1):19-31.

___ 1987 The Relationship Between Health Technologies and Health Education Strategies in Primary Health Care. In *Proceedings of the 12th World Conference on Health Education*. Pp. 213-221. Dublin: Health Education Bureau.

Brieger, W.R., J. Ramakrishna, S.U. Akpovi, and J.D. Adeniyi, 1984-85 Selecting Alternative Strategies for Community Health Education in Guineaworm Control. *International Quarterly of Community Health Education* 5(4):313-320.

Brieger, W.R., J. Ramakrishna, J.D. Adeniyi, and O.O. Kale 1988 Health Education Interventions to Control Onchocerciasis in the Context of Primary Health

Care. In *Primary Health Care: The African Experience*. R.W. Carlaw and W.B. Ward, eds. Pp. 341-376. Oakland, CA: Third Party Publishing.

Brieger, W.R., J. Ramakrishna, J.D. Adeniyi, C.A. Pearson, and O.O. Kale 1987 Onchocerciasis and Pregnancy: Traditional Beliefs of Yoruba Women in Nigeria. *Tropical Doctor* 17(3):171-174.

Clark, E., and R. Leavell 1958 Levels of Application in Preventive Medicine. In *Preventive Medicine for the Doctor in His Community*. H.R. Leavell and E.G. Clark, eds. Pp. 14-38. New York: McGraw-Hill.

Davies, I.K. 1973 *Competency Based Learning: Technology, Management, and Design*. New York: McGraw-Hill.

Glaser, B.G., and A. Strauss 1967 *The Discovery of Grounded Theory*. Chicago: Aldine.

Green, L.W., M.W. Kreuter, S.G. Deeds, and K.S. Partridge 1980 *Health Education Planning: A Diagnostic Approach*. Palo Alto, California: Mayfield.

Hare, A.P. 1969 Cultural Difference in Communication Networks in Africa, the United States, and the Philippines. *Sociology and Social Research* 54:25-41.

Havelock, R.G., and M.C. Havelock 1973 *Training for Change Agents*. P. 51. Ann Arbor: Institute for Social Research, University of Michigan.

Jain, I.C., B.V. Krishnamurthy, and P.M. Tripathi 1985 *Grass Without Roots: Rural Development Under Government Auspices*. New Delhi: Sage.

Lucas, A.O., and H.M. Gilles 1973 *A Short Text Book of Preventive Medicine for the Tropics*. Pp. 76-77, 203-207. London: Hodder and Stoughton.

Ojo, G.J.A. 1966 *Yoruba Culture*. Pp. 58-61, 278. London: University of Ife and University of London Press.

Patton, M.Q. 1980 *Qualitative Evaluation Methods*. Beverly Hills: Sage.

Pearson, C.A., W.R. Brieger, J. Ramakrishna, O.O. Kale, and J.D. Adeniyi 1985 Improving Recognition of Onchocerciasis in Primary Health Care: Consideration of Non-classical Symptoms. *Tropical Doctor* 15(4):160-163.

Ramakrishna, J., W.R. Brieger, J.D. Adeniyi, and O.O. Kale 1985-86 Illness Behavior in Guineaworm Disease. *International Quarterly of Community Health Education* 6(2):101-114.

Trice, H.M., and P.M. Roman 1974 Dilemmas of Evaluation in Community Mental Health Organizations. In *Sociological Perspectives of Community Mental Health*. P.M. Roman and H.M. Trice, eds. Pp. 119-178. Philadelphia: F.A. Davis.

Weiss, R.S., and M. Rein 1972 The Evaluation of Broad Aim Programs: Difficulties in Experimental Design and an Alternative. In *Evaluating Action Programs: Readings in Social Action and Education*. C.H. Weiss, ed. Pp. 236-249. Boston: Allyn and Bacon.

Wellin, E. 1955 Water Boiling in a Peruvian Town. In *Health, Culture and Community*. B.D. Paul, ed. Pp. 71-103. New York: Russell Sage.

Werner, D., and Bower, B. 1982 *Helping Health Workers Learn*. Chapter 10. Pp. 14-19. Palo Alto: Hesperian Foundation.

World Health Organization 1969 Planning and Evaluation of Health Education Services. Technical Report Series No. 409. P. 30.

___ 1981 *Managerial Process for National Development: Guiding Principles*. Geneva.

World Health Organization and UNICEF 1978 Primary Health Care: Alma-Ata 1978. Report of the International Conference of Primary Health Care, Alma-Ata, U.S.S.R. Geneva.

14

The Anthropologist and Primary Health Care

Dorothy S. Mull and J. Dennis Mull

As documented in the introductory chapter of this volume, enthusiasm for social science involvement in international health has waxed and waned over the years. During the present era of multiple primary health care (PHC) initiatives, organizational support for such involvement is at a record high. Currently, then, anthropologists have a particularly valuable opportunity to sustain and solidify their role in international health by demonstrating the important contributions that their discipline can make to movements such as "health for all." But whatever the vicissitudes in organizational demand for their services, history suggests that anthropologists will always be drawn to international health work--not only for its inherent interest and challenge but because it offers a chance to make a real difference in the lives of what Sacherer has aptly called "the destitute majority of humankind" (1986: 261).

In undertaking such ventures, anthropologists are likely to face obstacles of several types. First, if they are academics, their own colleagues may look askance at applied work, especially work done for agencies such as the World Health Organization (WHO) and the United States Agency for International Development (USAID).[1] Second, they themselves may find the underlying agendas and operational styles of the agencies uncongenial. Third, they will almost certainly have to contend with the formidable logistics problems inherent in carrying out virtually any type of sustained research in the developing world.

This chapter is an attempt to illuminate the basic challenges involved and to suggest possible solutions that follow from our own experiences while working and doing research in Mexico, Pakistan, Viet Nam, and Saudi Arabia over the past twenty-five years. It is a frankly personal account, offered here not with any claim of universal relevance but in the hope that it will find an echo in the experience of certain readers and will give others a behind-the-scenes glimpse of some important issues involved in international health work.

The Bias Against Applied Work

Until very recently, applied anthropological work has been marginalized within anthropology (Salzman 1989b: 44), and it is still disdained by many in academia. When we told colleagues of our intention to work with AID in Pakistan, for example, we received muted congratulations at best and at worst a prediction that our academic reputations would soon be in tatters. The dominant response was a worried, solicitous inquiry as to whether we were really sure we wanted to do "that."

A similar unease was apparent when one of us (DSM) attended a talk by a leading development anthropologist at a meeting of the Southern California Applied Anthropology Network in Los Angeles in September 1989. The anthropologist presented a rich, well-organized body of tips and strategies for conducting evaluations of health programs in developing countries, but at the end not one question from the audience dealt with such "how to do it" issues. Instead, people asked (1) whether she felt pressured to come up with positive evaluations of programs that her own aid organization employer or a "friendly" government had sponsored; (2) how she was able to participate in team evaluation efforts, since "we all know that anthropologists like running the show"; and (3) how she reconciled herself to working for agencies such as AID that "de-fund" countries whose policies are not to U.S. politicians' liking.

Although the anthropologist answered all of the questions extremely well and pointed out that she had organized an international women's health coalition with support from U.S. foundations to fund programs in countries de-funded by AID, one still sensed a lingering mood of doubt as the session ended. Since the audience was composed of people self-identified as having "a strong professional interest in applied anthropology," one can speculate that the discomfort level would have been even greater in a group of professionals more exclusively oriented toward academia. In short, within anthropology itself, engaging in applied international health work is often viewed as a highly questionable activity.

Reasons for the Bias

The reasons for this attitude are multiple. First and most obvious, most applied work takes place under the aegis of international aid organizations, and many people do not agree with the agendas of those organizations. Second, and related to the first point, there is guilt within anthropology about the history of the field, especially its cozy relationship with British colonialism in the early 20th century (see Kuper 1983: 99-120 for a discussion). Although it appears that the colonial anthropologists' advice was not only benign but had little if any impact on actual policy, the possibility that information gleaned from anthropological work might be used for purposes such as subordinating a population is still troubling. Thus anthropologists who speak even of "making themselves useful" are sometimes seen as relegating the field to handmaiden status or worse.

Another problem stems from anthropology's beginnings in evolutionary theory, which was based on the notion of a hierarchy ranging from the supposedly most "primitive" human upward to the supposedly most "civilized"--the latter bearing a curious resemblance to a 19th-century white European male. Sensitivities about this now completely rejected idea run so high that the very word "development" (as in "development work") is a pejorative term in some anthropological circles. Like "acculturation," it is thought to imply the ethnocentric view that the dominant Western nations represent the ideal toward which other countries should be moving.

A final charge leveled by academic anthropologists is that applied work "has no theory," and, by implication, those who engage in such work are intellectually inferior. Indeed, one of our anthropologist co-researchers on leprosy was so anxious to distance himself from anything "practical" that he refused to look at an actual patient with the disease when one appeared, explaining that he was "interested only in cognitive models."[2] Kuper reports that in the early 20th century, some British anthropologists regarded applied work as so intellectually undemanding that it was "best suited to women" (1983: 110). Yet in our experience, theory is often generated precisely *from* empirical findings. Thus the rejection of applied work as "atheoretical" seems to us to miss the point.

Health Bureaucracies: Styles and Agendas

Operational Style

We would agree, however, that there are jarring differences in style between academe and the agencies, both in terms of the individuals who tend to be drawn to such settings and in terms of the kind of product that is rewarded there. As Salzman has put it (1989b: 44), what is currently most valued in academic anthropological research is "liveliness, originality and vision rather than systematic, detailed and complete accounts. Too many data are boring, whereas elegant formulations are exciting." Agency reports require both a matter-of-fact style that can come across as wooden and a directness of statement that may seem to blur important distinctions in a reductionist manner. To an academic anthropologist sensitive to the implications inherent in such minor details as using the word "informant" as opposed to "subject," the blunt, quasi-military language used in and around agencies ("operations research," "engines of development," etc.) may seem almost repellent.

Yet those entering applied work need to move beyond this initial reaction to appreciate the methodological rigor and clarity fostered by "agency culture" at its best. Rigor and clarity have their own elegance, after all, and they are obviously essential when human lives, rather than academic promotions, are in the balance. Anthropologists in primary health care can satisfy their residual impulses toward subtlety and depth by publishing articles for their peers in the social science journals, and many do.

Political Ramifications

The answer to those who recommend standing aloof from involvement with international health organizations for ideological reasons has to be, first of all, that initiatives carried out by such organizations save lives. We suspect that few could read the spare, understated report of the dramatic success of an AID-funded diarrhea control project in reducing child mortality in Egypt (El-Rafie et al. 1990), for example, without feeling a sense of optimism. Further, as Pillsbury has pointed out (1986: 10), such initiatives "will proceed with or without anthropologists. Without us the interests of those people about whom we care [i.e. the poor] are far less likely to be considered or understood." Anthropologists will be replaced by marketing specialists, day-long "ethnographies" will be commissioned, and the rich understanding of cultural contexts so characteristic of the anthropological perspective will almost certainly be lost. Thus, while we share the view of some of our colleagues that anthropologists need to "study up," in Laura Nader's phrase, rather than ignoring the connections between biomedicine, the agencies, and capitalistic exploitation (see Singer et al. 1990), we feel that such exploitation is diminished rather than augmented by anthropological participation in PHC initiatives.

We would agree that there is a basic conflict between the nature of agencies such as WHO and AID and anthropologists' own historical theoretical orientation. Agencies typically value highly focused investigations, speed, and quantifiable results, while the fundamental tenets of classical anthropology are holism, maximum attention to cultural contexts, and an emphasis on descriptive research methods. Then, too, agencies must please the governments of developing countries, and the latter are often committed to preserving an elitist, hierarchical status quo, while anthropologists classically identify with those on the bottom of the socioeconomic pyramid (Bloom and Reid 1984: 184).

Organizational Constraints

These seemingly irreconcilable differences need not spell the end of meaningful and productive anthropological involvement in international health, however, especially if anthropologists strive to understand the agency's perspective and use that understanding to increase their own effectiveness within the organization. We feel that an important initial step is for anthropologists to recognize the severe constraints within which international agencies and Third World governments must function. As Bell and Reich have pointed out (1986), the developing world has been in a state of steady economic decline for the better part of a decade. There are various reasons for this, including decreased oil revenues, increased debt levels, the manipulation of global food prices by international cartels, and the protracted drought in sub-Saharan Africa. One of the major factors, certainly, has been the continued expansion of the world's population, which has doubled since 1940 and threatens to do so again within the next fifty years.

The affluent nations bear more than a little responsibility for this economic decline. WHO's former Director General Halfdan Mahler has commented, for example, that support for community development programs in international health has steadily deteriorated in recent years (personal communication). The United States has failed to pay its legally mandated contributions to UNICEF and UNESCO, while money that WHO originally intended to be spent on nutrition programs has had to be diverted to the AIDS struggle. Partly as a result of such funding problems, the developing world is experiencing rising rates of illiteracy and childhood malnutrition, growing political unrest, and consequent pressures on governments as they struggle to function with very limited resources.

Anthropologists working in international health should and indeed must keep these pressures in mind, attempting to understand the "culture of governments" and the "culture of the international agency" with the same energy they would devote to the study of any other of the world's societies. George Foster (1987a and 1987b) and Judith Justice (1986) have made particularly important contributions in this area, and in the present volume, Arthur Rubel describes major stresses that occurred when an inflexible centralized bureaucracy tried to deliver health care to a rural Mexican population (Chapter 7). In some cases that we know of, however, applied anthropologists have failed to give sufficient attention to organizational workings and constraints and have simply fallen into an adversary role vis-à-vis those in power. Sometimes this is overtly expressed, sometimes not, but the result is almost always reduced productivity and ill will. As Margaret Mead noted long ago, the problem is often exacerbated when bureaucrats are very senior and anthropologists are very young, and those working in the developing world usually *are* very young (Burgess and Dean 1962: 143).

Anthropologists and Physicians

One possible reason for this tendency to adopt an adversary stance is that people attracted to anthropology are usually not only lifelong sympathizers with the downtrodden, as noted above, but also highly independent and resistant to authority (Salzman 1989b: 44). Although all of these traits are admirable in most situations, one may yet ask, with the psychiatrist-anthropologist Arthur Kleinman (personal communication), whether it is fair for anthropologists to praise a given behavior in a *curandero* or shaman and to condemn the same behavior in a physician. (This observation could be generalized to include the typical anthropological view of priests and administrators as contrasted with village headmen and union leaders.)

With particular reference to the physicians who make decisions in international agencies, we feel that anthropologists need to develop greater awareness of the systems and circumstances that shape the behaviors--good and bad--of these individuals. (Ideally, physicians should do the same thing with regard to anthropologists, of course, but given the realities of life within the agencies, this is not likely to happen anytime soon [cf. Jansen 1989: 31].) Our point here is that such is the power of professional role requirements that if anthropologists were all suddenly licensed to practice medicine, it is very possible that in short order the majority would behave rather like doctors. In other words, there are large social and institutional forces that either cause doctors to be the way they are or permit them to be so.[3] We feel that more understanding of these forces would not only reduce the frustrations of anthropologists but could well increase the insightfulness of their academic contributions.

Simply put, physicians pay attention to anthropologists when anthropologists have something to say that is likely to improve people's health status. Naturally, they are unimpressed with mere "doctor-bashing" or championship of traditional practices that may be deleterious to health (cf. Velimirovic, Chapter 3). In fact, the only physicians likely to read such accounts are those who are already converts to the anthropological perspective. Further, what physicians and other international health leaders most need to know about in order to take action are examples where anthropological input made a positive difference, not where lack of such input resulted in program failure. Although examples of the latter are far easier to find that examples of the former, case studies such as Corinne Wood's description of the primary health care program she initiated in New Zealand (Chapter 6) and Marcia Griffiths' account of her group's successful nutrition intervention in Indonesia (Chapter 8) demonstrate that anthropological studies can indeed result in far-ranging benefits for Third World populations. (See Pillsbury 1986 for other examples.)

Anthropologists who accept assignments with international agencies are likely to find themselves interfacing with co-workers from other disciplines, e.g. health educators as well as physicians, who value the study of health beliefs and practices as a way of helping people to help themselves. Few of these co-workers will have degrees in anthropology, but many will respect its methods. In other words, they will understand that important insights can be gained from qualitative techniques such as depth interviews and household observations as well as from surveys. Although anthropologists tend to shun collaborative ventures (Salzman 1989a: 26), if they make an effort to welcome these co-workers as valuable colleagues they can make a strong contribution to the success of primary health care programs, bringing in fresh ideas. (In Chapter

13 of the present volume, for example, Ramakrishna et al. describe how health educators worked alongside of anthropologists in a guineaworm control initiative.) Thus we agree with Sacherer (1986: 261) that anthropologists should strive for a "teamwork" atmosphere rather than harboring exclusionary attitudes.

Logistics Problems

Lack of Trained Anthropologists

Bonding with non-anthropologists may be a necessity in view of the shortage of locally trained anthropologists in the developing world. This shortage is in fact one of the major limitations that international health agencies now confront in attempting to expand their primary health care programs. In Pakistan, for example, there is only one autonomous anthropology department in the whole nation of 100 million people, and such situations are far from rare. One reason for this is that job prospects are very poor for anthropologists in most developing countries. Another is the often extremely painful memory of what happened to those countries under colonialism (Pastner 1982). Indeed, one Algerian anthropologist trained in North America has written that when he reported for work at the University of Algiers, he found that all anthropology courses were suppressed for the stated reason that "ethnology is the colonial science *par excellence*" (Bennoune 1985: 363). Western anthropologists may be even more suspect than local ones, especially since many have no particular loyalty to the host country and have no compunctions about revealing unsavory truths. In other words, famous episodes such as that of the young doctoral candidate studying abortion of viable fetuses to control population growth in China have taken their toll, so that even mentioning the word "anthropology" may elicit negative and sometimes fairly paranoid responses.

Using Untrained Assistants

We feel that one can and should respond to the lack of formally-credentialed anthropologists by making use of the considerable expertise offered by other Third World nationals who speak the local language and understand the culture. Indeed, offering training in research skills to such individuals is wholly in the spirit of the community involvement that many feel is central to primary health care. Highly intelligent and potentially able people can be found in most settings. Still, problems can arise when one attempts to involve them in anthropological projects.

For one thing, in many countries there is no tradition of social science researchers deliberately working in unhygienic sites lacking sanitary facilities and electricity, i.e. undergoing discomfort for the sake of idealistic objectives. While conducting interviews in Mexican squatter settlements, we lost two very capable research assistants for essentially this reason. One failed to show up for work the day after she had had to climb a rickety ladder to reach a family living on a roof and the other said that she was unaccustomed to walking through "garbage dumps." On her last day on the job, this latter individual pressed a white, lace-trimmed handkerchief to her face as she picked her way along littered streets crowded with dirty, smiling children. In retrospect, we recognized that we had not given adequate attention to these workers' ability to adapt to field conditions before deciding to hire them.

Even when local helpers are truly interested in social problems and are willing to undergo physical hardships, they often find it difficult to understand the importance that anthropologists give to matters such as open-ended questions and the avoidance of bias. A vivid example comes to mind. The authors felt fortunate when they recruited a research assistant who was intellectually gifted, charismatic, and spoke several languages. She was a community activist who was highly motivated to promote change that would improve the health status of her people. After a brief training period, she became so enthusiastic about the concept of open-endedness that she took it on herself to lecture others about the importance of not asking leading questions. Soon after one such speech, she was overheard conducting her first interview.

The informant happened to have five children, none of whom were immunized against any disease. When the research assistant heard this, she threw up her hands and said, "What! You had five children and you didn't immunize any of them? For shame!" She then delivered a lecture on how the mother should behave in the future. The informant was so intimidated that she mumbled her replies to the rest of the questions, and the entire interview had to be discarded. Subsequent attempts to induce this research assistant to be less directive all failed. Eventually we concluded that her social action orientation was too compelling for her to approximate the unbiased stance needed for methodologically "pure" data collection. Rather than attempting to change her, we asked her to help us with health education. In that context, where her powerful motivating skills were not only appropriate but necessary, she was a striking success and a real asset to the program.

We have found that even when locally-recruited research workers have a very non-directive style, they often have problems in conducting interviews simply because they are perceived to have a good education and an upper-class "aura" about them. Although they speak the local language, they may not be able to put informants at ease, and all of the standard biases resulting from people's ideas of what the educated classes expect may be introduced into the interview context.

Hence the anthropological truism that it is best to choose research assistants who come from the same background as informants--who look like them, talk like them, and, to some extent at least, share their values. This is why community or village health workers often make good interviewers (and they are good informants as well, although those in positions of authority frequently neglect to solicit input from such people). Unfortunately, however, ideal interviewers are often impossible to find in the developing world, where literate individuals--i.e. people who can write down responses--are usually also members of the upper class.

Collaborating with Colleagues

Although anthropologists usually have at least some control over their research assistants, they are not always free to choose the best people with whom to collaborate as professional colleagues. It is often necessary to accept those individuals who are "assigned" to a particular project, and they may be so assigned because of powerful family connections rather than because of their inherent interest in the subject matter or their ability to perform the required tasks. In some cases they may be made authors of papers on which they did little or nothing, or they may be sent on junkets to Europe on the pretext that they are attending research-related conferences. Such events are commonplace in the developing world and one copes as best one can, trying at a minimum to ensure that these individuals have no adverse effect on the quality of the data collected.

Another difficulty related to professional collaboration is that developing countries generally lack research libraries in the Western sense, and local people may have few incentives to write up studies and publish them in scholarly journals. In Pakistan, for example, a talented, ambitious young academic usually writes for the newspapers, where at least his or her name will be seen and where a few people will feel the impact of his thoughts. Such a medium does not encourage rigorous intellectual and scientific analysis, of course, yet this situation is very difficult to change. In short, local researchers may be working in a tradition quite different from that of most Western-trained anthropologists, and compromises may have to be made.

Lack of Freedom in Research

It is also important to understand that Western-style academic freedom is often absent in Third World settings. Although every research situation is different, the power structure usually does not welcome findings that expose deficiencies in the existing system. For example, we have been forbidden to weigh and measure children in certain Mexican barrios because it might reveal widespread malnutrition, whereas the local health officer had reported malnutrition to be nonexistent. We have been prevented from questioning women about family planning in Pakistan because local authorities did not want such possibilities discussed. We have had our camera and film confiscated when we photographed a Saudi Arabian slum as part of a project on public health measures, the rationale being that such materials might be used abroad to portray the country as "primitive."

Thus the developing world is a thicket of potential problems for the unwary individual who does not realize that truth can be very much a cultural construct and that curiosity or individual research initiative may be viewed as a distinct threat. In Mexico, a local researcher who worked for an international agency on a full-time basis told us that she had to clear every single interview question with the agency before she asked it. The implications for inhibition of followup questioning and broad exploration of topics are painfully obvious. (This same researcher confided that she had "sneaked into" one of her official reports her own personal observation that a low rate of infant diarrhea in a particular region seemed to be connected with a high rate of breastfeeding; to us, this was the single most important piece of information in the entire document, yet she had had to be furtive about including it.)

Agency Research Biases

While most anthropologists would agree that their discipline draws a large part of its strength from its emphasis on qualitative data, the international agencies often see such data as essentially "soft" and difficult to interpret (Foster 1987a). To some extent this parallels a recent movement toward epidemiologic perspectives and methods within anthropology itself (see Coreil, Chapter 1). Not only has talk of "risk factors" become commonplace, but there is a new awareness of the importance of intracultural variation and the hazards of overgeneralization, as epidemiology offers a useful reminder that small numbers of cases may not be representative of the larger whole. Thus, truly random sampling is imperative in the modern era, and research consisting solely of opportunistic interviews in which one spends many hours talking with a few people who happen to have time to sit and talk would appear to be a thing of the past.

Although these developments have been generally salutary for anthropology, there is a danger that quantitatively-oriented agencies and governments will become so enamored of "big numbers" that they will preferentially support large-scale surveys of questionable reliability and validity. Everyone who has worked in international health has seen cases in which poorly-trained assistants were sent out to do interviews so that a bureaucrat could write summary reports in the comfort of his air-conditioned office later on. We recall one meeting with agency representatives in which focused and clearly presented ethnographic information painstakingly gathered in remote villages was belittled because the anthropologist had interviewed "only" 27 people, while approving remarks were made about a huge survey of 5,000 households despite the fact that an advertising agency had collected the data and the survey instrument contained questions such as, "Should a mother wash her hands before feeding a baby?" (The answer to this was almost always "yes" even though later participant-observer studies showed that such hand-washing was virtually never carried out.)

In general, anthropologists working with the agencies should recognize that they are likely to be asked for very specific and often isolated field observations with a direct payoff for program planners: who attends births, what percent of mothers breastfeed and for how long, what measuring containers for water are available in the home, and so on. Wide-ranging discussion of matters such as the reason for postpartum seclusion, the total cultural meaning of breastfeeding, or the symbolic significance of various types of water is not likely to be part of the agenda. Nevertheless, our experience is that compromise between what the agency initially envisioned and what the anthropologist might consider an ideal field study is usually possible if the anthropologist can demonstrate the programmatic importance of going into things in more depth. Examples of how inaccurate information can result from uncritical questioning by uninterested interviewers (see above) can be presented to make this point.

Agency Conservativism

The task of convincing the agency may not be so easy, however, when "going into more depth" would involve eliciting informants' views about what things need to be *changed* (or even investigated) in their country, in their neighborhood, or in a particular agency's or institution's health programs. This is not to say that such questions cannot be asked, but they are not usually given a high priority and may have to be introduced in a somewhat subversive fashion, given that agencies tend to be wary of anthropologists as tending toward negativism and exposés (Pillsbury 1986). Nevertheless, community participation in determining what the focus of research should be is clearly the ideal (see Ramakrishna et al., Chapter 13), and anthropologists should also keep their *own* mental lists of interesting topics in case an opportunity presents itself. For example, Gretel Pelto (1987) has suggested some important areas in the realm of maternal and child health that researchers can explore if they find themselves in a position to do so. In other words, an anthropological study can sometimes be "piggybacked" onto a more conventional survey, as will be described below.

In considering such options, anthropologists should bear in mind two unfortunate realities. First, despite their lip service to the ideals informing "health for all," program planners usually do not really want to empower the community. Such empowerment takes too long and has the potential to threaten the status quo (see Mull, Chapter 2). Although planners may be persuaded to foster community participation on the grounds that it will help their programs to have more impact, most such actions do not really stem from a commitment to sharing power with the people. They reflect a desire for expedience and rapid results rather than a true understanding of what community empowerment entails.

Second, anthropologists must not forget that although they may favor a leisurely approach to elicitation in the interest of thoroughness and accuracy, one of the major needs of bureaucracies is speed. The usual reason is that figures are urgently required to produce timely reports that justify the expenditure of money in particular ways. Not only do officials have their careers to think of, careers in which success is often measured in numbers of programs generated, but health crises can place enormous pressures on such people, especially since serious political disturbances are usually a very real possibility in the developing world.

Thus, recent proposals for a rapid method of ethnographic assessment (Scrimshaw and Hurtado 1987; Bentley et al. 1988) would appear to be an appropriate response to institutional demands. Indeed, we feel that this concept is one of the most novel and useful developments in anthropological interviewing technique to have appeared within the past fifty years. While some do not accept the legitimacy of such a high-velocity approach, it is a virtual necessity in an era in which international health funding for long-term participant-observer studies is scant and few would be willing to wait for the results in any case. Critics of "rapid" anthropological methods need to understand that relatively brief involvement in the field need not imply abandonment of high ethnographic standards if researchers are careful and bring to the project sufficient prior familiarity with the culture being studied. There is no doubt, however, that such ventures pose major challenges. The following case study of a rapidly-done reconnaissance survey illustrates some of the difficulties that may be experienced as well as some of the opportunities that may be presented.

Case Study: The Chitral Research Project

Background

In July 1987, we were invited by AID to conduct an anthropological survey of health beliefs and practices in the mountain villages of Chitral District in the extreme northwest corner of Pakistan. The survey had to be initiated and completed quickly for two reasons. First, the agency wanted to use the results in planning major primary health care initiatives it was about to start in the nation as a whole. Second, the climate in Chitral is such that interviewing had to be done during the relatively brief period between the spring thaw and the summer rains, both of which make the dirt roads of the area impassable. (Actual time spent in the field was less than a month.)

Although the agency was interested in all areas related to child health beliefs and practices, its prime concern was to obtain information related to the social marketing of packets of oral rehydration salts (ORS). Thus, we proposed to find out what word or words people used for diarrhea, how they diagnosed diarrhea and dehydration and whether they connected the two, who in the family would be likely to make the decision to obtain ORS packets, who would go to get the packets, who would prepare the rehydration fluid and how, whether people knew how much water should be mixed with the ORS powder, whether they had suitable water-measuring containers available in the home, and so on. The agency was also interested in any information that could be obtained about actual use of the packets in the area. Details of the survey design were left up to us, except that it was understood that respondents would be randomly selected and that about 150 people would be interviewed.

Research Methods

We decided to carry out this anthropological study in conjunction with a comprehensive epidemiologic survey (funded by a different agency) that one of us (JDM) was scheduled to direct in the same region. Personnel from the Aga Khan University (AKU) in Karachi were involved in both studies, and the logistical arrangements connected with each facilitated the other; for example, vehicles and lodging were shared.

Interviewers were two AKU nursing students and two AKU medical students, all female, who had volunteered to help. Interviewing took place in the homes of 150 mothers of children under 5 years old in 36 villages. Respondents were randomly selected in a manner suggested by a U.S.-trained epidemiologist: every tenth household was visited in every second village entered by the epidemiological survey team. The total population represented by these respondents was about 30,000, virtually none of whom had any access to physicians.

After consulting with a female AKU medical student who was a native of the region, we designed an interview schedule based on her information and on our prior experience with a similar survey in Karachi. What we were undertaking was in effect a form of rapid ethnographic assessment that took into account our prior research findings and incorporated methodology that we had found useful in the past. For example, we avoided hypothetical questions about breastfeeding, diarrhea management, and so on in favor of asking about specific children--frequently the youngest child. (One of the first items in the interview schedule asked the interviewer to obtain the age, sex, *and name* of every child in the family.) We had found that if specific children were asked about, the mother's interest was engaged and complicated histories were easier to keep straight.

Results

After completing the study, we sent a 35-page report of our findings to the agency, with a 3-page "executive summary" attached (D.S. Mull and J.D. Mull 1988). (The latter is almost a necessity, since agency officials are very disinclined to pore over lengthy treatises; see Coreil, Chapter 1.) The major topics covered by the report were child morbidity and mortality, childbirth practices, infant care, infant feeding, and finally (the main interest of AID) beliefs and practices regarding diarrhea and oral rehydration therapy. Findings in the latter area are summarized below as illustrative of the whole document.

We learned that child diarrhea was very prevalent in the region surveyed--about two-thirds of mothers had at least one child who had had a recent episode (an important piece of data allowing the agency to justify the extent of the problem). Ninety-nine percent of mothers said that diarrhea was potentially dangerous, especially if accompanied by fever, but only 5% saw it as dangerous because it caused dehydration; virtually all linked it with "weakness" instead. This latter finding was of interest to the agency for planning health education initiatives.

Other findings illustrated the hazards involved in relying on "survey"-type questions rather than observing actual behaviors. Sixty-three percent of mothers said that they had used packets of commercially-produced ORS for child diarrhea, and 69% of the latter responded correctly or nearly correctly when asked how much water should be mixed with a given quantity of ORS. (Packets distributed in this area are designed to be mixed with 1 liter of water.) When the women were asked to show us how they would ***measure*** the water, however, most were unable to do so since they had no container that held 1 liter. Virtually all did have metal drinking glasses in their homes, but even after much prompting, only about half were able to hazard a correct guess as to the number of such glasses that might be filled to approximate 1 liter of water. Further, when we asked the women to demonstrate how they had administered ORS to their children, we judged that only about one-fifth had administered sufficient quantities to replace the water lost via the loose stools. These findings helped AID to justify a nationwide distribution of 1-liter measuring containers to local health care facilities.

However, we were also interested in two issues not on AID's agenda. First, we wanted to collect data having to do with the status of women and the possible differential treatment of male and female children as reflected in child survival rates. Second, we wanted to learn how specific health-related behaviors in the area had changed so that we might gain insight into how health workers might change similar behaviors in the future. We decided to focus on a disease of great importance in the area, neonatal tetanus, and on the practice of "wrapping" newborn babies in dried cow dung--i.e. using it like talcum powder during diapering--as a major cause of this disease. (The bacterium giving off the tetanus toxin lives in the dung and the toxin enters the baby's body through the unhealed umbilical cord.) We found that although about three-quarters of mothers were still using the dung, it was being abandoned in favor of talcum powder, especially in areas close to village health workers.

From a theoretical point of view, the most interesting finding was that this behavioral change was occurring in the absence of any change in the underlying belief model. In other words, most people, even those who had switched to talcum powder, did not believe that anything in the cow dung caused neonatal tetanus. Rather, they believed that the disease was a form of fright sickness.[4] The data also made it clear that those people who had adopted the use of talcum powder had done so primarily because they were advised to do so by local health workers who, like themselves, were Ismaili Muslims. This finding had implications for bringing about behavioral change in the developing world, where foreign biomedical concepts such as "germ theory" are often very difficult to teach, and we later wrote it up for a social science journal (Mull et al. 1990).

Problems in the Field

Although the Chitral survey results satisfied the AID staff, we must add that the need to reach a large number of respondents within a brief time resulted in a variety of problems. First of all, it was physically impossible for us to be present in every one of the 150 interviews; thus the four young women who did the interviewing had to function as independent research assistants in about half of the cases. Every difficulty that an anthropologist might encounter as a result of using a rapidly-trained intermediary to interface with informants is accentuated in a milieu in which speed is of the essence and households cannot usually be revisited for clarification or followup.

For example, when issues related to maternal and child health are being studied, the informants are usually female and therefore female interviewers must be used. Given the realities of recruitment in the developing world, such individuals tend to be young women with no prior field experience. Further, most have not yet borne children, so that informants are likely to view them as "children" and to disclose less information to them (particularly in sensitive areas) than they would to a middle-aged mother, for example. Finally, because of the intimate connection between literacy and social class described above, such interviewers are usually "city girls" who may not be in physical shape for coping with rough conditions in the field.

In addition, young female interviewers often face special problems in male-dominated societies in which any male present in a household may try to "take over" the interview and answer "for" his wife. In Chitral, it was not only culturally unacceptable to ask men to leave, but also extremely difficult to persuade them to allow their wives to answer. After a few vigorous but largely unsuccessful attempts to circumvent such behaviors, we ultimately gave up. We advised the interviewers that it was not as important to maintain an impeccable research design as it was to respect local sensibilities and foster an atmosphere of good will.

Another difficulty is that, as in any situation in which interviewers new to anthropology are used, assistants may not pursue leads because of inexperience. In Chitral, for example, our interviewers reported back that there was "no" use of any medicines in the villages other than doctors' medicines. When we asked about the bunches of herbs that we had seen drying in virtually every home, they said that they had not thought of these as medicinal. As this experience suggests, it is crucial to debrief interviewers daily in order to identify problems with the survey instrument, to insert additional questions that seemeded important, and--above all--to clarify ambiguities in the data being collected. In Chitral, we also tried to be present in as many interviews as possible so that we could function as extra observers both of physical living conditions and of family dynamics. Finally, we did some hand-tallying of findings in the field so that we could share preliminary summary data with the interviewers. Our object was to involve them as collaborators in an important venture rather than as mere technicians, to boost morale, and to improve the quality of the data collection in the process.

As noted above, misleading or even erroneous findings pose a special danger when one has only a limited time in a particular area. Here is where the prior experience of the investigators can be crucial. For example, we asked about causes of child death in a survey done in another region of rural Pakistan in 1986 (J.D. Mull and D.S. Mull 1988). Virtually no one reported death due to diarrhea, yet we knew that it must have occurred. We went back to the homes and found that in most of the cases where death had been attributed to "fever," diarrhea was also present, but it was so common in the area that it was considered incidental and so was not even mentioned as a cause of death. This finding in turn led us to the insight that in the local conceptual model, diarrhea was strongly connected with "heat" in various forms (humorally hot foods, summer weather, etc.). Hence when we encountered the same problem with reported causes of death in Chitral, we were able to interpret the situation for the interviewers.

As in all anthropological endeavors, however, one does not really know what will be found--not even the universe of possible answers--until one is actually in the field. With rapidly conducted surveys, there are additional complications. First of all, one usually has little time to do pilot studies, and once mistakes are recognized, it is often very difficult to change the survey instrument because of a lack of duplicating equipment. As mentioned previously, before we went to Chitral we tried to minimize such problems by interviewing a female medical student who had been born in the area that was to be surveyed. Thus we were able to drop at least some of the inappropriate questions, e.g. those mentioning foods that were not available in the region. However, a large amount of hand-correcting of the survey instrument still had to be done in the field before each day's interviewing began.

Recommended Research Techniques

On the basis of our experience with projects such as the Chitral study, we agree with Bentley et al. (1988) that in order to provide maximally useful insights, rapidly conducted surveys should and indeed must be supplemented with other anthropological techniques. Use of key informants would appear to be essential, and participant-observer activities, however brief, can function as a cross-check on survey findings. When we came across a child with diarrhea in Chitral, for example, we modified the day's schedule and stayed in the home to observe how the illness was actually being treated. Too often, what is said is at odds with what is done, and it is the latter, of course, that is most important.

Other research strategies also have a role to play. For example, focus group discussions have proven their worth in helping to elicit data in a relaxed atmosphere and to illuminate patterns of intracultural variation. Use of clinical vignettes as described in note 4 below can provide a sense of the cultural context in which traditional diseases are embedded. Photographs can be similarly used as readily understandable and transportable visual stimuli (see Mull 1990). Judiciously employed, all of these techniques are capable of supplying an ethnographic context within which survey findings can fruitfully be interpreted.

Anthropologists and Primary Health Care

We feel that it is precisely because of anthropologists' traditional concern for contexts that their input is vital to primary health care initiatives. Behavioral research grounded in a holistic, inclusive frame of reference would seem to be a particularly appropriate way to begin to meet the broad goals of "health for all" as articulated at

Alma-Ata and as captured in the following statement (Guerra de Macedo 1987: i):

> Health is [now] recognized to be much more than merely the absence of disease. It is . . . a state of general well-being, manifested in a socially and economically productive life that can be lived in harmony with the environment. . . . Basic to this approach is the promotion of health by the people themselves.

Indeed, the words *health* and *whole* share the same Indo-European root. In keeping with this suggestive etymological association, many observers feel that "health for all" will never be reached in the absence of truly comprehensive approaches empowering the community in a radical and irreversible manner. As a discipline preeminently concerned with enhancing the dignity of humankind, anthropology has a vital role to play in catalyzing that empowerment. Especially in the developing countries, where three-quarters of the world's people live and all too often needlessly die, anthropologists can help to assure that, in William Faulkner's memorable phrase, humanity will "not only endure, but prevail."

Acknowledgements

We would like to thank Jeannine Coreil for helping us to clarify the thoughts presented in this chapter. Several anonymous reviewers were also helpful both in encouraging us to contribute such a personal account to a scholarly volume and in pointing out matters needing rethinking or amplification. Residual errors are, of course, our own.

Notes

1. Although some anthropologists have "gone it alone" in international health work with no institutional sponsorship, most people involved in primary health care--the term itself is a WHO creation--have been on the payroll of development agencies, private voluntary organizations (PVOs), or philanthropic groups. Hence the focus on agency work in this chapter.

2. In this and similar anecdotal accounts presented, names of countries, diseases, and so on have been changed.

3. Csordas (1988: 420) has pointed out that current concern with "biomedical hegemony" may lead to the error of "mistaking the medical profession for the real ruling class. The *latter* is the locus of hegemony, including hegemony over health and illness" (emphasis added). See Singer et al. (1990: vi) for a commentary on these remarks.

4. We learned this (and generated other folk models of illness) by using an elicitation technique developed by JDM in which informants are asked to diagnose illnesses presented in "clinical vignettes" (see Mull 1985). Briefly, after inquiring about what kinds of illnesses people get in a particular area, we construct vignettes in such a way as to reflect both important biomedical symptomatology and folk concepts that seem to be prevalent. The intent is to elicit free, undirected response. For example, one vignette used in Chitral was the following: "A woman has a cough and bloody sputum and feels very tired. What could have been wrong, what could have caused it, and what could cure it?" (Only 25% of respondents said that this was tuberculosis; the rest diagnosed it as a folk disease.) We have found that by using this and other open-ended elicitation techniques such as diagnosis of photographs (Mull 1990), we can maintain our informants' interest and also obtain a large amount of highly reliable data in a relatively short time.

References

Bell, D.E., and M.R. Reich, eds. 1986 *Health, Nutrition, and Economic Crises: Approaches to Policy in the Third World*. Dover, MA: Auburn House Publishing Company.

Bennoune, M. 1985 What Does It Mean to be a Third-World Anthropologist? *Dialectical Anthropology* 9:357-364.

Bentley, M.E., G.H. Pelto, W.L. Straus, D.A. Schumann, C. Adegbola, E. de la Pena, G.A. Oni, K.H. Brown, and S.L. Huffman 1988 Rapid Ethnographic Assessment: Applications in a Diarrhea Management Program. *Social Science and Medicine* 27(1):107-116.

Bloom, A.L., and J. Reid 1984 Introduction: Anthropology and Primary Health Care in Developing Countries. *Social Science and Medicine*, Special Issue 19(3):183-184.

Burgess, A., and R.F.A. Dean, eds. 1962 *Malnutrition and Food Habits*. New York: The MacMillan Company.

Csordas, T.J. 1988 The Conceptual Status of Hegemony and Critique in Medical Anthropology. *Medical Anthropology Quarterly* 2(4):416-421.

El-Rafie, M., W.A. Hassouna, N. Hirschhorn, S. Loza, P. Miller, A. Nagaty, S. Nasser, and S. Riyad 1990 Effect of Diarrhoeal Disease Control on Infant and Child Mortality in Egypt: Report from the National Control of Diarrhoeal Diseases Project. *The Lancet*, 334-338, February 10.

Foster, G.M. 1987a World Health Organization Behavioral Science Research: Problems and Prospects. *Social Science and Medicine* 24:709-717.

___ 1987b Bureaucratic Aspects of International Health Agencies. *Social Science and Medicine* 25:1039-1048.

Guerra de Macedo, C. 1987 Health Promotion. (Director's Letter.) *Bulletin of the Pan American Health Organization* 21(4):i.

Jansen, W.H. 1989 Future Directions of Development Anthropology. *Anthropology Newsletter* 30(7):27,31,36.

Justice, J. 1986 *Policies, Plans & People: Culture and Health Development in Nepal*. Berkeley: University of California Press.

Kuper, A. 1983 Anthropology and Colonialism. In *Anthropology and Anthropologists: The Modern British School*. Revised edition. Pp. 99-120. London: Routledge & Kegan Paul.

Mull, D.S. 1990 Traditional Perceptions of Marasmus in Pakistan. *Social Science and Medicine*. In press.

Mull, D.S., J.W. Anderson, and J.D. Mull 1990 Cow Dung, Rock Salt, and Medical Innovation in the Hindu Kush of Pakistan: The Cultural Transformation of Neonatal Tetanus and Iodine Deficiency. *Social Science and Medicine* 30(6):675-691.

Mull, D.S., and J.D. Mull 1988 *Health Beliefs and Practices of 150 Mothers in Rural North West Frontier Province*. Presented to USAID, Islamabad, Pakistan.

Mull, J.D. 1985 Medical Anthropology: The Art and Science of People Studying People. *Family Practice Research Journal* 5:67-78.

Mull, J.D., and D.S. Mull 1988 Mothers' Concepts of Childhood Diarrhea in Rural Pakistan: What ORT Program Planners Should Know. *Social Science and Medicine* 27:53-67.

Pelto, G.H. 1987 Cultural Issues in Maternal and Child Health and Nutrition. *Social Science and Medicine* 25(6):553-559.

Pastner, S. 1982 Pakistan and the Anthropological Endeavor. In *Anthropology in Pakistan: Recent Socio-Cultural and Archaeological Perspectives*. S. Pastner and L. Flam, eds. Pp. 2-10. Karachi, Pakistan: Indus Publications.

Pillsbury, B. 1986 Making a Difference: Anthropologists in International Development. In *Anthropology and Public Policy: A Dialogue*. Special Publication No. 21. Pp. 10-28. American Anthropological Association.

Sacherer, J. 1986 Applied Anthropology and the Development Bureaucracy: Lessons from Nepal. In *Practicing Development Anthropology*. E.C. Green, ed. Pp. 247-263. Boulder: Westview Press.

Salzman, P.C. 1989a The Failure of Solitary Fieldwork. *Anthropology Newsletter* 30(4):26,28.

___ 1989b The Lone Stranger and the Solitary Quest. *Anthropology Newsletter* 30(5):16,44.

Scrimshaw, S.C.M., and E. Hurtado 1987 *Rapid Assessment Procedures for Nutrition and Primary Health Care*. Los Angeles: UCLA Latin American Center Publications.

Singer, M., H.A. Baer, and E. Lazarus 1990 Critical Medical Anthropology: Theory and Research. *Social Science and Medicine*, Special Issue 30(2).

Contributors

Joshua D. Adeniyi, Department of Preventive and Social Medicine, University of Ibadan, Nigeria.

Margaret E. Bentley, Department of International Health, Johns Hopkins University, Baltimore, Maryland 21205.

William R. Brieger, African Regional Health Education Centre, University of Ibadan, Nigeria.

Jeannine Coreil, Department of Community and Family Health, College of Public Health, University of South Florida, Tampa, Florida 33612.

John M. Donahue, Department of Sociology and Anthropology, Trinity University, San Antonio, Texas 78284.

Marcia Griffiths, Manoff Group, Inc., Washington, D.C. 20009.

Suzanne Heurtin-Roberts, Department of Epidemiology and Biostatistics, University of California, San Francisco, California 94143.

Brigitte Jordan, Institute for Research on Learning, Palo Alto, California 94304.

Carl Kendall, Department of International Health, Johns Hopkins University, Baltimore, Maryland 21205.

Dorothy S. Mull, Department of Family Medicine, University of California, Irvine, California 92717.

J. Dennis Mull, Department of Family Medicine, University of California, Irvine, California 92717.

Mark Nichter, Department of Anthropology, University of Arizona, Tucson, Arizona 85721.

Gretel H. Pelto, Department of Nutritional Sciences, University of Connecticut, Storrs, Connecticut 06268.

Pertti J. Pelto, Department of Anthropology, University of Connecticut, Storrs, Connecticut 06268.

Jayashree Ramakrishna, Health Education Department, National Institute of Mental Health, Bangalore, India.

Efrain Reisin, Department of Medicine, Louisiana State University Medical Center, New Orleans, Louisiana 70112.

Arthur J. Rubel, Departments of Family Medicine and Anthropology, University of California, Irvine, California 92717.

Boris Velimirovic, Institute of Social Medicine, University of Graz, Graz, Austria.

Corinne Shear Wood, Department of Anthropology, California State University, Fullerton, California 92634.

Index